HOLY TEARS, HOLY BLOOD

HOLY TEARS, HOLY BLOOD

Women, Catholicism, and the Culture of Suffering in France, 1840–1970

Richard D. E. Burton

CORNELL UNIVERSITY PRESS
Ithaca and London

First published 2004 by Cornell University Press

Printed in the United States of America

Library of Congress Cataloging-in-Publication Data

Burton, Richard D. E., 1946–
    Holy tears, holy blood : women, Catholicism, and the culture of suffering in France, 1840–1970 / Richard D. E. Burton.
        p. cm.
Includes bibliographical references and index.
    ISBN 0-8014-4207-9 (alk. paper)
    1. Catholic women—France—Biography. 2. Christian women saints—France—Biography. 3. Suffering—Religious aspects—Catholic Church. 4. Catholic women—France—History—19th century. 5. Catholic women—France—History—20th century. I. Title.
BX4682.B87 2004
282'.092'244—dc22
                                        2003022173

Cornell University Press strives to use environmentally responsible suppliers and materials to the fullest extent possible in the publishing of its books. Such materials include vegetable-based, low-VOC inks and acid-free papers that are recycled, totally chlorine-free, or partly composed of nonwood fibers. For further information, visit our website at www.cornellpress.cornell.edu.

Cloth printing   10 9 8 7 6 5 4 3 2 1

Geneviève, Jeanne . . . Bernadette . . . Thérèse . . . When God wishes to
speak to France, he causes a young girl to rise up from the fields,
come out from the woods, burst forth from the springs.

—MARIE NOËL, *Notes intimes* (1959)

By bringing into the world the feeling for suffering,
Jesus Christ has increased enormously the ability to suffer.
His death was the death of physical and moral pagan health.
Neurosis comes from Golgotha.

—EDMOND AND JULES DE GONCOURT, *Journal* (15 MAY 1868)

CONTENTS

INTRODUCTION

The body of this book consists of accounts of eleven French women and their relationship to what I loosely call "the sacred," primarily, in the present context, in its Christian, and specifically Catholic, expression. These women were born between 1831 and 1909; most had brief, painful existences, and the one who lived the longest spent over fifty years virtually motionless, never sleeping and eating virtually nothing save the communion wafer she received once a week, until her death in 1981, just short of her seventy-ninth birthday. On almost every Friday for over half a century, she also bled from her forehead, hands, and sometimes right side in imitation, it was believed, of Christ's Agony on the Cross, after which she went into a coma lasting until the following Sunday when she was "resurrected" into full consciousness, again in conformity with the model of the Easter triduum. Bleeding and what, again loosely, may be described as eating disorders are, as we shall see, among the recurring themes in this book.

Of the eleven women discussed, one, at least, will be familiar to almost every reader: Thérèse Martin (1873–97), canonized in then record time in 1925, known formally as Sainte Thérèse de l'Enfant-Jésus et de la Sainte Face and more intimately to her tens of thousands of devotees the world over as Petite Fleur, Little Flower. Proclaimed a Doctor of the Church in 1997, only the third woman after saints Catherine of Siena and Teresa of Avila to be so honored, she remains, along with Mother Teresa of Calcutta, the most influential Catholic woman of the twentieth century. Almost every reader, too, will have heard of Simone Weil (1909–43) and know something, at least, of the extraordinary spiritual journey that took her from a comfortable secular Jewish background, via years of radical political activity that, for a time, involved her working on the factory floor, to the very threshold of the Roman Catholic Church, a threshold that she never formally crossed before dying effectively of self-starvation in a hospice in Ashford, England, in August 1943, in joint emulation of the malnourished people of occupied France and, once again, of Jesus's self-decreating—one of the key terms in her spiritual lexicon—offering of himself on the Cross.

The names of at least two of the other women are reasonably well known, though probably less for their own substantial achievements than for their relationships to brother, husband, or lover: the sculptor Camille Claudel

(1864–1943), sister of the great Catholic poet-dramatist Paul Claudel (1868–1955) and one-time mistress of Auguste Rodin (1840–1917), a relationship that undoubtedly contributed to, if it did not directly cause, her psychological collapse and eventual internment in a lunatic asylum; and Raïssa Maritain (1883–1960), a Russian-born Jewish convert to Catholicism, poet, mystic, and memorialist, whose life and work are inseparable from, if regularly subordinated to, those of her husband, Jacques Maritain (1882–1973), the virtual reinventor of Scholastic philosophy and, from, say, 1920 until the early 1960s, probably the most influential Catholic intellectual in the world. The turbulent life and fragmentary writings of a third woman, Colette Peignot (1903–38) are also becoming better known in their own right and not simply for the influence they had on those of her lover during the last years of her life, the self-styled "atheologist" Georges Bataille (1897–1962) who, along with others, was responsible for her posthumous mythologization as "Laure." Like Thérèse Martin, Colette was a victim of tuberculosis, which, like anorexia, is one of the leitmotifs of this book.

Five women, then, at least four of whom will probably be recognized by most readers, particularly those familiar with French literature, art, or philosophy. Beyond them, however, probably only Catholics will be able to identify Mélanie Calvat (1831–1904), the subject of chapter 1, though many others will have heard of the alleged apparition of the Virgin Mary of which she was the witness, along with the eleven-year-old Maximin Giraud (1835–75), a cowherd like Mélanie, in September 1846; for the hardline Catholic writers who dominate this book, the apparition at La Salette was much more important than the far better known one at Lourdes twelve years later, and Mélanie, despite (or, rather, precisely because of) her rejection by the hierarchy of the Church, a more authentic prophet by far than the duly canonized Bernadette Soubirous (1844–79), the pivotal figure at Lourdes and yet another casualty of tuberculosis. Similarly, the name of Marthe Robin (1902–81), the noneating, nonsleeping visionary mentioned above, will probably ring few bells beyond practicing Catholics, and practicing French Catholics at that, while one would need to be something of a Catholic scholar even to have heard of Eva Lavallière (1866–1929) and Claire Ferchaud (1896–1972), both typical products, in their different ways, of pre-1914 French ultra-Catholicism, though the latter lived on, spurned by the Church and embraced by the religious far right, into the post–Vatican II era. The final two names, Anne-Marie Roulé (1846–1907) and Pauline Lair Lamotte (1853–1918), the self-styled Madeleine Lebouc (*le bouc émissaire* meaning scapegoat in French), are unknown except, in the first instance, to literary scholars (Anne-Marie was the one-time mistress and inspiration of Léon Bloy [1846–1917], the most ultra of all the ultra-Catholic writers discussed in this book) and, in the second, to students of the history of psychiatry in France, Madeleine being one of the most spectacular cases of "hysteria" studied by the formidable Pierre Janet (1859–1947) at the famous—or is it notorious?—clinic of La Salpêtrière in Paris. Unlike Madeleine, who was "cured" of her so-called religious monomania, Anne-Marie spent the last twenty-five years of her life in a lunatic asylum in Caen where, for a time, one of her fellow inmates was none other than Louis Martin (1823–94), the father of Thérèse whose suffering expression was, as we shall see, the model of his daughter's devotion to the Holy Face of Christ from which she took the second part of her Carmelite name. The theme of reclusion, be it in convent (Thérèse, Mélanie), asylum, hospital or hospice (Camille, Colette, Anne-Marie, Madeleine), or home (Raïssa, Marthe), recurs throughout this book.

These eleven women were not chosen arbitrarily, but neither are they intended to be representative of French Catholic women as a whole from the early nineteenth to the mid-twentieth century. It was a period that began with Napoleon's Concordat with the Vatican, finalized in 1802, by which the Catholic Church in France became, in effect, an institution of the state, continued via the first Vatican Council of 1869–70, and the bitter conflict between Church and Republic that ensued and that was terminated, rather than resolved, by the formal separation of church and state in 1905, and came to a provisional conclusion with the Second Vatican Council of 1962–65, which appeared to mark the final reconciliation of the Church with the realities of democracy, freedom, and modernity. The lives of the women studied here span the spread of secularism, usually referred to in France as *"déchristianisation,"* between the late eighteenth and mid-nineteenth centuries, the rise, after the "terrible year" of 1870–71, of a reactionary form of Catholicism dominated by Marian apparitions (Mariophanies), the cult of the Sacred Heart of Jesus, and blind loyalty to the beleaguered pope "over the mountains" in Rome (whence its common name of "ultramontanism"), the parallel rise of "social Catholicism," which attempted to remedy the now almost unbridgeable "discordat" between the church of Rome and the mass of the French people, the unhappy association of both the bulk of the French Catholic hierarchy and, for a time, the bulk of French Catholics with the pro-Nazi Vichy regime between 1940 and 1944, and the seemingly irreversible liberalization of the church between the death of Pope Pius XII in 1958 and the accession of John Paul II twenty years later.

In the course of following—at some distance—more than 170 years of complex ecclesiastical, theological, and devotional evolution, the lives of many important French Catholic women are only touched on in passing, like that of Bernadette Soubirous, or omitted completely, like that of another saint, Elisabeth Catez (Saint Elisabeth de la Trinité), whose dates, 1880–1906, will probably be enough to indicate that she, too, was a victim of tuberculosis. I had originally intended to devote a chapter to Bernadette, until the publication of Ruth Harris's probably definitive *Lourdes: Body and Spirit in the Secular Age* in 1999 made such a project redundant; here Bernadette and Lourdes are referred to only in their contrast to Mélanie Calvat and the Marian apparition at La Salette in 1846. My original plan was also to discuss a representative selection of the countless nineteenth- and twentieth-century images—literary, visual, musical, and, above all, cinematic—of that pivotal and endlessly controversial emblem of female Catholic heroism in France, Joan of Arc. In the event, I was deterred both by the sheer volume and complexity of the material involved and, I readily confess, by the surpassing inanity of the latest cinematic version of her life by Luc Besson, starring his then partner Milla Jovovich. Jacques Rivette's dreary Maidathon *Jeanne la Pucelle* (1994) had already tested my patience to the limit, and I decided I could simply not take any more clanking armor, cropped hair, chains, and flames licking around successive *gamines* dressed *comme des garçons;* here only the unforgettable image of Renée Falconetti in Carl Dreyer's silent masterpiece of 1928 is retained, and this linked to my final emblem of female martyrdom in France, the *tondue,* cropped, smeared with swastikas or the letters "SS" in paint, pitch, or more noxious substances still, and symbolically guillotined or crucified during the "ugly carnival" (*le carnaval moche*) of June, July, and August 1944.[1]

There are, needless to say, other figures that I might have included had it been my purpose to give a representative picture of French Catholic women during the period in question: the poet Marie Noël (the pseudonym of Marie Rouget [1883–1967]) who scarcely ever left her hometown of Auxerre and whose quiet, intimate verse many poetically inclined French Catholics far prefer to the public and, at its worst, posturing and orotund writing of Claudel or Charles Péguy (1873–1914), the preeminent male Catholic poets of the twentieth century; or, in the crucial domain of charitable work, almost entirely passed over here, the remarkable Rosalie Rendu (1786–1856), one of the first Sisters of Charity to work among the Parisian poor (in her case in the now fashionable Quartier Mouffetard, south of the Latin Quarter); or, again, Pauline Jaricot (1799–1862), the founder, in 1826, of the Association du Rosaire Vivant, the first mass Catholic movement run by laypeople, and the main inspiration behind the Oeuvre de la Propagation de la Foi, founded in her native city of Lyon in 1822. But my concern is essentially with the themes of suffering and sacrifice, whence the omnipresence, I fear, of the two liquids that give the book its title. *Holy Tears, Holy Blood* is complete in itself but continues the lines of inquiry— as well as the central image—of my earlier book, *Blood in the City: Violence and Revelation in Paris 1789–1945* (2001). In that work, I addressed myself primarily to the question of *political* violence and suffering and to the way in which, for both "Right" and "Left," the paradigmatic sacrifice of Christ, renewed in the execution of Louis XVI and many others, offered a template for the understanding of the huge amount of bloodletting that occurred at irregular intervals in Paris between the seizing of the Bastille in

July 1789 and the Liberation more than a century and a half later. Here there is rather less blood, and considerably more weeping, but my focus is still on the centrality of Christ's Passion in French Catholic thought and practice during the period in question, that inaugural sacrifice which so many French Catholic women (and not a few non- or anti-Catholic women as well) felt it was their calling and duty to repeat, not just, or even primarily, in the case of Catholic women, for their own individual salvation but, more pertinently, for that of their nonbelieving fellow countrymen and women for whose sake they willingly assumed, and even actively sought out, pain, suffering, illness, and, ultimately, death in order to redeem them—literally "buy them back"—from the clutches of the Enemy whom, along with most ultramontanists, they commonly identified with Revolution, the "godless" Republic that had supplanted monarchy and Church, and with all those who they believed to be Satan's agents or puppets in his war against Christ: "Protestants," "freethinkers" (especially if they taught in the Republic's *école sans Dieu*), "freemasons," "socialists," "internationalists," "foreigners," and "Jews."

The prominence given here to the thematics of suffering does not mean, of course, that the voluntary assumption of pain in imitation of the Passion of Christ was the *only* way in which French Catholic women related to God during the hundred-plus years covered by this book. Tens of thousands of "ordinary" Catholic women lived lives of unspectacular dutifulness and devotion from which the extremes of so-called extraordinary phenomena discussed in chapter 5—excessive fasting, bleeding from head, hands, and side after the model of the stigmata of Christ, visions and "possession" both demonic and angelic—were absent. Indeed, most "mainstream" Catholic women devoted their lives to the *relieving* of the sufferings of others rather than to assuming, even actively seeking out, suffering for themselves in order more completely to resemble their Lord in his agony on the Cross. After all, the most popular Marian pilgrimage in the Virgin- and pilgrimage-obsessed half-century following the defeat of 1870 was not to La Salette where the Virgin's message was construed as predicting just such a catastrophe, but to Lourdes, in the promotion and organization of which women played, as Ruth Harris has shown, a determining role (see below), where her words were rather of healing and hope. Indeed, by the end of the century, Lourdes had become, as Emile Zola memorably demonstrated in his great novel of 1894 devoted to the pilgrimage, a semi-pagan celebration of *this* life rather than a Christian preparation for the life after death, which was precisely why adepts of the "culture of suffering" like the writers Joris-Karl Huysmans (1848–1907) and Léon Bloy not only placed it well below La Salette in terms of its spiritual significance but regarded it with something bordering on contempt (see chapter 1).

The culture of suffering was always, therefore, a minority calling within the devotional practice of the church, a Via Dolorosa chosen and assumed by a self-appointed religious elite, whose influence nonetheless spread well beyond the spiritual aristocracy that espoused it, legitimating and providing a meaning and outlet for the more down-to-earth, day-to-day sufferings and unhappinesses of thousands, and proposing models of sanctity to the mass of believers. It was not, needless to say, limited to women—indeed, its most ardent theoreticians, if not active practitioners, were men, as exemplified by such figures as the saintly curé of the village of Ars just north of Lyon, the Abbé Jean-Marie Vianney (1786–1859 canonized 1925); the missionary Théophane Vénard (1823–61), martyred by decapitation at Tonkin and an object of particular veneration by Thérèse Martin; and by Charles de Foucauld (1858–1916) who, after spending ten years as a hermit at Tamanrasset in the remotest Algerian Hoggar, was shot through the head by a fifteen-year-old youth in the course of a Tuareg raid on the village. To these emblematic martyrs and victims must be added the tens of thousands of "ordinary" Catholic men—amongst them such unordinary figures as the writers Charles Péguy and Ernest Psichari (1883–1914), both killed in the early months of the war—who underwent an individual and collective Golgotha in the trenches of 1914–18, and the much smaller number who offered up their lives in the struggle against the German occupation of their country in 1940–44, most famously the naval officer Honoré d'Estienne d'Orves (1901–41), executed for resistance activities at the fort of Mont Valérien just outside Paris in August 1941, whose final act was reputedly, an *alter Christus* to the end, to forgive, and ask God's forgiveness for, his executioners.

For all this, it was the Christlike sufferings of women that were foregrounded both by the post-1870 French Catholic hierarchy and, in particular, by the writers of the fin de siècle French Catholic literary renaissance, proponents and ideologues of what has been well named the Reactionary Revolution.[2] Of the eleven women studied in detail in this book, eight (Mélanie Calvat, Anne-Marie Roulé, Thérèse Martin, Madeleine Lebouc, Eva Lavallière, Claire Ferchaud, Raïssa Maritain, and Marthe Robin) were, in their different ways, and despite their very different backgrounds, personalities, and levels of education, representative, if not of female devotional practice as a whole, then certainly of the radical current within it that went by the name of "vicarious suffering" or "mystical substitution" (see below). Although never formally a Catholic, Simone Weil clearly belongs to the same spiritual tradition, though the route that she took to it was anything but orthodox. Camille Claudel's life was made up largely of suffering which, for a time, she succeeded in transmuting into art, but she was never a Catholic—indeed she was notably hostile to all forms of organized religion—and it was left to her Catholic brother Paul to transform her, in his literary works, into an icon of redemptive expiation and suffering. Finally, Colette Peignot spent her entire adult life rebelling against her Catholic formation, but, like her lover and mentor Georges Bataille, who at one time trained for the priesthood, replicated its teachings in sacrilegiously inverted forms even as she revolted against them, in such a way that, a "saint of the abyss," she appears as some kind of diabolic double of a Thérèse or a Raïssa, closer to them in spirit than she ever imagined. Taken together, the experiences of the eleven women studied here—whether they were intellectuals of the highest order (Simone Weil and Raïssa Maritain), simple peasant women of limited formal education (Marthe Robin), members of religious orders (Thérèse Martin), or "freelance" spiritual seekers both orthodox and decidedly heterodox (Eva Lavallière, Colette Peignot), or even close to insanity for at least part of their lives (Mélanie Calvat, Camille Claudel, Anne-Marie Roulé, Madeleine Lebouc, Claire Ferchaud)—illuminate what was from, say, 1870 to 1920, and, less insistently, into the late 1940s, the most publicized, if not the most generalized, expression of female Catholic spirituality in France.

Of course, if so rare and extreme a form of spirituality enjoyed such salience in French Catholic discourse and consciousness for fifty years and more, it was due in no small part to the talents of the Catholic artists and intellectuals who chose to describe, explain, and promote it, whence the prominence, in a book devoted to female religious experience, of male writers such as Bloy, Huysmans, Claudel, and, *mutatis mutandis,* Georges Bataille. To put the matter crudely, but not excessively: The women suffered, the men wrote about that suffering. To be sure, of the eleven women studied here, no fewer than seven (Mélanie, Thérèse, Raïssa, Claire, Eva, Colette, Simone) left extensive, if often fragmentary, writings of their own, writings that in many cases were collated, edited, and publicized by men: Jacques Maritain in the case of Raïssa, Georges Bataille, Michel Leiris, and Jérôme Peignot in that of Colette, the Catholic philosopher Gustave Thibon in that of Simone, the Franciscan Omer Englebert in that of Eva Lavallière. The "confessions" of Madeleine Lebouc are known to us solely through the study of her conducted by Pierre Janet, while Marthe's few writings and extensive dicta were mediated through a number of primarily male "filters," notably her priestly associate the Abbé Georges Finet (1898–1990) and the leading Catholic intellectual, Jean Guitton (1901–99). Anne-Marie Roulé is known solely through Bloy's doubtless highly mythologized account of her agonies and ecstasies, and, although Mélanie produced a narrative of her life, it is again through Bloy's hagiological *Celle qui pleure* (1907) that that account became known to the wider public; Claire Ferchaud's autobiography was not published in her lifetime. The "case" of Camille Claudel is rather more complex. A body of letters survives, and, of course, her sculptures remain (even though many of them have been lost) to bear witness both to the extravagance of her gifts and the intensity of her suffering. Nonetheless, it is difficult to dissociate her from her brother's promotion of her person and art, and her stature as an icon of female suffering was essentially his literary creation before it became—rather in the manner of the "sanctification" of Sylvia Plath—a topos of recent French feminist discourse.[3] Only Thérèse speaks to her public more or less directly (her writings and dicta, particularly the so-called *novissima verba* uttered on her deathbed, were at least originally collated, edited, and transmitted by her Carmelite sisters), though she, too, can only with difficulty be disentangled from the image constructed of her by her numerous male votaries, notably the great Catholic novelist and essayist Georges Bernanos (1888–1948), who, in many cases, inflected, not to say distorted, her experience in the direction of their own theological agenda. The ways in which these, and some other, male Catholic (and occasionally non-Catholic) writers conceptualized, interpreted, and, sometimes, fantasized about female suffering and inserted it into their broader theological, moral, political, and literary concerns is thus no less central to this book than the question of female suffering, in a religious or sacred context, itself. The two themes—female suffering and male appropriation of that suffering—are explored concurrently in the accounts that follow in chapters 1 through 6, before being confronted directly in the concluding chapter.

Doctrine of Vicarious Suffering

The Catholic doctrine of "vicarious suffering," or "mystical substitution," lies at the theological core of this book and will be illustrated and explicated as the chapters unfold. Its origins, discussed in detail in *Blood in the City*,[4] may usefully be recapitulated here, in view of the doctrine's probable unfamiliarity to most non-Catholic readers and to many modern Catholic ones as well. In the wake of the execution of Louis XVI (January 1793) and of his queen Marie Antoinette (October 1793), preceded or followed by that of hundreds of aristocrats, priests, nuns, and other royalist supporters, counterrevolutionary writers such as Joseph de Maistre (1755–1821), Louis de Bonald (1754–1840), and Pierre-Simon Ballanche (1776–1847) formulated the idea that every such "martyrdom" renewed and replicated the original sacrifice of Christ and, like that primary act of self-offering, had the potential to save not just the martyr him- or herself but the entire French nation, which, one way or another, had participated in the revolutionary "crime" and, above all, in the murder of that *alter Christus,* the King. In consequence of that unspeakable act, every French man, woman, and child, now and perhaps in perpetuity, was required to atone in blood, sweat, and tears in order to redeem, in the literal sense of "buy back," the nation from the diabolic forces that held it in thrall: the royal blood shed on the guillotine could only be expiated in the blood of the nation. The suffering body of Christ, the martyred body of the King, the wounded French nation, that *fille aînée de l'Eglise* (eldest daughter of the Church) who, every year, repudiated her Holy Mother a little more, the humiliated body of the Church and of its earthly Father, the pope, all became equivalents of each other, in a much more than merely metaphorical sense. With the restoration of the legitimate monarchy in 1815 lasting only until the Revolution of 1830, French ultra-Catholics did not want for further national crimes and woes to expiate in suffering: the inexorable spread of *déchristianisation* and parallel rise of "atheistic" socialism; the designs of Napoleon III, following his uncle, on Italy and, above all, on the Papal Lands; the defeat of 1870 followed by the virulently antireligious Paris Commune of March–May 1871, bringing it with it a fresh cortege of priestly victims; the virtual imprisonment of Pope Pius IX, yet another *alter Christus,* in the Vatican; the creation of a secular schooling system, *l'école sans Dieu,* or "Godless school," by the allegedly Jewish- and masonic-dominated Third Republic; the final separation of church and state in 1905, and the disbanding and exile of the religious orders; the massive bloodletting of 1914–18; the catastrophic defeat of 1940; even, for a few remaining diehards like Claire Ferchaud, the retreat from Empire in the 1950s and 1960s. By suffering with and suffering for afflicted monarchy, Church, and nation, individual Catholics, women, as effectively as and perhaps more effectively than men, could participate in their joint redemption. Women were attracted to the doctrine of vicarious suffering because it not only gave meaning and value to the pains and tribulations of their daily lives but also empowered them through the voluntary espousal of their powerlessness.

Ultraroyalist in origin and almost always ultrareactionary in its political implications, the doctrine of vicarious suffering derived its scriptural authority from a notoriously cryptic passage in Saint Paul's letter to the Colossians (1:24) in which the apostle tells his correspondents that (in the Jerusalem Bible translation) "it makes me happy to suffer for you, as I am suffering now, and in my own body to do what I can to make up all that has still to be undergone by Christ for the sake of his body, the Church." The key words "all that has still to be undergone by Christ"—which the Vulgate, used by most of the figures, male and female, discussed in this book, translates as *adimpleo quae desunt passionum Christi*—were taken to mean that Christ's death on the Cross was *not* the once-and-for-all "full and final sacrifice" that Protestant theology, for example, holds it to be, but that it was necessary for Christ's followers on earth to suffer further in their own bodies to bring his sacrifice to completion. The "merits" that they thus accumulate will then "revert" to the benefit not just of themselves but of the rest of nonsuffering, impenitent humanity, whence the name of "reversibility," which is also applied to the doctrine, and culture, of vicarious suffering. Thanks to the principle of reversibility, all human beings, Christian and non-Christian alike, become members of each other, participants, whether they know it or not, in a vast circulation of merits and graces through the universal Body of the Church, meaning here not the institutional church but the whole of humanity, living, dead, and still to be born.

Just as Christ suffered for us, so we must suffer for and, if necessary, *instead* of each other, "mystically substituting" our suffering selves for others, either to suffer in their place or to take their sufferings upon ourselves. It follows that no suffering is wasted or without value. Through suffering, we accumulate a spiritual capital on which we and others can draw to redeem ourselves from the clutches of the devil: by suffering, I collaborate in your salvation, just as you, by suffering in return, collaborate in mine. One can see both the solace that the doctrine could afford those who suffer, and also the misuses, even perversions, to which it might lend itself, as, for example, when the dying refused medication or sedation lest the salvific "merit" of their suffering be diminished.

From its original, highly politicized formulation, the doctrine of vicarious suffering reached a broader Catholic public through, in particular, the widely read *De la douleur* (1849) by the Catholic theologian and philosopher Blanc de Saint-Bonnet (1815–80), hailed by Léon Bloy as "one of the intellectual majesties of this century."[5] Thereafter, the thematics of vicarious suffering sluiced through the veins and arteries of Catholic France, pumped and primed by an increasingly vocal and influential Catholic intelligentsia: the convert-novelist Jules Barbey d'Aurevilly (1808–89) and the ultramontanist journalist Louis Veuillot (1813–83) in the 1860s and 1870s; Bloy, Huysmans, and the then-influential novelist and philosopher Ernest Hello (1828–85) in the 1880s and 1890s; Claudel, Psichari, Péguy, Maritain, and the orientalist Louis Massignon (1883–1962) during the belle époque and—if they survived the ordeal of war—into the 1920s and 1930s. In 1914–18 the doctrine of vicarious suffering may be said to have come into its own. No longer, if it had ever been, a theological abstraction, it offered consolation and inspiration to thousands of Catholic soldiers—and not a few non-Catholic ones, too—in the Time on the Cross that they spent in the trenches. "During this war no death is sad" (Pendant cette guerre, il n'y a pas de mort triste), wrote one priest of the death of the well-known Action Française militant, Dominique-Pierre Dupouey, in April 1915,[6] for every death, indeed every wound, blister, or louse-ridden greatcoat, could be turned to positive account in the great investment bank of sufferings, graces, and merits. For another ultraroyalist and ultra-Catholic activist, Georges Bernanos, all at the front, French and Germans alike, were members of "the universal church of combatants, living and dead," a monastic order whose mission was to expiate the sins of those at the rear: "We made [war] under the sign of expiation, it was a war of expiation, of redemption, of reciprocal expiation and redemption, each of the parties [the French and the Germans] rendering their service to each other, like monks exchanging disciplinary blows."[7]

After the real-life calvary of 1914–18, it is hardly surprising that the doctrine of vicarious suffering went into relative abeyance in the years following the war, despite the promotional verve of Bernanos, whose widely read

Sous le soleil de Satan (1926) and *Journal d'un curé de campagne* (1936), both featuring suffering priest-heroes explicitly modeled on the Curé d'Ars, were classic fictional expositions of the theology involved. But history again came to the doctrine's rescue in 1940–44, when the entire French nation, in emulation of Marshall Pétain's "gift of his person," was enjoined by Vichyist-Catholic ideology to suffer in expiation of the alleged sins of *l'entre-deux-guerres*: a declining birthrate, the abandonment of country in favor of city, the dangerous flirtation with "socialism" under the Popular Front (1936), even the collective overfondness for *pastis*. The impromptu sermon delivered to Jean-Paul Sartre's dejected prisoners of war in *La Mort dans l'âme* (1949) typifies the kind of expiatory discourse that would emanate from pulpit, press, and radio particularly during the first two years of the so-called Révolution Nationale:

> It was France, eldest daughter of the Church [*fille aîneé de l'Eglise*], that inscribed in history the dazzling succession of its victories; it was godless France [*la France sans Dieu*] that underwent the defeat of 1940. . . . So, my brothers, let us abandon the notion that our defeat is the fruit of chance: it is at once our punishment and our fault. . . . Harsh, unpleasant news, I agree, but good news nonetheless . . . , for if there is fault and if there is expiation, there is also redemption [*car si'il y a faute et s'il y a expiation, il y a aussi rachat*]. . . . Our Lord, who suffered for mankind, who took our faults upon Him, who suffered and is suffering still in order to expiate them, Our Lord has chosen you. Yes, all of you, peasants, workers, bourgeois, who are neither wholly innocent nor certainly the most guilty, He has chosen you for an incomparable destiny: He has chosen that your sufferings, like His, should redeem the sins and faults of the whole of France that God has never ceased to love and which He is punishing against His will.[8]

Just as the prisoners of war (POWs) are called on to expiate and redeem the sins and sufferings of those "back home," so those under occupation in France were required to suffer in order to "buy back" their loved ones from captivity; thousands, so to speak, "ransomed" themselves under the Relève program whereby, for every three Frenchmen volunteering for work in the Reich, one French POW would be returned to his homeland. Every French man, woman, and child was called on to become a sacrificial offering, following the Marshall himself who, according to Vichyist propaganda, sacrificed himself to "permit, like a new Christ, the redemption of defeated France."[9] Those, like Raïssa Maritain or Simone Weil, who found themselves abroad, often imposed further privations on themselves in emulation of their suffering compatriots; in Simone's case, as we have seen, pushing herself *usque ad mortem,* to the point of death and beyond, in pursuit of vicarious identification with the hungry and oppressed. As the psychologist Gérard Miller has written,[10] the ideology of Vichyist France gave voice to a kind of "expiatory delirium," indefinitely multiplied: the Marshall is suffering with you and for you, your priests, bishops, and cardinals are suffering with you and for you (and, needless to say, the Holy Father "across the mountains" is suffering with and for you as well), you the citizens are suffering for yourselves and each other, the prisoners in Germany are suffering with you and for you, we are all suffering together, and, as we join our sufferings to the super-sufferings of Christ, so the "merits" we accumulate will "revert" to the good of the entire nation so that, by suffering, we will collaborate with Christ and His saints in our collective redemption.

After this four-year-long litany of dolorism, it was predictable that, as in the 1920s, the return of peace and, more important, the restoration of liberty would cause the doctrine of expiatory suffering, tainted by its Vichyist associations, to recede in postwar French Catholic devotion, not, this time, a temporary eclipse but, to all appearances, a definitive decline. In the buildup to the Second Vatican Council (1962–65), so different from the first (1870), both Church hierarchy and laity turned to more activist and, above all, more life-affirming ways of living the faith. Although Raïssa Maritain and Claire Ferchaud lived into the 1960s, and Marthe Robin continued to receive and counsel penitents right up to her death in 1981, their form of devotion with its emphasis on the value, even the goodness, of suffering was notably out of tune with the mood of France's so-called Thirty Glorious Years (*les Trente Glorieuses*, c. 1950–c. 1980) of economic growth and upward social mobility. Virtually the last literary work—and it is arguably the greatest—to foreground the theology of vicarious suffering was Bernanos's posthumously published *Dialogues des Carmélites* (1951), written as a film script but now mainly known as the text of Francis Poulenc's magnificent opera of the same name (1957). Based on the story of the sixteen Carmelite sisters of Compiègne guillotined in Paris on 16 August 1794, text and opera take the doctrine of vicarious suffering back full circle to its counterrevolutionary origins and, in the words of Sister Constance, plainly modeled on the figure of Sainte Thérèse, give it its purest and most memorable formulation: "We die not for ourselves alone but for one another, or sometimes even instead of each other, who knows" (On ne meurt pas chacun pour soi, mais les uns pour les autres, ou même les uns à la place des autres, qui sait).[11] How eloquent that the last, and most moving, artistic expression of the doctrine of vicarious suffering should be of a procession of women filing, rapturously singing the *Salve Regina* and *Veni Creator,* to death by decapitation on the revolutionary scaffold.

Women in the Catholic Church

The relevant political, social, and cultural contexts will be progressively clarified through the portraits that follow, but it may be useful, at this stage, to make some brief general comments on the position of women in the Catholic Church in France during the period in question. That position may be characterized, succinctly if paradoxically, as both marginal and central. It was marginal in the sense that, from the Vatican down to the humblest rural parish, the principle of male, and specifically patriarchal, authority was unchallenged. The possibilities for real power for women—outside the closed world of convents, where even the Mother Superior was ultimately subordinate to her local bishop—were effectively non-existent. The role of the Catholic woman (and it was a view from which few, if any, of those studied here deviated in thought, let alone in deed) was to serve, obey, care for the suffering, and to suffer herself. On the other hand, women were absolutely central to the political and social project of the French Catholic Church—as they were to every Christian denomination in Europe and elsewhere at a time of escalating secularization[12]—and were explicitly targeted by the Church as key figures in its increasingly explicit struggle with modernity, be it in its political, social, intellectual, or ethical expression. From the early 1800s, when the ten years' war between Revolution and Church was formally ended, it was obvious to every priest in the land, urban or rural, rich parish or poor, that women outnumbered men at his offices by something like two to one; even those men present at mass were, in the consecrated expression, more often "accompanying" their wives, children, and servants rather than taking communion themselves. At confession (an essential preliminary to making even the obligatory once-a-year Easter communion), the predominance of women was even more marked, and an abundant anticlerical literature, often scabrous in content as well as intent, dwelt on the power exercised by priest over female penitent in dimly lit confessional. While boys, particularly middle-class boys, were educated in their majority in secular schools, it was normal, and remained so until well into the twentieth century, for the daughters of even nonbelieving fathers to be educated by nuns, and the anticlerical father of Mouchette, the desperate teenage heroine of Bernanos' *Sous le soleil de Satan* (1926), is only recycling the platitudes of his kind when he complains that "the nuns work on girls in favour of the priest" and so "ruin in advance the authority of the husband"; moreover, "what with his youth club [*patronage*], the *enfants de Marie* and the rest, the priest gets hold of them for an hour every Sunday. Watch out for what goes on underneath!"[13] The result was what one leading historian of French Catholicism has called a sharply marked "sexual dimorphism" in religious beliefs, attitudes, and practices:[14] an increasingly non- (and sometimes anti-) religious masculine population in all classes of society confronted with a still largely believing female population, especially, but far from exclusively, in the upper and middle classes, for whom, however, frequenting the sacraments was often inhibited by the now widespread use of one or another form of artificial contraception (usually "dry copulation" [*le coït sec*] or withdrawal) which made the encounter with the priest in the confessional an occasion of evasion, embarrassment, or outright condemnation.

Thus it was that, in France as in Britain, if "men were the religious problem," women came increasingly to be seen as "the religious solution."[15] Given the perceived "maleness of impiety,"[16] the Church acted accordingly, and as early as 1801 there appeared in Paris a book bearing the significant title of *Des services que les femmes peuvent rendre à la religion* in which the author, the Abbé Gaspard Jauffret, declared outright: "Christian wives, you are responsible for the conversion of your husbands."[17] The following year—the year of the formal signing of the Concordat—the Abbé Baudoin, incumbent at Chavagnes-en-Paillers in the ultraconservative and ultra-Catholic Vendée in the west of France, underlined the importance of "forming Catholic mothers" to combat unbelief and its consequences, sexual immorality, drinking, and (though he did not say so in so many words) political revolution. There is much evidence that French Catholic women responded in large numbers to the call of their clergy, and in 1855 a visiting Italian cleric opined that "it is to woman that France owes its not having remained in the religion of schism, deism, or idolatry that impiety had successively laid upon it"; to the extent that secularization has been withstood, it is the "new priesthood" (*sacerdoce nouveau*) of women, both religious and lay, that provided the bulwark. Such female initiative was most evident in the founding, almost always at the prompting of a single devout woman, of all manner of charitable, educational, and evangelical "associations," "congregations," or "works" (*Oeuvres*), not just religious orders—though these were numerous—but lay organizations run by women for women, subordinate, ultimately, to (male) ecclesiastical authority, but, in practice, a domain where women could exercise far greater influence than in any other sphere open to them at the time. Nor, contrary to widespread beliefs, were the founders and, still less, the members of such organizations all of upper- or middle-class origin. Some, of course, were scions of the old aristocracy, like Thérèse de Bavoz who restored the Benedictine tradition in France or Emilie de Vialar whose Soeurs de Saint-Joseph de l'Apparition were established in Algeria a mere five years after the beginning of French colonization in 1830. But others, their names now forgotten, came from the lower-middle classes, the skilled working classes, and even the peasantry: Marie-Sophie Barat, Anne-Marie Javouhey, Alexandrine Conduché, Julie Chauchard, Jeanne-Antide Thouret, Jeanne Jugan, Elisabeth Eppinger. Rosalie Rendu, and Pauline Jaricot have already been mentioned. Here let us record just three other typical nineteenth-century female initiatives: Anne-Marie Rivieu (1768–1838), still illiterate when she made her first communion at Montpezat-sous-Bauchon in the Ardèche, but, by 1792—a time of mounting hostility to the Church—a teacher of the catechism "doing the work of three vicars" and, two years later, living with four female companions in a makeshift "convent" in the small town of Thueyts nearby. With the signing of the Concordat, her teaching order, the Présentation de Marie, began its remarkable expansion, so that by the time of her death it had no fewer than 141 "branches" with three hundred sisters devoting their lives to being, in her words, "an open Gospel in which everyone may read Jesus Christ!" Or, again, Charlotte Dupin (1770–1805), a priest's servant in Lyon, who, imprisoned during the Terror for her religious beliefs and associations, turned her sufferings to divine account by founding, on her release, a lay organization devoted to visiting prisoners. After her death, the "Charlottes," as they were known, joined the Soeurs de Saint-Joseph and, in 1841, became a separate order known as the Soeurs de Marie-Joseph. As early as 1811, the Charlottes were preparing four thousand meals a day in Lyon alone and taking them to prisoners whose cells they also offered to clean; a branch of the order, known as the "Peigneuses," later devoted itself to the humble task of washing patients in hospitals and combing their hair.[18] Or finally, another Lyonnaise, Françoise Perroton, born in 1798 or 1799, a member of Pauline Jaricot's Propagation de la Foi by 1820, who, in 1845, no longer a young woman, decided to go, unaccompanied, to the island of Wallis in the Pacific, a journey that took her ten months, to establish a religious foundation. There she remained, known as "Carméli" to the local people whom she served, until her death in 1873 from the effects of elephantiasis, writing in her last letter: "When one has merited hell a hundred times over, one can put up with transient suffering no matter how long it lasts. I count on the charity of my friends, but above all on the infinite mercy of Jesus Christ. Kolopelu, 17 April 1873."[19]

Along with this "gender shift in the centre of religiosity"[20] apparent in both France and Britain, went a marked "feminization" of the content and, above all, the imagery of Christianity in both countries. In Britain, as well as feminizing piety, evangelicalism "pietized femininity. Femininity became sacred *and nothing but sacred.*"[21] In France, this process went even further, aided, of course, by the central position of the Virgin Mary in the Catholic faith and, not least, by the huge number of women—130,000 in 1880—in religious orders of all kinds.[22] As God the Father became more remote even for believers, so his place was taken, first, by a discreetly feminized Christ and then, particularly after 1870, by a hyperfeminized Virgin. Curiously androgynous, with his wispy beard, doelike eyes, and delicate, soft-limbed body, the nineteenth-century French Catholic Christ wept and bled like a woman. Both the cult of the Sacred Heart and that of the Holy Face, so dear to Thérèse Martin that she took it as the second part of her Carmelite name, were directed at a comprehensively feminized image of Christ; even the angels, previously male or asexual, took on the attributes of women.[23] Increasingly, female saints such as Philomena, whose tomb was discovered in Rome in 1802, eclipsed their male counterparts in popularity, with women typically taking the lead in the promotion of their cult; the rapid diffusion of the image of Philomena, not to mention the popularity of Philomena as a first name for girls, was largely due to Pauline Jaricot's pilgrimage of 1835 to her shrine from which she returned with fragments of the virgin martyr's body which she passed on to the Curé d'Ars, who in turn promoted Philomena as a healer of bodies and souls.[24] At a time when God the Father was either distant, angry, or both, the cult of female saints such as Philomena "opened the way to [a] *tender* ultramontane piety."[25] The role of the female saint was, like that of the androgynized Jesus, to bleed, weep, and love unconditionally; small wonder, as we shall see, that Mary Magdalene occupied so central a place in the devotions of many of the women we shall study.

But the core of what has been well called "affective ultramontanism"[26] was undoubtedly the cult of the Virgin Mary, known technically as "hyperdulia," being superior to the veneration (*dulia*) appropriate to saints but falling short—in strict theological orthodoxy if not always in practice—of the worship (*latreia*) appropriate to the Three Persons of the Trinity. The nineteenth century was the hyperdulic century *par excellence,* and Catholic France surpassed every other country in the intensity of its Marian devotion. It was not simply that Marianism foregrounded what we may call the "Anima aspect" of the sacred. The cult of the Virgin was, in many respects, centered on, and often organized by, women, not least in the case of three of the four alleged Mariophanies that the church formally recognized in France between 1830 and 1871. Of these, the first (at the Rue du Bac in Paris between July and November 1830) and the third and most famous (at Lourdes in February and March 1858) involved a single female witness (Catherine Labouré and Bernadette Soubirous, respectively), while at La Salette in 1846 the testimony of Mélanie Calvat was adjudged superior to that of Maximin Giraud; only at Pontmain in Normandy (January 1871) were the two boy witnesses (Eugène and Joseph Barbedette, aged twelve and ten) considered more central than the eleven-year-old Françoise Richer and the nine-year-old Jeanne-Marie Lebossé.[27] Not only this, but, as Ruth Harris has shown, Lourdes, the most popular of the new Marian shrines, "was an enterprise jointly imagined by priests and women, and its distinguishing feature—the care of the sick and dying—was the brainchild of the female participants."[28] "It is difficult to think," she concludes, "of any sphere in the parallel universe of the republic where women had such constant, institutionalized influence."[29] "We have the women and children," declared (with considerable exaggeration) Bishop Dupanloup of Orléans, one of the few members of the French hierarchy to resist the ultramontanist trend, the implication being that the Church's archenemy, the Republic, had the bulk of French men in its thrall.

To many such male Republicans it did indeed seem that the Church was a conspiracy between priests and laywomen, in which the former preyed on the latter even as they prayed with them and for them with a view to neutralizing, or supplanting, the influence of their fathers or husbands; this was the case made by Jules Michelet (1798–1874) as early as 1845 in his *Du prêtre, de la femme, de la famille,* and it was one of the reasons why many Republicans viewed with alarm proposals to extend the suffrage to women. Churches were widely viewed as a feminine space—"boudoirs" Charles Baudelaire called them[30]—with their muted candlelight, incense, flowers, and lacework, and religious feelings were considered a feminine quality and preserve. In the preface to his *Souvenirs d'enfance et de jeunesse* (1883), Ernest Renan (1823–92), whose *Vie de Jésus* (1863) had, by submitting the gospel narratives to historical and textual criticism, undermined the faith of thousands of Catholics, wrote that "woman puts us [i.e., men] back into communication with the eternal source in which God is reflected": "The more man's head is developed, the more he longs for the opposite pole, namely the irrational, repose in utter ignorance, woman who is only woman, instinctive being which acts only by virtue of an obscure consciousness. . . . That is why it is only through women that religion survives in the world."[31] Dominated by male celibates, the nineteenth-century Catholic Church concealed its patriarchy beneath explicitly feminine trappings; never was the term "Mother Church" more pertinent to the reality of its power. "On the femininity of the Church," Baudelaire noted with typical ambiguity around 1860, "as the reason for its omnipotence."[32]

Such, very briefly, is the general background against which the following chapters should be read. The themes and images that they severally raise will be brought together and discussed synoptically in the final chapter. My own attitude to the subject(s) of this book will become clear in due course. Suffice it to say that, no matter how much I, a still believing liberal Catholic convert (lapsed), recoil from the "sanctification of sadness and pain"— the expression, meant critically, is that of André Gide[33]—that dominated the lives of most, if not all, of the women studied here, I have nothing but respect, and sometimes much more, for the women themselves, be they intellectual high-flyers like Simone Weil or uneducated peasant women like Marthe Robin or Claire Ferchaud. Of all of them it could be said, as it was of the "woman in the city, which was a sinner," who, kneeling, washed Christ's feet with her tears and wiped them with her hair, that they "loved much" (Luke 7:47), and that, in their passion, they balked at no suffering or privation to manifest that love. Parts of this book have not been easy either to research or to write, and parts of it, too, may not be easy to read. How could it be otherwise when blood and tears, shed for the holiest (or, sometimes, the unholiest) of causes, are present on almost every page?

HOLY TEARS, HOLY BLOOD

Rouen
Lisieux
Reims
Villeneuve-sur-Fère
Paris
Alençon
Chartres
Solesmes
Saint-Benoît-sur-Loire
Vézelay
Tours
Loublande
Loudun
Paray-Le-Monial
Ars
Morzine
Châteauneuf-de-Galaure
La Salette
Avignon
Saintes-Maries-de-la-Mer
Lourdes
Saint-Maximin-la-Sainte-Baume

I

SHE WHO WEEPS

Mélanie Calvat

LA SALETTE, 19 SEPTEMBER 1846

La Salette (1846) was not the first Marian apparition in nineteenth-century France to be officially accredited by the Church, nor did it ever achieve anything like the national and international popularity as a place of pilgrimage later enjoyed by Lourdes (1858) or, in Portugal, by Fátima (1917); there are, however, grounds for seeing the La Salette "fact" or "event" (*le fait de La Salette*), as its supporters confidently termed it, as historically and spiritually more important than either of its better-known successors, if only because it set the model or paradigm for almost all subsequent apparitions. The first nineteenth-century French Mariophany to receive formal Church validation occurred in 1830 when, on three separate occasions between mid-July and mid-December that year, the Virgin allegedly "appeared" to a twenty-four-year-old novice of the Ordre des Filles de la Charité named Catherine Labouré (1806–76, canonized 1947) at the Order's Mother House on the rue du Bac on the Left Bank in Paris.[1] On her second appearance on 27 November, the Virgin, Catherine averred, had revealed to her the design of a "miraculous medal"—a letter *M* surmounted by a cross with, underneath, the Sacred Hearts of Jesus and Mary herself—that, according to the Virgin's instructions, she, Catherine, was to have struck and reproduced in order that all who wore it and repeated the prayer "O Mary conceived without sin, pray for us who have recourse to you" should benefit from the Virgin's especial solicitude and protection. As shown in *Blood in the City* (chapter 6), the speedy acceptance of Catherine's vision by the Church and the extraordinary diffusion of the Miraculous Medal in the years that followed owed not a little to the critical circumstances of the early 1830s, particularly in Paris. The first of the Virgin's appearances occurred just days before the Revolution of July 1830, which toppled the old Catholic-legitimist monarchy of Charles X and was followed, in its turn, by four years of generalized sociopolitical panic marked by repeated strikes and riots and, above all, by the cholera epidemic of 1832 that caused twenty thousand deaths in Paris alone. By the end of the decade, *ten million* exemplars of the medal were in circulation, not just in France and neighboring countries but also in the United States, Russia, China, even Abyssinia. The popularity of the Miraculous Medal offers ample proof that, though attendances at mass might be in decline, there was an enormous diffuse public eager for tangible proof—or what it considered to be such—of supernatural intervention and protection, and that while Christ, let alone his Father in heaven, might be becoming a remote, shadowy presence, even an absence, for many, his Mother, making light of the gap between heaven and earth, supernature and nature, was capable of stepping into, and filling with the gracious light of her presence, the spiritual void opened up by the increasing remoteness of the Three Persons of the orthodox Trinity.

The identity of Catherine Labouré was not made publicly known until 1855, shortly after the promulgation by Pope Pius IX of the doctrine of the Immaculate Conception of the Virgin Mary (1854). By this time another Marian apparition had occurred to witnesses, in circumstances very different from those of July–December 1830 and, despite its controversial nature, had been formally accredited by the Church.[2] The location of this new revelation—a bare mountainside high above the scattered village of La Salette-Fallavaux (population 734) seventy miles southeast of Grenoble in the French Alps—could not have been more unlike the convent chapel on the rue du Bac, nor could its witnesses have less resembled the devout and (belatedly) literate Catherine Labouré.

Mélanie Calvat (1831–1904) and Maximin Giraud (1835–75) were not from La Salette but hailed from the nearby *bourg* of Corps where their poverty-stricken parents had separately hired them out as cowherds—the usual term *berger* and *bergère* both sentimentalizes the nature of the children's work and fits them into an image of conventional piety—to acquaintances in La Salette, a commune noted for its low level of religious practice and, correlatively, for its ingrained addiction to what scandalized clerics called *le vice français,* not some sexual deviation but the custom of working on Sundays and other feast days of the Church.

In common with other villages and towns in the region, indeed in common with much of France and Europe as a whole, La Salette had suffered from severe potato blight in both 1845 and 1846, and the dry spring and wet summer of 1846 had led to a calamitous grain harvest, with bread prices doubling in Grenoble as a result and making winter famine a virtual certainty in outlying towns and villages. Mélanie and Maximin were certainly aware of this situation, but this was the probable limit of their social consciousness. At fourteen and eleven years respectively, both were patois-speakers with no more than a few words, if that, of French at their command, and both had been refused first communion on the grounds of their ignorance of even the basics of the faith. Maximin's mother had died in

1837, and his father had remarried almost immediately to a woman who, it appears, treated her new stepson with considerable harshness whence, according to one psychological interpretation of *le fait de La Salette,* the threatening and punitive character of the "great news" the Virgin disclosed to the children.[3] For supporters of the La Salette revelations, it was the very ordinariness of the children, indeed their positive unattractiveness (Mélanie was described by her employer as "sulky, idle, disobedient," while Maximin struck almost all those who later questioned him as "habitually coarse and vulgar"), that guaranteed the veracity of the story they would shortly have to tell, as though, in the words of the Magnificat, Mary had herself set out to "put down the mighty from their seats and [exalt] them of low degree" (Luke 1:52) by revealing herself to two illiterate urchins on a barren mountainside in the absolute back of beyond.[4]

Although both from Corps, Mélanie and Maximin did not meet until two days before the alleged apparition, further grounds, in the view of their defenders, for believing that their story was not some collusive fabrication but a straight narration of a "fact" or "event" that had undoubtedly occurred. They met again the following day and arranged to meet and look after their cows together on the day after that, Saturday, 19 September 1846, not just—apologists and symbol-seekers would quickly point out—the regular Our Lady's Saturday but the eve of the important, and, given the Virgin's doleful message on the 19, spiritually supercharged Marian festival of Notre-Dame des Sept Douleurs. On Saturday morning, the two children, accompanied by Maximin's dog Loulou, took their combined herd of eight cows up to an *alpage* (mountain pasture) on the Mont Planeau overlooking La Salette, at an altitude of some 1,800 meters above sea level, where they joined several other children similarly occupied. At midday, having left their cows grazing in a nearby valley, Mélanie and Maximin ate some bread and cheese (*de la tome un peu sèche*), and the other children joined them for *un brisounou* (a little while), as Mélanie put it in the local patois, before moving off down the mountain with their cows, leaving Mélanie and Maximin to take a well-deserved nap after their morning's exertions.

The story of what happened when they awoke is based on a conflation of several accounts given by the children (principally by Mélanie) at intervals over a period of more than thirty years, supported by various interviews conducted by clerics again over an extended period, either to satisfy their private curiosity (like the inquiry undertaken by the patois-speaking Abbé François Lagier in February 1847) or as part of the Church's official investigation into the validity, or otherwise, of the apparition, which culminated in its formal recognition on the fifth anniversary of the "event" itself, 19 September 1851. Each of Mélanie's accounts is more elaborate and, above all, more theologically loaded than its predecessor, particularly in the version that was published, with the approval of her local bishop, when she was at Castellamare in Italy in 1879. Variations, interpolations, and pious fictions apart, each gives essentially the same account of the Virgin's appearance, actions, and utterances (other than the notorious "secrets" that she disclosed privately to each child in isolation) that Mélanie and Maximin gave to a series of individuals on the evening of 19 September and throughout the Sunday that followed: first to their employers and their families (it was *la vieille mère Pra,* mother of Mélanie's patron Benjamin Pra, who first "identified" the children's *Belle Dame* as the Virgin); then, on Sunday morning, to the local priest, the Abbé Perrin, who promptly delivered a tearful sermon at Mass revealing to the few villagers in attendance that the Virgin had appeared among them; followed, in the afternoon, by a lengthy interrogation by the village mayor, M. Peytard. Finally, on the evening of 20 September, Benjamin Pra, helped by Maximin's employer Pierre Selme, known as "le Bruit," and another neighbor, Jean Moussier, took down in stumbling French the account that—using patois except for those words that the Virgin had uttered in French (which the children were somehow able to reproduce even though they had not understood them)—Mélanie and Maximin gave to their suitably stunned audience. When it was complete, the peasant redactors decided to entitle their ill-spelt document *Lettre dictée par la Sainte Vierge à deux enfants,* thus placing it within the ancient rural tradition of the *lettre tombée du ciel,* copies of which, hawked by itinerant colporteurs and bearing such titles as *Lettre trouvée à Jérusalem miraculeusement de la part de Notre Seigneur Jésus-Christ, écrite de sa propre main en lettres d'or* (Letter miraculously discovered in Jerusalem written by Our Lord Jesus Christ in his own hand in golden letters), were undoubtedly still circulating in areas such as the French Alps in the mid-1840s; not surprisingly, critics of the "relation Pra," as it is technically known, regard the whole thing as a simple fabrication, redeploying the well-worn topoi and expressions of an established quasi-literary prototype.[5]

What, reduced to its essential elements, purportedly happened on the early afternoon of 19 September is as follows. Awaking from their sleep around 3 P.M., Mélanie and Maximin went to look for their cows and, having made sure that they had not gone astray, returned to the rocky hollow where they had left their baskets. There, hovering above the site of a dried-up spring, Mélanie beheld a brilliant globe of light, called on "Mémin" to come and see, and dropped the stick she was carrying, prompting Maximin to cling all the tighter to *his* stick in case "it"—the light—should do anything to threaten them. Then the luminous orb opened up to encompass the two children in its light, and a still brighter globe was revealed within that gradually took the form of "une très belle dame," sitting on a bench of stone, head in hands and elbows resting on her knees, weeping uncontrollably; perhaps, Maximin thought, interestingly in view of his troubled relationship with his stepmother, she was "a mother [*une maman*] whom her children had beaten and who had fled into the mountains to cry her heart out [*pour y pleurer tout son saoul*]."[6] Then the Belle Dame stood up, walked toward them, weeping still, and, speaking in French, told them not to be afraid but to come forward and hear the "great news" (*une grande nouvelle*) that she had come to bring them. She was wearing a headdress, scarf, white dress, and apron, but there the resemblance with any other local woman ended, for both her headdress and shoes were surrounded with roses of every imaginable color, while on her breast she wore a pair of chains, one bearing a crucifix complete with Christ, together with, still more ominously, a hammer and a pair of pincers (*des tenailles*), the traditional "instruments of the Passion" with which Christ had been first nailed to the cross and then taken down when dead. Without further ado, and still speaking in French, the Belle Dame began to deliver her down-to-earth but baleful tidings:

> If my people refuses to submit, I shall be forced to let my Son's hand do what it will. It is so heavy and weighty, that I can no longer hold it back. How long have I been suffering for you! If I want my Son not to abandon you, I am obliged constantly to pray to Him, and you, you take no heed of it. No matter how much you pray, no matter what you do, never will you be able to make up for the trouble that I have taken for you. I gave you six days on which to work and I kept the seventh for myself, and people are unwilling to grant it to me. That is what so weighs down the arm of my Son. Men driving carts are unable to swear without putting my Son's name in the middle. These are the two things which so weigh down the arm of my Son. If the crop fails, it is solely because of you. I showed this to you last year by way of the potatoes; you paid no heed to it; on the contrary, when you found they were spoiled, you swore, using the name of my Son. They will continue to spoil, and at Christmas there will be none left.

It was only as she uttered the words *"pommes de terre"* (potatoes) that the Belle Dame realized that the children could understand barely a word of what she was saying, prompting her to switch instantly and effortlessly into their patois: "Si las truffas [potatoes] se gastoun ay rien que peu vous aoustres, vous oiou fa veire l'an passa n'aïa pas vouga fas conti, qu'era ou countraire quant troubava de trufas gastas jurava, l'y bitava l'ou nou de moun fils oou meo . . ." Still further threats then followed: Any seeds that were sown would be eaten by animals, corn would crumble into powder when it was threshed, there would be a great famine, children under the age of seven would be seized with the shakes (*prendent un tramble*) and would die in the arms of those who held them, nuts would go bad, and grapes would rot (*la nouses vendrent baufas et lous rasins purirent*); though, if people changed their ways, stones and rocks would be transformed into heaps of grain (*de mounteous de bla*) and the earth would produce potatoes in superabundance . . .

At this point, the Belle Dame paused and beckoned the children to approach separately to hear the "secret" that she whispered *in French* to each, to Maximin first, then to Mélanie. Then, reverting to patois, she continued her dialogue with the children, asked them whether they said their prayers—not much, they replied—and, shifting her line of attack from humanity in general to La Salette in particular, complained that only a few elderly women attended mass on Sundays while the other villagers worked or, on the rare occasions when they had nothing better to do, attended only in order to poke fun at religion; as for observing Lent, the Salettins flocked to the butcher's like dogs (*la caréima van à la boutsaria couma lou tsis*). Then she reminded Maximin that, some time earlier, his father had told him that the harvest would fail and that they would go hungry at Christmas, an item of "inside information" that convinced both Maximin and his father of her supernatural powers and origins. The Belle Dame then switched back to French as she concluded by ordering the children to pass on her tidings and warnings "to all of my people." Her mission accomplished, she crossed the bed of the dried-up stream, repeated her final instructions in French without looking back, moved up the mountain supposedly along the S-like curve inscribed by the present Stations of the Cross, skimming over the grass as though she was weightless, before "melting like butter in a frying pan" into the air, as one of the children subsequently put it.[7]

No sooner had Mélanie and Maximin disclosed what had allegedly happened on the mountainside above La Salette than the site began to attract the pious and the curious first from the villages around, then from the region, and, finally, by the first anniversary of the "event," from France as a whole; forty thousand pilgrims, including two hundred priests, are reported to have gathered at the site on 19 September 1847, and masses were said continually from three in the morning until midday. Two days after the apparition, on 21 September 1846, the dried-up spring by which the Belle Dame had stood began "miraculously" to flow again. Over the coming weeks a succession of cures were reported, including that of Maximin's father whose asthma attacks ceased after he visited the site with Pra and Selme. His instantaneous conversion seems to have been replicated a hundred times over throughout the vicinity. Religious practice increased almost overnight in both La Salette and Corps, and Sunday work and swearing effectively ceased; clearly the Belle Dame's warning that she could no longer restrain her Son's chastising arm concentrated more than a few local minds.

The first publications began to appear in the spring of 1847, with one account of the "event" allegedly running at 300,000 copies; the vast and diffuse public that had responded to the Miraculous Medal was plainly still hungry for evidence of supernatural intervention, even if it took the menacing form of the *grande nouvelle* of La Salette. That the apparition was accepted so rapidly by so many as true was due in no small part to the fact that so many of the Belle Dame's prophecies were almost instantly realized. There *was* a calamitous shortage of potatoes and corn in 1846–47, not just in the Alps or even in France as a whole but in large parts of Europe, in

Catholic Ireland above all, and it was not long before the vineyards of France did indeed succumb to a combination of phylloxera and mildew. Still more ominously, young children *did* die in unprecedented numbers (forty-three in Corps alone in 1847; sixty-three in 1848), and in 1849 the scourge of cholera returned to afflict France. Add to this the political turmoil of the late 1840s and early 1850s both at home and abroad—revolutions throughout Europe in 1848, massive discontent across rural France throughout the Second Republic (1848–51), the threat to the papacy and its lands from Italian nationalism, civil war in Catholic Spain, international conflict in the Crimea—and the climate could scarcely be more favorable to the kind of millennialist anxieties and hopes to which the Belle Dame gave voice. "The pilgrimage becomes every day more frequented," the bishop of Grenoble, Monseigneur de Bruillard told his assembled priests in September 1852, a year after he had recognized the apparition as authentic, "the peasants [*cultivateurs*] are starting to recognize the terrible truth of what was announced six years ago."[8]

The Bishop's words may smack of triumphalism, but in reality he and the rest of the ecclesiastical hierarchy were at least as anxious as they were delighted about the apparition and the apparent religious revival it had unleashed in the diocese and beyond. On the one hand, *any* evidence of supernatural intervention was welcome in an age of, as they saw it, rampant materialism and rationalism, and any substantial return to religious observance in a region as notoriously apathetic as the Alps could not but be applauded, even though the mix of emotions associated with the "event" clearly contained a dubious, and perhaps dangerous, sociopolitical component; more broadly, the apparition might boost the standing of the Church in the face of the semi-official anticlericalism, or at best religious indifferentism, of the Bourgeois Monarchy, so seemingly entrenched that none could imagine that it would collapse within eighteen months of the Belle Dame's appearance. Against this, and in addition to its traditional caution regarding all manner of reported miracles, apparitions, and signs, the hierarchy feared any religious or quasi-religious movement that it had not initiated or could not control, as was the case at La Salette. Many priests had responded to the outbreak of popular religious enthusiasm, but again they had done so on their own individual initiative, leaving the hierarchy following in their wake when its instinct was to lead from the front.

Furthermore, there were grave doubts concerning the character of the two moody, patois-speaking visionaries, though even those who least took to them had to admit that the childrens' surliness ceased as soon as they began to speak of "their" Lady. There were doubts, too, concerning the apparent triviality of what the Belle Dame had to say: all potatoes and nuts, Sunday working and carters' oaths, and nothing, or next to nothing, about the Church's real fears (creeping rationalism, "socialism," anticlericalism, religious laxism in general), and, above all, *nothing about sex*.[9]

The seeming banality of the Virgin's public utterances made the question of what she had said secretly to each child all the more serious and contentious. Despite all manner of threats, bribes, and enticements, Maximin never revealed what the Belle Dame whispered to him, and speculation centered for decades around her revelations to Mélanie. In the months following her admission into the Couvent de la Providence in Corps in November 1846, Mélanie learned not only to speak French but to read and write, and in July 1851, by now a novice with the Soeurs de la Providence at Corenc near Grenoble, she was persuaded, against her will, to write down in conditions of great secrecy what the weeping Virgin had told her. Only Monseigneur de Bruillard saw what she had written (and he, appropriately enough, broke forthwith into tears),[10] and the document was immediately taken under sealed cover to Rome where it was presumably read by Pius IX before being consigned to the Vatican archives. Rumors circulated throughout the 1850s and 1860s concerning its content, but it was not until 1873 that a genuine, though expurgated, version of the secret was published, in Italy where by now Mélanie had been virtually banished, and only in 1879, following the death of Pius IX, that the full text, discussed below, was at last made known to the world, bearing somewhat surprisingly, the *imprimatur* of Mélanie's local bishop, Monsignore Zola de Lecce.

Knowing (or suspecting) what Mélanie's sealed envelope contained, the Church had as its priority to separate vision from visionaries and, above all, to sever the Virgin from whatever private discourse she may have had with the children. To this end, or so defenders of Mélanie and Maximin would argue, the hierarchy set out to discredit—to "demonetize," in the words of the ultra-Catholic novelist and journalist Léon Bloy (1846–1917)[11]—the witnesses while defending the authenticity of what they claimed to have witnessed. Accordingly, despite some opposition from within the Church, much of it orchestrated by the archbishop of Lyon who feared that the growth of La Salette would take away pilgrims and funds from his own Marian shrine of Notre-Dame de Fourvière,[12] the apparition was accepted as authentic by a commission of enquiry, by twelve votes to four, and the decision made public, with full papal approval, on 19 September 1851, just two and a half months before a military coup put an end to the Second Republic and prepared the way for its erstwhile Prince-President Louis Napoleon to become Emperor Napoleon III in emulation of his illustrious uncle. Rumors—fully justified as it turned out—that Mélanie's secret document was highly critical of the whole Napoleonic tradition appeared to be confirmed when Monseigneur de Bruillard was replaced by Monseigneur Ginouilhac, a noted supporter of the new imperial regime. On 19 September 1855, before a huge throng of pilgrims gathered at the site of the apparition, the new bishop made the following significant pronouncement:

The mission of the children is finished, that of the Church is beginning. Let [the children] go where they will, anywhere in the world, let them become bad Christians and ignore what they have announced to all the peoples of the world, let them trample underfoot all the graces they have received and will still receive, all that will have no effect on the Apparition which is certain, canonically proven and will never seriously be shaken.[13]

The message could hardly be clearer: The Church had its apparition and pilgrimage, let Mélanie and Maximin go hang!

Like the waters of the once dried-up stream in the mountain, the flood of popular piety was now channeled into the formal institutions of the Church; the miraculous had been regulated, the extraordinary rendered ordinary, its potential disruptiveness neutered to the benefit of the ecclesiastical hierarchy. A sanctuary was built at the site, housing a community of monks who, according to critics, were as keen to demote the visionaries as to promote their vision, indulgences were offered to all who made the pilgrimage, and a nationwide Archiconfrérie de Notre-Dame Réconciliatrice de La Salette was set up to capitalize on the boost that the "event" had given to the Church as a whole. What the Virgin had actually said, let alone the secrets she had confided to the children, was firmly hidden under an institutional bushel. The whole thing, wrote the novelist-convert Joris-Karl Huysmans (1848–1907), looked suspiciously like a "revolt (*sédition*) of the upper clergy against the Holy Virgin, an order to take no account of her promises and threats; it was an injunction to disobey Her, even the right to accuse Her!"[14]

As the apparition and pilgrimage were regulated and officialized, so a systematic campaign was undertaken to discredit and marginalize Mélanie and Maximin who, by now, were children no more but potentially dangerous young adults: such, at least, was the charge regularly made by ultra-Catholic proponents of the integrity—apparition *and* secrets—of *le fait de La Salette*. Maximin was by far the easier target, given his evident fondness for drink and the erratic course of his life that led him from a failed religious vocation to a succession of unskilled or semi-skilled jobs interspersed with periods of idleness, a spell as a papal *zouave* in Rome, and, finally, to a partnership in a failed business enterprise involving the production and marketing of a supposedly restorative *liqueur de La Salette*. In the late 1840s, when still barely into his teens, Maximin was contacted and cultivated by supporters of the self-styled Baron de Richemont, one of several pretenders to the French throne claiming to be the "lost king" Louis XVII, who evidently believed that Maximin's jealously guarded "secret" could be used to further their cause. In an attempt, presumably, to wheedle it out of him, they took him to Ars, just north of Lyon, to speak with its celebrated priest-confessor, the Abbé Jean-Marie Vianney (1786–1859, canonized 1925). In the course of their interview, Maximin allegedly denied that the apparition had occurred, though, when Maximin subsequently protested that it had, the future saint retracted the doubts he had initially expressed concerning the adolescent's genuineness: he had, apparently, misheard him. Maximin had further contacts with the fantasy world of French ultra-royalism, was mobilized during the Franco-Prussian war of 1870, made a final pilgrimage to La Salette in November 1874, and died the following March. He never married and supposedly told one of the La Salette missionaries that "when one has seen the Blessed Virgin, one can attach oneself to no-one on earth."[15] For all his weaknesses, Maximin does not seem to merit the derision, even the obloquy, of which he has so often been the victim.

Mélanie was a more substantial figure, and the evidence of systematic persecution by the Church hierarchy correspondingly more telling. After consigning her secret to the safekeeping of the Vatican, Mélanie was admitted into the community at Corenc as Soeur Marie de la Croix, but soon came up against the hostility of Monseigneur Ginouilhac who, in the course of an episcopal visitation, reprimanded her for lack of "Christian simplicity" and for succumbing all too readily to the personality cult of which she was understandably the object. He refused her permission to take final vows, and, suffering from an acute stomach disorder, Mélanie was transferred to the Filles de la Charité at Vienne (Isère). There, too, she ran foul of authority and, after an incident in which she bit her new Mother Superior, was sent back to Corps in disgrace. There, now in her early twenties, Mélanie was visited in September 1854 by two Catholic dons from Oxford who were on pilgrimage to La Salette and so impressed them that they arranged with Monseigneur Ginouilhac, no doubt to his considerable relief, for her to move to a Carmelite convent in Darlington where her presence, they believed, would hasten the return of the heretic English to the fold of the true Petrine church.

But Mélanie—or Soeur Victime de Jésus as, almost too eloquently, she became on taking her Carmelite vows—was no more settled in the northeast of England than she had been in the southeast of France. In her unhappiness, she became increasingly obsessed with founding her own religious order, to be known apocalyptically as Les Apôtres des Derniers Temps (the Apostles of the Last Days) as, she insisted, the Belle Dame had ordered her to do. Desperate to leave the enclosed Carmelite order, but forbidden to do so, she was reduced to throwing a letter addressed to the postmaster of Darlington over the convent wall appealing for help before her superiors were prepared to release her from her vows.

And so her ordeal as a nomadic visionary continued: back to France in September 1860 as Soeur Zénaïde in the Ordre de la Compassion in Marseille, then to Cephalonia in Greece, back again to Marseille, where the disclosure of her identity led to her expulsion from the order in April 1867, then, after a pilgrimage to La Salette, to Italy where, intervals apart, she was to spend the rest of her long and turbulent life. Still forbidden to establish her own order and, after the revelation of her "secret" in the 1870s, an object of veneration on the part of many ultra-Catholics, especially in France, she remained a dangerous loose cannon in the eyes of the Church as, under Pope Leo XIII, it sought some kind of *rapprochement* with the secular world including, not least, the French Third Republic. Back in France from 1898 to 1904, at Saint-Pourçain-sur-Sioule and Diou in the department of the Allier, Mélanie drafted her autobiography, the diffuse and spiritually saccharine *Vie de Mélanie, Bergère de La Salette, écrite par elle-même,* with the help of a local priest, the Abbé Combe, whose own works *Le Secret de Mélanie et le Grand Coup* and *Le Secret de Mélanie et la crise actuelle* were in due course placed on the Vatican's Index of Prohibited Books.

After a final pilgrimage to La Salette in September 1902, Mélanie returned to Altamura near Naples where she died on 15 December 1904. Unlike Catherine Labouré and Bernadette Soubirous, Mélanie Calvat has received no official recognition, let alone blessing, from the Church that nonetheless accepts the authenticity of her testimony, and on 21 December 1915, while reaffirming the validity of the apparition, the Holy Office formally prohibited all further commentary on the notorious "secret." In May 1923 the *Secret of Mélanie* was itself placed on the Index, and the original document of 1851 has now been fortuitously or conveniently "lost."[16]

So what did the Belle Dame whisper to Mélanie on the afternoon of 19 September 1846? Or, more to the point, what did the Mélanie of the 1870s, a frustrated and possibly mentally disturbed visionary deliberately sidelined by the Church that wanted her testimony but not her, say that the Virgin had said to her and which—notwithstanding the *imprimatur* of her local bishop in Italy—the Church was clearly anxious to suppress? The text published in 1879, and written by Mélanie the previous year, begins with the Virgin telling Mélanie that the "secrets" she is about to confide could be made public in 1858—precisely the date, as Léon Bloy would point out in triumph,[17] of her next, and still more dramatic, public appearance at Lourdes. What follows is a mixture of prophecies, objurgations, and threats delivered in a French that Mélanie would indeed have needed supernatural inspiration to recall in such detail and which must, at the very least, differ significantly in style, if not necessarily in substance, from the original document of 1851. First—and surely most seriously from the point of view of the Church—the priesthood, and by implication the hierarchy, is denounced out of hand and in virtual entirety for its immorality, greed, and ingrained impiety: "The priests have become sewers of impurity [*des cloaques d'impureté*]," the Virgin declares, "and vengeance hangs over their heads. Woe to priests and others consecrated to God who by their infidelities and loose living crucify my Son anew! . . . There are no more generous souls, no-one worthy of offering the stainless Victim to the Eternal One on behalf of the world." After a generalized condemnation of the world's rulers comes the announcement that "Society is on the eve of the most terrible scourges and the gravest events; people must expect to be governed by an iron rod and to drink the cup of God's anger to the lees." Pius IX (whose death in 1878 probably prompted Mélanie to publish) is advised not to leave Rome "after 1859" and warned specifically against "Napoleon": "His heart is double, and when he seeks to be both pope and emperor, God will soon abandon him; he is that eagle which, always seeking to soar, will fall on the sword that he wanted to use to oblige humanity [*les peuples*] to raise themselves up." If uttered by the Virgin in 1846, when Louis Napoleon was but a half-baked conspirator, or even if written down by Mélanie in 1851 before the military coup that would in due course transform prince-president into emperor, these words were prophetic indeed, and supporters of Mélanie who read them in 1879 and beyond would recognize in them clear predictions of the third Napoleon's Italian adventure of 1859–60 and its appropriate nemesis, his ignominious fall from power in September 1870; to opponents and skeptics, they had simply been added by Mélanie, or whoever advised her, *after* the events they referred to had happened. And so too of all the other events specifically "predicted": wars between, or involving, France, Italy, Spain, and England (but not, interestingly, Prussia or Russia), civil wars between Italian and Italian, Frenchman and Frenchman (the burning of Paris in May 1871 is clearly referred to), the expropriation of the papal territories and the confinement of Pius IX to his remaining fragment in Rome. Otherwise, the "secrets" consist of the familiar tropes of Christian apocalyptic, perhaps intercut with Nostradamus, whom Mélanie is known to have read[18]: fire, famine, floods, warfare and plague, rampaging demons, Lucifer, Antichrist (who will be born of a "Jewish nun [*une religieuse hébraïque*], a false virgin in league with the serpent of old, the master of impurity," presaging the destruction of the old order and the birth of a New Heaven and New Earth: "Water and fire will purify the earth and consume all the works of man's pride, and everything will be renewed: God alone will be served and glorified."[19]

Why, if the Virgin's specific predictions could be readily explained as simple *ex post facto* additions, and if her overall message merely recycled conventional figures of millenarian discourse, was the Church evidently so concerned to prevent their diffusion? And why were so many of the finest minds of the turn-of-the-century French Catholic revival—the poet-dramatist Paul Claudel (1868–1955), the philosopher Jacques Maritain (1882–1973), the orientalist Louis Massignon (1883–1962), as well as the firebrand novelists Huysmans and Bloy—convinced not just of their veracity but of their absolutely crucial importance to the destiny of both France and the Church?

The Church, as we have seen, wanted to separate "La Salette I"—the apparition—from "La Salette II"—the secrets—and to keep vision and visionaries, especially Mélanie, scrupulously apart.[20] The position of Mélanie's supporters was precisely the reverse: La Salette I and La Salette II formed a single supernatural occurrence, and both apparition and secrets were inseparable from the persons and experience—before, during, and after 19 September 1846—of the two witnesses, above all, needless to say, of Mélanie herself; quite simply, the Church (and the world) could not have the vision minus the visionaries, nor the latter without the disquieting, if scarcely original, messages they had received. Over and above the doubts the Church had regarding flaws in the witnesses' character—flaws that, in Mélanie's case, were exacerbated by its official attitude toward her—there were cogent political reasons for keeping the secrets suppressed.

Assuming—and it is a quite massive assumption—that the text of 1879 is close to the original document of 1851, it was obviously in Pius IX's interest, prior to 1870, to prevent the diffusion of a text that placed a scathing denunciation of the clergy in the very mouth of the Mother of God, predicted that unnamed disasters would befall him, and, finally, would needlessly complicate the Vatican's already troubled relations with Napoleon III. After 1870, a virtual prisoner in the tiny enclave that remained of his former possessions, Pius plainly had no wish to permit a publication that predicted, and gave implied supernatural sanction to, his present predicament, and every reason still to fear the Virgin's anticlerical diatribe. Thereafter, the secrets could do nothing to further Leo XIII's policy of engagement with the secular world and, above all, of *ralliement* to the French Third Republic, and the interdicts of 1915 and 1923 may owe something to Church's desire to quell apocalyptic speculation during and after the greatest conflict in history, combined, no doubt, with a desire to bring Mélanie posthumously to heel and to prevent the Church from being outflanked on its right by ultra-Catholic extremists.

Doubtless, too, Mélanie's rebelliousness, so unlike Catherine Labouré's quiet dutifulness or Bernadette Soubirous' pious withdrawal, rankled in an institution chronically ill-equipped, then as now, to deal with any expression of female autonomy. And so, even after the supposed ban on discussion of Mélanie's secrets, the campaign of defamation against her continued, with the friars of La Salette in its vanguard. In 1928, the Jesuit Hippolyte Delehaye dismissed even the original "relation Pra" as a "miserable rhapsody" that merely stitched together the conventional formulae of the *lettre tombée du ciel*,[21] and the approach of the centenary of the apparition in 1946 provoked a further salvo of denigratory comment, with Mélanie standing accused, inter alia, of hysteria, "pithiatism" (bogus prophetism, after the Pythia of Delphi), and fraud.[22] Not without justice could supporters of Soeur Victime de Jésus claim that her faithfulness to the whole of her vision had transformed her, both during her long life and after, into Soeur Victime de l'Eglise.

It was precisely her status as victim that made Mélanie so potent a figure in the eyes of the ultra-Catholic right. For men like Bloy, Huysmans, and

Massignon, the apparition, the secrets, and Mélanie's personal suffering form a unity so tight that Belle Dame and *bergère* become virtual doubles of each other, with the title of Bloy's *Celle qui pleure* (1907) applying equally to weeping Madonna and the tearful life of her votary. Mary and Mélanie "compenetrate" so completely that, says Bloy, "it is sometimes difficult to distinguish them, to know which is she who speaks and she who is silent, she who weeps and she who looks on, she who threatens and she who prays. All that can be seen is a whirlwind of painful light" (*un tourbillon de lumière douloureuse*).[23] Pain, indeed, is the core of the La Salette event and experience, and it was this that commended it to Catholic extremists such as Huysmans and Bloy, the crux—quite literally—of whose theology was the doctrine of "reversibility" or vicarious suffering according to which suffering "purchases" not merely the salvation of the individual sufferer, but that the "merits" that so accrue then "revert to," and "ransom," the entire community of the faithful.[24] His thought teetering, as it so often does, on the brink of blasphemy, Bloy argues that God's redemptive project for man has *failed,* or at least remains incomplete, that Christ's sufferings on the Cross were not enough in themselves to atone for man's sins and to redeem (that is, buy back) him either from the clutches of the devil or the wrath of his Maker, and that the whole universe—including, scandal of scandals, his own mother—must continue to suffer to bring Christ's Passion to completion.

For Bloy and his like, *le fait de La Salette* was, before all else, proof of "the simple Catholic truth . . . that it is absolutely necessary to suffer in order to be *saved*" and that "we are made for that [suffering] and for that alone." This, he maintains, is why La Salette can only scandalize the mass of "ordinary" Catholics, not to mention nonbelievers, for whom "suffering is a simple accident of earthly life" and not, as he believes, its very essence, even, still more starkly, its *purpose.* The whole of modern culture, both secular and religious, is dominated by a "hatred of Pain"; "people absolutely refuse to believe than pain is necessary"[25] and, in their pursuit of earthly happiness and health, are abandoning the *"Absolute Christianity"* of which Mélanie is the "annunciatrix and prophetess"[26] in favor of the waters and watered-down Christianity of Lourdes if they are Catholics or, if they are not, of "sport, which must be one of the English words for Damnation."[27] For Bloy, La Salette replaces the suffering of the Cross at the core of human experience, and Mary's words to Mélanie and Maximin are "the most painful sigh heard since the *Consommatum.* Who would dare to say that the Virgin Mary is 'blessed' when, for so many centuries, she has seen Her Son's blood flowing in vain?"[28]

Bloy was born in 1846, just "seventy days before the Apparition," and felt that he "mysteriously belonged" to La Salette and the religion of suffering it expressed.[29] He first visited the site in August 1879 in the company of the shadowy Abbé Tardif de Moidrey, one of the earliest promoters of

Mélanie's cause, with, in all likelihood, advance access to her "secrets," who, as it happened (though nothing, for Bloy, ever merely "happened"), died at La Salette on 30 September that year, almost thirty-three years to the day after the apparition that reactualized the dying agony of the thirty-three-year-old Christ.[30] To go to La Salette, as Bloy did again in 1880 and 1906, was a major undertaking prior to the advent of motorized transport, requiring several changes of train and a final ascent by foot or on mule-back from the village of La Mure up to La Salette itself. Both Bloy and Huysmans, whose first visit took place in July 1891 a year before his "final" conversion,[31] give memorable accounts of the formidable scenery they pass through on their way to the site, and for both its physical inaccessibility is further proof of La Salette's superiority over its "democratic" counterpart Lourdes: Our Lady "descended at Lourdes for everyone and at La Salette just for a few" (*pour quelques-uns*), wrote Huysmans with ill-concealed spiritual *hauteur*.[32] But physical remoteness was not the sole reason for setting La Salette above Lourdes. To the extent that the Virgin's message at Lourdes was in essence one of healing and love, it could ultimately be reconciled not just with existing society with its visceral "hatred of Pain" but also with the will to existence itself, the sheer animal instinct to live and to be, whence the site's huge popularity with the mass of "ordinary" life-loving, pain- and death-fearing Catholics. But when the Virgin spoke to Mélanie and Maximin on the mountain, she seemed to be opposed to *everything*: to society as it is, to the contemporary Church, to reason, to the body, and, ultimately, to earthly existence itself. Only spiritual supermen (or the occasional spiritual superwoman like Huysmans's amiable ascetic Mme Bavoil) could bear the absolute demands that the "Madonna of suffering" made of those she had chosen, and herein lay her appeal. "Notre-Dame de Lourdes is a joyful Madonna, for the masses [*les foules*]," declares Huysmans's Abbé Gévresin, "I would even say under my breath, if I dared, a Madonna for mugs [*une Madone pour les mufles*]!"

A preference for She Who Weeps over She Who Smiles goes to the heart of the ultra-Catholic sensibility, its mixture of eroticism and elitism, its selective recasting of the faith in the mold of its sadomasochistic obsessiveness and its incipiently fascistic politics. "I will confess," proclaims the Abbé Gévresin,

that the Virgin of the Stabat Mater touches me infinitely more than the joyful and triumphant Virgin of the Ave Regina and the Regina Caeli. I will add that at La Salette She has been despised by the clergy and duped by it. I thought I would make an act of reparation by coming to see Her undergo—and that you will see—the silent outrage of the priests attached to Her Person. Finally, at Lourdes, She has friends, because She is happy and here She is not; She is abandoned because She is suffering; between these two pilgrimages, there was no doubt as to my choice.[33]

As was his wont, Bloy went still further along this Via Dolorosa:

> I am writing this on the Feast of the Assumption. Others see Mary in glory, I see her in ignominy. Whatever I do, I cannot imagine the Mother of the suffering Christ [*du Christ douloureux*] in the gentle light of Lourdes. That is denied me. I feel no attraction towards an Immaculate Conception crowned with roses, white and blue, bathed in suave music and perfumes. I am too soiled [*trop souillé*], too far from innocence, too close to the goats, too needful of forgiveness [*trop voisin des boucs, trop besoigneux de pardon*]. What I need is the Immaculate Conception crowned with thorns, My Lady of La Salette, the Immaculate Conception stigmatized, infinitely bloody and pale . . . , the Virgin of the Swords, as the entire middle ages beheld her: a Medusa of innocence and pain who change into *cathedral stones those who looked on as She wept*.[34]

At La Salette, it is "integral, absolute Christianity in its splendour," at Lourdes Christianity made tolerable and possible for the masses, as though, having wept "infinite tears" over each one of humanity's prevarications in 1846, the Virgin decided, twelve years later, to conceal her suffering and appear in the "disguise [*travestissement*] of a mother who, with death in her heart, puts on her party clothes [*habits de fête*] to reassure her children."[35]

Of Mary's sorrowful tears, Mélanie is not just the witness but the emissary, the channel, her mission on this earth being to transmit and continue the tears of the Virgin which are themselves a continuation of the outflowing of Christ's saving Blood. It was Mélanie's destiny to be rejected and suffer and, following her own autobiographical account, Bloy describes how, from earliest childhood, she was the victim of a "strange, hyperbolic, monstrous hatred" on the part of her mother and how the price of having found a new mother in the Belle Dame on the mountain was to suffer still further and more painful rejection continuing even after her death, "Christian society having been as much a cruel stepmother [*marâtre*] to her as her mother."[36] But "this continual wandering, this incessant migration necessitated by unpardoning hostility"[37] is precisely what enables Mélanie to accomplish her supernatural mission, for the "merits" accrued by her tears and her suffering "revert," through the spiritual economy of vicarious suffering, to humanity as a whole and help pay for its "ransom" or "redemption." The whole of the universe, from Christ and his Mother, through the communion of saints and down to the humblest of sufferers, becomes a kind of spiritual exchange and mart in which the blood and tears of the unhappy few are the coin in which the sins and demerits of the happy hordes of degenerate humanity are "paid for" and "redeemed." God's anger is "bought off" by the sufferings of his substitutes, be they Christ, his Mother, or a peasant girl in the Alps, who offer up their unhappiness for the salvation of the happy: "The core of my thinking is that in this fallen world, any joy takes place in the order of nature and any pain in the order of the divine."[38]

Bloy saw Mélanie as the successor of one of his other Christ-substitutes, the royalist pretender Charles Guillaume Naundorff, self-proclaimed son of Louis XVI, who, after a life of exile, rejection, and misery, died at Delft in Holland on 10 August 1845, "slightly more than thirteen months before the Apparition of La Salette," as Bloy is naturally quick to point out.[39] Just as Maximin had been approached by supporters of the "Baron de Richemont" shortly after the apparition and, later in life, visited the Comte de Chambord (the recognized pretender) at Frohsdorf in Austria, so Mélanie seems to have accepted that Naundorff's son, whom Bloy also met in mysterious circumstances,[40] was the "legitimate King, King FLEUR DE LYS," thus proving to Bloy's satisfaction the "analogy or affinity, correspondence or mysterious relationship between the Miracle of La Salette and the Miracle of the destiny of the Son of Louis XVI."[41] Ultra-Catholicism and ultraroyalism feed into and reinforce one another, and a kind of apostolic succession of suffering is established linking Christ on the Cross to "Louis the Last" on the guillotine, and thence to the lifelong crucifixion of his putative son Naundorff and the Passion of Mélanie, Soeur Victime de Jésus, herself. Writing in the centennial year, 1946, Louis Massignon, who made the pilgrimage to La Salette on at least five occasions between 1911 and 1953, likened Mélanie to Marie-Antoinette, another expiatory victim, set apart, in his view, persecuted, and finally put to death to atone for the sins of the French monarchy.[42] Later in the same article, he set Mélanie's meaning to France alongside that of the ultimate nationalist-Catholic martyr, Joan of Arc.[43] "When God loves one of his servants," Massignon declares, "the sign of His predilection is that He incites others to persecute him or her." Thus Mélanie's childhood was both "full of suffering and full of grace"—full of grace *because* full of suffering—and she was set apart from the beginning by "the seal of solicitude with which God marks His substitutes, whom He causes to 'complete' the Passion of the Son through Compassion with His Mother." Called to "a saving vocation as substitute for the 'Soledad' of the Madonna," Mélanie truly becomes a Victim of Jesus, a "vexillary of the Passion," whose whole life is a continuation and completion of the suffering on the Cross.[44]

La Salette, says Massignon, was "a spiritual navel" (*un ombilic spirituel*), the epicenter of a worldwide Catholic upheaval.[45] It never became a place of mass pilgrimage like Lourdes, and therein lay its importance. It did not call the sick in body but the troubled in spirit and mind, not "the satisfied and the wise, but the anxious, those who are heavy with secret tears"[46]; it was, before all else, an intellectuals' apparition. Its primary meaning for men like Bloy, Huysmans, Massignon, Maritain, and Claudel was that, in Massignon's words, it marked "a supernatural intervention [*ingérence*] in the established order that threatened to call that order in question," a miraculous breach in the "integral incarceration"—spiritual, economic, cultural, political—that Massignon believed characterized contemporary life.[47]

Whereas the Church hierarchy wanted to keep the apparition minus Mary's discourse and secrets and, above all minus Mélanie and, to a lesser extent, Maximin, dissident Catholics believed, as Bloy put it, in "the profound and magnificent unity of the Revelation of 19 September 1846."[48] Unlike the hierarchy, they were untroubled by the anticlericalism of the secrets because they themselves were anticlericals of the Right, believing, in Bloy's singeing words, that "any priest who does not aim at Sanctity is truly, rigorously, absolutely, a Judas and a shit [*une ordure*]."[49]

What delighted ultra-Catholics about La Salette was that each of its elements—the apparition, the discourse, the secrets, Mélanie's subsequent life—was totally irreconcilable with the contemporary zeitgeist. The Virgin who wept on the mountain revealed herself to be implacably, unconditionally, *antimoderne,* to use the title of Maritain's polemic of 1922: anti the contemporary world's edulcorated religion, its secularism, its rationalism, its day-to-day mores, its attachment to this life and the body, its conviction that Man—capital M—is master of his own destiny, and that, all in all, *tout s'arrange très bien sans le bon Dieu,* that *ce n'est pas la peine de s'occuper de Dieu,* as Claudel puts it in his exegesis of the Belle Dame's denunciation of Sunday working and swearing.[50] Unlike Lourdes, La Salette could not be "recuperated" either by the established Church or by established society. It was fundamentally *other,* and so established itself, in Massignon's words, as "the preferred pilgrimage of those whom the social condition of the nation torments."[51] And not just social, but also, and above all, *political.* La Salette was, and remains, the mecca—if that is not a contradiction in terms—of all who opposed, and oppose, the French Republican order from the Right, royalists of every faction and hue, *Pétainistes,* fascists, *Frontistes, Intégristes,* all for whom 1789 was the beginning of the end and the Enlightenment the source of all western civilization's distortions and lies. To go to Lourdes, for a Catholic, is, ultimately, to opt for reconciliation and life; to place La Salette above Lourdes, as did a whole generation of French ultra-Catholics, is to espouse a radically antihumanist worldview, at once reactionary and revolutionary in its political implications, in which suffering becomes the supreme value, indeed the sole purpose, of living.

All this is summed up in the person and experience of Mélanie who, in the ultra-Catholic perspective, both rejected, and was rejected by, the established order of things, her uncompromising vision inciting both Church and state—ultimately allies, despite their surface antagonism—to hound her throughout a lifetime of wandering and misery. But social rejection is the sign of supernatural election and, like the Man of Sorrows before her, the Woman of Sorrows offers herself up as a sacrificial victim whose sufferings and death will "buy back" the French nation from the hell that otherwise awaits it. The Revolution had already produced exemplary female martyrs in the persons of Marie-Antoinette and the sixteen Carmelite sisters whose execution in July 1794 would inspire Georges Bernanos's posthumous drama of vicarious suffering, *Dialogues des Carmélites* (1949). Mélanie takes over from them the vocation of expiatory victim, along with all the other female ecstatics, stigmatics, and holy anorexics discussed later in this book who believed they were bleeding, swooning, or starving for the redemption of the Church, the French nation, or humanity as a whole. In the postrevolutionary French Catholic imagination, the spiritual function of woman is to weep, bleed, and starve for the salvation of others, to offer herself up as a holocaust to appease a revengeful male deity. Of the women, holy and unholy, under consideration here, only Thérèse Martin appears to have escaped or transcended the expiatory Catholicism of her times, but only, as we shall see in the next chapter, at the price of assuming to the full the painful life and still more painful death that their spiritual vocation imposed on her.

2

LITTLE FLOWER

Thérèse Martin

ALENÇON—LISIEUX, 1873–1897

Christmas 1886 marked a critical turning point in the lives of two French adolescents whose writings and personal example would, in their different ways, contribute decisively to the twentieth-century revival of Catholicism in their country and beyond. At Vespers on Christmas Day, listening to the singing of the Magnificat as he stood beside the now famous "second pillar at the entrance of the chancel to the right of the sacristy" in Notre-Dame, the eighteen-year-old Paul Claudel (1868–1955) had the revelation, as he later put it, "of a God who was stretching out his arms to me" which, by dint of some simplification and not a little self-dramatization, he would forever after present as the crucial threshold separating a non- or semi-believing "before" from a fully believing "after."[1]

Some eighteen hours earlier, returning home from midnight mass in the Normandy market-town of Lisieux, the thirteen-year-old Thérèse Martin, in religion Sainte Thérèse de l'Enfant-Jésus et de la Sainte-Face (1873–97, canonized—in then record time—in 1925), underwent what she would later describe as her "complete conversion," thanks to which she was definitely liberated from the "narrow circle" of emotional-spiritual turmoil and psychosomatic illness that had afflicted her at regular intervals since the death of her ultradevout mother Zélie in August 1877 when Thérèse was four and a half.

In their different but overlapping spheres, the conversion experiences and subsequent lives and writings of the two unhappy youngsters would dominate the French Catholicism of the first half of the twentieth century: Claudel as its greatest poet and dramatist (and most visible intellectual "conquest"), Thérèse as its foremost exemplar of a living, attainable, and fully realized saintliness. After the Second World War, helped by his embarrassing enthusiasm for Maréchal Pétain, Claudel's reputation first waned and then nose-dived—"*Plus jamais Claudel!*" chanted the students of May

1968—and now barely extends beyond academe and a diminishing band of committed Catholic intellectuals. That of Thérèse, however, has recently undergone a remarkable revival, having declined somewhat after its early peak during the First World War and its immediate aftermath, largely on account of her elevation, in 1997, the centenary year of her death, to the rank of Doctor of the Church, the youngest of only thirty-three saints so honored and only the third woman after Saint Catherine of Sienna and the founder of the Carmelite order for women to which she belonged, Saint Teresa of Avila. Her autobiographical *Histoire d'une âme* (first published in 1898) continues to outsell any other devotional work, and, in commemoration of her centenary, a reliquary of "polished jacaranda decorated with exquisite gold and silver filigree" containing half of her remains underwent an extended premillennium "world tour" taking in Russia, most of western Europe, Argentina, Brazil and the United States, where 114 "appearances" were scheduled at churches and monasteries, before it moved on to the Philippines in January 2000.[2] In short, the "little flower" who was at pains to stress her littleness in all things save in her love of God still bulks very large indeed both among rank-and-file Roman Catholics and, thanks to sedulous cultivation, in the official panoply of the Church. Probably no saint other than Saint Francis is so universally revered and, with the obvious exceptions of Popes John XXIII and John Paul II and Mother Teresa of Calcutta, no recent Catholic has had so great an impact inside and outside the Church. She experienced no visions or ecstasies, and few physical "cures" or other miracles are credited to her—though another French woman endowed with a charisma far beyond her diminutive build, Edith Piaf (1915–63), always claimed to have been cured of infant blindness as a result of having been taken to Lisieux at the age of three.[3] If, in the hundred years since her death, Saint Thérèse has lost none of her capacity to move, comfort, and inspire, it is above all on account of the self-proclaimed ordinariness that she pursued in her day-to-day existence and projected in her writings with quite extraordinary zeal.

"To become a great *Saint!!!*"[4] by dint of remaining little: such was Thérèse's self-conscious project, and it is unlikely that any other saint of the Church has so deliberately pursued sanctity from so early a stage in her life. Inevitably the singleness and self-consciousness of her purpose not only repel her critics but exasperate some of her greatest admirers; even the great Swiss theologian Hans Urs von Balthasar (1905–88), author of one of the finest discussions of her thought and experience, has chided her for succumbing to the temptation of "conscious auto-canonization."[5] Her holy simplicity can seem all too *voulu,* her renunciation of self alarmingly self-centered, while her cult of childlikeness sometimes degenerates into what Vita Sackville-West, certainly no enemy of the *petite voie* she prescribed, memorably described as a "treacly dulcification," not so much child*like* as child*ish*. Whatever their beliefs, many readers will also share the same writer's view that Thérèse's style, with its little-girl breathlessness and interminable troping on the figures of flowers and birds, all of them "coloured in . . . lollipop pinks and blues," can sometimes be "as nauseating as a surfeit of marsh-mallows." Yet, "sugary, namby-pamby, and silly"[6] though the saint and her writings may seem, there lies at the core of each a toughness of experience and reflection that distinguishes Thérèse from the bulk of her female contemporaries in the Church, while her emphasis on God's mercy and love, rather than on his judgment and anger, sets her apart from virtually all the male Catholic writers of her time, and above all from those like Huysmans and Bloy who placed the theory and practice of expiatory suffering at the heart of their religion. It is her distance, notwithstanding appearances, from this characteristic fin de siècle distortion of Christianity, and her stress, correspondingly, on the self-sacrifice that manifests God's love rather than the self-sacrifice that seeks to appease or deflect his anger, that will provide the guiding theme of the discussion that follows.

Thérèse was born in the prosperous Normandy town of Alençon, renowned throughout France for its lace, on 2 January 1873, the youngest child of Louis Martin (1823–94) and his wife Zélie (1831–77), both of whom had sought, but been refused, religious vocations and who, when they married in 1858, had privately pledged never to consummate their union and to live together as "brother and sister." After a year of connubial chastity, they were reminded by their spiritual director of the Christian (and particularly Catholic) duty to "go forth and multiply," an injunction to which they responded by producing nine children in rapid succession. Four of them, two boys and two girls (one of them named Thérèse), died in early infancy, while the surviving five, all girls, would all eventually enter religious orders: Marie (1860–1940), Pauline (1861–1951), Céline (1869–1959), and Thérèse in the Carmelite house at Lisieux, where the family moved in 1877 after Zélie Martin's death, Léonie (1863–1941) in the Visitandine convent at Le Mans until ill health forced her to abandon her vocation in 1895. Zélie's sister Elise Guérin (1829–77) was also a Visitandine sister at Le Mans, while her brother Isidore (1841–1909) was a leading lay figure in the Catholic community at Lisieux, renowned above all for the fiery proclerical (and increasingly anti-Masonic and antisemitic) articles he contributed to the local Catholic newspaper *Le Normand* of which, as a prosperous pharmacist, he was also the principal financier; in 1895 his daughter Marie Guérin (1870–1905) would join her four cousins in the Carmel as Soeur Marie de l'Eucharistie. It would, in short, be impossible to imagine a more thoroughly *bien pensant* milieu for a future saint to be born into—utterly unlike the warring and basically nonreligious atmosphere that prevailed in the Claudel family home at Villeneuve-sur-Fère in the Champagne in the 1860s and 1870s (see chapter 3).

Along with the Martin family's deep Catholic faith went a series of devotional practices—pilgrimages, the cult of the Sacred Heart, an obsession with "merits," "works," and expiatory self-sacrifice—that Thérèse would in large part reject or transcend. She also inherited an associated set of political-religious beliefs; some, notably monarchism and the cult of Joan of Arc, she would subscribe, but others, above all the antisemitism to which Isidore Guérin, a disciple of Drumont, was giving increasingly violent expression by the late 1880s[7] nowhere feature in her writings. To the extent that she thought about politics, Thérèse was undoubtedly a royalist of sorts—to speak, as she habitually did, of her father as her "petit Roi," even her "roi de France et de Navarre" and of herself as his queen was rich in political, as well as psychological, resonances—and she appears to have swallowed whole the Catholic nationalism of her times, inscribing the words "Vive le Dieu des Français," the rallying cry of the *zouaves pontificaux* (French members of the Pope's personal guard) at the battle of Loigny in December 1870, on the *tricolore* borne by a French soldier on the cover illustration of the school exercise book in which she began her account of her life in 1895.[8] Despite a tangential and accidental involvement in the anticlerical controversies of the 1890s (see below), and despite an obsession, during her last months, with the spread of atheism in France, she appears to have held no especially strong views on the increasingly threatened position of the Church in republican France, and is notably indifferent to the whole question of "social Catholicism" that so exercised her fellow religionaries, including both her father and uncle who were active members of the local branch of Albert de Mun's Cercles Catholiques. Poverty of spirit, not poverty *tout court,* was the abiding focus of her preoccupations and prayers.

Since, to a degree exceptional even among Catholic devotional writers, her own family provides the template of Thérèse's spiritual vision, and since, in particular, the notions of paternity and maternity are so central to her thought, it is necessary to dwell at some length on the lives and characters of her parents, on her relations with them and her four elder sisters, and, not least, on her preoccupation with the four siblings who had died before she was born. Until her death in August 1877, her mother was undoubtedly the focal point of her existence, and the psychoanalytical historian Jacques Maître is only reformulating the obvious when he states that "Thérèse's project" (*démarche*) is "largely oriented by a luxuriant proliferation of spiritual creativity animated by her maternal imago."[9] Prior to his wife's death, Louis Martin was a comparatively remote and inaccessible figure where Thérèse was concerned, dividing his attentions unequally between his clock-maker's shop on the main street of Alençon, where he spent less and less time, and his passion for fishing that, along with an equal passion for reading and prayer, he pursued in a *retiro* or *pavillon,* as he called it, that he had purchased just south of the town on the Sarthe before he got married. He was also frequently away on the pilgrimages that proliferated as never before in the climate of apocalypticism that prevailed in Catholic

France in the wake of the military, social, and religious disasters of *l'anneé terrible*[10]: pilgrimages to Chartres and Notre-Dame de la Délivrande, both with their spiritually potent Black Virgins, to the Church of the Immaculate Conception at nearby Sées, to the sanctuary of Notre-Dame du Sacré-Coeur at Issoudun, as well as to lesser centers in the locality such as Notre-Dame de Recouvrance, Notre-Dame de Lignerolles, Notre-Dame du Repos at Courteilles, all of them evidence, if evidence were needed, of the extraordinary salience of Mary in Catholic devotional practice in the troubled atmosphere of the times.

In 1870 Louis sold his shop to a nephew in order to assist his wife who, by this time, had established herself as one of the most successful middle-women in the Alençon lace industry, putting out orders and materials to local craftswomen and selling on the results of their labor at considerable profit to herself and her husband who remained the nominal head of the enterprise; the bulk of the 280,000 *francs-or* that Louis Martin left on his death in 1894 he owed to the unrelenting efforts of his wife between 1871 and 1877 when she was already suffering from the breast cancer that would kill her.[11]

It was time-consuming and exhausting work, and Zélie complained bitterly at how harsh her life had been made by "that wretched Alençon lace" (*ce coquin de point d'Alençon*), making her "a slave of the worst kind of slavery," and her trials at work, combined with a childhood that, in her own words, had been "sad as a death-shroud" (*triste comme un linceul*), her grief at the loss of four children one after the other, and her own deteriorating health, caused her to intensify the rigors of her already strict religious life and to inflict on her daughters the harsh, guilt-ridden, and guilt-inducing education she had received at the hands of her own mother. Believing among other things that her much-loved daughter Hélène (1864–70) was in purgatory because she had told a lie on her deathbed which she, Zélie, had failed to get absolved by a priest, Mme Martin resorted to a so-called *chapelet de pratiques* as the principal "teaching aid" in her spiritual pedagogy. This was a rosary containing thirty beads that had to be completed each day by each daughter, advancing by one bead for every "sacrifice" or "invocation" accomplished, and correspondingly regressing by one bead for every "sin" committed or "impure thought" that flashed across the mind: Small wonder that Thérèse would later say that, if there was one science that God did *not* possess, it was surely mathematics (*calcul*).[12]

It is hardly surprising, either, that, having been exposed from earliest childhood to this daily calibration of virtue and vice, all of the Martin daughters, including Thérèse, suffered at one time or another, and some of them continuously, from crippling feelings of guilt and inadequacy that expressed themselves, spiritually, in the form of "scruples" about frequenting the sacraments of penance and communion and, psychosomatically, as eating disorders and illnesses, particularly migraines, for which there was no apparent physiological causes. Both Marie and Céline alternated at times between self-starvation and bulimia, and the unfortunate Léonie, the least attractive and most rebellious, in Zélie's eyes, of her daughters, suffered particularly from her mother's unrelenting computation of "sacrifices" and "faults"; the eczema caused by wearing her Visitandine headdress day and night that led her to abandon her vocation in 1895 was almost certainly psychosomatic in origin.[13] Even Pauline, the sister to whom Thérèse was closest and, after Thérèse, the most "saintly" of the five, never really transcended the belief, instilled in her by her mother from earliest childhood, that she had to "earn" her right to God's love by good works, self-sacrifice, and voluntary suffering and, despite all her youngest sister's efforts to assure her, continually suffered from scruples and a terror of purgatory.[14]

Subjected by her own mother to the harshest of Catholic upbringings (and a victim, too, of migraine attacks as a child),[15] Zélie Martin in turn imposed on her daughters the rigors of what Jean-François Six calls a "dolorist and reparationist education"[16] that mirrored and transmitted the ultramontanist obsession with expiatory suffering. She may not have quite been the "phallic mother" that the Freudian Jacques Maître depicts,[17] but she was undoubtedly inhabited by a range of "death-dealing impulses" (*pulsions mortifères*),[18] themselves derived from her upbringing, for which her four eldest daughters, in particular, paid in the coin of anxiety, depression, and psychosomatic illnesses and which fostered a religious life dominated by fear of judgment and purgatory and by the omnipresence of "scruples." Above all, given Louis Martin's economic inactivity, his emotional passivity, and frequent absences from home, it was his wife who assumed most of the roles and tasks conventionally performed by the father. There can be little doubt that in the Martin household it was Zélie who embodied the superego and its values.

In October 1866, Zelie, the mother of three daughters ages six, five, and three, had given birth to Joseph, her first son. Perhaps already suffering from the breast cancer that would eventually kill her, Zélie was unable to feed Joseph and, having been forced to send him to a wet nurse in the nearby village of Sémallé, blamed herself when he died at the age of five months in February 1867. Another infant son, also named Joseph, died aged eight months in August 1868, and in 1870—truly an *anneé terrible*—two more children died within six months of each other, Marie-Hélène in January at the age of five and a half and, in August, having lived barely two months, the evocatively named Marie-Mélanie-Thérèse.

It was, therefore, into an atmosphere of acute anxiety and hope that Marie-Françoise-Thérèse was born in January 1873. Almost immediately Zélie's worst fears seemed about to be realized: In mid-March, after two months of sickly existence, the child refused, or was unable, to take Zélie's milk. In desperation, Zélie walked the five or six miles to Sémallé to find the wet nurse, Rose Taillé, who had suckled the first of the two Josephs. The two women walked back to Alençon, and, the following day, Zélie came downstairs to see Thérèse "fallen as though dead," as she put it, on her nurse's breast. As she began to thank God for having given her daughter "so gentle a death," Thérèse opened her eyes and, "completely cured" from that moment on, bestowed on her mother and sisters the first of those iconic smiles with which she would be forever associated.[19] It was, however, necessary for her to be taken back to Sémallé where, growing stronger by the day, she would remain for more than a year, deeply attached to her nurse, crying as soon as she went away, and smiling and laughing when she returned and, not unexpectedly, preferring her and the other women on the farm to Zélie when she came on one of her regular visits. This rural idyll ended when, in April 1874, Thérèse was brought back to Alençon, the first—or, if one includes the initial separation from Zélie, the second—of a succession of losses of this or that mother-figure that would dominate her existence.

From her return to Alençon until her mother's death in August 1877, Thérèse's behavior shows signs of disturbance as she sought to adjust both to the loss of Rose Taillé and to the distinct style of mothering practiced by Zélie Martin. Like her elder sisters, she suffered from intermittent eating disorders, and she developed a phobia for milk that would last all her life.[20] In a gesture significant for one whose writings and thought would be dominated by the image of the flower, Thérèse refused to accept a rose that her mother had cut especially for her: a cut rose (*une rose taillée?*). Above all, she was clearly desperate for her censorious mother's approval, forever running after her to confess some "sin" she had committed and sometimes refusing to eat until she had received "absolution": "She stands there like a criminal awaiting condemnation," Zélie wrote to Pauline in a letter that Thérèse cites in her first autobiographical manuscript, "but she has in her little head the idea that she will be forgiven more easily if she accuses herself."[21] Another significant anecdote has Mme Martin standing at the top of the stairs with Thérèse clambering toward her, crying "Maman, maman!" at each step and refusing to go on to the next until her mother says "Oui, ma petite fille!," and so on and so on, a (presumably much repeated) episode that must bear distantly on Thérèse's later, and much celebrated, rejection of "the harsh stairs of perfection" (*le rude escalier de la perfection*) in favor of the Christ-operated elevator (*ascenseur*) of grace.[22] On another occasion, Thérèse told her mother to her face that she wished that she (Zélie) would die so that she could "go to heaven" forthwith, a wish she also extended to Louis Martin. Clearly, as Jean-Françoise Six puts it, Thérèse was torn between a desire, on the one hand, to preserve her mother and win her approval and, on the other, to be rid of her and her *pratiques* in order fully to live. And though Thérèse undoubtedly suffered from, and

unconsciously blamed herself for, Zélie's death shortly afterward, it is difficult not to feel that, ultimately, she benefited psychologically and spiritually
from the early removal of her repressive, guilt-breeding presence. It is surely
no accident that, alone of the Martin sisters, it was Thérèse, the youngest,
who came to experience God as love and compassion rather than as justice
and judgment.[23]

Release from the tyranny of Zélie's Medusa-like gaze enabled Thérèse instantly to find more satisfactory mother-figures among her immediate family. On the day of her mother's funeral, 29 August 1877, the family servant,
Louise, looked at the five grieving sisters and sighed "Pauvres petites, vous
n'avez plus de Mère," whereupon Céline, the closest sister in age to Thérèse,
threw herself into the arms of Marie, the eldest (and Thérèse's godmother),
with the words, "Eh bien, c'est toi qui seras Maman," prompting Thérèse to
turn toward Pauline, the second oldest sister, and exclaim, "Eh bien! moi,
c'est Pauline qui sera Maman!"[24] With this transfer of hitherto frustrated
affection, Thérèse began to construct an incestuous emotional-spiritual ma-
triarchy in which, under the benign, quasi-maternal tutelage of Monsieur
Martin (see below), each of her sisters, with the partial exception of Léonie,
became simultaneously her metaphorical mother and daughter—and even,
as we shall see, her metaphorical father and son.

Her relationships with Pauline and Céline were particularly intense and
possessive. When Thérèse entered the Carmel in April 1888, Pauline who,
having entered in 1882, was by now responsible for novices, became her
"mother twice over" (*deux fois ma Mère*),[25] and in 1893 attained to the status of super-mother when she was elected prioress in place of Mère Marie
de Gonzague (1834–1904), another substitute mother with, however, a
Zélie-like passion for self-mortification (including flagellation with nettles)
and a corresponding zeal for disciplining her charges.[26] At home Thérèse
was known as the "petite fille à Céline,"[27] but when she entered the Carmel
in advance of her elder sister, it was she who became Céline's spiritual
mother and, like most mothers of the time, one who was most anxious lest
her "daughter" choose a partner other than the one (Jesus) that she had pre-
selected for her. "It was impossible for me to see her give her heart to a
mere mortal," wrote Thérèse in the first of her autobiographical memoirs,
and she was doubtless delighted when her cousin and principal suitor
Henry Maudelonde, put off by Céline's eternal demurring, transferred his
attentions to another. But even this was not enough for Thérèse. When, in
April 1892, Céline was invited to Maudelonde's wedding reception, Thérèse
prayed that her sister would be unable to dance lest some mortal entice her
away from her predestined *cavalier* in heaven. For some reason, Céline was
indeed unable to do other than walk woodenly to the music, to the exasper-
ation of her first, and only, suitor that night who forthwith escorted her
back to her seat: "That adventure, unique in its kind," wrote Thérèse,

"caused me to grow in confidence and in love of Him who, in placing *his sign* on my brow, had at the same time imprinted it on that of my beloved Céline."[28]

Here and elsewhere it is clear that, under the guise of religion, though quite sincerely in her own lights, Thérèse was engaged in reconstructing in the Carmel the all-female household under its feminized father-figure that had taken shape at Les Buissonnets, the house in Lisieux to which Louis Martin and his daughters had moved in November 1877, an ideal sorority-cum-matriarchy whose unity and completeness were disrupted when first Pauline (October 1882) and then Marie (October 1886) left to enter the Carmel, with, as we shall see, dire psychological, spiritual, and physical consequences for the youngest of their sisters. Having lost both her "second mother" (Pauline) and sister-godmother (Marie), Thérèse intended to join them as soon as possible in the Carmel, draw Léonie and Céline in her train, and so reunite the sisters, along with their dead siblings, under the protective gaze of a still more sublime mother-father, the crucified Christ, whose physical resemblance to her "petit Roi," Louis Martin, is stressed by Thérèse herself with what, to post-Freudian eyes, is an embarrassing lack of embarrassment. Louis Martin's death in July 1894 enabled him to enter the Carmel in spirit, to be reunited there with his widow, divested now of her negative aspects, in the form of the Virgin, and also permitted Céline, who had been looking after him, to join her sisters in September that year. Only the unfortunate Léonie remained on the outside, but the arrival of cousin Marie Guérin in August 1895 restored the sisterhood to its ideal number of five. In the months that followed Thérèse even acquired two brother-sons in the form of Père Maurice Bellière (1874–1907) and Père Adolphe Roulland (1870–1934) with whom she corresponded and whose spiritual sister and protectrix she became.[29] After years of travail and suffering, the fragmented Martin family was together again, with each of its members mother-father, daughter-son, and sister-brother to the others: the primitive horde reconstituted as a spiritualized super-family under the roof of the Carmel.

All this lay some considerable way in the future, not so much in terms of time as of ordeals endured, assumed, and transcended; whatever her resistance to the idea of *expiatory* suffering, Thérèse would always insist that "*suffering alone* can give birth to souls."[30] Following her mother's death, Thérèse reconstructed her life around the twin pillars of Pauline and her father, both of whom presented a characteristic blend of "masculine" and "feminine" features. Pauline's tough disposition earned her the family nickname of "petit Paulin,"[31] and if Louis Martin was Thérèse's "roi de France et de Navarre," he also "joined to the love he already possessed [while his wife was alive] a truly maternal love" that came to the fore after her death.[32] Just as Zélie had been her daughters' mother-father at Alençon, so Louis became their father-mother at Les Buissonnets; indeed, his legal power as their father over them was formally transferred to his brother-in-law Isidore Guérin in September 1877.[33] But now Thérèse had no real rivals for her father's affection; he was "mon Roi à moi toute seule" and she was his "petite reine," and whenever the "Reine à Papa" and her father-brother-husband went out walking together, as they frequently did, people stopped in the streets to look with wonderment at "such a *handsome* Old Man with such a *little daughter.*"[34]

Louis Martin was like some provincial Père Goriot whose daughters would successively abandon him in favor of a greater Father-Lover-Husband-and-Boychild in Heaven. At the age of six or seven, her father being away on one of his pilgrimages, Thérèse had a vision in the garden of Les Buissonets of "a man dressed exactly like Papa, having the same build and the same way of walking, except that he was *much more bowed down,*" his head shrouded in a kind of apron that prevented the terrified girl from seeing his face, the first instance of the crucial Theresian theme of the veil. It was not until fourteen years later, when she was in the Carmel, that Thérèse was able to grasp the prophetic significance of what she had seen. The mysterious figure was both a premonition of her aged Father, broken down by a succession of strokes beginning in May 1887, and a doppelgänger of Christ, his Holy Face veiled during the hour of his Passion.[35] When, as Soeur Thérèse de l'Enfant-Jésus et de la Sainte-Face, Louis Martin's favorite daughter made the cult of the Holy Face the center of her devotions, she preempted simplistic analysis by herself drawing attention to the preternatural resemblance between the face of Jesus imprinted on Veronica's handkerchief and that of her *"incomparable* little Father" who, like Jesus, was both great and small, strong and weak, rich and poor, broken and triumphant. Perhaps no Christian has ever been more comfortable with the analogy—almost the identity—between "Papa le bon Dieu" and her own "pauvre petit Père."[36]

In an unexpected aside in her first autobiographical essay, Thérèse asks Pauline (to whom, as Mère Agnès de Jésus, the text is addressed) whether she "remembers the masculine and the feminine."[37] It is a revealing admission—apparently Thérèse had great difficulties with genders when learning to read and write, regularly confusing and transposing the masculine and the feminine—for, as we have seen, gender combinations and confusions lie at the heart of her family experience and accordingly contribute greatly to her emerging family-based spirituality. Thus not only are Zélie, Louis, and "Paulin" androgynous figures—"Paulin" even becomes "mon Jésus vivant"[38]—but Céline is addressed as Thérèse's "petit Valérien," the reference being to the chaste marriage between Saint Valérien and Sainte Cécile that Louis and Zélie had already used as the model for their own projected *mariage blanc.*[39] If in this instance Thérèse is in the feminine position, elsewhere she assumes unambiguously the masculine role. In her longing to "embrace all the vocations" for Christ's sake, she imagines herself as a warrior (in the masculine form, *guerrier,* priest, apostle (*apôtre,* of indeterminate gender), *docteur* (in the sense of *Docteur de l'Eglise*), martyr (again in the masculine form), a Crusader (*un Croisé*), or a *zouave pontifical* in order to "die on a battlefield for the defense of the Church."[40] And her supreme "role model," as we shall see, was the androgynous warrior and martyr Joan of Arc for whom Thérèse wrote a number of canticles and plays (always "starring" herself), signing one such work "Un soldat français, défenseur de l'Eglise, admirateur de Jeanne d'Arc"—all masculine—and dedicating it to the equally masculine "valeureux chevalier C. Martin."[41] It is not so much that there shall be "neither male nor female" (Gal. 3:28) in Thérèse's heavenly family, but all shall be both male *and* female, united within the maternal-paternal love of Jesus who is simultaneously and inseparably God and Man, man and woman, suffering redeemer and sleeping child, father and son, mother and daughter. Perhaps when Thérèse was proclaimed *Docteur de l'Eglise Universelle* in the centenary year of her death, she finally achieved her goal of "embracing all the vocations" by combining, and transcending, the masculine and feminine in herself.

The first, and greatest, challenge to Thérèse's reconstituted family came in the autumn of 1882 when the nine-year-old girl overheard her "second mother" Pauline telling her godmother-sister Marie about her imminent, but hitherto undisclosed, departure for the Carmel. It is no exaggeration to say that Thérèse's separation from Pauline—, following the separations from Rose Taillé and her mother and exacerbated by seeing Pauline each week on the other side of the grill in the convent—caused her reconstructed world to shatter into fragments. In the months following Pauline's entering the Carmel on 2 October 1882, Thérèse developed a whole range of symptoms—incessant migraines, insomnia, bouts of uncontrolled trembling, panic attacks, fainting fits, and bursts of verbal delirium—which she ascribed to demonic interference but which were clearly psychosomatic reactions to the trauma of renewed maternal deprivation. In late March 1883, while staying at the Guérins, Thérèse's condition degenerated still further and, according to the testimony given by her sister Marie in 1910 as part of the canonization inquiry, she was seized by a series of "terrifying visions" in which, inter alia, nails in the wall of her room seemed to stick out at her "like thick charred fingers" (*de gros doigts carbonisés*), causing her to shriek with terror. When her father came to visit her, she was terrified by his hat (which had also featured in the hallucination of the veiled man in the garden), calling it a "fat black beast" (*grosse bête noire*): black fingers, black hat, perhaps, speculates Jacques Maître, emblems of paternal anger and judgment singling her out for "killing" Zélie.[42] Thérèse was able to attend, and enjoy, Pauline's clothing as a Carmelite sister on 6 April 1883, but it was not until five weeks later, on Pentecost Sunday (13 May), that she was finally, if incompletely, delivered of the "strange illness" (*étrange maladie*) brought on by her "second mother" abandoning her, thanks to a "miracle" that bulks very large indeed in the standard hagiological accounts of her life.

Back at Les Buissonnets and lying in bed with Léonie for company, Thérèse began to murmur, "Mama . . . Mama . . ." with more than usual pain in her voice, bringing Marie and Céline to her bedside as well, at which point all three girls began to pray to the statue of the Virgin that, a gift to Louis Martin before he was married, he had brought from Alençon to Lisieux, installing it in Thérèse's room when she fell ill. Louis had also recently arranged for a novena of masses to be said for Thérèse's recovery at the church of Notre-Dame des Victoires in Paris, the epicenter of a nationwide Marian cult[43] and a regular place of pilgrimage for Louis and Zélie whenever they visited the capital. In other words, with three of her four sisters around her, and with her mother and father present "in spirit" in the statue, Thérèse had recovered five-sixths, at least, of her family, and it was at that moment that, prompted, Thérèse believed, by the fervor of her sisters' prayers and by her own "ineffable goodness and tenderness," the Virgin looked down on her with a "ravishing smile" that "penetrated to the depths of her soul." It was as though, having regressed to a condition of infant catalepsy, Thérèse was suddenly brought back to life by a smile in which the love of mother, sister, and maternalized father mingled with that of the Mother of God. This was certainly how Thérèse interpreted her experience, using the inevitable floral imagery, as a rebirth and, above all, as a fortification of the wilting flower she had become which, its corolla drawn upward by the "blessed Star" that had shone down on it, would enable it, five years later, to "burst into blossom on the fertile slopes of Mount Carmel."[44]

"Complete Conversion": Christmas 1886

The *sourire de la Vierge* (smile of the Virgin) marked, however, only the beginning of a prolonged healing process that the "complete conversion" of Christmas 1886 would bring to a triumphant conclusion. Thérèse's continuing anxiety expressed itself through recurrent migraine attacks and, in terms of religious observance, through further recourse, undoubtedly encouraged by her sisters, to the obsessive and self-defeating rituals of "earning" and "meriting" God's love. Thus, between 1 March and 8 May 1884, the date of her first communion, Thérèse performed a total of 1,949 "sacrifices" (an average of 28 per day) and said no fewer than 2,773 "invocations" (40 per day), all of them duly recorded in a specially prepared notebook given her by Pauline.[45]

Yet what Thérèse experienced at the communion itself was, according to her own account, precisely the revelation that God's love, mediated through his Son, is gratuitous, unconditional, and freely bestowed without regard to the "merits" of its receiver. "There were no demands, no struggles, no sacrifices" involved as, "like a drop of water losing itself in the bosom of the ocean," she and Jesus, "the master, the King," met and merged in a "fusion" that made her feel that she was loved unconditionally and could love unconditionally in return. As in the earlier "miracle" of the *sourire de la Vierge,* all the members of Thérèse's family, living, absent, and dead, were "really present" at the moment when she received the host in her mouth:

> The absence of Maman caused me no suffering on the day of my first communion: was not heaven in my soul, and had not Maman long since taken her place there? Thus, in receiving the visit of Jesus, I also received that of my beloved Mother who blessed me and rejoiced in my happiness. . . . I did not weep for the absence of Pauline, no doubt I would have been happy to see her at my side, but my sacrifice had long since been accepted and, on that day, joy alone filled my heart, and I united myself with her who gave herself irrevocably to Him who was giving Himself so lovingly to me![46]

Just as she and Jesus—himself almost, if not quite, identified with her earthly "master and King"—"were no longer two," so Thérèse is united via the host with both her mother and "second mother" and with the rest of her family. Receiving the host put an end, temporarily, to the sufferings of her "*exiled* heart" and showed her that, though life, as Pauline's departure had taught her, was indeed an experience of "continual separation,"[47] the broken unity of the family could be re-created through God's love as made present, above all, in the sacrament of Holy Communion. Small wonder that, ever after, and in sharp contrast to the eucharistic practice of the times, Thérèse sought regular, indeed daily, communion, convinced as she was that "it is not in order to remain in the golden ciborium that God descends *every day* from His Heaven."[48]

All this, however, did not prevent Thérèse from being seized by "the terrible sickness of scruples" when she went on retreat to prepare for the solemn renewal of her first communion in May the following year:

> It is necessary to have gone through this martyrdom [*ce martyre*] in order to understand it: it would be impossible for me to say what I suffered during *a year and a half.* . . . All my thoughts and the simplest of actions became a source of anxiety for me; my only respite was to tell them to Marie, which cost me greatly, because I felt obliged to tell her the outlandish thoughts I had about her herself. As soon as I had unburdened myself, I enjoyed a moment of peace, but this peace vanished in a flash and soon my martyrdom resumed.[49]

The ostensible cause of these scruples was fear lest she had deceived herself, and consequently others, about the authenticity of the *sourire de la Vierge,* though her retreat notes also indicate that she was also greatly alarmed by the officiating priest's dire warnings about mortal sin and the danger of taking communion "unworthily"; the onset of puberty was also probably a factor.[50] There followed the familiar round of headaches and weeping fits that, with Marie's help, she negotiated as best she could until a further, and this time double, "separation" occurred with the departure, in early October 1886, of Marie to the local Carmel and of Léonie, briefly and unsuccessfully, to the Poor Clares at Alençon. At this point Thérèse sought the intercession of her four dead brothers and sisters, and—yet another "miracle" brought about by the presence of her ideal family around her—the "ugly malady" (*vilaine maladie*) instantly ceased: "When I think of these things, my soul plunges into the infinite, I seem already to be reaching the shores of eternity. . . . I seem to see My Mother in Heaven coming to meet me with Papa . . . Maman . . . the four little angels. . . . I seem at last to be enjoying forever the true, the eternal family life [*je crois jouir enfin pour toujours de la vraie, de l'éternelle vie en famille*]."[51]

Psychologically and spiritually, the way was now open for her "complete conversion" at Christmas 1886. Returning to Les Buissonnets after midnight mass, full of joy at having received "the *strong, powerful* God" (le Dieu *fort* et *puissant*) in Holy Communion, Thérèse rushed as she had from earliest childhood to open her Christmas presents hidden, according to the "ancient custom" of the household, in a row of shoes placed in front of the fire when she overheard her father saying to Céline, "Fortunately this is the last year it [the hiding of the presents] will happen" (Enfin, heureusement que c'est la dernière anneé!), presumably because Thérèse would become "grown-up" on her fourteenth birthday a week or so later. In tears, Thérèse ran upstairs, followed by Céline who, seeing her distress and still wanting "to treat me like a baby because I was the youngest one in the family," urged her not to go back down and upset herself further. But, according to her own account written nine years later, "Thérèse was no longer the same, Jesus had changed her heart," and, fighting back her tears, she went downstairs and, taking her shoes and placing them in front of her father, "*joyfully* drew out all the objects, looking as happy as a queen," to the obvious delight of Monsieur Martin and the equally obvious amazement of Céline. It seems a trivial incident, but Thérèse interpreted it as the crucial division between the second period of her life, inaugurated by the death of her mother, and the third, "the most beautiful of all, the most full of the graces of Heaven." It was, she wrote, the moment when she emerged form "the *swaddling clothes* of *childhood*" (*les langes de l'enfance*), when Jesus "wishing to show me that I must free myself from the defects (*défauts*) also deprived me of its innocent joys"; in a word, "little Thérèse had recovered the strength of soul that she had lost aged four and a half and it was for ever after that she would keep it."

That this rebirth occurred on the anniversary of Christ's birth is obviously crucial. Thérèse is freed from her swaddling clothes on the night that the infant Jesus was wrapped in his and laid in a manger, his becoming a "sweet *little* Child" enables the less than sweet little child Thérèse to grow up, or, as she puts it, "on that *night* when He made Himself *weak* and suffering for my love, He made me *strong* and courageous, He bestowed upon me his arms [Il me revêtit de ses armes] and since that blessed night I was never beaten in combat, but rather marched from victory to victory and began, so to speak, to '*run like a giant*' [et commençai pour ainsi dire, 'une course de géant']."[52]

All this suggests that, metaphorically, Thérèse was "masculinized" on the night of 24/25 December 1886, first by receiving the "strong, powerful God" in communion and then, immediately afterward, be being temporarily denied the "feminine," or at least childish, pleasures of Christmas. Through the exasperated words of her earthly Father and King, his heavenly counterpart tells her, as it were, that she is behaving like a silly little girl and, as he does so, provides her with the psychological and spiritual strength to overcome her distress and redefine herself as an adult. But her heavenly Father and King is both weak and strong, infant and adult, feminine and masculine; Thérèse is made strong by a helpless babe, armed by a man-child broken, stripped, and nailed to a cross, transformed from a girl into a warrior of Christ through the prevenient grace of a divine man-woman. For the first time, she begins to "run like a giant," words taken and adapted from Psalm 19:5 in which the sun is likened to "a bridegroom coming out of his chamber" (as the transformed Thérèse comes out of her bedroom) who "rejoiceth as a strong man to run the race." Still more strikingly, a few weeks before her death, Thérèse likened her "act of courage" in coming downstairs on her "night of light" to that of Judith in beheading Holofernes: "You acted with a man's heart and your heart was made strong" (Vous avez agi avec un coeur viril et votre coeur s'est fortifié).[53] With the enemy occupying her spirit now slain, she emerges like Judith from the tent of Holofernes in full possession of herself. She goes downstairs, opens her presents, and stands before her earthly father as his consort and equal and before the woman-manchild in heaven as future bridegroom and bride. It is no longer a question, as it was at her first communion, of the Eros of *fusion* with the multiple objects of her love but of the relation-in-separation of Agape: "In a word I felt *charity* enter my heart, the need to forget myself in order to give pleasure and since then I was happy!"[54] Having now put away childish things and ceased to speak, understand, and think as a child (1 Cor. 14:11), she can now become *childlike* and, as an autonomous, individuated young person, a spiritual androgyne, enter into reciprocal relations with others. Secure in possession of herself, she need no longer seek her own but devote herself fully to her calling.

With the crucial breakthrough accomplished, the path to Mount Carmel was swiftly negotiated. On 29 May 1887, just four weeks after her father's first stroke, she sought, and obtained, his consent to enter the Carmel when she was fifteen and, with remarkable determination and audacity, took steps to obtain the necessary permissions. Abandoning the little-girl curls that symbolized her psychic dependence, she put up her hair,[55] and, accompanied by her father whose "patriarchal simplicity" she never more admired, was received first by a hesitant bishop of Bayeux and then, on a diocesan pilgrimage to Rome (November 1887) that she called her *voyage de noces,* broke every Vatican convention to put her request directly to Pope Leo XIII who, to her dismay, intimated that she should wait for, and obey, the decision of Monseigneur Hugonin. It was, she later wrote, as though "Jesus was silent, he seemed absent, nothing revealed his presence to me"; she had offered up herself to the Christ-child as "his *little toy*" and now he had chosen to break it (A Rome Jésus perça son petit jouet), not, however, to destroy it but to "see what was inside and then having seen it, and pleased with His discovery, He dropped his little ball and fell fast asleep."[56] Playing and sleeping: however cloyingly expressed, they are crucial Theresian themes to which we shall return, here noting only that, from her point of view, the sleep of the Christ-child brought almost instant results for, three days after Christmas, Bishop Hugonin relented and acceded to Thérèse's request. It being considered unwise for her to enter the Carmel in midwinter, Thérèse was finally reunited with her sisters Pauline (Mère Agnès de Jésus) and Marie (Soeur Marie du Sacré-Coeur) on 9 April 1888, three months after her fifteenth birthday.

Two months later her father, showing signs of both mental and physical breakdown, ran off to Le Havre, the first of several such escapades accompanied by strokes that would lead to his hospitalization, in February 1889, in the Maison du Bon-Sauveur in Caen where a fellow patient was Anne-Marie Roulé, the deranged former mistress and Pythian oracle of Léon Bloy, interned there from her breakdown in 1882 until her death twenty-five years later.[57] "Papa's three years of martyrdom" began shortly after he attended her clothing on 10 January 1889, and Thérèse, blamed by many for his plight, began to center her devotions around the image of the Holy Face. On 8 September 1890, clad in a bridal gown "of white silk trimmed with swansdown" and with her "long fair hair . . . curled for the occasion," Thérèse made her formal profession of vows, wearing, as was the custom, a hand-written *billet de profession* addressed to her bridegroom against her heart under the dress.[58] Later that month, on the 24th, Thérèse had her curls cropped off and "exchanged the white headdress of the novice for the black one of the professed nun"[59]; her incorporation into the Carmelite community was complete.

The Pranzini Episode (1887)

There is one further episode that needs our attention before we move on to discuss Thérèse's revolutionary doctrine of the *petite voie* (little way), an episode that was critical in her spiritual and psychological development and provides an unexpected recurrence of the theme of the guillotine that figured so prominently in *Blood in the City*.[60] In July 1887, more or less midway between her Christmas conversion and departure for the Carmel, Thérèse learned, by secretly reading her father's copy of the notoriously ultra-Catholic and antisemitic *La Croix*,[61] of the trial and condemnation to death of one Henri Pranzini for the triple murder of a prostitute, her "maid," and the latter's eleven-year-old daughter in an apartment on the rue Montaigne in Paris the previous March. On the strength of having once traveled to Russia, Pranzini was projected by the Catholic press as an atheistic nihilist bent on the destruction of God, property, and society, and it was confidently predicted that, impenitent to the last, he would go blaspheming to hell. Thérèse began to pray for Pranzini's salvation in the "certainty," however, that God "in His infinite mercy" would forgive him even if he showed not a single sign of contrition, and it was only for her own "consolation" and "encouragement" that she prayed that he would indeed give such a sign. Although Thérèse prayed without ceasing and asked Céline to have a mass said for her intentions, "not daring to do so myself for fear of having to admit that it was for Pranzini, the great criminal," it needs to be stressed that she did not feel she had to *earn* forgiveness for Pranzini by fasting, inflicting pain on herself, or performing any of the other "sacrifices" required by the theory and practice of vicarious suffering. She does not, in other words, "substitute" herself for Pranzini in order to deflect God's anger from him to her, for the very good reason that she does not believe that God is angry or that his Justice is anything other than his Mercy and Love. It is not, therefore, she who "purchases" Pranzini's forgiveness through her prayers and "merits," but God who gives that forgiveness freely and gratuitously, as in his loving kindness he freely gives everything; there is no ransom to offer, no sacrifice to perform, only freely given love to be freely accepted. And, to show Thérèse that he has indeed forgiven the murderer, God induces Pranzini to give precisely the sign of contrition that Thérèse has been praying for. Knowing that Pranzini was due to be executed at dawn on 31 August outside the Grande Roquette prison in Paris, Thérèse peeked at her father's copy of *La Croix* while he was taking a nap and learned to her joy that, at the very last moment, even as his head was being placed in the *lunette* of the guillotine, Pranzini had called on the prison almoner, the celebrated Abbé Jean-Baptiste Faure (1833–93), to offer him the cross, whereupon he kissed it twice—three times according to Thérèse's own account—before the blade descended.[62] With that, in Thérèse's words, Pranzini's soul "went to receive the *merciful* [*miséricordieuse*] sentence of him who declares that there is more joy in Heaven for one sinner who repents than for 99 of the just who have no need for repentance": she has obtained a *sign* of God's forgiveness of Pranzini, but she has not "earned" or "bought" that forgiveness itself. She has adopted as her "first child" (*mon premier enfant*) a man whom *La Croix* averred to be beyond all hope of forgiveness, not because she doubts God's mercy and love and hopes, through her prayers, to dare, almost force, him to exercise them on Pranzini's behalf, but because she is convinced that God in his grace has *already* adopted him as *his* child. There is indeed an exchange between Thérèse and God, mediated by Jesus, but it is, as she says, an "exchange of love," not the *do ut des* of a sacrifice offered by Thérèse and then returned with interest by God: quite simply, there is nothing to be purchased since everything is free.[63]

The moment when Pranzini placed his lips on the "sacred wounds" (*plaies sacreés*) of the crucified Christ was absolute proof for Thérèse that God's love and his justice are identical. It showed her, if she still had any doubts, that he wills the forgiveness of *all* of his children, no matter how great their sins, and only those who freely refuse that forgiveness are damned, not because God, like a piqued patriarch, seeks vengeance but because, having freely created man to be free, he cannot, even in his love, counteract the free choices man makes; the damned are self-damned, but God does not for that cease to love them. But the death of Pranzini was crucial not just to the formation of Thérèse's theology of grace, but to her whole spiritual and psychological development. Clearly she identified with Pranzini, and she may also have identified with his alleged victims,[64] the prostitute, the maid, and, above all, the eleven-year-old girl, and transferred on to him all the guilts and anxieties of her childhood; in freely acknowledging her sin, she also receives God's forgiveness. Pranzini's severed head is, like the severed head of Holofernes, the past self she cut off when, to use her own image, she emerged like Judith, transfigured and reborn, on the night of her "complete conversion." But Pranzini is also a figure of the martyred, wounded Christ, helpless as a child in the hands of his executioners, and in adopting him as her "first child" she also adopts the man-child Jesus even as she is adopted by him.[65] It is the usual Theresian imbroglio of familial, marital, and martial connections—she is both Jesus' child and his mother, his bride and his bridegroom, a helpless babe and an androgynous soldier of Christ, a Joan or a Judith—but above all she is confirmed in her mission, which is to love him who first loved her and, through prayer, to transmit that love to the whole of humanity. With this we can move on to discuss the main elements of the *petite voie*, the path to sainthood for all, with which Thérèse's name is forever associated.

La Petite Voie

Thérèse received no formal theological instruction, nor, apart form the Bible, had she read widely. Her spiritual models were those of her order, Saint Teresa of Avila and Saint John of the Cross (though her *petite voie* was to differ significantly from their dizzying ascents of Mount Carmel), reinforced by the acknowledged masters of French devotional writing: Saint

François de Sales (1567–1622); the Abbé Jean-Joseph Surin (1600–65), celebrated above all as the exorcist at Loudun; and Père Jean-Pierre Caussade (1675–1751), author of the classic *L'abandon à la Providence divine* which, after more than a century's neglect, was republished in 1860. She was also influenced by Father Frederick Faber's *The Foot of the Cross* (1858) which she read in translation, and also learned much from at least two of her spiritual directors: Père Almire Pichon (1843–1919), the Jesuit who heard her general confession on 28 May 1888 and who, having himself suffered form scruples "to the point of insanity," was able to reassure her and steer her decisively away from "the path of fear" (*la voie de la crainte*),[66] and the Franciscan Père Alexis Pror (1844–1914) who, preaching the convent's annual retreat in October 1891, scandalized the sisters, but not Thérèse, by asserting that "our faults cannot hurt God."[67] Her correspondence with her spiritual brother and sons, Pères Bellière and Roulland (see above), helped her to crystallize her ideas, and in her final ordeal she gained much consolation from the writings of Saint Théophane Vénard (1829–61), who had undergone martyrdom by decapitation in Tonkin in 1861.[68] Otherwise, her spiritual thinking was developed through prayer, meditation, and day-to-day interaction with her fellow Carmelite sisters whose all too obvious servitude to the God of Justice, expressed in the form of scruples, spiritual anxiety (particularly on the subject of purgatory), and an obsession with "works," encouraged her to go ever more confidently along the *petite voie* of trust in God's love. In this spirit, she gave Soeur Fébronie de la Sainte-Enfance (1819–92), the Carmel's ultrastrict subprioress, the following memorable advice: "Sister, if you want the Justice of God, you will get the Justice of God. The soul receives exactly what it expects from God."[69]

Given the constraints on her freedom of expression, her limited experience of life, and her circumscribed intellectual horizons, it is remarkable how far, simply by obeying her spiritual instincts, Thérèse was able to break with the devotional practices of her day and the expiatory theology that underpinned them. She found saying the rosary a torment and was indifferent to the cult of the Sacred Heart, at least as it was currently practiced, telling her sister Céline, who was visiting Paray-le-Monial with Léonie for the bicentenary of the death of Saint Marguerite-Marie Alacoque, the founder of the cult, in October 1890, that she did not "see the Sacred Heart like everyone else," not, in other words, as the all-too-familiar bleeding strawberry with its reparationist undertones but as the locus of a one-to-one dialogue with Christ.[70] Similarly, while making the Holy Face the center of her personal devotions, Thérèse distanced herself from the expiatory dimension foregrounded in the original vision of Marie de Saint-Pierre (1816–48) and further stressed by the significantly named Confrérie Réparatrice de la Sainte-Face founded in 1851 by Louis Dupont (1797–1876), the so-called holy man of Tours, in which Thérèse had been enrolled, along with the other lay members of her family, in April 1885.[71]

In general, and seemingly as a matter of principle, Thérèse had no time for the so-called *voies extraordinaires* of "abnormal" religious experience—the visions, ecstasies, stigmata, inedia, and the like that would feature so prominently in the "cases" of women like Louise Lateau, Claire Ferchaud, and, most recently, Marthe Robin (see chapter 5). And, in marked contrast to her father, Thérèse considered pilgrimages a distraction from the day-to-day "monotony of sacrifice" of her own inner journey[72]; her lack of interest in La Salette and Lourdes, to say nothing of the nearby Marian shrine of Pontmain, distinguishes her from virtually every other Catholic thinker of her time. Though constantly stressing the spiritual value of suffering, she was opposed to self-mortification in all the forms in which it was still commonly practiced in monastic life, not least at the Carmel in Lisieux (e.g., excessive fasting, flagellation, the wearing of the cilice and similar instruments of self-torture), and, again in marked contrast to the standard practice of her times, advocated frequent, indeed daily, communion. There is an illuminating exchange of letters between her and her cousin Marie Guérin on the occasion of the latter's visit to the Paris exhibition in May 1889—in itself a perilous adventure for a good Catholic girl, given that it commemorated a hundred years of revolution in France.[73] Visiting the galleries and pavilions that month, Marie was exposed to one "nudité" after another and, fearing for the moral and spiritual state of her soul, ceased taking communion, so great was the terror of doing so "unworthily." As soon as she heard, Thérèse wrote back urging her cousin to resume taking communion, confident that she had committed no "fault" and that, even if she had, this was no reason for withdrawing herself from God's love: The only thing that "offends Jesus and hurts His heart is lack of confidence." In other words, the host is not a reward but a gift, and it is not necessary to be "clean" or "pure" before receiving the gift of God's love, any more than—to use Thérèse's favorite analogy—a child should draw back from the love of its parents because it has been naughty or is dirty.[74]

Sicut parvuli

Apart from her near-contemporary Charles Péguy (1873–1914), no French Catholic of her time dwelt more insistently than Thérèse on Christ's injunction to his followers that they "become as little children" in order to enter the kingdom of God (Matthew 18:3). But it is only possible to approach God as a child because God places Love before Judgment or, more precisely, because, in Thérèse's view, God's Love and his Judgment are the same. The form of Thérèse's spiritual infantilism may owe something to Carmelite tradition (see below), but its source lies deep in her own experience of childhood and, above all, in her relationship with her idealized father-and-mother Louis Martin. Thérèse's God, and, still more, her Jesus, is, like her father, an androgynous being, combining the power and authority of the archetypal father with the tenderness and mercy of the mythical mother, with the latter ultimately transcending and subsuming the former; the actual authoritarianism of Thérèse's "phallic mother" is eclipsed in favor of the "maternal" loving kindness of her feminized father. "God is more tender than a mother" is her clearest statement of a theme on which she would work endless variations,[75] and there was no biblical passage that she more enjoyed citing than Isaiah 66:31: "As one whom his mother comforteth, so I will comfort you."

There were, of course, numerous precedents in devotional writing, beginning with Saint Bernard of Clairvaux, for this stress on the motherhood of God and, still more, of his son,[76] and Thérèse would have found in her reading of Saint François de Sales many elaborate permutations of this well-worn spiritual topos.[77] It was, however, a tradition that had largely "gone underground" in postrevolutionary Catholic Europe, resurfacing in some, but not all, of the forms of Marian devotion that were so characteristic a feature of the age. As God-the-Father, followed, more often than not, by his son, became both more abstract and more threatening, so popular piety, with or without the sanction of the Church hierarchy, installed Mary as a shield of mercy and kindness in the face of divine anger. In reviving the tradition of the motherhood of God, Thérèse did not so much render Mary redundant as accentuate an underlying movement toward the comprehensive feminization of Catholicism, whence, in part, her immediate popularity as a spiritual model. A mother at heart, Thérèse's "Papa le bon Dieu" is utterly incapable of anger—and utterly unlike the actual mother she had known. In shifting from the God-Father-Justice paradigm that dominated the official spirituality of the Church, not least at the Carmel at Lisieux, to that of God-Mother-Love,[78] Thérèse paradoxically repudiated her own mother and installed her mother-father in her place. No longer the threatening superego-figure that obsessed her from earliest childhood until Christmas 1886, God revealed himself/herself as unconditional love seeking "only" unconditional love in return, and from this core experience of divine mother-fatherhood all the main strands of Theresian spirituality spontaneously unwind: the child-parent relationship as the model and ground of the soul's relationship with God; the primacy of love over merit; the thematics of playing, sleeping, and hiding; and, perhaps above all, the need for "loving audacity" (*amoureuse audace*),[79] not caution or restraint, in all human dealings with God. The last strand was epitomized for Thérèse in the "woman in the city" of Luke 7:37 (whom, in common with Church tradition, Thérèse identified with Mary Magdalene), kneeling in tears at Christ's feet, wiping them with her hair, and breaking over them her precious alabaster box of ointment and so, in her fearless self-surrender, winning the ultimate prize: "Her sins, which are many, are forgiven; for she loved much" (Luke 7:47). There is no need for a formal exposition of Thérèse's "doctrine"; it is the images and metaphors that count, and it is on these that we shall concentrate in the discussion that follows, postponing critical comment until the end of this chapter.

When, following the Gospels, Thérèse spoke of entering the kingdom of heaven "as a child," she did not conceive the child as "innocent," "selfless," or "pure."[80] Like virtually every other Catholic of her day, she believed that original sin was transmitted more or less organically from parents to child, though, like Simone Weil (see chapter 5), she had the gravest misgivings concerning official church teaching on the fate of unbaptized infants.[81] It was not the selflessness of the child that she admired but its greedy, selfish clamoring for love, its refusal to hold back or take no for an answer. One of her favorite images depicted Christ with two children, one of whom sits semi-naked on his lap and paws at his neck, lifting its head to be kissed, while the other, fully clothed, stands head bowed at his side, in a posture of dutiful respect: "The second child," wrote Thérèse "does not please me so much. He stands like a fully grown person [*une grande personne*]: someone has said something to him . . . He knows that Jesus must be treated with respect."[82] The first child is an infant version of Mary Magdalene, the second of Martha: Both are loved, but the confident self-surrender of the former pleases Christ (and Thérèse) more than the anxious self-attention of the latter.[83] Littleness, for Thérèse, is the ultimate state of grace: smallness is greatness. The word *petit* occurs no fewer than 1,175 times in her correspondence and 374 times in the remarks made and taken down in the course of her last illness, far more often even than "Dieu" or "Jésus" (whose name is coupled with "petit" 31 times in her letters), and invariably in a positive sense.[84] *Petite fleur, petite Thérèse, petite voie, petit Jésus:* For many, Thérèse's compulsive miniaturism will be one of her least palatable traits, for others the key to her thinking. Her heaven is a Lilliput peopled by diminutive saints, and the only way to join them is to become little oneself. Next to Isaiah 66:13 and Luke 7:47, Thérèse's most common biblical quotation is Proverbs 9:4, which she renders as "Whoever is *very little,* let him come to me" (Si quelqu'un est *tout petit,* qu'il vienne à moi), where the French Jerusalem Bible gives "simple" and its English version "ignorant"; she also quotes Wisdom 6:7 as "Mercy is granted to the little" (La miséricorde est accordeé aux petits, cf. "The lowly will be compassionately pardoned").[85] In one of her last letters, dated 18 July 1897, Thérèse reassured her anxious brother-son, the Abbé Bellière, with the following parable of her own:

Imagine that a father has two cheeky, disobedient children. Coming to punish them, he sees one of them shudder and run away from him, feeling in the depths of his heart that he deserves to be punished; his brother, on the other hand, flings himself into his father's arms, saying that he is sorry for having caused him pain, that he loves him and that, to prove it, he'll be a good boy from now on. Then, if this child asks his father to *punish* him with a *kiss,* I do not believe that the heart of the happy father could possibly resist the filial confidence of his son whose sincerity and love he knows well. He is not, however, unaware that his son will more than once fall into the same faults, but he is inclined always to pardon him if his son always seizes him by the heartstrings [*si toujours son fils le prend par le coeur*]. . . . I will say nothing about the first child, my dear little brother, you will have to decide whether his father can love him as much, and treat him as indulgently, as the other.[86]

If even an angry father is swayed by a son's love, how much more merciful still is Thérèse's mother-father in heaven from whom all anger is absent. For Thérèse, as for Péguy of *Le Porche du mystère de la deuxième vertu* (1911), the parable of the Prodigal Son was "the word of Jesus that has had the greatest resonance (*retentissement*) in the world": "Even to think about it brings a sob to the heart. . . . Hundreds and thousands have wept over it."[87] But, like Péguy, Thérèse knew that the father was even more prodigal than the son—prodigal with his love—and that the tears of joy shed by the former far exceeded the latters' of gratitude and relief. "I do not like, says God, those who mistrust me" (Péguy);[88] "What offends Jesus, what wounds Him in His heart, is lack of confidence" (Thérèse)[89]: For both, trust, not fear, is the beginning of wisdom, and both see the naughty child who expects and *demands* forgiveness as the epitome of that trust.

Approaching God and Christ "as a child" is only the beginning of Thérèse's "paidolatry," or cult of childlikeness, for her Christ is above all the Christ enshrined in the two parts of the name that she took when she entered the Carmel: the Christ-child asleep in his crib and the Holy Face imprinted on Veronica's handkerchief, both equally helpless. Between the infant and the crucified Christ there is for Thérèse virtually no interval or transition; the adult Christ of the temptation, the healings, the parables, and the sermon on the Mount scarcely features in her writings. Her Christ rarely speaks, and in the images of the Christ-child and Holy Face around which she centered her devotions, the eyes of her Savior are almost always closed, as they are in the images that she herself created.[90] The seamless continuity between Christ-child and Holy Face is vividly illustrated in the double-shielded coat of arms that Thérèse designed for herself and placed at the end of her first autobiographical memoir completed in January 1896. Dimidiated diagonally, the left-hand escutcheon depicts in its lower half a sleeping Christ-child with, dropping over him, a bunch of grapes attached to a vine that winds into the upper half where it serves as a support for a conventional handkerchief-image of the Holy Face; the Holy Face is flanked on one side by another bunch of grapes and on the other by a harp, also suspended from the grapevine. Derived self-evidently from John 15:5 ("I am the vine, ye are the branches"), the vine and its two bunches of grapes are intended, writes Thérèse in her accompanying commentary, to represent her "one desire on this earth: that of offering herself as a little bunch of grapes to refresh the child Jesus, to amuse him and to let herself be pressed by Him as the fancy takes Him (*au gré de ses caprices*) and also to be able to staunch the burning thirst that He feels during His passion." Locked indissolubly together, the two shields represent the betrothal and marriage of "JHS" (Jesus) and "FMT" (Françoise-Marie-Thérèse); Thérèse is the child-bride of a child-groom and a dead man. The whole image embodies a dictum of Saint John of the Cross: "Love is paid only with Love" (*L'Amour ne se paie que par l'Amour*).[91]

Thérèse's picture of the sleeping Christ-child reflects the thousands of such images that circulated in France, most of them linked to the cult of L'Enfant-Jésus founded by the seventeenth-century Carmelite Sainte Marguerite de Beaune (1619–48).[92] But, just as the Holy Face so plainly replicates that of her father (and increasingly so as he entered his "passion" of breakdown and illness),[93] so Thérèse's cult of the Christ-child reaches far beyond a conventional devotion and into the depths of her psyche. The Christ-child is both herself, her child, and her brother, an image of the two little Josephs whose intercession she sought in her prayers. But if she is the child's mother, she is also his child, for, even as he sleeps, he watches maternally over all of his children, and particularly, of course, over his *petite Thérèse*. When he awakes, he plays with her, and she plays with him; she is a "useless toy" in his hands, a "little ball of no value" which sometimes it pleases him to "pierce" (as his own hands and feet will later be pierced) to see what, if anything, is inside.[94] Sometimes he just drops it and goes back to sleep, making the little ball feel lost and neglected, but it never rolls away and, even if it does, Jesus is always there to retrieve it and continue his playing.

As so often with Thérèse, the frequent mawkishness of expression conceals the profoundest of spiritual intuitions. Instinctively she had rediscovered the ancient theme of *play* as an expression of divine grace, of what, in a classic study, the Jesuit Hugo Rahner called the practice of "eutrepelia," which centuries of puritanism and obsession with "works" had driven underground along with the whole tradition of spiritual childhood of which it forms part.[95] The Christian God, says Rahner, is a *Deus ludens* who creates through the sheer playful love of creating; the creation has no "point" beyond its simple existence as God's loving gift, it is *Gottespiel*, his plaything, his toy, and all that he requires of his playmates is that they play along with him, like the David of 2 Samuel 6:21 ("Therefore will I play before the Lord") in imitation of the divine spirit that creates and sustains the whole of the universe: "I was by his side, a master craftsman, delighting him day after day, ever at play in his presence, at play everywhere in the world, delighting to be with the sons of men" (Proverbs 8:31–32, Jerusalem Bible translation).

If Adam's fall was in a profound sense a fall into seriousness, into purposeful action, into business and busy-ness, into a work ethic whose religious counterpart was a "works ethic" of accumulating merits like capital, then salvation may be construed as a recovery of the childlike playfulness and carefreeness of the origins: "and the streets of the city shall be full of boys and girls playing in the streets thereof" (Zechariah 8:5). It is in this light that we should interpret Thérèse's ball games with Jesus, as a playfully pointless response to the sublime pointlessness of creation. Like the seventeenth-century Welsh poet-divine Henry Vaughan (1621/2–95), Thérèse truly believed, in opposition to the works-centered piety of her age, that it was possible "by mere playing [to] go to Heaven."[96] There is ample evidence that she had laughed and played with Rose Taillé on the farm at Semallé but also that, by her own repeated admission, the ability to play disappeared once she returned to the *pratique*-dominated world of the family home in Alençon.[97] Not for the first time, liberation for Thérèse came from repudiating the influence of her own mother and placing herself under the tutelage of a whole series of idealized mother-figures, supreme among whom is the infant, child, brother, and mother rolled into one, who is only too delighted to "play ball," in every sense of the term, with his playmates if they will abandon their anxious self-attention and, freely and joyfully, "play ball" with him.

Thérèse takes the theme of playing with Jesus an audacious step further when she speaks of gambling her all with him on the "bank of love"—a loaded image, indeed, at a time when so many Catholics, including the Guérins, had lost heavily on the crash of the Union Générale in 1882. But Thérèse's speculation on divine love is as far removed from Pascal's tortured epistemological wager in favor of God's existence as it is from Georges Bataille's later and still more anguished theory and practice of the *mise en jeu* of the self (see chapter 6). For Thérèse it is sufficient "simply" to risk everything one has and let Christ "play the market" in one's place, either by enhancing the initial value of the stake by careful investment or, better still, by squandering the lot in one rash speculation after another because, on the heavenly stock market, all investors are winners, provided only that they hand over everything to the divine broker in advance: "I am playing the bank of love and I am playing for high stakes" (Je joue à la banque de l'amour. . . . Je joue gros jeu).[98] In risking all she has saved, Thérèse *dares* her Savior to save her. If Christ is a thief (Luke 12:39 etc.), not only does Thérèse offer herself up to be stolen, but, far from calling out "Stop thief!" when she sees him approach, beckons him on with cries of "This way! This way!"[99] Then, with typical boldness, Thérèse goes one step further and announces that, disdaining to purchase entry into heaven through "merits" or "good works," she will both steal and steal into it like the penitent thief at the Crucifixion: "I will imitate thieves, I want to get it [heaven] by cunning, by a trick of love [*une ruse d'amour*] which will open its entrance to me, to me and other poor sinners."[100] Jesus comes to humanity as both beggar and thief; on the one hand, the "divine Beggar of love" (*le divin Mendiant d'amour*)[101] solicits man's love empty-handed, apparently offering nothing in return, while on the other he turns thief and steals human hearts when they allow themselves to be stolen or else lovingly tricks them into surrendering their goods. The only response is to approach Jesus as beggar and thief in one's turn, to stretch out one's hand, and, as Thérèse does not hesitate to say, to pester (*importuner*) him until he delivers[102]; failing all else, one can trick him and rob him of the hidden riches he carries secreted under his rags. Time and again Thérèse insists that only the empty-handed and courageous receive the fullness of God's gifts; heaven is not to be purchased (though it can be wheedled, stolen, and obtained by ruse), it is enough to stand as one is and have the courage to ask and in due course, perhaps not immediately, "it shall be given you" (Matthew 7:8). Thérèse's whole work is an extended *Essai sur le don,* with the crucial distinction that God, unlike man, does not give in order to receive a countergift in return. He gives absolutely, gratuitously, unconditionally. Or, as one of Thérèse's greatest admirers Georges Bernanos (see below) put it in *Les Enfants humiliés* (1949), "Amongst us, there is only exchange, God alone gives, only He."[103]

One of the principal elements of Thérèse's *petite voie* is the notion of hiding and being hidden, and, as always, the roots of this theme reach deep into her childhood experience.[104] As a tiny child, Thérèse would hide under her blankets from her mother, hoping that Madame Martin would forgive her some real or imagined misdemeanor when she "revealed" herself; her pleasure in rituals of this sort was so intense that, wrote Madame Martin to Pauline, it was "like playing at dolls," a most significant analogy in view of Thérèse's later desire to be a mere toy in Christ's hands.[105] Subsequently, this longing to be tucked in, hidden, and cosseted reappeared in her desire to conceal herself within the folds of Mary's "virginal mantle"—the Virgin being explicitly addressed as "Maman" in the passage in question—or to throw herself into Jesus's arms "like a little child hiding myself in His hair"; experience, she says, has taught her that "happiness consists solely in being hidden" (or in hiding oneself, *le bonheur ne consiste qu'à se cacher*), and the Carmel itself is likened to the cloak of the virgin in which she and her sisters can hide.[106] But Thérèse's Jesus also takes pleasure in hiding himself, not in order to deny himself to those who would find him, but precisely for the joy, after teasing and leading them on, of being discovered and captured, as—to use the inevitable analogy—in a game of celestial hide-and-seek. Thus it is only proper that the Holy Face should be partly hidden by a veil, like the apronlike covering that half-concealed the face of the stranger in her childhood hallucination and which she later construed as the "sign" of her own father's "*glorious* ordeal."[107] Just as Thérèse's daily meditations centered around "the mysteries of love hidden in the Face of our Spouse" (*les mystères d'amour cachés dans le Visage de notre Epoux*),[108] so in daily communion Jesus offered himself to he "hidden beneath the species [*apparence*] of a white host."[109] *Larvatus prodeo*: like a masked actor, Jesus proceeds surreptitiously, keeping his secrets hidden as a matter of principle "from the wise and the prudent" and revealing them only "unto babes" (Matthew 11:25; "aux *plus petits*" in Thérèse's translation).[110] But, like a baby playing peek-a-boo with its mother, the best way to please the hidden Christ is to hide, for only to the hidden will his secrets be revealed: "In order to find something hidden (*une chose cacheé*), we must remain hidden ourselves, our lives must thus be a *mystery,* we must imitate Jesus . . . whose *face was hidden.*"[111] Jesus is both hider and seeker, as are his play-mates; the pleasure of both lies equally in catching and being caught.

While basing her *petite voie* primarily on the paradigm of mother-father and child, Thérèse does not neglect the equally traditional paradigm of the Bride of Christ and her heavenly Bridegroom. She quotes copiously from the *Song of Songs,* the principal source of this spiritual tradition, especially as mediated through the commentaries of Saint Bernard of Clairvaux,[112] and, in her little-girl way, reproduces, almost to the point of parody, the major images and themes of epithalamic devotion. She even devises a "Letter of invitation" in which guests are informed of the forthcoming marriage, to be celebrated on Mount Carmel on 24 September 1890 (the date of her formal taking of the veil), between "Soeur Thérèse de l'Enfant Jésus de la Sainte Face" and "Jesus, the Word of God [*le Verbe de Dieu*], second Person of the Adorable Trinity who by the operation of the Holy Spirit became Man and Son of Mary Queen of Heaven." The invitation is issued in the joint names of "Almighty God, Creator of Heaven and Earth" and "Monsieur Louis Martin, Proprietor and Master of the Demesnes [*Seigneuries*] of Suffering and Humiliation and Madame Martin, Princess and Lady-in-waiting [*Dame d'Honneur*] of the Celestial Court."[113] The invitation is typical of Thérèse's tendency to miniaturize and prettify everything. Her vision lacks the frank sensuality encountered, for example, in the work of Hildegard of Bingen, Mechtild of Magdeburg, or Angela of Foligno whose spiritual raptures would so preoccupy Bataille, to say nothing of the earlier Teresa after whom she was named. She does not so much make love with her Spouse as flirt with him, as he flirts with her in return; it is a matter of caresses and cuddling, at the very most of a little light petting. Yet there is no mistaking the intensity of her identification with the "astounding or rather the amorous audacity" of Mary Magdalene, or the ardor of her self-surrender as she allows herself to be "drawn," "a poor little fragment of useless iron," into the "divine brazier" of Christ's love, there to be "penetrated" and "flooded" (*imbibeé*) by its "burning substance"[114]; it is a characteristic mixture of sexual metaphors in which Thérèse is, like her Lover, simultaneously masculine and feminine, penetrating only in order to be penetrated in her turn. But, with Thérèse, it is rarely a question of orgasmic fusion between the Bride and her Groom—the iron, however brightly it glows, always remains distinct from the fire—and her mildly erotic spirituality stops well short of the ecstatic *Liebestod* of the founder of her order; between Teresa and "Thérésita" the distance is ultimately as great as that between the baroque splendor of the Bernini in Santa Maria della Vittoria and the simpering statuettes of "Petite Fleur" to be found in a thousand parish churches of France.[115] But, then, it was never Thérèse's ambition to be a *great* saint or at least not in any conventional sense of the word "great."

It should be clear from the preceding discussion that Thérèse's *petite voie* turns the spiritual orthopraxy of her times on its head. Convinced that God is Love and not Judgment, or, rather, that his Love and his Judgment are one and the same, Thérèse was able to assert with absolute confidence that he and his Son have "no need of our works, but only of our love"[116] and, in so doing, broke decisively with the merit-obsessed piety of both her upbringing and of the vast majority of her Carmelite sisters. All of her preferred metaphors—and above all the famous Christ-operated elevator to heaven[117]—express the key Christian teaching that it is the divine, as incarnated in Christ, that *descends* to mankind and not mankind that *rises* to the divine via the stairway of "works." It is Thérèse's genius, her admiration for Joan of Arc notwithstanding, regularly to *refuse* to "fight the good fight." When she encounters an obstacle on her *petite voie* to heaven, her instinct is not to climb over it but, to use her own characteristic image, to slip underneath it like a child crawling beneath the legs of a horse that stands in its path[118]; her final resort is, quite simply, to desert, for it is better to fail, and offer up one's failure to Christ, than to believe that one has overcome through one's unaided efforts.[119] Thérèse's spirituality is a spirituality of *Gelassenheit,*[120] of "letting go" and self-surrender, and above all of liberation from the tyranny of the superego (incarnated in her case by her mother) and its associated works ethic. Playing, sleeping, and hiding lead further than constant striving and straining; like the lilies of the field that "toil not [and] spin not" (Luke 12:27), the Little Flower opens its petals to receive the rays of divine grace and allows itself to be drawn gently upward to Heaven. If such images repel by their sugary profusion, it is through them that Thérèse recovered and reformulated some of the all but forgotten spiritual traditions of the Church. In essence, she was a fool for Christ's sake through whom the ancient themes of holy infancy, holy folly, and holy play acquired an energy that had been denied them for centuries.[121] In coming empty-handed, even empty-headed, to the self-emptied Christ, she renewed the whole tradition of *kenosis,* or self-emptying [cf. Phil. 2:7]; truly her *petite voie* is not the way of the World.

Thérèse and the Doctrine of Mystical Substitution

Yet there was one respect above all in which Thérèse broke with the prevailing spirituality of her order and her times, and this concerns her attitude toward the theory and practice of vicarious suffering, otherwise known as the doctrine of mystical substitution. The more or less canonical *Trésor du Carmel,* which Thérèse had certainly read, defined the divinely ordained mission of the order as follows: "To pray for sinners, and to offer oneself up on their behalf to divine justice, and to make up [*suppléer*], through the rigors of an austere, crucified life, for the penance that they fail to do themselves. The order therefore requires generous, humble and zealous souls, that renounce themselves and courageously offer themselves up as victims in place of our divine Master who has now [i.e., since his resurrection and ascension into heaven] become incapable of suffering [*devenu impassible*], in order to be sacrificed [*immolées*] like him for the glory of His Father and for the salvation of souls."[122]

This injunction to "stand in" for both sinners and Savior—for those who refuse to suffer and repent and for him who, in his Glory, can suffer physically no more—was followed with a particular rigor and ardor at Lisieux where the local Carmel's cofounder, Soeur Geneviève de Sainte-Thérèse (1805–91), was a devoted member of the Confrérie Réparatrice de la Sainte Face (see above) who committed herself to a life of physical sufferings and privations in order to deflect onto her person the divine wrath that would otherwise have been visited on the sinful French nation; she died in great pain in December 1891, and her heart was preserved and exposed as an example to the sisters of what the doctrine of mystical substitution ultimately involved.[123] Still more extreme was the case of another Lisieux Carmelite, Soeur Marie de la Croix (Louise Désirée Gosselin, 1811–82), who in 1849 "offered herself up" as a victim to secure the promulgation of the doctrine of the Immaculate Conception. Not long afterward she went out of her mind, but, when the doctrine in question was officially proclaimed in 1854, both she and her Carmelite sisters took it as a "sign" that God had "accepted the offering" of her sanity and rewarded her accordingly. She lived on until 1882, denied the sacraments on account of her madness, and apparently convinced that she would suffer for all eternity in limbo for the greater glory of the Virgin; her sacrifice of her own sanity and salvation for the sake of the Church was still cited as an example when Thérèse entered the Carmel six years after her death.[124]

As the enmity of Church and Republic intensified after 1880, so acts of holocaustal self-offering took on a more and more explicitly political coloration, and it was, for example, by no means untypical when, in 1897, the year of Thérèse's death, the newly elected prioress of the Carmel at Epernay, Soeur Marie-Thérèse, consecrated herself to a life of self-denial and suffering in order to obtain "the destruction of freemasonry" in France and so help purify a nation that she considered "rotten with pride to its roots."[125] At Lisieux the pressure to mount the Calvary of vicarious suffering was intense, and it is, therefore, all the more striking that Thérèse chose not to join those "souls that offer themselves up as victims to God's Justice in order to divert [*détourner*] and draw onto themselves the punishments reserved for the guilty."[126] To enter the lists of expiatory sacrifice would have gone flat in the face of her two deepest convictions, namely, that God's forgiveness is freely given not earned and that, in any case, there is, and can be, no punitive impulse in God that could require diversion or appeasement: He really is Love, and Love only, for Thérèse. Thus, even in her final agony when her fellow Carmelites, even her own sisters, were casting her as an exemplary immolatory victim, she would have none of it and, except to please others, refused to "offer up" her sufferings for this or that cause:

> My little life is made up of suffering and that's all there is to it! I could not say: My God, this is for the Church, my god, this for France, etc. . . . God in His goodness [*le bon Dieu*] knows full well what to do with it; I gave everything to Him to give Him pleasure. And then it would tire me too much to say to Him: Give this to Peter, give this to Paul. I only do it very quickly when a sister asks me to, and after I think no more about it. When I pray for my brother missionaries, I don't offer up my sufferings, I say very simply: My God, give them everything that I desire for myself.[127]

With these and similar words, uttered in the last weeks of her life, Thérèse demonstrated how far she had moved from the *do ut des* mentality that dominated the Catholic piety of her age. She gives to give pleasure, not to "ransom" this or that sinner or to wring this or that favor from a tight-fisted God. Her God gives absolutely, and so, insofar as it is humanly possible, does Thérèse. There are no deals to be settled in the currency of pain, no debts to be paid off through the "merits" of suffering. The only exchange is that of reciprocal love.

Thus when Thérèse speaks of sacrifice, as she frequently does, it is invariably to God's love and not to his Justice that she makes it, and she never "substitutes" herself for sinners since there is no need to do so; there is simply no anger in God to be bought off or placated. As the English Dominican Simon Tugwell has written, "heroic souls who offer themselves as victims to divine Justice presuppose their own separation from the sinners who offend that justice; but Thérèse totally identifies herself with 'my brothers, the sinners.'"[128] Accordingly, she offers herself up exactly as she is, not to "purchase" her salvation or that of anyone else, but solely to express her love for the God of Love and his Son:

> I am only a child, powerless and weak, and yet it is my very weakness that gives me the courage [*l'audace*] to offer myself as a *Victim to your Love, O Jesus!* Formerly only pure and stainless hosts [*les hosties pures et sans taches*] were acceptable to the God of Strength and of Power [*le Dieu Fort et Puissant*]. In order to satisfy Divine *Justice,* perfect victims were required, but the law of fear was superseded by the *law of Love,* and *Love* chose me as a holocaust, feeble and imperfect creature that I am. . . . Is not this choice worthy of *Love?* . . . Yes, in order for Love to be completely fulfilled, It must humble itself [*il faut*

qu'Il s'abaisse], humble itself until it is nothing and then transform this nothing into *fire*.[129]

These words were written in September 1896, when Thérèse knew she was dying, and repeat the image of fire that comes increasingly to the fore in the writings of the last two years of her life. In January 1895, Thérèse played the part of the heroine in the second of the two plays, *Jeanne d'Arc accomplissant sa mission,* on the theme of the Maid that she wrote for performance in the Carmel. A photograph taken at the time shows her standing in the court of the convent, wearing what appears to be cardboard armor over her robes, to the dress of which paper *fleurs de lys* have been sewn. She wears a black wig over her headdress, and in one hand carries a banner and in the other a sword: It is a memorable image of the androgynous warrior-martyr whom Thérèse so admired. The play was to climax, naturally, in the execution of the heroine, and a number of portable stoves had been laid on to simulate the pyre. But simulation turned to reality when the makeshift scenery burst into flames that almost caught Thérèse's highly combustible costume.[130] Six months later, on the Feast of the Holy Trinity (9 June 1895), she formally offered herself up as a "Holocaustal Victim to God's Merciful Love" (Victime d'Holocauste à l'Amour Miséricordieux du Bon Dieu), beseeching him to consume all her imperfections, "like the fire which transforms everything into itself." Thérèse does not offer up her "merits" to the flames of God's Justice since she knows that "all our justices are stained [*ont des taches*] in your eyes"; it is her love that she offers to the source of all love, in accordance with the motto, taken from Saint John of the Cross, on her own coat of arms: "Love is paid only with love." Thérèse's fire is the Fire of Love not of Justice; its "waves of *infinite tenderness*" lap around the beloved, consuming imperfections and sins but preserving identity, promising not the total union of mystical fusion-in-death but an "Eternal Face to Face" between the Bride and her Groom.[131]

It was into this intimacy that Thérèse felt called—perhaps even experienced—in the summer of her twenty-third year. Nine months later, with preternaturally apposite timing, Thérèse first coughed up blood in her cell while keeping vigil on the night of Maundy Thursday–Good Friday (2–3 April 1896). Shortly after Easter, her Groom left the bridal suite and abandoned His Bride to her sufferings: her terrible, and still obscure, final ordeal had begun.

Calvary 1896–97

Theresian scholars, biographers, and hagiologists still debate the nature of the crisis that the future saint traversed between Easter 1896 and her death on 30 September 1897—almost eighteen months during which, in addition to the increasingly intolerable pain that she endured without ever being administered morphine, she felt, in her own words, "a wall rise up to the heavens and cover the starry firmament," plunging her soul into "deepest darkness" and causing the very "thought of Heaven [which had been] so sweet to me" to become a "subject and struggle" without end.[132] Was it, as some commentators contend, Thérèse's version of Saint John of the Cross's "Dark Night of the Soul" in which, wholly abandoned by God like Christ in his Passion, she was exposed to the worst temptation—despair—that the devil can devise, as a result of which she came close to losing faith and even to believing herself to be damned? Or was it, as others maintain, an acute attack of spiritual dryness, appalling in its timing and intensity, which she endured in confident prayerfulness so that, despite her losing, as she put it, "the *enjoyment of Faith*" (*la jouissance de la Foi*),[133] that faith itself was never seriously challenged? To the very limited extent that the present writer is qualified to judge, her ordeal seems somewhat less than a total *noche oscura de la alma* and considerably more than simply the loss of the "enjoyment" of faith. Let us examine the evidence, inconclusive though it is.

On 8 January 1897, another Sister Thérèse in the Carmel, Soeur Thérèse de Saint-Augustin, had a dream about her namesake that she hastened to tell her. In her dream, the second Soeur Thérèse had found herself in "a very dark apartment, with a heavy black door, beneath which a brilliant ray of light" shone through from the adjoining apartment. From the other side of the door, Soeur Thérèse heard a voice saying "Call Soeur Thérèse de l'Enfant-Jesus!" (On demande Soeur Thérèse de l'Enfant-Jésus!) and, a little later on, "Make sure that she is very beautiful!" (Il faut qu'elle soit très belle!), and it seemed to Soeur Thérèse that her namesake was somewhere in the dark room with her and that she was being prepared for an imminent journey to heaven. For Thérèse herself, this was not so much a dream (*un rêve*) as a vision (*un songe*) in which the current state of her soul was embodied:

> I do not believe in eternal life, it seems to me that after this mortal life there is nothing. I cannot express to you the darkness into which my soul is plunged. What you have just told me is exactly the state of my soul. The preparation I am receiving and above all the black door perfectly capture what is happening in me. You only saw red in this dark door [*vous n'avez vu que du rouge dans cette porte si sombre*], that is to say that everything has disappeared for me and that all that remains for me is love.[134]

Thérèse's interpretation of the dream not only diverges from that of the dreamer (for whom, incidentally, she did not greatly care—the feeling was mutual)[135] but significantly alters some of its details: the door itself appears to glow red, and neither the voice nor the light behind it is mentioned. Furthermore, the subject of the dream questions, even denies, the eternal life that the dreamer affirms, yet nonetheless finds huge consolation in what she has heard, telling another sister two days before her death how much it had helped her withstand her illness and its accompanying spiritual crisis.[136] The discrepancy between the two versions of the dream suggests that, even though her faith has been tested to the core, leading her to doubt the existence of anything resembling "heaven," Thérèse's love for God persists even in her darkest dereliction; she even seems to love the door that keeps her in darkness—if it glows red, it is not from any light shining behind it, but with a light with which she herself invests it—almost as though it is not necessary to believe in God in order to love him. This is what she calls her "folly": to love and to hope even in the absence of faith, to love God as much in his absence as in his presence.[137] Small wonder that, in her darkness, Thérèse identified with Job, and loved to quote (after the Vulgate) Job 13:15: "Even if God were to slay me I would still hope in him" (Quand même Dieu me tuerait j'espérerais encore en lui).[138]

In the spiritual wasteland into which she was cast, Thérèse was led to reflect with anguish on the reality and extent of unbelief in the France of her times and was forced to abandon her earlier conviction that, as she put it, nonbelievers were "speaking against their thought" when they denied the existence of God.[139] As she came to accept that nonbelievers genuinely did not believe, so she fell victim to "terrible thoughts" (*affreuses penseés*) that more and more placed her own faith in doubt: "The reasoning of the worst kind of materialists gains a hold on my mind" (C'est le raisonnement des pires matérialistes qui s'impose à mon esprit).[140] Her own doubts led her to identify with those without faith and to suffer along with them—for she could not conceive that nonbelief might not involve pain—for as long as it pleased God for her to do so. In the hope of alleviating both their darkness and hers, she pledged herself to eat "the bread of pain" (*le pain de la douleur*) sat alongside "poor sinners" at the "table of bitterness" (*cette table remplie d'amertume*) and not to rise "from the table they have soiled (*la table souilleé par eux*)" until it is purified, if such is God's will, "by a soul that loves you."[141] It is the closest Thérèse comes to endorsing the doctrine of vicarious suffering, the only difference—and it is crucial—being that she undertakes to suffer *with,* not *for,* nonbelievers whom she does not believe to be subject to God's wrath: this is compassion, *Mitleid,* in the strict sense of the word.

Above all, even as her faith in God falters, she does not cease to hope in and love him, nor, ultimately, does she doubt his love for her, consoling herself with the thought, which she found in Lamennais's notes in her edition of *The Imitation of Christ,* that "Our Lord on the Mount of Olives enjoyed all the delights of the Trinity, and yet his agony was not for that any less cruel"; "it's a mystery," adds Thérèse, "but I can assure you that I understand something of it through what I am experiencing myself."[142] Thérèse's final ordeal clearly partakes of the *Via negativa* of the Carmelite and other mystical traditions, but, in the view of the best of her exegetes, stops short of being the "full" Dark Night of the Soul.[143] As she wrote to Céline in July 1889, "to love Jesus without feeling the sweetness of that love" (*aimer Jésus sans sentir la douceur de cet amour*) is "love pushed to the point of heroism" (*l'amour poussé jusqu'à l'héroïsme*). When she herself had to suffer this "martyrdom without honour, without triumph," neither her love nor her courage were found wanting.[144]

The Cult of Thérèse

Studies of Thérèse usually conclude with a month-by-month, week-by-week, and day-by-day, even hour-by-hour, chronicle of her appalling final illness, with admiring references to her endless good humor, her kindness to those looking after her, her willing acceptance of suffering, above all her sheer guts in the face of pain unrelieved by either medicinal or spiritual solace. If the present account fails to follow this pattern, it is not simply because, in Stendhal's words, *le dire surpasse le disant* but because to dwell, as so many writers do, on the splendors and miseries of her death at the expense of her life can lead to a serious distortion of both her example and her "message." That Thérèse willingly espoused, and at times actively sought, suffering is not to be doubted, even though, with the partial exception of the passage cited above, she distanced herself from the whole theology and practice of "mystical substitution." She did not believe that suffering was necessary to "purchase" God's grace—that grace was freely bestowed—no more than she believed that Jesus requires "useless sufferings" of his followers.[145] On the other hand, she did believe that "*suffering alone* can give birth to souls"[146] and, when physical suffering became inevitable, she went toward it and embraced it with something approaching alacrity; although the decision to deny her morphine was not hers,[147] it seems likely that, had it been offered her, she would have refused. Those who are less than convinced by the traditional Catholic teaching of sanctification by suffering will find one particular incident—searingly presented in Alain Cavalier's prize-winning film *Thérèse* (1986)[148]—especially appalling. In mid-August 1897, driven almost out of her mind by the pain, she instructed her sister Céline (now Soeur Geneviève de Sainte-Thérèse) to reply, "Tant mieux" (so much the better) every time she herself uttered, "Je souffre"[149]: no doubt it helped her to withstand the intolerable, but the underlying (and doctrinally sanctioned) attitude toward pain it implies will leave many feeling decidedly uncomfortable.

The association between sanctity and pain is reinforced by the intensely moving photographs of Thérèse taken by Céline during the last eighteen months of her life—photographs that show her tense and anxious even before she was bedridden, with none of the alertness, glow, and almost palpable sense of happiness that suffuse the photographs taken before the onset of her illness and accompanying spiritual crisis. By then, Thérèse was, in her own terrible but barely translatable expression, *un bébé qui est à la mort,* a baby belonging or going to death,[150] and doing so without any of the spiritual comforts that her earlier experience would have led her to expect. The last photograph of her alive, taken in the cloisters of the Carmel on 30 August 1897, shows her being wheeled dwarfed by the huge pillows on which she is propped up, for a final visit to the Blessed Sacrament, scattering rose petals over the crucifix she holds in her hand.[151] This is probably how most people picture Thérèse, and such is the power of the image that we can all too easily forget that, from her "complete conversion" of Christmas 1886 to the double crisis of Easter 1896, Thérèse not only enjoyed excellent physical health but was almost completely liberated from the psychosomatic disorders, translated into religious terms as scruples and spiritual anxiety, that had troubled her at regular intervals between the death of her mother and Christmas 1886. In other words, for almost ten of her twenty-four years, Thérèse was anything but the ailing and hysterical girl-saint whom even some of her admirers continue to foreground, and it was, of course, during this decade of happiness, marred only by anxiety over her father's physical and mental well-being, that the lineaments of her *petite voie* were laid down. Appearances and, above all, her language to the contrary, Thérèse is in reality the least neurotic of saints, though this has not prevented Catholics and non-Catholics alike from twisting both her life and the "doctrine" that was inseparable from it into a grotesque parody of what they actually mean.

Thérèse, it has to be said, offers a sitting—or, more often, a recumbent, bed-ridden—target for adversaries of Catholicism or of Christianity in general. Late in her life, Thérèse inadvertently fell into a trap laid by the notorious anticlerical hoaxer Léo Taxil (real name Gabriel-Antoine Jogaud-Pagès),[152] author of such scurrilous classics as *Les Amour secrètes de Pie IX* (1881) and *Les Crimes du haut clergé empoisonneur* (1883), who, in a typical spoof designed to ridicule the Church, invented the story of "Diana Vaughan" which, for almost two years, kept French Catholics' hearts in their mouths until the nature of the hoax was revealed. On 21 June 1895 *La Croix* triumphantly announced the conversion of "Diana Vaughan," supposedly an American woman resident in France who had long been a member of the so-called Palladian sect founded in 1870 by "Albert Pike" with the object of "preparing the reign of Antichrist" through the worship of Asmodeus, Astaroth, and any number of other rebellious angels and spirits. *La Croix* had previously urged its reader to pray to Joan of Arc for "Diana's" conversion, and when it duly occurred, it was taken as proof of the Maid's active intervention in the struggle against the coalition of Satan, world Jewry, and the Masonic International. The Carmelite sisters at Lisieux fell predictably into the trap, and on 21 June 1896, put on a play,

Le Triomphe de l'humilité, written by Thérèse and starring her as "Diane Vaughan," the new Joan of Arc, in her war against a trio of malevolent spirits. In her innocence, Thérèse sent photographs of herself and Céline dressed, respectively, as Joan and Saint Catherine to Miss Vaughan's accommodation address in Paris, and it was these, projected onto a screen, that were mockingly displayed at the press conference held on 19 April 1897 on the premises of the Société de Géographie on the Boulevard Saint-German at which Taxil revealed that he had concocted the whole story from beginning to end.[153] The Church's obsession with diabolic and Masonic conspiracies had been held up to ridicule, as had its cult of the Maid as defender of France and the Faith, which reached its climax at this time. Thérèse was deeply hurt when she learned of this abuse of her innocence, and it may have been of Taxil and his like that she was thinking when, in the last of her autobiographical manuscripts, written in June-July 1897, she reluctantly accepted that there really were "souls who lack faith, who by abuse of the graces [they have received] lose this precious treasure, the source of the only pure and authentic joys that exist."[154]

This was Thérèse's only, indirect contact with national politics during her lifetime, and though her cult, which developed with remarkable rapidity after the publication of *Histoire d'une âme* in 1898, was vigorously promoted by the Carmelite order, it took shape outside the formal control of the Church and, from the outset, reached beyond the ranks of the religiously committed to the great "church of the un-churched" in the wider world without. Miraculous healings and other favors were reported as early as 1899, and the gathering cult received a major boost when, in May 1908, a four-year-old blind girl named Reine Fauquet reportedly recovered her sight when taken by her mother to visit Thérèse's grave in the Carmelite cemetery at Lisieux.[155] But it was essentially by text and by image that the cult of Thérèse multiplied and spread, with *Histoire d'une âme,* usually in an abridged edition distributed free of charge by the Carmel, rapidly overtaking any other work of devotion, while translations into English (1901), Polish (1902), Italian and Dutch (1904), German, Portuguese, Spanish, and Japanese and Russian (1905) made Thérèse an international celebrity within ten years of her death. In addition, between 1898 and 1925 no fewer than 30,328,000 images of Thérèse, usually based on one of several posthumous portraits painted by her sister Céline, were disseminated globally, complete with iconic roses and smile, the latter often accentuated by Petite Soeur's lightly rouged lips.

But Thérèse's admirers were not content merely to read her own words. They wrote back in their turn, and by 1911 the Carmel at Lisieux was receiving an average of fifty *lettres à Thérèse* every day, a figure that was to rise to between eight hundred and a thousand per day during and immediately after the Great War; a selection of letters and other submissions, running to seven volumes and 3,200 pages, was published under the title *Pluies de roses* between 1911 and 1926 and played a significant part in the beatification proceedings that, responding to pressure from below, the bishop of Bayeux, Monseigneur Lemonnier, formally, and somewhat reluctantly, set in motion in August 1910.

Already considerable before 1914, the cult of Thérèse received a further injection of energy with the outbreak of war, and not just among the French, soldiers and civilians, and their allies but on the German side as well; even Muslims in France's colonial regiments are said to have invoked the help and protection of "la petite sainte d'Allah." Thérèse quickly outstripped her heroine Joan of Arc as the *poilus'* preferred intercessor and protectress, and the Carmel at Lisieux received not a few mutilated copies of *Histoire d'une âme* that their owners claimed had saved them from bullet or shrapnel; "we may well have Jeanne d'Arc," wrote one soldier from the front, "but *la petite soeur* is much closer to us."[156] When, therefore, Thérèse was beatified in 1923 and canonized two years later, both were French as much as Catholic occasions and placed her not far beneath Joan (canonized 1920) as a national icon, one, moreover, that evoked none of the political opposition that, even in the 1920s, the figure of the Maid was still able to arouse.[157]

The first place of worship to be formally dedicated to Thérèse, the chapel of the Orphelins-Apprentis d'Auteuil in the 16th arrondissement, was consecrated in October 1930. Since then almost two thousand churches worldwide have been placed under her patronage. Meanwhile, almost every place of worship in France had installed its own mass-produced copy of the familiar statue by Père Marie-Bernard of the Trappist monastery at Soligny, putting Thérèse alongside the Virgin, Joan of Arc, and Marianne as the most profusely represented woman in the land. By the early 1930s, the cult of Thérèse was becoming discreetly politicized, and both Pope Pius XI and his newly appointed Secretary of State Cardinal Pacelli, the future Pius XII, gave it their strong personal backing, receiving energetic local support from the new bishop of Bayeux, Monseigneur Suhard, who, as archbishop of Paris, would disgrace himself under the German occupation.[158] All three saw in Thérèse's *petite voie* a possible "third way" between the rival claims of Marxists and Fascists and, against the background of the Popular Front and the Spanish civil war, the consecration of the new basilica at Lisieux, which Pacelli conducted in person on 11 July 1937, took on the character of an implicit political statement.[159] Petite Soeur was no longer—if she had ever been—ideologically neutral.

Thérèse Attacked: Pierre Mabille

Given the increased visibility and growing politicization of the cult of Thérèse, it is almost certainly no coincidence that the first sustained attack on her personality and message was also published in 1937, the fortieth anniversary of her death. Its author, Pierre Mabille (1904–52), had trained as a surgeon but, something of a polymath with particular interests in the occult, sociology, and psychoanalysis, had collaborated with, among others, Bataille on the dissident art review *Minotaure* (1930–39) before joining the surrealist group in 1934; in 1940, the year in which he published his best-known work, *Le Miroir du merveilleux,* he fled to Haiti where he in due course became an adept of *vaudou,* supposedly "initiating" André Breton when the Surrealist "Pope" visited that country in 1945.

Combining Freud and Marx with a virulent hostility to Christianity, particularly in its Catholic expression, Mabille's *Thérèse de Lisieux* is best read in the context of the Surrealists' promotion of the erotic as a subversive revolutionary force, as exemplified in Breton's *Amour fou,* another key text of 1937. Over and above its possible political significance, Thérèse's "case" is linked, says Mabille, to the broader "problems of love" particularly as these are experienced in a repressive, petit bourgeois society.[160] Her importance lies in her location "at the exact intersection of Christianity and the petite bourgeoisie," each, in Mabille's view, in a state of terminal decline.[161] Mabille argues that the entire Martin-Guérin clan was inhabited by a death wish typical of the French petite bourgeoisie as a whole; this suicidal urge expressed itself first in the wish of Louis and Zélie Martin to live together "as brother and sister" and then, when they were dissuaded from this, in their desire that each of their surviving daughters follow a religious vocation and so in effect extinguish the family line. "For in Thérèse, life flounders and comes to a halt" (*car en Thérèse, la vie échoue*),[162] not just the life of the Martins or the life of the petite bourgeoisie, but the very principle of physical existence itself, for Christianity systematically devalues nature, the body, and sex, all in the name of some chimerical transcendent reality to which Thérèse offered herself up as a sacrifice. "Since the general theme of Thérèse's thought is provided by essentially pessimistic and negative Christian doctrines, it can be said without exaggeration that the saint's behavior is characterized by a mechanism of auto-destruction, auto-disintegration, which can lead only to suffering and death."[163] Thus, according to Mabille, Thérèse's life was driven by the "boundless masochism" characteristic of Catholic women of her class, and if she became "such a pitiful victim of the order of society and of its imposed religious conceptions,"[164] it was because, deep down, suffering and martyrdom were all she had ever desired. Her incestuous desire for her father was sublimated and transposed into love of "Papa le bon Dieu," and the act of taking communion was a transparent simulation of "an oral sexual relationship" (*un rapport sexuel buccal*).[165] Terrified of adult existence, she regressed into a deliberately cultivated infantilism; terrified of the mind, she placed "the heart" above everything and "hypertrophied" the imagination and emotions at the expense of the intellectual tradition of the Church.[166] In short, Thérèse's *petite voie* leads only to death—death of the body, death of the mind—and if humanity is ever to become fully alive both the Thérèse-myth and the Christ-myth (*mythe christique*) to which she offered up her life must be jettisoned: "The corpse of Jesus must cease to interpose itself between men and women."[167] Stop looking for salvation in some mythical hereafter, Mabille urges his readers in conclusion, and seek instead to realize "the unity of your being" in the kingdom of this world, rather than letting it be shredded and crushed, as Thérèse did, in the "terrible mill" (*terrible laminoir*)[168] of bourgeois conformity and the teaching of Christ. Whence the conclusion "Thérèse=Catholic ideology combined with the action of a bourgeois milieu."[169]

Thérèse Defended: Georges Bernanos

An entirely different view of Thérèse is proposed in another, much greater work of 1937, Georges Bernanos's blistering polemic *Les Grands Cimetières sous la lune*. In his novels *L'Imposture* (1929) and *La Joie* (1931), Bernanos had already used Thérèse as the basis for the young Chantal de Clergerie who, along with the saintly Abbé Chevance, shines forth as the one beacon of hope in a world otherwise given over to mendacity, greed, self-hatred, and despair; as she memorably says, "With Satan, sadness came into the world" (*Avec Satan, la tristesse est entrée dans le monde*).[170] Chantal's childlike simplicity of spirit is an earthly manifestation of "the great simplicity of God"[171]; her confidence, her temerity, and, above all, her "perpetual joy" (*perpétuelle allégresse*)[172] mark her out as a true child of Christ, opposed point for point to that embodiment of Christian imposture, the embittered and hypocritical Abbé Cénabre, who has neither faith, hope, nor charity, and whose sinister laugh is as sure an expression of the emptiness of his soul as Chantal's radiant smile is of the fullness of hers.

In short, Bernanos's enraptured Thérèse-Chantal is the antidote to the poisonous combination of "ideological" Christianity—Christianity as perverted by legalism and power—and bourgeois conformity that Mabille's self-torturing martyr is said to express and endorse. Neither can survive: the latter because she is in love with suffering and seeks only to die, the former because her joyful affirmation of life in the spirit cannot but incite the self-hating violence of those, like her father's drug-addict chauffeur, in whom every vestige of the spirit is dead. And so, at the end of *La Joie*, Thérèse-Chantal offers her life up as a ransom for a world that has rejected God's love not out of self-love but out of the far greater sins of self-hatred and despair. Her compassion mirrors "the prodigious compassion of God"[173], her self-offering that of Christ on the cross. She has "the gaiety of the saints"[174] but also, and inseparably, the "terrifying, fundamental solitude of the children of God" whose mission is both to radiate joy and to proclaim "the good news of divinized Pain" (*la bonne nouvelle de la Douleur divinisée*), to experience God's presence but also to know "in the depths of the soul, in the very marrow of the bone, the state of sacred abandonment [*le délaissement sacré*], threshold and portal of all saintliness."[175] The reference to Thérèse's final agony is clear, even if the expiatory interpretation is Bernanos's rather than that of Thérèse herself.

In October 1934 Bernanos moved with his family to Majorca and it was there, between Christmas 1934 and January 1936, that he wrote his finest novel, *Journal d'un curé de campagne,* in which the priest-hero's dying words "Tout est grâce"—are a direct quotation, acknowledged by Bernanos only on *his* deathbed, from Thérèse's *Novissima verba* (entry for 5 June 1897):

> If one morning you were to find me dead, don't be afraid: it's only *Papa le bon Dieu* who has come looking for me. No doubt it is a great grace to receive the Sacraments; but when God does not permit it, it's good all the same, everything is grace [*tout est grâce*].[176]

Historically a man of the right, a former *camelot du roi* and author, in 1931, of a panegyric to the founding father of modern French antisemitism Edouard Drumont (*La Grande Peur des Bien-Pensants*),[177] Bernanos was ideologically predisposed to support the Francoist-Falangist cause when the Spanish civil war broke out in July 1936. Many French Catholics did, not least another fervent admirer of Thérèse, Paul Claudel, whose initial "conversion" occurred, as we have seen, on the very day that Thérèse made her decisive spiritual and psychological breakthrough.[178] But what Bernanos witnessed in Majorca during the opening weeks of the war—the "purging" (*épuration*) of up to three thousand supporters of the Republic and others by local Nationalist forces, all with the spiritual blessing and encouragement of "the personage whom protocol requires that I name as His Excellence the Bishop of Majorca"[179]—plunged him into a turmoil of horrified pity and wrath that issued in two coruscating masterpieces written almost concurrently: the thunderous four-hundred-page invective *Les Grands Cimetières sous la lune* and the masterly *Nouvelle histoire de Mouchette,* the story of the rape and suicide of a French peasant girl directly inspired, according to the author, by the sight of lorry-loads of Republican prisoners being taken away under armed escort, "poor creatures, hands on their knees, faces covered in dust, but erect, quite erect, with heads held high, with that dignity that the Spanish possess amidst the most atrocious misery."[180]

But *Les Grands Cimetières sous la lune* is much more than a denunciation of Fascist atrocities—even of Fascist atrocities committed under the sign of the Cross, with a priest in attendance, up to his ankles in blood, dispatched by his local bishop to grant absolution—to the perpetrators? the victims?—between "two volleys of gunfire."[181] Above and beyond the bloodletting in Majorca, Bernanos targets his most familiar and obdurate enemy, *les bien-pensants,* the mass of fearful, straight-thinking, right-doing French Catholics whose joyless conformism masks the depths of their betrayal of the spirit of Christ, who go on the parish pilgrimage to Lisieux and come back with their pictures of Thérèse and copies of *Histoire d'une âme* that they flip through once or twice, not realizing how the empty imposture of their lives is a perversion of "the spirit of childhood" that they nonetheless praise—within reason, of course—when they sit down with Monsieur and Madame X for their next evening of bridge.[182] But this world, indeed the world as a whole, "is going to be judged by children," "the spirit of childhood is going to judge the world."[183] And what child is better qualified to judge the world of the faithful than "a tiny tuberculous Carmelite" who, "through the heroic observance of duties as humble as herself," has sown here below "a seed whose germination nothing can halt"?[184] If Thérèse is to be judge, the role of prosecutor is assigned, in a superb rhetorical twist, to a nonbeliever who, on the saint's feast-day, is allowed to mount the pulpit and address the ranks of the faithful and ask them, point blank, how well their lives measure up to the "spirit of childhood" to which they (and their priests) pay annual lip service. The list of charges is read out remorselessly: you, *les bien-pensants,* have comprehensively betrayed both the letter and the spirit of the Gospels "which are always young, it is you that are old," since you have "failed to live your faith, your faith is no longer alive," it is as though the Word made flesh has been rendered disincarnate and abstract, above all we, who do not believe, ask what you, the believers, are doing with the grace of God you have received, "should it not be shining out from you? Where the devil are you hiding your joy?"[185] The answer, of course, is that most Catholics have no joy to hide. Their "faith," like that of the Abbé Cénabre, is an imposture, and only the joy—and the willingness joyfully to suffer—of a Thérèse-Chantal can remedy "the disincarnation of the Word, the true cause of our woes."[186] Whence the "tragically urgent character" of Thérèse's message, for it really is necessary to become as little children again, which, for Bernanos, means staying loyal, as an adult, to one's experience as a child: "What does my life matter to me! all that I want is for it to remain faithful right up to the end to the child that I was."[187] "I do not know for whom I am writing, but I know why I write. I write in order to justify myself—In whose eyes?—I have already told you, and I shall risk ridicule by telling you again. In the eyes of the child that I was."[188]

But could Thérèse's "spirit of childhood" have prevented the massacres of Majorca? Or could her "tiny innocent hands"[189] at least have deterred His Excellency the archbishop-bishop of Parma from "waving his venerable hands over Italian machine-guns"[190] and giving his blessing to weapons and killers alike? Bernanos undoubtedly believed that they could; Mabille, had he posed the question in those terms, would have concluded just as certainly that Thérèse and the bishop were on the same side. In seeking, in the words of his nonbelieving alter ego, to "use [Thérèse's thought] *humanly*, for the settling of the affairs of *this* world" (italics added),[191] Bernanos unwittingly reveals the limitations of that thought: the fact that (unlike Bernanos) she had little sense of either the radicalness or the banality of evil, that, with her abundance of love, she was a stranger to the violence and hatred, the will to power and the greed, that govern "this" world and that while her *petite voie* may point us toward God, there are sometimes material obstacles across it more substantial than the nerve-racking grating noise made by a fellow sister at evening prayer that it is simply not possible to "pass under."[192] And Mabille is right: there *is* a masochistic streak—more indeed than a streak—in her temperament and teaching, which means that, however much her *petite voie* challenged the devotional orthodoxies of her time, it could always be "recuperated" by those who, unlike Thérèse, and for whatever reason, cannot get outside of the idea that God's love has to be earned, and earned, moreover, through suffering and penance, whence the necessity, as Claudel put it in his essay on Thérèse in *Trois figures saintes pour le temps actuel* (1953), that there be "people and"—a significant precision—"more especially women" prepared to "purchase [*racheter*] minute by minute" the salvation of sinners by offering themselves up in their stead:

> Now what did Christ come to do on earth? He came to suffer, He came to merit. He came to purchase His Father for us. Why should there not therefore be a tribe of men and of women entirely dedicated to the task of continuing Christ, *of making up what is lacking in the passions of Christ,* of Christifying, so to speak, the event, of meriting, of using sin, of giving a redemptive value [*une valeur de rachat*] to everything by way of suffering associated with sin that the passage of time brings our way? This is what is known as expiation. People who have incorporated the cross and constituted themselves as a ransom. [Des gens qui ont intégré la croix et qui se sont constitués rançon.][193]

This is the sacrificial, substitutive mission that Claudel assigns to Thérèse in the teeth of almost all of her writings and so draws her back into the merit- and suffering-based economy of salvation that she had almost transcended. Thérèse enjoys an exemplary status in this book because, virtually alone, and in defiance of more or less all of her upbringing and milieu, she really did believe in a God of unconditional love who seeks only the love of his children in return. "There is no anger in God," wrote Thérèse's closest English equivalent, Mother Julian of Norwich (1342–c.1420),[194] and "whether we are filthy or clean is all the same to his love."[195] Thérèse is unique in that, reading her, one really can believe that "all shall be well and all manner of thing shall be well,"[196] which is why she is remembered and revered to this day when almost all of her contemporaries are forgotten.

3

BROTHER AND SISTER

Paul and Camille Claudel

VILLENEUVE—MONTDEVERGUES, 1868–1943

"A traveler and a man with roots" (*un voyageur et un enraciné*) was how the eighty-two-year-old Paul Claudel described himself at the beginning of his celebrated radio interviews with Jean Amrouche in 1951–52:[1] a *voyageur* by choice, career, and compulsion who had spent the bulk of his adult life outside of France, principally in China, Brazil, Japan, the United States, and Belgium, before retiring to Brangues in the Ain in 1935 and, at the same time, an *enraciné* who, physically and, still more, in imagination, kept returning to the tiny hamlet of Villeneuve-sur-Fère in the Tardenois where he had been born next to the church on 6 August 1868 and which would later provide the setting and many of the principal themes of the theatrical work for which he remains best known, *L'Annonce faite à Marie* of 1912.

In November 1937 Claudel gave a formal public lecture entitled "Mon pays" in which he evokes, in highly conventional language, the "indelible kinship between a poet and his origins [*terroir*]." The audience is told of the "terrible wind" that almost never ceases to gust through the village, of how, when it rains, it rains "harshly, violently and, so to speak, passionately" and, above all, of the view of the four cardinal points that opens up from the "kind of promontory" on which Villeneuve is built: (1) the great plains to the north with the farms and villages that would later feature in his work (Combernon, Bellefontaine, Arcy Sainte-Restitue), often supplying his characters with their curious and evocative names (Coeuvres, Violaine, Coûfontaine), and (2) beyond them, the "great invisible cathedrals" of Laon, Soissons, and Reims, which, he claimed, were already beckoning to him as a child; (3) the forest of la Tournelle to the south; and (4) to the west, la Hottée du Diable, that extraordinary collection of sandstone rocks apparently dumped at random amid the surrounding plains with, at its heart, the massive humanoid rock known to locals as le Géyn (*le géant*) where Claudel conceived his first major drama *Tête d'or* in 1887–88, between his conversion experience of Christmas 1886 and his formal return to the church four years later and from which, looking out "toward Paris, the world, the sea, the future," he first became aware, as he puts it elsewhere, of both his vocation as a writer and, simultaneously and inseparably, of "the vocation of the Universe."[2] There are a few references to local history, to his forebears, and to one or two local characters, but it is essentially a polished, noncommittal performance by a sixty-nine-year-old smiling public man that notably omits any reference to his immediate family. The overall picture given of life at Villeneuve is one of order and stability, of stolid, uncomplaining resistance to the elements. Nobody listening to the speech, or reading it later, would gain any inkling of the tensions and conflicts that lurked beneath the surface of village life and, above all, of the Claudel's family home which, perhaps giving away more than he knew or wished, the poet-diplomat would late in his life compare to Wuthering Heights.[3]

How striking, then, that in the month following his lecture, Claudel should, in the privacy of his diary, have revealed at length what the men and women of Villeneuve were *really* like, people like the Valentins and the Philippons, Spémant the blacksmith and Vaternelle the carpenter, "all of them alcoholics from father to son, and prone to committing suicide," Paillette the day-laborer with his Romany blood, the plasterers, the shepherds, the loggers: "What was most characteristic about all those people was *hatred*. They all hated each other, especially amongst relatives. Acts of violence, grievances, long meditated revenge. Appalling scenes from time to time." If the lower-class villagers were "crushed, brutalized by toil, with deformed, hunched, dejected bodies," bourgeois families like the Claudels themselves were no better with their endless obsession with the unpaid rents they were due, while *grands notables* like the Thierrys ended up "in debauchery and dissipation." "That's Humanity for you": three hundred people living on top of each other in mutual hatred and suspicion, and of whose idea of God—if they considered him at all—Claudel did not care to think, "a painful and appalling milieu which explains the deep pessimistic cast of my younger years. All of it engraved in my child's mind with incredible force."[4]

As in the village as a whole, so in the Claudel family home to which, having moved away in 1870 for one temporary address after another, they returned every summer, "a very peculiar, inward-looking family, living very much on itself, with a kind of prickly, embittered pride," perpetually riven with quarrels, father with mother, children with parents, children with each other, "incessant disputes, one scene after another."[5] A minor civil servant and convinced anticlerical, Louis-Prosper Claudel (1826–1913) was desperate that his only surviving son—a first son, Henri, had died in infancy in 1863—should enter the Ecole Normale Supérieure, and it was to this end that mother and children moved to Paris in 1882 when Claudel enrolled at

Louis-le-Grand, his father remaining at Wassy and then Rambouillet and visiting them only at weekends. Claudel's failure, at the early age of fifteen, to pass the *baccalauréat* at the first attempt predictably led to a further round of intrafamily dispute and recrimination.

Louise Claudel, née Cerveaux (1840–1919), appears to have been a strict, withdrawn woman, perhaps permanently maimed by the death of her firstborn—"our mother never embraced us," Claudel revealed in an article of 1949—not unlike the mothers of Thérèse Martin or Colette Peignot, except that her religion was no more than a public formality.[6] Claudel seems to have felt no more than respect for his father, perhaps accompanied by a deeper unacknowledged hostility that surfaces in the salience of parricidal themes in his work,[7] and, when learning of his final illness in March 1913, delayed going to see him "through idleness and a secret desire to arrive too late," a desire that in the event was fulfilled, leaving Claudel full of remorse that he had not been present at the deathbed to encourage his recalcitrantly antireligious father to confess.[8] For his mother, too, there was a mixture of respect and compassion, but little sign of real affection or grief in the prayer that he wrote for her in his diary when receiving news of her death: "My God, have pity on the soul of *Louise Athénaïse Cerveaux*. She was poor, simple, deeply humble, pure of heart, resigned, devoted to her daily duty, working with her hands from dawn until dusk. How did this woman whose character consisted above all of modesty and simplicity come to have two children like my sister Camille and like me?"[9]

My Sister Camille . . .

In the Wuthering Heights that was Villeneuve-sur-Fère, Camille Claudel (1864–1943) stands out with all the passionate vividness of Catherine Earnshaw herself, with her younger brother cast in the role of an equally passionate and incestuous Heathcliff. The figure of Camille haunts the whole of Claudel's work from beginning to end. A female Proteus, combining good and evil yet transcending ultimately both, she is present in all the majestic, doomed, or suffering women who almost always determine the course of his plays, either through their own actions and loves or through the actions and loves they inspire, from Violaine in the successive avatars of *L'Annonce faite à Marie* (but also her murderous sister and antitype Mara), Lâla in the second version of *La Ville* (1897), Lechy Elbernon in the two versions of *L'Echange* (1893, 1952), Ysé in *Partage de midi* (1905), Sygne and Pensée de Coûfontaine in the linked plays *L'Otage, Le Pain dur,* and *Le Père humilié* (written between 1909 and 1916) to Doña Prouhèze in *Le Soulier de satin* (1919–24), a figure both positive and negative embodying what Claudel, independently of Jung, called the Anima in all its contradictory wholeness, both Wisdom and Folly or, rather, the Wisdom of Folly and the Folly of Wisdom, an amalgam of muse, Madonna, and maenad whose disruptive, bewitching message (here spoken by Lâla in *La Ville,* act 3) is always the same:

> Je suis la promesse qui ne peut être tenue et ma grâce consiste en cela même.
> Je suis la douceur de ce qui est avec le regret de ce qui n'est pas.
> Je suis la vérité avec le visage de l'erreur, et qui m'aime n'a point le souci de
>   démêler l'une de l'autre.
> Qui m'etend est guéri du repos pour toujours et de la pensée qu'il l'a trouvé.
> Qui voit mes yeux ne chérira plus un autre visage et que fera-t-il si je souris?
> Qui a commencé de me suivre ne saurait plus s'arrêter.
> Mais je sens que la mort est proche![10]

[I am the promise that cannot be kept and my grace consists precisely in that. / I am the sweetness of what is along with the regret of that which is not. / I am truth with the face of error, and whoever loves me is not concerned to separate one from the other. / Whoever hears me is cured of rest for all time and of the thought that he has found it. / Whoever sees my eyes will never cherish another face and what will he do if I smile. / Whoever starts to follow me will never be able to stop. / But I feel that death is at hand!]

The original of this hallucinating vision was born at Fère-en-Tardenois, the market town of which Villeneuve is an outlying hamlet, on 8 December 1864, sixteen months after the death of the infant Henri Claudel, and all her life Camille would believe, probably not without reason, that her mother resented her because she had not been born a boy.[11] In February 1866 her sister Louise was born, with whom she was to have as tempestuous a relationship as with her similarly named mother, and Claudel would later admit that the rivalry between the two sisters that provides the mainspring of the action of the successive versions of *L'Annonce faite à Marie* was based on a "transposition" of the turbulent relationship of his two elder sisters.[12]

From an early age Camille manifested a distinct talent for drawing, molding, and carving that was encouraged by her father (as he would later also encourage Claudel's early career as a writer) but discouraged and mocked by the two Louises acting in concert, with Claudel himself evidently siding with Camille, whose earliest model he became. After her first communion, Camille, following her father, became increasingly antireligious. It was she, according to Claudel,[13] who introduced Renan's *Vie de Jésus* into the household and so indirectly led to his loss of religious faith that would be so dramatically reversed at Christmas 1886 when it was a copy of the Bible given to Camille that, accidentally or providentially opened at Proverbs chapter 8, gave him the first intuition of the female figure of Wisdom that so haunts his work. As Claudel also, and almost certainly wrongly, held Camille responsible for the family's move—minus Louis-

Prosper Claudel—to Paris in 1882, that move which, he says, was such a "catastrophe" in his life, "tearing" it in two,[14] we can begin to see something of the complexity of his sister's role in his life. Inadvertently (or, once again, providentially), Camille is the source of both her brother's fall and redemption, the author of the *felix culpa* that destroys his faith and condemns him to exile in Paris, but, in so doing, also leads him to Notre-Dame and conversion. Camille is *Eva* and *Ave,* the inscrutable instrument of Providence, the temptress who redeems, the corruptrix who saves.

Once in Paris, Camille continued the formal training she had begun with the sculptor Alfred Boucher at Nogent-sur-Seine by enrolling at the Académie Colorossi and, while continuing for the time being to live with her family, sharing a studio on the rue Notre-Dame-des-Champs. Exactly when she met her nemesis Auguste Rodin (1840–1917) is unclear, but, whenever the initial encounter occurred, she "graduated" rapidly from pupil and model to assistant and thence to collaborator and mistress, their lives and works evolving synergistically from the mid-1880s to the mid-1890s when, again at an indeterminate date, Rodin abandoned Camille in favor of Rose Beuret, the long-term companion from whom he had never separated throughout his liaison with Camille. A caricature by Camille of 1892 entitled "Le Collage" depicts two figures, clearly herself and Rodin, stuck together by the buttocks, trying in vain to pry themselves apart.[15] It is an apt image of their personal and creative osmosis during this time, but also of at least Camille's lacerating attempts to tear herself free and establish her own existential and artistic autonomy. For, however intense their emotional, physical, and creative interpenetration, it was always, ultimately, Rodin who was the proverbial dominant partner. Although, as Rodin said, the artistic "gold" that he had helped her discover within herself was "hers and hers alone,"[16] she, however much she initiated, suggested, and helped, was never the crucially determining influence on him that he was on her. Their creative trajectories evolve in tandem with each other, with her *Çacountalà* echoing or inspiring his *Eternelle Idole,* his *Galateé* replicating or provoking the pose of her *Jeune fille à la gerbe,* often so close together in conception if not in completion, that it is impossible to tell which work has primacy over the other, but always the greater public success—and the consequent public commissions—came not to the mistress but to the Master. That the sexual stereotypes of the time counted for much in this inequity of outcome is not to be doubted, and gave an underlying basis of fact to Camille's later obsession that her ideas, her work, even her life, had been "stolen" from her by "that brigand Rodin."

The separation of Rodin and Camille was, her brother wrote in 1951, a "necessity" for him and a "total, profound, definitive catastrophe" for her. In this he exaggerates, at least in the short term and in respect of her artistic output, for it was in the decade following the *rupture* that Camille produced her finest work: the audacious miniature *La Vague* (1898) in which a superbly carved onyx wave is about to descend on a group of three female bathers in bronze, the wonderfully rhythmic *La Valse* (1905), the intensely moving *L'Implorante* (also 1905) in which is expressed all the artist's sense of yearning and loss, and the bronze group *L'Age mûr* (1902) in whose plangent female figure on the right Claudel revealingly saw an embodiment of his sister as "Anima torn from her encumbering Animus [presumably Rodin, or could it be Claudel himself?], imploring, humiliated, kneeling and naked."[17]

Yet even as she produced this impressive body of work, which together justifies Claudel's description of her as the creator of a new kind of "interior sculpture,"[18] Camille's life was beginning palpably to disintegrate. The magnificent features present in César's stunning photograph of 1884 became thicker and heavier, perhaps under the influence of alcohol, her public behavior became more erratic, and by the end of the 1900s she rarely ventured out from the two-room apartment on the Quai des Bourbons on the Ile Saint-Louis into which she had first moved in 1899. From 1905 on, her conversation and letters became dominated by her obsession with Rodin and his "band" whom she accused of plagiarizing her ideas, stealing her works, breaking into her home and studio, and plotting against her at every turn, even enlisting her mother and sister in the conspiracy against her. Chillingly, the unbelieving Camille becomes the target, in her imaginings, of all the nefarious forces that the Catholic middle classes from which she stemmed believed to be assailing France as a whole: thus her sister Louise "is in league with the Protestants" (*donne dans les protestants*), Rodin is a "Huguenot," the Freemasons are dividing her work up among them—only the Jews appear to be missing.[19]

In 1909 Claudel describes her as being "bloated, with a soiled face, speaking incessantly in a monotonous, metallic voice" and living in the squalid surroundings of the Quai des Bourbons, its wallpaper in tatters and the one armchair broken and torn.[20] Not surprisingly, the neighbors began to ask questions and complain, and on 10 March 1913, just a week after the death of Louis-Prosper Claudel that left his son so singularly unmoved, "K-mille," as she now sometimes signed herself, was interned against her will, but at the family's initiative, in the mental asylum at Ville-Evrard on the outskirts of Paris, two male nurses having had to break into her apartment to apprehend her. Diagnosed, now aged 48, as suffering form "systematic persecution delirium," she remained at Ville-Evrard until the outbreak of war caused her to be transferred, along with the other patients, to the asylum of Montdevergues at Montfavet near Avignon.

Here she would remain for the rest of her life, still blaming Rodin and his allies, the art dealers, for the failure of her career and for her physical internment, living in terror of poisoners and spies (and apparently surviving solely on a diet of raw eggs and jacket potatoes that she insisted on cooking herself), begging Claudel to obtain her release and to allow her to return to

Villeneuve and holding "his" God responsible for allowing her to rot in a madhouse. The two Louises refused to permit her to return, along with the other patients, to Ville-Evrard at the end of the war and never once visited her in thirty years' sequestration. To his credit, Claudel went to Montfavet as and when foreign postings and other commitments permitted, and last saw her in September 1943, just a month before her death from a heart attack at the age of 78, her last words apparently being *"Mon petit Paul."* She remains buried at Montfavet, though a commemorative plaque has been placed on the church wall at Villeneuve above the Claudel family tomb, and a memorial cross stands at one of the entrances to the village.

Camille's Influence on Paul

Simply to recount the tragedy of Camille Claudel suggests, without specifying, the enormous, if usually unacknowledged, influence it must have had on her brother's life and work,[21] and a parallel suggests itself between the greatest twentieth-century French Catholic poet and dramatist and his closest Anglophone counterpart, T. S. Eliot, and his unfortunate first wife, Vivien Haigh-Wood.[22] Camille's influence was at its strongest between 1882 and 1893, when Claudel left France for his first diplomatic posting in the United States, and again after 1943, but her spirit impregnates almost all his leading female characters, even when, like Ysé in *Partage de midi,* their immediate biographical source lies elsewhere. There was, in the first instance, her sheer physical presence, so memorably captured in César's portrait, already referred to, of 1884: "I can see her again," wrote Claudel in 1951, "that superb young woman, in the triumphant radiance of her beauty and genius," with her waist-length auburn hair and the dark blue eyes he would later bestow upon his supreme female creation, Violaine in *L'Annonce faite à Marie.* But Claudel also alludes, in that same moving article, to the "often cruel ascendancy that she exercised over my early years," to the "terrible violence of character" and "ferocious gift for mockery" that coexisted with the "impressive air of courage, frankness, superiority and gaiety" she exuded.[23]

There seems little doubt that, like the Sacred itself, Camille was to her brother both *fascinans et tremenda,* to be desired and dreaded simultaneously, and when she first appears in his work, as "Marie" in a fragment of an early, unpublished drama written in 1888, it is in the double form of *peccatrix* and *redemptrix,* desired by her brother (with whom she has apparently conspired in an act of parricide) and by her lover (to whom Claudel gives the name of his deceased brother Henri), but inspiring in both of them a terror that causes them to flee from her presence. If Camille had been the unwitting instrument of her brother's conversion—it was she, as it were, who, by helping him "slay" his false, earthly father and mother, had brought him back to his true Father and Mother in heaven—she was also, in the crucial years between 1886 and 1890, the principal obstacle to his making public that conversion and returning to full, active membership in the Church.[24]

In *Tête d'or* Camille again embodies the double aspect of the Anima, appearing first as the former lover whom the eponymous hero buries at the beginning of the play and then as the crucified princess—the daughter of the emperor whom Tête d'or has killed in his pursuit of power—whose sufferings point the way to salvation at its close. Claudel's lifelong obsession with the *Oresteia,* all three parts of which he translated, the last two in the very year of Camille's internment, must owe something to its themes of brother-sister love and their joint killing of their mother and (false) father.[25] In the long poem *La Messe là-bas* written in 1917 while Claudel was in Brazil, the soul is figured by a "once beautiful woman on her hospital bed" and by a woman in prison (*bagne*) who "beneath her clothes violently squeezes her identity tag"; the poem concludes with the vision of "the smile of that sudden sister" who relays God's love and forgiveness.[26] The image of the soul as a "sequestered sister," a "forgotten sister, with whom we have parted company," that appears in *Seigneur, apprenez-nous à prier* (1942) is almost too poignant when read in the context of Camille's personal tragedy and of Claudel's sense of guilt at his own professional and artistic success.[27]

L'Annonce faite à Marie

But it is Claudel's best-known play, *L'Annonce faite à Marie,* that is most infused with the spirit of Camille, though, in the course of its multiple versions, the author gradually camouflaged its origins in his family's intestine divisions. In its successive avatars, *L'Annonce* occupied Claudel for half a century and more, from its earliest version as *La Jeune Fille Violaine* of 1892–93 to the substantially revised text under the same title completed in China in 1898–99, followed by a still more radical rewriting in 1910–11 under the new title of *L'Annonce faite à Marie,* with a "definitive version for the stage" being produced much later, in 1948. To follow the play through its successive transformations of period, plot, characterization, and theme is a fascinating task, but one impossible in the present context where only the principal constants and variants can receive our attention.

The core of the play from beginning to end lies in the relationship between two sisters, Violaine and Mara (called Bibiane in the first extant version), which, as already noted, Claudel admitted to be based on the relationship of Camille and the younger Louise, albeit "extremely transposed." Claudel's critics and biographers have commonly associated Mara with Camille, seeing Violaine as an idealized imaginative creation, and have accordingly opposed the sisters as black to white (Mara is repeatedly referred to as "la noire" or "la noirpiaude"), as flesh to spirit and evil to good, in short as Eve to Madonna—this being in the days before another Madonna had effectively destroyed the possibility of all such clear-cut binary opposites. Although Mara clearly owes much to Camille, notably her hatred of her parents, so also does Violaine, and the difference between the two sisters diminishes significantly from version to version: after all, only an *O* separates Violaine from the *vilaine* Mara, and Mara in her turn is only an *I* away from Maria.

Names were all-important to Claudel who believed that words, even letters, are hieroglyphs that physically embody what they mean rather than mere arbitrary signs, and the name Mara is clearly intended to suggest the bitter undrinkable waters of Marah in the wilderness that Moses, with God's help, is able to purify and sweeten (Exodus 15:23–25). The name Violaine (originally derived from that of a village between Château Thierry and Soissons) bears almost too many semantic associations: Violaine is both an instrument and victim of *viol*ence; she *viol*ates the existing order of things and is violated in her turn; the final syllable, *-laine,* of her name suggests the wool of the Lamb of God that must be shorn, washed, and purified before it can be woven into the white raiment of holiness (cf. the suffering Marthe Laine in *L'Echange*); and, when coupled with the first syllable of her family name Vercors, produces the poet-convert Verlaine whose first "Catholic" collection was entitled, precisely, *Sagesse.* In its turn, Vercors suggests the *Verum corpus* of the Blessed Sacrament, and her father's androgynous Christian name, Anne, posits him as a fusion of Animus and Anima (like the pope whom he visits in Rome in the first version of the play, who is both mother and father of his flock),[28] whose daughter Violaine is an externalization "of that which was feminine in me" (*l'épanouissement de ce qu'il y avait en moi de féminin*).[29] But if Anne on his anima-side suggests Anna mother of Mary, on his Animus-side he figures Annas (in French Anne) who binds and hands over Jesus to Caiphas and the Romans and who, by knowingly playing a part in Christ's crucifixion, unknowingly contributes to his resurrection and man's ultimate salvation. In the same way, it is Anne Vercors' decision to hand over Violaine to Jacques Hury as his wife, not knowing or not caring that Mara loves and desires him, that precipitates the whole drama, while his leaving the family home of Combernon—a farmstead a few hundred yards from the Claudel's house at Villeneuve—bound, variously, for Rome, the United States, and, in the final version, for the Holy Land, creates the space in which the tragedy can unfold, just as Louis-Prosper Claudel's absence in Wassy and Rambouillet in 1882–86 triggered the family crisis in Paris that, indirectly and after much suffering, led Claudel himself back to his "true" Father in heaven. The complexity, mutability, and frequent incomprehensibility of the plot of *L'Annonce* suggestively figures the complexity and inscrutability of God's soteriological "plot" for his creatures.

Knowing of her younger sister's love for Jacques Hury, Violaine—who is also in love with him, as he is with her—feigns involvement with another man (Baube in the first version, Pierre de Craon thereafter) and voluntarily renounces Hury in favor of Mara. But Mara is still jealous and angry, and, in versions one and two, throws burning ashes in Violaine's eyes and, despite having secured husband and inheritance, chases her out of the family demesne. Blinded, Violaine flees to a rock-strewn wilderness clearly based on the Géyn where, living in conditions of extreme privation and suffering, she becomes renowned as a healer and consoler of the poor. It is this reputation that, some time later, brings Mara to her in the hope of restoring the sight of the blind child Aubin she has borne to her husband Jacques Hury. Violaine duly performs the miracle cure, but Mara still resents the fact that her husband's real love is for Violaine, not herself, and, in the first two versions, attacks Violaine with a stone, inflicting on her the injuries from which she will eventually die. In the meantime, the sisters' mother, Elisabeth (named, presumably, after the mother of John the Baptist), has also died, and Anne Vercors returns from his pilgrimage to find the household he had hoped to secure by marrying Violaine to Hury effectively in ruins. But, by willingly assuming her agony and forgiving her for her crimes, Violaine brings the family back together again and ensures, through her suffering and death, the restoration of the patriarchal order that Anne Vercors (and, beyond him, the pope) so grandiloquently embodies. "It is not bad to suffer," she declares in the first version of the play,[30] and her willingness to suffer for the sake of the household makes possible the return, after her death, of the fertility of the land. Like the grapes that have to be crushed before the wine can ferment, so the "crushing" of Violaine in the *pressoir* of family conflict creates the conditions of fruitful communion with which all four versions of the play triumphantly, if somewhat glibly, conclude.

The second version of the play gains considerably in thematic richness through the introduction of the character of the architect Pierre de Craon in place of the colorless and somewhat absurd figure Baube. Once again the name is highly significant. Based originally on the village of Craonne to the north of Villeneuve, which was to be razed to the ground during the Great War, the architect's initials are those of Claudel himself, and the word *craon* means stone (thus reinforcing "Pierre" and clearly intended to evoke the traditional founder of the Church) but also suggests "crayon" and hence a parallel between architect and writer. Finally, it has been suggested that the aristocratic particle "de" (which runs against Pierre's apparently plebeian origins) is introduced to enable Claudel to weave the name of Rodin—detested as a man, but ultimately admired as an artist—into that of his hero.[31] The introduction of the architectural theme gives the Church as institution and edifice a much greater prominence in the second version of the play that, not without verbosity, adds the culminating vision of the "dwelling-place of god with man"[32] to the explosion of fertility, germination, fermentation, and communion that brought the original text to its resoundingly positive conclusion. Water gushes forth, a rainbow appears in the sky, bells ring out, the "interior egg" (*oeuf intérieur*) of the Church opens out to deliver new life, and Anne, Mara, Jacques, and Pierre are reconciled through the atoning self-sacrifice that Violaine has made for their sakes, willingly accepting to be ground and crushed to create the bread and wine of their future communion. "He who sacrifices himself is consecrated," says Pierre de Craon, encapsulating the whole official message of the play.[33]

The theme of atoning self-sacrifice is even further highlighted in the third, and best, version of the play—the first to bear the inspired title of *L'Annonce faite à Marie*—which Claudel completed in 1910–11 and which was first performed on stage on 23 December 1912 at the Théâtre de l'Oeuvre in Paris, the timing underlining the new play's almost liturgical character. The decisive scenes of the play now take place on Christmas Eve, and the setting is the divided, semi-occupied France of the 1420s when there is no crowned king on the throne and, with no fewer than three "popes" contending for overall supremacy, "everything is entering into conflict and movement, being no longer sustained by a superior weight."[34] There are frequent references to Joan of Arc (with whom Violaine is implicitly compared), and Violaine's resuscitation of Mara's now dead rather than merely blind firstborn child is made to coincide not merely with Christ's birth but with the coronation of Charles VII at Reims which, for the sake of the play's symbolic coherence, is advanced from 17 July 1429 and so falls on the anniversary of Clovis' baptism in the selfsame cathedral in the year 496, 499, 506 or whenever—and also, of course, on the date of Claudel's own conversion and return to the Church. Other changes occur, most notably the fact that, prior to the play's actual beginning, Pierre has made an unreciprocated sexual advance toward Violaine and has been afflicted with leprosy in apparent punishment for his deed. He is engaged in constructing a chapel in Reims that will house the relics, above all the milk teeth, of the eight-year-old girl-saint Justitia that have recently been discovered in the city; it will be milk from Violaine's breast that will revive the dead child Aubaine (its change of gender is to be noted), pointing forward to Claudel's later metaphor of grace as a "gush of milk" (*une poussée de lait*).[35] Learning that the women of Reims are giving Pierre their jewelry to finance the project, Violaine, with Mara watching unseen, hands over the ring that Jacques Hury has given her and willingly kisses him on the face and so knowingly takes on herself his disease and the fault that occasioned it. Informed by Mara of the gift and the kiss, Jacques concludes that Pierre and Violaine are lovers and, in the absence of Anne Vercors who has left for the Holy Land, rejects and banishes Violaine and marries her sister.

From this beginning, the theme of vicarious suffering is enormously expanded, partly, it has been shown, under the influence of Claudel's reading of Huysmans's *Sainte Lydwine de Schiedam* (1901) and partly in consequence of his own personal experience since the completion of the second *Jeune Fille Violaine*: the rejection of his attempted religious vocation, his affair in China with the woman (Rose Vetch, née Rosalia Rylska) who served as the model for the character Ysé in *Partage de midi* and the illegitimate child it produced, and his own remorse and repentance, followed by his marriage to Reine Sainte-Marie-Perrin in 1906.[36] Now it is not just for the faults and failings of the Vercors household that Violaine chooses willingly to suffer, but for the sins of the world, and, having been fatally injured in an "accident" in fact engineered by Mara, is laid by a now leprosy-free Pierre de Craon on the kitchen table at Combernon like a sacrificial victim on the altar. Having taken on Pierre's disease, miraculously revived Mara's dead child, and forgiven Mara her crime, she now offers her life up to restore health, vitality, and order not just to one family but the entire cosmos. But, whereas, in the earlier versions of the play, suffering is first passively undergone and then actively assumed ("It is not we who choose," says the 1898 Violaine, "it is we who are chosen"),[37] in the 1912 version it is willingly and, indeed, actively sought out. If, as the dying Violaine says to Jacques in the last act of the play, "it is too hard to suffer and not to know for what purpose," "happy," on the other hand, "is he [*sic*] who suffers and knows why he does so," underlining her earlier remark that "powerful is suffering when it is as voluntary a sin."[38] The object of life is not earthly happiness— "I am tired of being happy," says Anne Vercors, explaining why he is leaving—and it is not even to live, he declares at the end of the play when he has absorbed the redemptive meaning of his daughter's self-offering: "It is not to live, but to die, and not to construct and erect [*charpenter*] the Cross but to mount it, and, laughing, to give all that we have. There is joy, there is freedom, there is grace! And long live god if the old man's blood on the sacrificial cloth beside that of the young man does not make a stain as red, and as fresh, as that of the year-old lamb!"[39]

It is at this point that the contemporary reader, alerted by feminism to the whole question of "inclusive" and "exclusive" language, may begin to balk at Claudel's almost unvarying use of masculine nouns and pronouns when expounding his, and much of his age's, theology of vicarious suffering. It is in no way to advance a reductive or tendentious reading of his plays to remark that, in them, it is primarily, if not exclusively, the female characters who suffer physically, and primarily, if not exclusively, the men who reap the soteriological benefits of their sufferings. Violaine herself acknowledges that the general human vocation of suffering is one that women can assume with particular dedication and vigor, especially in view of their exclusion from the priesthood: "The male is priest, but it is not forbidden to woman to be a victim." God, she continues, is

greedy, and does not permit any of His creatures
to be set on fire,
   Unless an element of impurity is consumed in it,
   Its own, or that which surrounds it, like the embers
Of the censer that are stirred to life!
   To be sure, the suffering of this time is great.
   They have no father. They look and no longer know
Where is the King or the Pope.
   That is why my body is here in travail in the place
Of disintegrating Christendom.
   Powerful is suffering when it is as voluntary as sin![40]

The merits of the sufferings undergone by the daughter revert in the end to the Father and the patriarchal values he embodies, so that *L'Annonce* becomes progressively a holocaust of *female* victims—Elisabeth dies, Violaine dies, *la Pucelle* is burnt to death, the last nuns of the nearby convent of Monsanvierge also die—while Anne, Jacques, and Pierre are left on stage at the end of the play to proclaim the triumph of order, hierarchy, and, not least, *property*. "Everything belongs to you, Father," says Jacques to Anne, from whom he will duly inherit, as they survey the Combernon lands in the final scene of the play, while Anne, in a positive ecstasy of ownership and belonging, declares how, fittingly sat on the "mountain" that his surname suggests, "before me, beside me, around me, I do not cease seeing the earth, like a fixed sky painted all over in changing colors." His wife and eldest daughter are dead, Jeanne and the last nuns are dead, but, says the Father, "the King and the Pontiff are once again restored to France and the Universe, the schism is ended, and once more the Throne rises above all of the men." The women may be dead, "but I, I am alive, on the threshold of death, and an inexplicable joy is within me!" Likewise Pierre de Craon: "Now I have everything," he declares, "I possess everything in my hands," and, armed with these powers, he will, "a father of churches," draw the chapel of Justitia from his side "like an Eve of stone," and will place on its summit an effigy of "Violaine the leper in her glory, Violaine the blind in the look of all," seen but unseeing, her symbolic empowerment concealing the actual powerlessness of her sex. As for the surviving females, Mara and Aubaine, the voice of the one and the cries of the other are silenced by the sheer volume made by the all-male trio of voices as they merge with the Angelus bells at the end of the play. "There are no flowers," proclaims Anne Vercors, "there are now only fruit," but the fruits are all for the men, and the death of the woman whose sufferings brought them forth has been all but forgotten.[41] This is not the last, far from it, that we will hear of the doctrine of vicarious suffering that pervades Catholic writing of the late nineteenth and early twentieth centuries, but it is sufficient to permit an interim verdict: sacrificial theory *always* ultimately reinforces the existing order and hierarchy, and it is *always* the Father who ultimately benefits from the sufferings of the Daughter, or, for that matter, the Brother who is ultimately redeemed by the self-offering of the sister. And so, in the end, we come back to Camille whose internment is so mysteriously prefigured in that of Queen Marie of France as sister in the enclosed order of Monsanvierge—even the name points forward to Montdevergues, two years before Camille was sent there—and in the prophetic words uttered by the 1898 Violaine:

> I am like the poor sister cloistered behind the grill and the curtain,
> Whom a relative has come to visit, and he gives news of the family.
> "So and so is dead," he says.
> I have my own body as a cell, it has no window, and the key of the
> One door it has is held by one man.
> I do not know where I am any longer, I am in him whom I love![42]

Faced with misery of this kind, irredeemable at least on this earth, the Angelus bell that rings out the Good News at the end of *L'Annonce* will, to some, have a hollow sound indeed.

4

BEGGARS OF HEAVEN

Jacques and Raïssa Maritain
PARIS—VERSAILLES—MEUDON, 1900–1939

On 20 June 1905, Léon Bloy, the self-styled "pilgrim of the absolute" and, at 58, still the most extreme French Catholic of his age, received an unsolicited money order for twenty-five francs accompanied by a letter signed by two complete strangers, Jacques and Raïssa Maritain. It was the feast of Saint Barnabas, the companion of Saint Paul, which, that year, had been postponed because its usual date, 11 June, clashed with Whit Sunday, a fact of no little significance for Bloy who, before all else, believed in the providentiality of all earthly affairs and for whom nothing "happened" here below without the active intervention of one or another member of the communion of saints, Barnabas being one of the intercessors whom he was wont to invoke with particular fervor. For the last fifteen months, Bloy had been living with his wife, Jeanne, and their daughters, Véronique and Madeleine, in a ramshackle house on the Butte de Montmartre, no more than a couple of hundred yards from the Basilica of Sacré-Coeur, which, characteristically, Bloy detested with all the passionate hatred of which he was capable, on a street named after the nineteen-year-old Chevalier de la Barre who had been tortured and executed at Abbeville in 1766 for having sung "impious songs" and refused to doff his hat as a procession of Capucin monks passed by.[1] It was an ironically appropriate address for a Catholic who, more than any other, was obsessed with the experience of martyrdom, expiation, and pain.

Bloy and his family had for many years been reduced to something like indigence, contriving just to survive off the meager earnings of his increasingly dotty writings, supplemented by gifts of money from friends and benevolent readers. As befits one who dubbed himself *le mendiant ingrat* (the ungrateful beggar), Bloy was often less than thankful toward his benefactors, as he regarded such gifts as acts of reparation by the giver for the "enormous injustice" that he, Bloy, was condemned to endure for the sake of his unswerving commitment to what he called "absolute, integral Christianity," the apocalyptic Catholicism of Mary's secret message to Mélanie Calvat (see chapter 1). For Bloy, money was the lifeblood of modern society, at once an expression and parody of the saving blood Christ had shed on the Cross, and, like the Precious Blood of the Savior, it must be *exchanged* if it is to be as effective in its sphere as the Lord's Blood is in that of salvation: not for nothing, Bloy believed, did the Host resemble a coin.[2] To hoard money is to keep grace for oneself and so render it inoperative; to pass it on in the form of a charitable offering is both to give, and not give, of oneself, the gift of money being a synecdoche and substitute for the total self-offering of the martyr or saint.

But even a token gift of twenty-five francs requires a countergift in return, especially when that very morning the receiver had been obliged to borrow some money from his barber in order that his wife and children might have something to eat. Accordingly, Bloy wrote back to his latest benefactors the following day, enclosing copies of the first two volumes of his journal, and on 23 June sent them an open invitation to visit, together with detailed instructions concerning the route they should take.[3] It was the opening exchange in one of the most crucial encounters in the history of twentieth-century French Catholicism.

Jacques and Raïssa Maritain were unlike almost all the other intellectual converts of the fin de siècle and the belle époque in that neither had been baptized, or brought up, within the Catholic faith. Jacques Maritain (1882–1973) was the grandson of Jules Favre (1809–80), Freemason, freethinker, and republican stalwart, who, coincidentally, first came to public attention in 1857 in connection with La Salette as the defender of a woman wrongly accused of having hoodwinked Mélanie and Maximin by posing as the Weeping Virgin eleven years earlier. His mother, the remarkable Geneviève Favre, had become a Protestant along with her father when he married the daughter of an Alsatian pastor toward the end of his life, and of the two children of her brief marriage to Jules Favre's secretary Paul Maritain—she was one of the first French women to benefit from the new divorce law of 1884—the elder, Jeanne, was baptized a Catholic and the younger, Jacques, according to the nominal faith of his mother; in reality his upbringing was secular, the forthright Geneviève, who reverted to her maiden name and never remarried, making no secret of her hostility to Christianity in all of its forms.

When, at the turn of the century, Jacques left the Lycée Carnot to study philosophy at the Sorbonne, he appeared as an especially brilliant product of the left-leaning, freethinking, republican milieu in which he had been raised: an ardent defender of Alfred Dreyfus and supporter of Jean Jaurès, a volunteer teacher at the *universités populaires,* an admirer of Charles Péguy in his earliest socialist-humanist guise.[4] Fittingly, his closest friend at this time and later was Ernest Psichari (1883–1914), grandson of the archetypal liberal secularist Ernest Renan, who likewise gave no hint of the religious avocation that would take him to north and west Africa with the French colonial army, conversion, and death as a self-styled "centurion" of Christ at Rossignol in Belgium in the first weeks of the Great War.[5] A closet homosexual, Psichari had tried to commit suicide in 1903 when Maritain's sister Jeanne had rejected his proposal of marriage.

Raïssa Oumansov (1883–1960) was even further removed from the Catholic mainstream for she was both Russian and Jewish and, when she and Maritain met in late 1900 or early 1901 (he was collecting signatures in the Latin Quarter for a petition protesting against the repression of radical students in Russia), she had abandoned even the vestigial religious beliefs of her childhood in the Ukrainian port of Mariupol on the Sea of Azov. Fearing the endemic antisemitism of late-nineteenth-century Russia and anxious above all to further the education of his gifted eldest daughter, Ilia Oumansov had left Mariupol in the summer of 1893 to take his family to New York, but like many Jewish refugees before him and after, decided to stay in Paris where his wife and two daughters (Véra was three years younger than Raïssa) joined him later in the year, lodging first in the "classic" Jewish catchment area of the Marais on the rue des Francs-Bourgeois and then, equally classically, moving to the rue de Montreuil in the Faubourg Saint-Antoine where Oumansov pursued his trade as a tailor. In 1898, the whole family received French nationality and, like most naturalized French Jews, Raïssa would always identify passionately with France, though, much less typically, "her" France would always be the France of Notre-Dame, Chartres, and, above all, La Salette rather than the France of 1789 and the universalist republican tradition. At seventeen and already a student of philosophy at the Sorbonne, Raïssa had seemingly left Russia and Jewishness far in her wake, though, like the man who would become her husband in 1904, she felt increasingly ill at ease within the antimetaphysical straitjacket of French intellectual orthodoxy at the turn of the century.[6]

Three points defined the intellectual geography of the Latin Quarter in the early 1900s: (1) the Sorbonne with its narrowly conceived scientific positivism, hostile in principle to any notion of the supernatural or spiritual; (2) Péguy's "boutique" on the rue de la Sorbonne from which, beginning in January 1900 and under the very nose of his arch-enemy, he edited the hugely influential *Cahiers de la Quinzaine;* and (3) just the other side of the rue Saint-Jacques but, philosophically, an ocean apart, the Collège de France where Henri Bergson (1859–1941) was appointed to the chair of philosophy in 1900 and where he was already exploring the theories of psychic dynamism, intuitionism, and the *élan vital* at the heart of all being that, as formulated in *L'Evolution créatrice* (1907), would strike at the core of what Raïssa later described as the "empty, colorless world of universal mechanicalism" routinely expounded in the *amphithéâtres* of the Sorbonne.[7]

In their pursuit of the metaphysical nourishment both instinctively craved, the couple sampled the wares on offer at each of these three outlets, before realizing, as Raïssa put it much later, that only a fourth site in the symbolic geography of the Quartier, the Eglise Sainte-Geneviève, could truly satisfy their spiritual hunger.[8] They quickly dismissed the monistic determinism of the philosophers of the Sorbonne, but found the anti-intellectualism of the *boutique de Péguy* antithetical to their need for philosophical order and authority. And, while Bergson's lectures at the Collège de France successfully challenged the intellectual rigidities of the Sorbonne, they too notably failed to provide any meaning, justification, or ultimate *telos* for the profusion of psychic and physical vitality that the philosopher so powerfully evoked.

In *Les Grandes Amitiés,* written in exile in New York in 1940–41, Raïssa recalls a crucial exchange that took place between Jacques and her one afternoon in the Jardin des Plantes where, surrounded by courting couples and nannies with children and against a background of exotic flora and fauna, they reviewed the available philosophical options and concluded that, in the absence of any ultimate metaphysical justification for existence, all that remained was the "*Nunc dimittis* of despair" and its logical corollary (for the Maritains were nothing if not logical), namely suicide. It was Camus's *mythe de Sisyphe* forty years in advance and, like Sisyphus, they decided to give the rock of absurdity a final heave up the mountain, with joint suicide the solution if existence failed to respond to the vehemence of their challenge for meaning: "We wished to die through a freely willed refusal if it was impossible to live according to truth."[9]

Having decided, in Raïssa's words, that a life of pain was acceptable but not a life of absurdity, they began, logically enough, to look for a meaning in suffering, and it was this quest that, following a remark made by the playwright Maurice Maeterlinck in *Le Matin,* led them in the direction of Léon Bloy's remarkable novel *La Femme pauvre* (1897). Like so many of Bloy's readers, they were riveted by his evocation of suffering and poverty and enthralled by the possibility of meaning that they glimpsed in two of the novel's most famous statements of Bloy's theology of sanctification through pain: "One does not enter Paradise tomorrow, or in ten years' time, one enters today when one is poor and crucified," "there is only one sadness, that of not being saints" (Il n'y a qu'une tristesse, c'est de n'être pas des saints).[10] To the offer of hope that Bloy's words had given them, they responded with their gift of twenty-five francs and their hope of his friendship, which Bloy reciprocated in his turn with his offering of books and open invitation to visit.

On the morning of Sunday 25 June 1905, the two "beggars of heaven" (*mendiants de ciel*)[11] duly mounted the huge flight of steps up the Butte de Montmartre to meet the notorious *mendiant ingrat,* alias *le Vieux de la Montagne,* in his curious lair at its summit, mysteriously confident that their appeal for meaning was at last about to be answered. Jacques's third-person account continues as follows:

They crossed a tiny old-fashioned garden, then entered a modest house, its walls adorned with books and beautiful pictures, and first encountered a kind of white-haired embodiment of goodness that was Mme Léon Bloy; her two daughters Véronique and Madeleine looked on with eyes wide with astonishment. Léon Bloy seemed almost shy, he spoke little and in a low voice, trying to tell his young visitors something of importance that would not disappoint them. What he revealed to them cannot be recounted: the tenderness of Christian brotherhood, and that kind of trembling of pity and fear that seizes one in the presence of a soul marked by the love of God. Bloy appeared to us as the absolute opposite of other men, who conceal their grave spiritual shortcomings, and so many crimes, beneath the carefully maintained distemper [*badigeonnage*] of conventional sociability. Rather than the whited sepulchre of Pharisees of all ages, he was a charred, blackened cathedral. The whiteness was within, in the depths of the tabernacle. Through having crossed the threshold of his house, all their values were displaced, as though by the flick of an invisible catch. They knew, or they sensed, that there was only one sadness, that of not being saints. And everything else became a twilight in comparison.[12]

After this first visit, the Maritains regularly returned to 40, rue de la Barre, drawn by the household's air of living and lived saintliness, and, even allowing for retrospective revisions, it is clear that Bloy's brand of Catholicism, however extreme and eccentric, struck them from the outset as the way out of their metaphysical impasse and the personal unhappiness that went with it. But before formal conversion could even be envisaged, one major obstacle—the fact of Raïssa's Jewishness—had to be resolved, and on it Bloy held a typically extremist position.

The Maritains' exchanges with Bloy in the summer of 1905 focused on one of his key works, *Le Salut par les Juifs,* first published in 1892, in which, with a characteristic combination of wrong-headed fury, hermeneutic ingenuity, and sudden explosions of stunning lyric beauty, *le mendiant ingrat* explores, with a subtlety pushed to the point of dementia, the multiple meanings of Jesus' enigmatic statement to the woman of Samaria in John 4:22: *Salus ex Judaeis est,* "for salvation comes from the Jews." It is also one of the most repulsively antisemitic works of a decade that outdid all others in the virulence of its Judaeophobia and, reading it, Raïssa must often have recoiled in disgust, particularly at Bloy's extraordinary description—a masterpiece in the rhetoric of loathing—of the *Judenmarkt* in Hamburg with its nightmare vision of *das ewige Jude,* always identical to itself, cloning itself *ad infinitum,* and inexorably taking over the globe. Yet over and above its racist obscenities, *Le Salut par les Juifs* addresses two issues that, as well as being among the supreme paradoxes of the Christian religion, were of the most immediate concern to Raïssa herself: the fact, inescapable, unacceptable, that Christianity's savior of humanity was a Jew and, correlatively, that, in the biblical account of his arrest, trial, and execution, it was the Jewish nation *in its entirety* that was held responsible for his death and hence, by an extreme dialectical reversal, for the redemption-by-sacrifice of the whole of mankind—minus, precisely, the Jews.[13]

God's Chosen People are thus the "instruments of Redemption," as Bloy, following Church tradition, describes them, but are denied the fruits of the sacrificial murder they committed; they are Christianity's ultimate scapegoats, divinely ordained Christ-killers on whom Christians can project the responsibility—and their own sense of guilt—for the atoning death of their Savior.[14] But, once more in keeping with the ancient teaching of the Church, Bloy believes that the Second Coming of Christ will occur only when Jews repent of their crime and convert to Christianity en masse, whence the further paradox that Christians, having already benefited from their crime, are dependent on the deicidal enemies of Christ for their full and ultimate salvation: "The Jews will be converted only when Jesus descends from His Cross, and precisely Jesus will be able to descend from it only when the Jews are converted."[15] In short, Jews are sacred in the double sense of that word, blessed *and* cursed, victimizers *and* victims, who must be both persecuted and preserved in order that they may play their role as double agents in the Christian drama of redemption. More than any other writer of his time, Bloy foregrounded what most Christians had either never recognized or were at pains to repress, namely the irreducible Jewishness of their Lord and Savior, not to mention the Jewishness of his Mother, whence the triple scandal, as Bloy put it in a letter to another female correspondent, quoted by Raïssa, that "I eat, every morning, a Jew named Jesus Christ" (Je mange, chaque matin, un Juif qui se nomme Jésus-Christ), that, furthermore, "I pass a part of my life at the feet of a Jewess with a transfixed heart of whom I have made myself the slave" and that, horror of horrors, in his wager for salvation, "I have placed by confidence in a bunch of Yids" (J'ai donné ma confiance à un troupeau de Youpins).[16]

By the time the Maritains met Bloy, *Le Salut par les Juifs* had been out of print for some years, and, with Bloy's agreement, they decided to have it reprinted at their own expense; in return, Bloy duly dedicated the new edition to Raïssa in the name of "the Catholic glory of the God of Abraham, Isaac, and Jacob." In her discussion of the book in *Les Grandes Amitiés*, Raïssa lets Bloy off lightly for having reformulated "in sometimes inadmissible terms" what she calls "the medieval horror of the Jewish people which he considered to be still engaged in its deicidal action, just as he saw the Passion of the Redemption as forever present and actual."[17] But, antisemitism apart, Bloy's argument, expressed with his usual extremism but in substance wholly orthodox, removed the principal obstacle to her eventual conversion:

[His] testimony was in the first instance the revelation for me of the unity of the two Testaments. One passes from one to the other through Christ. He said so Himself; He, Salvation, comes from the Jews. Through Him, the Old Testament flows into [*se déverse*] into the New, which is not its antithesis, but its fulfillment, its perfection.[18]

As a Jewish woman in quest of conversion, Raïssa was herself about to accomplish the transcendence of the Old Dispensation by and in the New, and, by offering herself up in renewal of Christ's sacrifice, could be sure that her renunciation of the faith in her forebears—and both her mother and father were still alive—was in fulfillment of God's salvific purpose not just for herself but for mankind as a whole, *including,* not excluding, the Jews. *Le Salut par les Juifs,* Bloy wrote to her on 25 August 1905, might have been written with her and her situation explicitly in mind:

> "I am not a Christian," you say. "I am only groaning and seeking." Why should you continue to seek, my friend, since *you have found.* How could you like what I write, if you did not feel and think as I do? You are not merely a Christian, Raïssa, you are an ardent Christian [*une chrétienne brûlante*], a beloved daughter of the Father, a bride of Jesus Christ at the foot of the Cross, a loving servant of the mother of God in her antechamber of queen of the Worlds. . . . Only you do not know it, or rather you did not know it, and it was in order to learn it that you were sent to us . . . the importance, the DIGNITY of Souls, cannot be expressed, and the souls of the two of you, Jacques and Raïssa, are so precious that it required nothing less than the Incarnation and agony [*supplice*] of god to redeem [*racheter*] them—exactly like mine . . . *empti estis pretio magno,* you have been brought at great price. That, my friends, is the key to everything, in the Absolute. One has been bought back and redeemed, like slaves of great price, by the ignominy and voluntary torture of Him who made heaven and earth. When one knows that, when one sees it and feels it, one becomes like gods and yet one weeps without ceasing. . . . It is in the strict sense of the word the desire for Redemption, accompanied by the presentiment or the intuition of what it cost Him who was in a position to pay. That is Christianity, that is, and there is no other way of being a Christian.[19]

It was Bloy's ultraliteralist theory of Christ's buying back of mankind from the devil at the price of his life, restated to meet the situation and needs of the two "beggars of heaven," and directed with particular sharpness at Raïssa herself. Not two months after their first visit to the rue du Chevalier de la Barre, the Maritains were already on the brink of paying the price of total commitment to the God-Man who, their mentor assured them, had purchased their souls at the price of his very existence.

Unlike Claudel and Huysmans before them and still more unlike Simone Weil in the future, Jacques and Raïssa moved rapidly, though not without anxiety and conflict, toward formal reception into the Church. In September 1905, they made the ritual initiands' pilgrimage to Chartres and found in the cathedral's statuary and windows encyclopedic confirmation of the completion and perfection of the Old Testament in the New. Shortly afterward, Raïssa had the first of many experiences of the presence of God as, traveling by train through a forest, it suddenly seemed to her that the trees became "bigger than themselves" and began to "speak of an Other," their sole "function" being to "*designate* the Creator."[20] As in Chartres cathedral, so now on a train, she seemed to be moving through "a forest of symbols" toward God; nature, art, and supernature formed a specular whole, each reflecting and designating the other in an intuited order to which the reading, some years later, of the *Summa Theologica* would bring intellectual coherence.

Under Bloy's direction, Jacques and Raïssa read a selection of devotional works whose titles resonate from one chapter to another of this book: the *Revelations* of the German stigmatic Anne Catherine Emmerich (1774–1824); the *Memoriale* of Blessed Angela of Foligno (1250–1309), another stigmatic, anorexic, and ecstatic whose mystical-erotic trances were grist to Bataille's "atheological" mill; and the *Catéchisme spirituel* of Jean-Joseph Surin, the exorcist of Loudun, much read by Thérèse in the Carmel at Lisieux. That all these were in some way physically and/or psychologically ill seems hardly fortuitous, not least because in February 1906 Raïssa herself fell victim to a mysterious sickness, possibly psychosomatic in origin, that rendered her semicomatose for some weeks, recovering after Bloy's wife had fastened the "miraculous medal" of Catherine Labouré around her neck.[21] Henceforth, sickness and spirituality would go hand in hand in her life, each feeding into the other as, more and more, she withdrew into intense interior contemplation.

On 5 April 1906 Jacques and Raïssa informed Bloy that they wished to be baptized, along with Véra who, when told of their decision, replied that she was ready to follow them; unbeknown to them, she too had been reading *La Femme pauvre*.[22] The baptism of all three took place at the recently constructed church of Saint-Jean de Montmartre at the foot of the Butte on June 1906 (the Feast of Saint Barnabas) with Bloy, his wife, and elder daughter Véronique acting as godparents: "and immense peace descended upon us, bringing with it the treasures of faith. There were no longer any questions, any anguish, any ordeals—there was only the infinite response of God."[23] First communion followed at Sacré-Coeur itself on 3 August, and at the end of the month, without telling either the Oumansovs or Geneviève Favre what had happened, the Maritains left for Heidelberg where Jacques, his vocation as a philosopher as yet undefined, had been awarded a scholarship to study embryology; Véra joined them there at the end of the year. In January 1907, Raïssa fell dangerously ill with amoebic enteritis and received the Sacrament of Extreme Unction on the 17th of that month; she interpreted her recovery soon afterward as absolute proof both of the rightness of their decision and of the efficacy of the sacraments of the Church.[24]

Returning on a visit to Paris in the spring of 1907, Jacques discovered that the Oumansovs had been informed of their daughters' conversion and that they considered it, quite simply, as a betrayal of themselves, their religion, and their people. Still worse, when Jacques belatedly told *his* mother of his reception into the Church, Mme Favre angrily dismissed the whole thing as a conspiracy jointly mounted by Bloy and Raïssa, Catholics and Jews operating hand in glove with each other to take what she treasured most in life away from her; her worst fears and suspicions were confirmed when, accompanying her to the Gare de l'Est on his departure, he was accosted by a priest with whom he was clearly familiar.[25] In the still paranoid atmosphere of post–Dreyfus Affair France, any such encounter suggested a ramifying network of spies, agents, and behind-the-scenes manipulators of minds, and in September 1907 Mme Favre wrote to her son's friend Ernest Psichari, by then with the French colonial army in Africa and engaged, unbeknown to her, on a spiritual quest of his own, telling him how, when she learned of Jacques's conversion, she had burst into tears at seeing him thus "annihilated, reduced to such slavery," the result, she was sure, of "supple, lying, skilful individuals working, without his knowledge, at breaking his intelligence." Watch out, Geneviève tells Psichari, "Jacques is awaiting your return with impatience, devoured with proselytizing zeal, and has told me that he hopes to bring you to him! It's enough to make one weep."[26]

Geneviève Favre's belief in the existence of a conspiracy of conversion was not altogether fantastical, for the years following the separation of Church and State in 1905 brought a steady stream of conversions among, in particular, the educated upper middle classes, above all at the Ecole Normale Supérieure where mass-attending students known in *normalien* slang as *talas* (from *il va-t-à la messe*), almost nonexistent at the time of the Affair, were a conspicuous and often raucous presence by the time Henri Massis and Alfred de Tarde, writing under the pseudonym of "Agathon," published their celebrated survey on contemporary (upper-class) youth, *Les Jeunes Gens d'aujourd'hui,* in 1913. Such converts were usually well to the right in their political views, ardent defenders of the honor of Joan of Arc from any alleged republican slight, and, more often than not, members or sympathizers of the royalist movement Action Française, founded in 1898 at the height of the Dreyfus Affair.

There are signs, too, that the Maritains were moving toward the fringes, if not into the heart, of the ultra-Catholic reaction. At Bloy's suggestion, they spent several days at La Salette, shrine of the religious far right, in late June and early July 1907, in preparation for their confirmation that took place at Grenoble on 6 July. In his notebook, Jacques described La Salette as "the paradise and the house of our heart"[27] and began work on a study of the apparition that would have endorsed the most "radical" position regarding the authenticity of the Virgin's secret "message" to Mélanie (see chapter 1). In the event, the study fell under the papal interdict on further publications on La Salette and remains unpublished, presumably destroyed, to this day, though in 1918 Jacques and Raïssa traveled to Rome for an audience with Pope Benedict XV when they tried, unsuccessfully, to have the ban lifted in their case.[28]

They took a further step to the right—or the right took a further step toward them—when in late 1908, at the suggestion of Dom Delatte, leader of the exiled Benedictine community at Appuldurcombe on the Isle of Wight that Jacques had visited in August 1907,[29] they approached the Dominican Hubert Clérissac to act as their spiritual adviser. Clérissac was celebrated for having been present at Oscar Wilde's deathbed conversion, and it was he who suggested that the Maritains study Saint Thomas Aquinas, and so may be considered, after Bloy, as the greatest single influence on their lives. If, however, Clérissac was an ardent Thomist, he was an equally ardent supporter of Action Française who believed that Catholicism and monarchism formed a single seamless whole and for whom modernity in all of its forms, be it in politics, philosophy, or theology, was quite simply the work of the devil.[30] The title of Jacques's postwar collection of essays, *Antimoderne* (1922), might be seen as an act of posthumous homage to their mentor, and when, in October 1908, he, Raïssa, and Véra left Paris for Versailles where the Dominican was based, it partook of an orthodox *hegira* from the City of Error, the spiritual counterpart, as it were, of Thiers's abandonment of Paris on the day the Commune was declared (18 March 1871). For the next thirty years, Versaillais of the spirit, the Maritains would live on the fringes of Paris, directing repeated intellectual mortars on the largely unheeding city below.

Jacques's notebooks of 1909–11 show how, under the influence and guidance of Clérissac, the faith of all three grew in intensity through a combination of reading (Aquinas above all, but also Angela of Foligno, Saint Catherine of Genoa, Jan van Ruysbroeck, Tauler, and—Raïssa's particular favorite—Saint Gertrude [1256–1301/2]), prayer and meditation, regular communion at Versailles cathedral, singing of hymns after dinner, and, not least, regular bouts of illness that seem to have acted as a spiritual catalyst not only for Raïssa but for Jacques and Véra as well. More and more the house at 16, rue de l'Orangerie took on the character and atmosphere of a miniature religious community, with its daily round of prayers and other rituals, and even its own private oratory in which a statue of Our Lady of Salette, spotted by Clérissac in an antique shop, was installed in February 1911.

In March that year, Ilia and Hissia Oumansov, by now largely reconciled to their daughters' conversion, moved to a nearby house in Versailles, and pressure began to mount on them to follow Raïssa and Véra into the Church. According to Raïssa's account in *Les Grandes Amitiés*, Ilia began to show signs of Catholic "sympathies" as early as 1910 and started visiting churches, drawn at first by his love of the organ; Mme Oumansov, however, was much more reserved, and neither can have been exactly inspired by the letter they received from Mme Bloy in which she casually informed them that "you"—meaning Jews as a whole—"crucified our Lord Jesus Christ."[31] When Ilia fell seriously ill in February 1912, Raïssa and Véra, aided and abetted by Jacques, pressured him to enter the Church, and though the decision to request baptism came from him, many readers of Raïssa's account will feel that the three of them overstepped the limits of propriety in wresting it from an elderly man in extremis. Be that as it may, on Ash Wednesday, 21 February 1912, Ilia was baptized Jude-Bernabé by Jacques himself using a flacon of water from La Salette for the purpose; a "miraculous medal" was duly fastened round his neck (he apparently already carried one in his wallet), and on 22 February he took communion, was confirmed on the 23rd, and died later that night. By Raïssa's own admission, Mme Oumansov was "troubled and irritated against us" by what must have seemed to her conversion under duress, and it would be many years before she would follow her daughters and son-in-law into the Church.[32]

In 1911, again at Clérissac's instigation, the Maritains had subscribed to Action Française's eponymous newspaper, but to their director's derision and disgust, jibbed at formerly adhering to the movement itself, not least, one presumes, because of the vicious antisemitism of its leader, Charles Maurras (1868–1952).[33] As a sign of the intensification of their faith, Raïssa, Véra, and Jacques went in May 1911 to the abbey of Oosterhout in Holland with a view to becoming oblates of the Order of Saint Benedict and in September 1912, after a year's preparation, became tertiary members as Soeur Gertrude, Soeur Agnès, and Frère Placide respectively. Returning to France, Jacques and Raïssa made a formal vow of chastity in Versailles cathedral on 2 October 1912 and lived thereafter "as brother and sister," foregoing the possibility of children in the name of their commitment to God, though they stopped short of separating completely and each entering a religious order, as did (for a time) their friends and fellow converts Pierre and Christine van der Meer.[34]

Refusing an orthodox academic career at the Sorbonne, the Collège de France, or the Ecole Normale Supérieure, Jacques began to teach at the Collège Stanislas, the preeminent Catholic school in Paris and France, and later at the Institut Catholique in Paris, and so began his lifelong campaign to reinstate Thomism as a truly *contemporary* philosophy, embracing the natural and the supernatural, the human and the divine, in a supremely ordered and rational synthesis to which, in his most famous single work, he would give the name of *Integral Humanism* (1936).[35] Because, presumably, of his suspect health, Jacques did not see active service in the war that, in its first few weeks, saw the deaths of Psichari, by then himself an oblate of the Dominican order (22 August 1914), of Péguy (5 September), and then, of natural causes, of Clérissac on 16 November; their first and greatest spiritual mentor, Léon Bloy, died on 3 November 1917, still sharp-witted and pugnacious enough in his death throes to correct his wife's murmured *Ave o Crux spes unica* to *O Crux ave spes unica*.[36]

In 1917 Jacques began an intellectual and spiritual correspondence with a serving soldier named Pierre Villard who, after his death in combat in

June 1918, was found to have left Jacques a substantial sum of money, part of which he used to found and finance the celebrated Cercles Thomistes with their regular meetings and annual retreats that would be held annually from 1922 to 1938, providing a unique forum for secular priests, religious and laymen and women, philosophers, theologians, and artists, French and foreign alike. The legacy also enabled him to devote much more time to his writing, and by the late 1920s works such as *Art et scolastique* (1920) and *Primauté du spirituel* (1927) had established him beyond doubt as the premier Catholic intellectual in France. Most important of all, the Villard bequest enabled the Maritains to buy the house in Meudon, on the western outskirts of Paris, which throughout the interwar years would be the center of much that was most dynamic and creative in French Catholic intellectual and artistic life. Raïssa, Véra, and Jacques moved into 10, rue du Parc in June 1923, having had one of its rooms consecrated as a chapel in which, by special dispensation, they were permitted to keep the Blessed Sacrament. The most fruitful and influential period of their lives was about to begin.

Meudon, 1923–39

"Every Christian," Raïssa wrote in *Les Grandes Amitiés,* "is essentially a 'separated' being, separated from the world by the death-shrouds of Christ." For the most part, however, it is "in the world" that he or she must remain, struggling every day "to live at once according to the eternal and the temporal: the disproportion is infinite. How to adjust our actions between these extremes?"[37] To the physical problem of how to be both apart and related, the house at Meudon brought an immediate practical solution: It was well away from the center of Paris, but easily reachable by train or by car, though still sufficiently distant to deter the casual visitor. Above all, it made possible a moral and intellectual distance verging on a sense of spiritual superiority, as Raïssa's poem "Terrasse de Meudon," written sometime between 1926 and 1934, perhaps unwittingly reveals:

> Du Sacré-Coeur les pendeloques
> Et les deux tours sur l'échiquier
> Où joue et gagne Notre-Dame
> Immobilisent ta clarté
> Et l'insolite Tour Eiffel
> Est une aile couleur du temps
> Qui s'aventure dans ton ciel.[38]

[The pendants of Sacré-Coeur / and the two towers on the chessboard / Where Notre-Dame plays and wins / Arrest your clarity / And the incongruous Eiffel Tower / Is a time-colored wing / Venturing into your sky.]

From the terrasse Paris is spectacular but silent, devoid of disrupting human presences, ordered like a chessboard on which only the victorious Sacré-Coeur and Notre-Dame truly belong, and on which the Eiffel Tower, symbol of the detested modernity,[39] rises up like an unwonted (and unwanted) interloper. Visitors—pilgrims rather—to 10, rue du Parc had first to traverse, admittedly in the comfort of a railway carriage or car, the wasteland of shanties surrounding the city—the infamous *zone*—and then climb the suburban Mount Carmel to the house where, in the words of one frequent visitor, the young Maurice Sachs (1906–45, see below), "everything [was] at rest, except thought; everything [kept] watch around the Real Presence of God. Gentleness, sweetness, calm, and serenity."[40] Once inside, it seemed that the occupants of the house—even the chubby-faced, smiling Mme Oumansov—had somehow risen above not merely the cares of the quotidian world but terrestrial matter itself, floating free of their bodies like rarefied spirits. Sachs had never seen any beings less bound to the earth: "It is not clear whether they sleep, it is difficult to imagine that they do, it is always a surprise to see them eat, and the toilets in the house seem completely redundant. Once when I saw Jacques Maritain get out of his tiny camp bed and wash himself with cold water in the kitchen, it seemed rather farcical and unreal."[41]

If Jacques struck many visitors as the very image of Christ—with his drooping left shoulder and tilted head, it seemed to Sachs that he was constantly bearing an invisible cross—Raïssa and Véra were always seen as, respectively, Mary and Martha, Véra round-faced like her mother and "careful and troubled about many things" in the house, while Raïssa, slender to the point of emaciation, sharp-featured, and with a fiery orange glint in her eyes, "sat at Jesus' feet, and heard his word" (Luke 10:39–41).[42] Jean Cocteau, one of the Maritains' numerous (if, in his case, temporary) converts (see below), famously described Raïssa as "frail as gossamer and strong as a steel blade" (*fragile comme un fil de la Vierge et robuste comme une lame d'acier*),[43] while Sachs, who both admired and feared her, sensed something rather more disturbing in her combination of ardor and severity:

> That rather sickly body had concentrated all its strength in the spirit. A rectilinear, logical, apostolic spirit, hard-edged and powerful, loving with passion, adoring with violence, Raïssa Oumansov emerged straight and spare from the Russia that prepared the Revolution. Ah! If only Marxism had seized her instead of Catholicism, if Hegel had triumphed in her over Thomas Aquinas, and Lenin over Saint Paul, if she had preferred *The Possessed* to *La Femme pauvre,* loved Thorez rather than Maritain, what a party militant she would have made, this steel-like, battle-hardened woman, who felt burning within her the invincible flames of love and sacrifice which sometimes lit up her transparent cheeks with a yellowish-white glow.[44]

Every Sunday afternoon around four, the Maritains held open house for their increasingly large flock of disciples, neophytes, and seekers, and, while

Raïssa and Véra served tea, Jacques might begin by explaining the circumincession of the three Persons of the Trinity with the aid of a blackboard and chalk, after which those present would debate and ask questions until late in the evening. Sometimes individuals slipped away into the garden for private conversations with this or that priest or religious, for there was no secret about the desire to proselytize among those who, for whatever reason, had seen fit to attend.

The "congregation" varied from week to week and from year to year, but always included a high proportion of converts, both religious and lay, the latter mostly artists and writers. The nucleus was composed of priests and religious known to the Maritains, above all their new spiritual director, Father Reginald Garrigou-Lagrange, and Prince Vladimir Ghika who, having converted from Orthodoxy to Catholicism in 1902, was ordained in 1923 with the Maritains in attendance; "more victim than sacrificer," in Raïssa's words, he frequently said mass in the private chapel at Meudon.[45] Among the better-known writer-converts regularly to attend were Henri Ghéon (1875–1944) and Henri Massis (1886–1970), both of them, like Garrigou-Lagrange, supporters of Action Française; they were joined, as and when circumstance and inclination permitted, by Max Jacob (1876–1944), once a near-neighbor of the Bloys at Montmartre who, since his conversion, was more often at the Benedictine monastery at Saint-Benoît-sur-Loire than in Paris; the poet Pierre Reverdy (1889–1960) who, in 1926, would likewise leave Paris to live in the shadow of the Benedictine house at Solesmes; and the young Julien Green (1900–1998), a convert from Protestantism in 1916 and already acclaimed as a leading "Catholic novelist" thanks to his *Adrienne Mesurat* of 1927. The painters included Georges Rouault (1871–1958), a prewar acquaintance through Bloy on whom Jacques published an influential essay in 1926[46] and Raïssa's compatriot Marc Chagall (1887–1985), the subject of her monograph *Chagall ou l'orage enchanté* of 1948. Another regular visitor was the great Catalan pianist Ricardo Viñes (1875–1943) who numbered among his pupils not only Francis Poulenc (1899–1963), a future Catholic convert whose only other connection with the Meudon circle was through fellow-composer Georges Auric (1899–1983), a youthful disciple of Bloy, and, remarkably, Colette Peignot who, as an apparently model Catholic teenager, was a highly talented pianist; such was the interconnectedness of the Parisian artistic milieu that her brother would marry the soprano Suzanne Rivière who gave the first performance of some of Poulenc's early songs.[47] That Ghéon, Jacob, Green, and Poulenc were all homosexuals may be seen, in the light of what follows, as something other than mere biographical coincidence.

The Meudon circle was an impressive if unequally gifted collection of individuals, sufficiently ecumenical to embrace at one time or another a left-wing Catholic (and crypto-homosexual) like Mauriac and a future Vichyist like Massis. And, most famously of all, it briefly included the Maritains' prize catch, the star and epitome of *le tout-Paris* of the 1920s, Jean Cocteau (1889–1963), whose highly publicized "return to the sacraments" in the summer of 1925 reveals the Meudon circle at both its generous-hearted best and its gullible, bullying worst.

Jean Cocteau

Devastated by the death in December 1923 of his companion, the *Wunderkind* novelist Raymond Radiguet (1900–23), Cocteau had left Paris for Monte Carlo where, in the company of Auric and Poulenc, he had been introduced to the musicologist Louis Laloy, author of *Le Livre de la fumeé* (1913) and a dedicated user of opium; that Laloy was also a Meudon "regular" offers still further evidence of the extraordinary incestuousness of the artistic and intellectual life of the period.[48] Under Laloy's proselytizing influence, Cocteau was soon smoking opium copiously and regularly, but, his grief unassuaged, began—according to his own highly mythologized account of his conversion in his public *Lettre à Jacques Maritain* of 1926—to look for consolation and hope in the Church in which he had been baptized but whose sacraments he had long since abandoned:

> I was asking for mercy. It was so simple to ask for Grace [*Je demandais grâce. Il était si simple de demander la Grâce*]. Like those people of Nice whose window shutters are covered with the huge letters of an advertisement, I was living in God [*j'habitais Dieu*] and I had never gone out to look at my window from outside.

He wrote to his fellow poet (and fellow homosexual) Max Jacob at Saint-Benoît-sur-Loire and was urged to confess and take communion "the way one goes to a doctor." "What!" Cocteau wrote back, "You advise me to swallow the Host like an aspirin tablet."[49] In July 1924 Auric took Cocteau to Meudon—Jacques and he had previously corresponded on literary matters but had not, apparently, met—where he received further spiritual encouragement, discreet but undeniably urgent, and in September Jacques promised, to Cocteau's evident delight, to pray for him while on pilgrimage to the Marian shrine of Notre-Dame-des-Bois near Violot in the Haute-Marne;[50] a further meeting took place at Meudon in December.

The Maritains' genuine concern for an artist both admired concealed an ulterior motive. Jacques was eager to establish a combined literary review and collection to challenge the hegemony of the *Nouvelle Revue Française* and to combat the influence of the Surrealists; to "capture" Cocteau might be a major coup for the Church and a positive example to "youth," but it would also put his publishing venture on the map and in all likelihood attract other nonaffiliated modernists.

Moreover, Cocteau's recovery of faith inaugurated a period of intense proselytizing activity. In the course of 1925 Pierre Reverdy—a major "catch"—and Maurice Sachs—a very minor one—were both received into the Church, and the Maritains and their friends also secured two notable deathbed conversions: that of Erik Satie (1866–1925) in June—according to Sachs, he agreed to take communion[51]—and, early in 1926, the twenty-year-old André Grange, tersely described as a "victim of the Surrealists" by Raïssa.[52] Much closer to home, Raïssa, Véra, and Jacques were beginning to "work" on Mme Oumansov and, after considerable pressure, she was baptized as Elisabeth-Marie on 2 August 1925.[53] But Cocteau's conversion was the most sought-after prize, and the Maritains set about securing it with almost military precision.

However sincere Cocteau might be in proclaiming his newfound beliefs (and, according to Sachs, he spoke continually of Maritain and God, though not, to be fair, in that order),[54] formal membership of the Church was a more complicated matter. At Maritain's insistence, he agreed to tackle the immediate obstacle—the ten pipes of opium he was now smoking each day, three at nine in the morning, four at five in the afternoon, and three at eleven in the evening[55]—by entering a clinic in February 1925. There he remained for six weeks, supposedly in complete isolation, sustained by letters from Maritain, Max Jacob, and—here was the much deeper second problem—the nineteen-year-old Jean Bourgoint (1905–66) whom he had met just before entering the clinic and to whom he gave "his first whiff of opium in a kiss."[56] On his discharge at the end of April, Cocteau resumed not only his double addiction but also his friendship with the Maritains and eagerly accepted an invitation to Meudon on 15 June to discuss Jacques's various publishing projects. The car that was due to take him on to a performance of the Ballets Russes failed for some reason to turn up and, before he could leave, there arrived at 10, rue du Parc, almost as though prearranged by the Maritains or by some higher agency still, one of the more remarkable, if only occasional, members of their circle: Father Charles Henrion.

Henrion was a prewar convert whom the Maritains had known since 1913 and who, at the time of his serendipitous arrival, was permanently based in Tunisia where, along with another convert, the former Admiral Malcor, he had founded the Confraternity of Sidi-Saad, a contemplative order that also provided medical care for the local population. Henrion's conversion had been assisted by Claudel, and, like him and the Maritains, he was devoted to Mélanie and to the idea of the Apostles of the Last Days (*Apôtres des derniers temps*) that she had taken over from the eighteenth-century contemplative and prophet Louis-Marie Grignion de Montfort (1673–1716, canonized 1947). But Henrion's particular devotion was to the latter-day desert hermit Father Charles de Foucauld (1858–1916) who, converted in the same year as Claudel and Thérèse (1886), had died a martyr's death deep in the Sahara, at Tamanrasset in Algeria, in December 1916.[57] On the evening in question, Henrion arrived wearing a white *burnous* emblazoned with the emblem that Foucauld had supposedly devised to stop the infidels in their tracks, a blood-red Sacred Heart surmounted by a crimson cross. It certainly worked its magic on Cocteau, pitching him by the end of the week into the bosom of the Church as though propelled by some preternatural force of which the Maritains were only the instrument.

"Jacques, was that your trap?" Cocteau wrote in the open letter be began shortly afterward, "Had you been lying in wait for just that moment?"

> A heart entered, a red heart surmounted by a red cross, in the middle of a white shape that glided in, bent over us, spoke, shook hands. The heart hypnotized me, diverted me from the face, beheaded the burnous. The heart was the white shape's real face: it was as though Charles were holding his head on his breast, like the martyrs. No wonder the sunburned head was like a mirror-image of the heart, a mirage in all that African light. . . . Let me come to the most important point—the man's easy grace: compared with it I felt my best to be mere stagey charm. He smiled, told stories, exchanged recollections with Massis. I, stupid, "groggy," as boxers say, was gazing as through a thick windowpane at the white shape moving against the sky. I suppose that your wife and your guests must have realized what was going on: room, books, friends—nothing existed any longer. It was at that moment, Maritain, that you gave me a push. A push from your athletic soul. Everyone saw that I was losing my footing. No one came to my aid, because they knew that to help me, at that moment, would be my ruin. . . . A priest gave me the same shock as Stravinsky and Picasso.[58]

The severed head, the acephalous body, the Sacred Heart, and the Cross: the combination of four of the key motifs of this study was enough to send Cocteau, to continue his own image, reeling on to the ropes, whereupon the ever-alert Raïssa moved in for the knockout: "I see Jean Cocteau standing silent in the recess of the window, *caught*. Here then is the crystal-clear answer of God to our prayers, to our anxiety; for several weeks we had been wondering to which priest we should send Cocteau, for the time had come—and we could think of no-one. Once more our most gentle God has responded to a very great difficulty with the most effective of help."[59] What if Cocteau's car had arrived according to schedule? Jacques strongly hinted that angelic influences were at work:

> God was hurrying you on. . . . Reverdy and I felt that the moment had come when you would need a priest. To whom should we send you? It was then that you met Father Charles. If there was a conspiracy, it was a conspiracy of angels. I had been informed by telegram of his arrival on the very day you were to dine at Meudon. As soon as he came in, thanks to a great swirl of silence in our souls that lasted to the end, we knew instantly that he had come only for you. He was wearing on his breast the heart that you put at the end of your letters,

but with the Cross planted in it. Solitude sent you a contemplative; the contemplative and the poet understand each other, a man used to the workings of Heaven was at ease with your sense of the invisible.[60]

When Cocteau's car eventually arrived, the *coup de grâce*—literally—had been landed and, accompanying him out, Raïssa invited him to attend the mass that Father Henrion was due to say at the house the following Friday—which, inevitably, was the Feast of the Sacred Heart . . . "Cocteau saw, I am positive, the sign of his destiny appear on the heart of a man. The heart with which he signs all letters had suddenly become *the heart of Jesus*."[61]

The following day the Meudon conversion machine moved swiftly into action. Véra telephoned the bishop of Versailles, requesting that Father Charles be given permission to hear confessions at 10, rue du Parc; Henrion had not been consulted in advance and was unhappy about the whole thing, but, in Raïssa's words, "he could not refuse the task that we [imposed] on him without mercy." On Wednesday the 17th, after a thorough working-over by Jacques and Reverdy ("Take the earphones [*écouteurs*]! Take the earphones!" urged Reverdy, referring to the sacraments without which Cocteau "would understand nothing"), Cocteau agreed that he would *speak*—nothing more—to Henrion the next day, which he duly did in the drawing room at Meudon, while Jacques and Raïssa, though receiving two other friends at the time, "prayed inwardly" and listened for any tell-tale sounds of submission. Eventually, they heard Cocteau and Henrion go up to the chapel, Jacques was summoned, Cocteau made his confession and left "deeply shaken" (*tout bouleversé*). Finally, on Friday 19 June, Cocteau took communion in the chapel along with the Maritains, Henri Ghéon (a former cruising companion of André Gide in both Paris and North Africa, and a future Pétainist to boot), and the orientalist Louis Massignon (yet another homosexual who had converted to Catholicism in 1908), with the as-yet-unbaptized Mme Oumansov present as an observer; "another example for her," wrote Raïssa, "*Misericordias Domini* . . ."[62] Still "groggy" no doubt, "JC" had been safely delivered into the welcoming arms of J-C: Cocteau always liked "coincidences" like that.[63] A convert, Maritain famously wrote in his response to Cocteau's open letter, is "a man whom God has turned inside out like a glove. All the seams are outside, the leather [*l'écorce*] is inside, it no longer has any use."[64] Cocteau's life had certainly been shaken, even shattered, since Radiguet's death, but had it been truly "turned inside out"?[65]

Cocteau's immediate response was that of any writer: to write. Begun in August 1925 and published along with Maritain's *réponse* the following year, his *Lettre à Jacques Maritain* gave a dramatic account of the circumstances of his conversion, committed its author to the cause of "Art for God's sake," and notably failed to condemn or foreswear the smoking of opium—though it did concede that "opium resembles religion to the extent that an illusionist resembles Jesus." Not only did Cocteau continue to smoke opium, but it seems likely that he sometimes—notably at Midnight Mass at Meudon at the end of the year—took communion under its influence.[66] He also pursued his relationship with Jean Bourgoint whom he persuaded—either by way of squaring his own conscience or to entangle his lover in the same moral dilemmas as himself—to be baptized in August 1925. After a highly colorful and erratic existence, Bourgoint was admitted to the Trappist monastery at Cîteaux as a lay brother in 1947 and remained there for sixteen years as Frère Pascal, dividing his time between dairy, laundry, and the study of theology, before having himself transferred to Cameroun where, a true holy fool, he worked in a leper colony at Mokolo, "the poorest village in the world," as he called it, making orthopedic footware for sufferers of leprosy of the feet, and dying there of cancer in 1966.[67]

Cocteau's Catholicism was far less enduring. A man of the theater who lived his "private" life in public, he could hardly remain immune to the accusations of hypocrisy that soon fell upon him. On his "return to the sacraments" Père Charles had urged him to "remain free" (*rester libre*), words which Cocteau, to Maritain's dismay, interpreted as meaning that he could do—and, above all, publish—what he liked. Maritain soon had to ask him to withdraw his long poem *L'Ange Heurtebise*—written before his conversion and celebrating with lyrical bravado his passion for Radiguet—from its projected publication in the Meudon circle's literary collection. Cocteau would not compromise and, publishing his poem elsewhere, distanced himself from the Maritains without, however, breaking with them completely. In July 1927, Maritain wrote to Cocteau explaining how, in the eyes of the Church, homosexual love, however passionate and sincere, is an infraction of both the divine and the natural order and, as such, "a profound refusal of the Cross," to which Cocteau replied that he "needed love and to make love to souls," scarcely bothering to conceal that he preferred such souls to be enclosed in a beautiful masculine physique.[68]

The beginning of the end came in February 1928 when Cocteau contributed a rapturous preface to the first published work, provocatively entitled *J'adore*, by his latest companion Jean Desbordes (1906–44). To add insult to the injury he was knowingly inflicting on the Maritains, Cocteau's words appear alongside a photo-portrait of Desbordes wearing a sailor-suit. *J'adore* is a collection of homosexual fantasies and confessions, parts of which seem to have been written—possibly with Cocteau's aid and encouragement—deliberately to offend and antagonize the Maritains. Here, for example, is Desbordes's gay anticredo:

> I declare that the Holy Sacrament which is a loving presence exists in affection.
> I declare that when this miraculous affection brings together two beings, to the

point of causing them to die for each other, the divine presence is no longer in the church, but in the lovers' soul. . . . Jacques Maritain murmurs that human love is a disfigured, violated love, grace betrayed. Love is royal. It reigns over the many Versailles of the heart. It stops Satan as fire stops wild beats.[69]

This mixing of "God and the genitals" was too much for Maritain, and though, he told Cocteau, he was not judging Desbordes ("I leave that to God"), "it is a question of knowing whether masturbation and homosexual love [*l'onanisme et l'amour pédérastique*] form an appropriate reliquary for the Names of Jesus, the virgin, and the saints."[70] "Maritain thinks that Jean [Desbordes] is a devil in disguise," Cocteau retorted to an American friend, "He is mistaken. Jean is a love."[71]

The following June, Maritain learned that Cocteau was about to publish, albeit anonymously and in a limited edition of thirty-one copies, an explicit account and defense of his homosexual experiences entitled *Le Livre blanc,* and he again wrote to Cocteau urging him to withdraw it: "This project belongs to the Devil. It is the first time that you have made a public act of adhesion to evil." Refusing once more to comply, Cocteau made a resolute defense of artistic and personal freedom ("follow your road without compromise and let me follow my own. In imitating yours I would distort myself and distort human beings as they are")[72] and published *Le Livre blanc* in which he affirmed both his homosexuality and his faith, ending his apologia on a courageous note of defiance: "A vice of society makes my uprightness [*droiture*] a vice. I am withdrawing. In France, this vice does not lead to prison on account of Cambacérès' proclivities and the longevity of the Code Napoléon. But I will not accept being tolerated. That offends my love of love and of liberty."[73]

And that, more or less, was that. After undergoing a further detoxification cure, Cocteau tried to reestablish contact with 10, rue du Parc, but the Maritains had had enough, and they would maintain only the most formal relationship with Cocteau thereafter. In retrospect, the whole business seems a tragic blunder on both sides, with the Maritains, for good reasons and bad, putting undue pressure on an individual whose emotional vulnerability and taste for the theatrical led him to take a step against which the slightest self-knowledge should have forewarned him. How can either party have seriously supposed that Cocteau would have been able—even if he had been willing, which he was not—to contain his artistic and personal freedom within the moral straitjacket of the Church? And when it came, as it inevitably must, to choosing between the opium pipe and the "aspirin" of the Host, or, still more, if it may so be put, between JB (Bourgoint), JD (Desbordes), and J-C, can either proselytizers or proselytized have doubted which way JC would jump? The only individuals to emerge with credit from the affair are, ironically, Bourgoint and Desbordes, both of them authentic martyrs to their respective beliefs, Bourgoint in the circumstances described, Desbordes as an agent for the Polish resistance tortured to death by the Gestapo in July 1944, as the Maritains prepared to return from America in honor and while Cocteau, with typical slipperiness, endeavored to cover up his equivocal career in occupied Paris.[74]

Maurice Sachs

If Cocteau's botched conversion mingled pathos, posturing, and an alarming lack of insight on all sides, that of his one-time companion and secretary Maurice Sachs was a typically grotesque episode in a life of self-destructive dissipation that ended in horror and ignominy in Germany in April 1945.[75] Born in 1906 into a Jewish family that, in his own words, "married and divorced with incredible vivacity," Sachs seems not to have known his father and was brought up by his spendthrift mother, aided and abetted by the first wife of her father (not her mother), who had later married Jacques Bizet, son of the composer, dandy, alcoholic, and opiomane, whose life and death (by suicide in 1922) seem deadly harbingers of Sachs's own. After a Catholic schooling and early initiation into drugs and homosexuality, Sachs was, by his mid-teens, a familiar figure in the whirl of post-war Parisian nightlife, meeting Cocteau, as it was almost fated that he would, in February 1924. The pudgy-faced Sachs had little to commend him as a sexual partner, but Cocteau adopted him as one of his *gosses*, using him as a combined secretary, errand boy, and sounding board for his wit. Cocteau later described Sachs as "a chameleon, stricken with the disease of mimeticism," and it seems indeed to have been partly in emulation and envy of his mentor that Sachs set foot on his own singularly ill-advised road to Meudon-Damascus.

Like Cocteau, Sachs was in the throes of emotional turmoil, and the church seemed likely to fulfill the "desire for a framework" that he was always seeking and then rebelling against. In July Sachs begged Cocteau to guide him into the church ("Jean, lead me, you who bear the initials of the savior" [*vous qui avez les initiales divines*]), Cocteau gave his name to the Maritains, and on 1 August Sachs duly made his way to Meudon. There he was received with the customary courtesy and concern, and—remember he was not yet nineteen—felt himself "melt and become small and quite child-like" before Jacques's Christlike mien. Having arrived friendless and forlorn, he left feeling he had found nothing less than a Messiah, though whether that was Jesus or Jacques—or, for that matter, Oedipus or his true self—it would take him many years to decide. On the train back to Paris, he decided to be "REUNITED with humanity" in the form of "300 million Catholics," overwhelmed with joy at having at long last discovered an "oasis," a "warm inn," in which he could be at one with "the *eternal* father, the *virgin* mother and the son who had *sacrificed* himself for me."

As with Cocteau, the Maritains were anxious to expedite Sachs's entry into the Church and recommended him to another priest in their circle, the aptly named Père Pressoir ("Father wine-press"), director of the Carmelite seminary in Paris. After little more than a month of instruction, Sachs was baptized in the chapel at 10, rue du Parc on 29 August, having, according to his baptismal certificate, formally "renounced the errors of the Jews" and adopted the principle of *nulla salus extra ecclesiam* (no salvation outside the Church), with Jacques, Raïssa, and Cocteau (not present at the ceremony) acting as godparents. First communion and confirmation followed almost immediately: another triumph, if a minor one, for the celestial conversion machine, though not without Raïssa's confiding to her diary her disquiet concerning "something obscure" in the most recently acquired of her godsons.

Thus far, no harm, and possibly some good, had been done, and matters might have rested there had not Sachs, through a mixture of postconversion euphoria, guilt, pride, and a desire to emulate the holiness of the Maritains and Pressoir, decided that being an ordinary practicing Catholic was not enough and that he was being called to a higher religious vocation. With what seems a culpable lack of psychological, let alone spiritual, discernment, the Maritains, with Cocteau in support, encouraged Sachs to pursue his vocation, and on 2 January 1926 he entered the Carmelite house on the rue d'Assas in the sixth arrondissement.

For the first few weeks things went passably well, and Sachs was able to receive cigarettes and other creature comforts *ad libitum*. As a special concession elicited by Jacques, the neophyte was permitted to wear a cassock from the outset; reputedly, Sachs had one run up by Coco Chanel and delighted in hitching it up "like a young woman" as he went up the altar steps to take Holy Communion. But soon "the struggles between Jacob and the Angel" began with a vengeance, and all the hair shirts, spiked iron bracelets, and scourges in the seminary could not quell the clamorings of sexual desire. Each night's prayers swarmed with masturbatory fantasies, and the fantasies won; in July 1926, after Maritain's intervention, Sachs was granted leave of absence to go on holiday with his "grandmother." If Sachs's superiors thought that Mme Bizet would preserve her charge from temptation, they were grievously in error, for grandson and "grandmother" headed directly for Juan-les-Pins, then just establishing itself as an ultra-fashionable resort, where Sachs met and fell madly in love with an American teenager named Tom Pinkerton with whom, wearing a pink bathing suit under his cassock, he promenaded hand in hand on the beach.[76] Pinkerton's mother wrote a letter of protest to the bishop of Nice, sending Sachs back to Paris via Solesmes and a stay with Jacob at Saint-Benoît-sur-Loire;

to his very considerable relief, Père Pressoir refused to readmit him into the seminary, telling him that it would be much better for him to be a good Christian than a bad priest.

With desire and devotion vying within him, Sachs continued to practice (with Jacques's encouragement, though Raïssa seems to have suspended relations with him) until finally the conflict became too much for him to bear; in one of his last desperate letters to Jacques he describes how, on his knees at Benediction one evening, he was reduced to gnawing the chair in front of him "because the Blessed Sacrament sent me into a state of terrible rage. I think of God with FEAR and REVOLT." Then in November 1926 military service took him out of France, out of the Church, and out of the Maritains' life, pending further adventures, humiliations, and deceptions.

His end was predictably sordid. After playing the black market[77] and informing for the gestapo in occupied Paris, Sachs tried in desperation to preempt deportation by volunteering as a laborer in Germany. Working as a crane operator in Hamburg, he continued to spy and inform on fellow foreign workers until his arrest and imprisonment in November 1943 for black-market and other illicit activities. Though known to be Jewish, he managed to survive in prison for almost a year and a half, trading information on other prisoners for drugs, food, and writing materials. As the Allies advanced, the inmates were force-marched in the direction of Kiel, an ordeal that proved too much for Sachs; unable to continue, he was taken to one side and dispatched with a bullet in the back of his head. Hardly surprisingly, the Maritains were scandalized by *Le Sabbat* when it appeared posthumously in 1946, though, unaware of his fate, Raïssa wrote of him with sympathy in a letter of November 1947 to a French Canadian priest:

> Whatever evil he did, he never used false theories to disguise that evil as good, as many renowned and illustrious authors have done, but he always called evil by its name; and, if he did not have the strength truly to seek after the good, at least he aspired towards it, and certainly suffered at not being able to reach it. God alone can know the extent of his responsibility in the evil [he has done]; as for ourselves, knowing the heavy burden he inherited from his family—we do not judge him. May God have mercy on him, living or dead. And you, my most dear friend, do not refuse him your prayers.[78]

After 1926, the Maritains—or, more precisely, Jacques, for Raïssa's existence remained essentially inner-oriented—and their circle were increasingly drawn away from their primary philosophical and spiritual focus into public controversy amid the endless to-and-fro of manifesto and counter-manifesto, attack, response and counterresponse that made up French political-intellectual life during *l'entre-deux-guerres*. The papal condemnation of Action Française in December 1926, followed by the placing on the Index of the newspaper of the same name, divided the Meudon circle as it divided French Catholic opinion as a whole. Maritain (who, to repeat, had never been a member of the movement but had subscribed to its newspaper in deference to Father Clérissac) supported the papal interdiction, thus incurring the enmity of his long-term associate Henri Massis, infuriating Maurras himself who had paid occasional visits to Meudon, and prejudicing his growing friendship with Bernanos, not a member of the circle, whose first novel, *Sous le soleil de Satan* (1926), he had hailed as a breakthrough for Catholic literature.[79]

In the 1930s, unlike many French Catholic intellectuals, Maritain was notable for his early opposition to fascism and for his refusal to take the "Holy War" line on the Spanish civil war that was espoused, among others, by Fathers Henrion and Garrigou-Lagrange, "that sacred monster of Thomism," as Mauriac later described him.[80] Along with Mauriac, Emmanuel Mounier, Gabriel Marcel, and various other "left Catholics," Maritain signed the protest "Pour le peuple basque" against the bombing of Guernica that was published in *La Croix* in May 1937. He was stung by Claudel's disgraceful poem "Aux martyrs espagnols" ("eleven bishops, sixteen thousand priests massacred, and not a single apostasy") of June 1937 into denouncing, in an article in *La nouvelle Revue Française* entitled "De la guerre sainte" (1 July 1937), the whole idea, so widespread among Catholics in France and elsewhere, that the Nationalist cause was some kind of "White Crusade" against the combined evils of socialism, atheism, and democracy.[81]

Associated nationally and internationally with Mauriac and Bernanos (see chapter 3) as Catholic supporters of Republican Spain, Maritain found himself denounced as a "Judio convertido" by Luis Serrano Suñer, interior minister in the provisional Nationalist government in Salamanca, and fell victim to a right-wing whispering campaign regarding the alleged influence on him of the two "Russian Jewesses," Raïssa and Véra, with whom he shared the house at Meudon.[82] The whispers became howls of anger and hate the following year when, in a series of articles and speeches, Maritain, bravely declaring himself to be "semitic" by marriage, association, and intellectual heritage, publicly aligned himself with the plight of Jewish people in Germany and elsewhere, to the predictable fury of professional Jewbaiters like Lucien Rebatet of *Je suis partout*:

> M. Jacques Maritain is married to a Jewess. He has judaized [*enjuivé*] his life and his doctrine, his theology, his dialectic, are as forged as a Jewish spy's passport. M. Maritain represents, body and soul, what the Germans so rightly call a *Rassenschander,* a polluter of the race.[83]

With many former allies (notably Garrigou-Lagrange) speaking and conspiring against them[84] and alarmed and despondent at the rising tide of antisemitism in France,[85] Jacques, Raïssa, and Véra were glad to escape to the United States for an academic visit in October 1938.

Back in France by early 1939, the Maritains let 10, rue du Parc to their friend Olivier Lacombe (it would be requisitioned during the Occupation, and they would never live there again) and spent the summer and early weeks of the war at various locations in the provinces, including Kolbsheim in the Alsace at the home of Antoinette and Lexi Grunelius where the Centre Jacques et Raïssa Maritain is now located and where Jacques and Raïssa are both buried. Invited on a further academic visit to the United States, Jacques, Raïssa, and Véra sailed from Marseille on 4 January 1940: It was not planned as a long-term exile but that, in effect, is what it became, and, after four years in New York and Princeton (1940–44) followed by three years in Rome (1945–48) where Jacques was appointed French ambassador to the Vatican by De Gaulle, the Maritains would never again enjoy the influence in France that was theirs during *l'entre-deux-guerres*. With existentialism in the ascendant in France, Jacques kept neo-Thomism alive from across the Atlantic where the trio spent most of the following decade.

Véra died at Princeton in December 1959, and Raïssa the following November at the Grunelius's Paris apartment on the rue de Varenne where, thirty years after their estrangement, Cocteau came to pray for her soul on the night of her death.[86] Shortly afterward, fulfilling a long-held desire, Jacques withdrew to the community of the Petits Frères de Jésus in Toulouse, writing his best-selling critique of post–Vatican II developments in the Church *Le Paysan de la Garonne* (1966) and visiting Kolbsheim annually to meditate at his wife's grave, until his own death in 1973.

If we thus skim over the outward events of the Maritains' last three decades, it is not because they lack interest, honor, or importance but because our concern lies elsewhere: in Raïssa's journal, edited and published by Jacques after her death, first in a small private edition in 1962 and then, to universal acclaim, by Descleé de Brouwer the following year. In his preface to the work, Brother René Voillaume, founder of the order of the Petits Frères de Jésus, likens Raïssa's spiritual experience to that of Thérèse and implicitly places her journal alongside *Histoire d'une âme* as a spiritual "classic."[87] How far is either of these comparisons justified?

Raïssa's Journal

Raïssa began keeping a diary—or, rather, a regular record of her spiritual reflections, interspersed with brief references to her day-to-day life—in 1914, and continued to do so throughout her life, though after 1939 the entries become increasingly irregular; only between 1915 and 1926 and again between 1931 and 1939 does the journal have any kind of continuity and coherence. Jacques knew of the diary's existence—indeed it was he who first suggested to Raïssa that she keep it—but had no idea, until after her death, of what it contained. It is, by definition, not a systematic exposition of her experiences and ideas, nor a work of testimony written for others, like *Histoire d'une âme;* still less is it any kind of devotional manual. It is intensely private, self-effacing, and austere, with none of the emotional effusiveness that marks—and, for many readers, disfigures—Thérèse's autobiographical writings, but little, either, of the sense of a rejoicing, suffering human presence that makes reading the latter so memorable. However intensely Raïssa may have experienced the divine presence, she does not communicate this in her journal but in her poetry—sparse, sharp-edged, and intense as her person itself—and the sense of a personal bond between spiritual bride and divine bridegroom, the core of most comparable writings by women, is largely absent from its pages. Yet Raïssa's starting point, or rather the spiritual principle she reached after long hours of daily meditation and prayer, is, like that of Thérèse, God's ineffable love for his creatures that leads him to take on their human nature as Christ, "in such a way that everything which partakes of that nature, suffering, pity, compassion, hope . . . , all those things became so to speak attributes of God."[88] Thus, for Raïssa as for Thérèse, it is always god who initiates and man who responds, both on the collective and the individual level:

> The Word [*le Verbe*], like a giant, has spanned [*franchi*] the infinite distance from God to the creature. . . . Henceforth nothing can stop the Savior's love for us. He has spanned the infinite in order to take on a flesh similar to ours. (1916, 30)

> I await for everything on God. For from me to Him it seems that all the bridges are broken. But not from Him to me. (Saint-Benoît-sur-Loire 1924, 147)

Raïssa's God, like Thérèse's, is Love before all else. He can "never present Himself as an enemy" (1958–59[?], 369) and, in all his dealings with humanity, his love always transcends and supersedes his justice: "Love is incapable of judging" (1934, 226); "The law is not god. God is not the law.—He is Love" (1958–59[?], 369). Thus far we are entirely within the spiritual universe of *Histoire d'une âme.*

But while Thérèse's "Papa le bon Dieu" is almost embarrassingly human, with a doting father's predilection for spoiling and pampering his children, Raïssa's is much more remote and forbidding, and his love often runs contrary to mere human conceptions of care, concern, and compassion: "The goodness of God is not like human goodness" (1960, 30–39). A *deus excelsus terribilis* (the title of Raïssa's poem of 1943 on the suffering and abandonment of European Jewry),[89] he rarely presents himself with maternal attributes and feelings,[90] and seems, if not to will, then at least to expect, that those whom he loves will suffer; Raïssa was fond of quoting God's words to Blessed Angela of Foligno, "It is not in order to laugh that I loved you" (1917[?], 206), and took as her motto Mélanie's belief that "He wounds in order to heal" (1915, 23).

Owing her conversion to Bloy, it is probably inevitable, and certainly understandable, that she should have taken over his ideas on sacrifice if not on vicarious suffering. Though Raïssa believes herself to be "a victim accepted by God" (1917, 50) and believes sacrifice to be "the absolutely general law of perfecting the creature" in that "everything that passes from an inferior to a superior nature must pass through self-sacrifice, mortification, death" (1917, 55), she does not, except at times of acute *public* crisis (as in 1939), offer herself up as a *substitute* for others in order to ransom by her own sufferings the sins of the world; her general position is rather that "sacrifice is not essentially expiation, but testimony, homage. 'Except a corn of wheat'" (1917, 53) [fall into the ground and die, it abideth alone: but if it die, it bringeth forth much fruit]. But to bear witness and to be a martyr are, etymologically, one and the same, and a Christian must consent to "the total immolation of oneself" (1918, 73) in order that God's love may be made manifest through him or her. Because "the whole created world has been rendered bitter by sin" (1918, 65), it follows that "the fulfillment [*l'épanouissement*] of nature is contrary to the life of grace, in the state of nature as fallen [*dans l'état de nature déchue*]" (1931(?), 209). "Nature," and above all "human nature," and in that nature the body above all, must be offered up to God for cleansing, refashioning, and, if necessary, for mortification: "Can there be a mystical life without death? An essential question. 'Except a corn of wheat fall into the ground and die.' [*Si le grain ne meurt*]" (ibid.).

Thus it is that, if Thérèse's Christology focuses on the childhood of her Savior and on his face *after* his death, Raïssa's dwells on the horrors of the Passion itself, with which she feels called on to identify. "Bound like a victim laid out [*disposée*] for sacrifice" (1940, 269), she relives Christ's abandonment on the Cross.

> God my God the distance between us is not
>   endurable,
> Show me the path, straight and bare and boundlessly
>   true,
> From my soul to Your spirit—without the screen
> Of anything men have raised between earth and heaven.
>   "DE PROFUNDIS" (*LETTRE DE NUIT* [1939])[91]

God "wills all our agonies [*déchirements*]" (1918, 32), and his saints must "do more than accept suffering—they ask it of God for the love of God and the salvation of souls" (1959[?], 308).

Like Bloy, Huysmans, and Claudel—indeed like virtually all French Catholic writers of our period—she returned continually to the idea, derived from Colossians 1:24, that Christians must "make up" or "complete" "what is lacking in the sufferings of Christ" (*adimpleo quae desunt passionum Christi*) now that he, ascended into heaven, is no longer able to suffer himself (1934, 228). Those whom God chooses he first allows to experience his gentleness and then, "once assured of their faithfulness—and it is He himself who assures it—He spares their hearts no suffering. He does not make them live like people restored to life [*comme des ressuscités*], but like the dying and martyrs. . . . These poor souls who have married Him in faith thus enter into the mystery of Redemption. And then they see that there is no reason to their martyrdom except that it completes what is lacking in the Passion of Christ [*ce qui manque à la Passion du Christ*]" (1925, 172–73). Suffering both *with* Christ and *instead of* Christ, Christians must "add [their] small change [*petite monnaie*] to the golden river of the Passion of Christ in order to repair the injury [*le mal*] done to the divine substance itself by sin" (1922, 117–18) and, by a "supplement of meritorious suffering" (1947, 291), bring the work of reparation to completion. Given their shared indebtedness to Bloy, it is hardly surprising that Jacques should have stressed "the implacably *sacrificial* manner in which God treated [Raïssa] in her final illness": "And during all this time she was implacably destroyed, as though blow by blow with an axe, by this God who loved her in His terrible fashion and whose is only 'gentle' in the eyes of the saints or of those who do not know what they say."[92]

It is within the context of this reparationist theology that we must examine the place of illness in Raïssa's life. In the summer of 1904, a few months before her marriage (and a good year before her conversion), Raïssa almost died when, on holiday in the country, she had to be operated on by the light of a paraffin lamp held by Jacques for a pharyngeal blockage, whereafter, she says, her health was never again to be other than precarious.[93]

Illness became a recurring feature of her life, with particularly serious crises in 1905, 1906, 1908, 1921–22, 1932 (a cure at Bagnoles de l'Orne after the death of her mother), and, above all, 1934–35; this last was accompanied by a major spiritual crisis, the onset of which is linked by Raïssa herself to the fascist riots of 6 February 1934 in the center of Paris, followed by the retaliatory general strike called for 12 February (214, 218–19). The possibility of all, or most, of these illnesses being partly psychological in character can neither be proved nor dismissed. What is certain, however, is, in the words of Judith D. Suther, the "symbiosis between intense *recueillement* and physical suffering" throughout Raïssa's life: "Health was not a state of well-being which she sought or enjoyed. It was a relative condition of the flesh, contingent and precarious like all other fleshly attributes, and to lose it, especially to relinquish it voluntarily, was to approach God."[94] When asked by Bloy in 1906 why she was ill, Raïssa replied that it was "because illness is salutary for me,"[95] not least because it enabled her to withdraw from "the world" and focus her attention within:

All my attraction is towards the interior. What I do on the exterior is now contrary to my innermost life. I am only really in repose, at peace, spiritually active, when I am alone, at prayer. Everything else does me injury [*me fait violence*]. Makes me live on the surface of myself—whereas I am drawn inwards—in a kind of insincerity since I seem to be interested in things that do not truly interest me. All that wearies me and brings me nothing in compensation for my effort. (1924, 151–52)

Most visitors to Meudon were struck by—and photographs confirm—her extraordinary physical frailness. There is no clear evidence of anorexia, though it is noteworthy that, after her serious illness of 1908, she adopted a diet "reduced more or less to rice and water and dubious vegetarian products. An absurd diet, without doubt, in which vitamins played little part, but which I long found marvelous because it reduced the suffering to a minimum, made me as light in my body as in my spirit, and enabled me to read and pray as I would."[96] When Raïssa speaks of food, it is less of eating than of being eaten by God: "We are the food of God. Utterly terrible to be assimilated by Him." Feeding God with the whole of her being ("it is my substance that I must offer up to God, so that he may transform it" [1934, 225]), she becomes "assimilated by Him into Himself," her whole life an agony of *morir sin morir*: "Generous souls die quickly. But I never finish dying. One thinks one is dead, and suddenly one is reborn so to speak completely. Then the labor [*le travail*] starts over again. God directs his purifying flame into all the corners of the heart, for He takes care of me" (1934, 229–30).

All this is so like a widespread image of Thérèse—essentially the Thérèse of her last eighteen months—that it is easy to mistake the differences. Thérèse never sought to isolate herself from others—even in her last illness she spoke (and laughed) volubly with her carers—and always found meditative prayer (*oraison*), Raïssa's forte, beyond her powers of concentration. Her spiritual life was a *game* not, as it was for Raïssa, a lifelong wrestling match with the angel in which defeat and physical suffering are proof of God's love for his creature: "The sign of God's triumph is in Jacob's limp. And Jacob won over God by letting himself be mortified in the flesh" (1934, 225). While Thérèse's "Papa le Bon Dieu" is almost identical with her father, Raïssa's God is altogether more remote and austere than either Ilia Oumansov—of whom her first memory was seeing him in tears outside the room in which his wife was giving birth to Véra—or her beloved maternal grandfather "Dedushka"; it is as though, somehow dissatisfied with her kind, but weak, father, she sought an altogether more demanding taskmaster. In a way reminiscent of Thérèse, she treats her father with "an almost maternal compassion," and, up to the age of eleven, played at being the little boy "Pifo" with Véra, her younger, but stronger, sister in the role of his/her mother "Mimo";[97] all her life, Véra would effectively "mother" her. But, once in France, and at school, any such playfulness seems to have left her: The overwhelming quality of Raïssa is her *seriousness*.

There is a revealing incident related in *Les Grandes Amitiés* in which the twelve- or thirteen-year-old Raïssa is left in charge of her classmates. Onto the blackboard go, in one column, the names of all the girls who are naughty and, in the other, the names of those who are good. Result: a whole classroom of *dissipées,* and just one solitary *sage,* Raïssa Oumansov herself.[98] In her pursuit of a much higher form of *sagesse,* she similarly distanced herself from her fellows. Her way is anything but "little": It is harsh and heroic, and above all it is not for the many but for the few.

Thérèse democratizes holiness; Raïssa restricts it to an elite. An authoritarian by nature or formation, she sought and needed an authoritarian God, just as Jacques, in reaction against the defection of his father, seems to have sought structure and order in the hierarchies of neo-Thomist philosophy. Powerful father-figures dominated their joint lives—Bloy, Clérissac, Aquinas, Garrigou-Lagrange, the successive popes whose authority they never once questioned—and they, in their turn, had a powerful appeal for disciples who both needed, and feared, a strong patriarchal framework for their lives: Cocteau, whose father committed suicide when he was eight;[99] Sachs, who seems never to have known the mysterious Ettinghausen who fathered him.

The Maritains' spirituality was that of La Salette, not Lourdes; their model was Mélanie rather than Thérèse. Where Thérèse almost completely escaped the sacrificial paradigm of relations with God, the Maritains—and Raïssa in particular—put it at the very center of their thought and existence: blood and tears, not smiles, were the currency in which she conducted her transactions with God. Her closest spiritual sister is not Thérèse but Simone Weil or even Colette Peignot whose life and death both resemble and invert her own (just as Bataille's *Somme athéologique* subverts Jacques Maritain's beloved *Summa theologica*), so that even the place of Colette's birth—none other than Meudon—establishes a bizarre kinship between her and Raïssa.

5

FASTING, BLEEDING, SEEING

"Extraordinary Phenomena" in France
C. 1870–C. 1950

For many nineteenth- and early twentieth-century French Catholic priests, particularly those in the country, the church had no greater enemies than drinking and dancing. Often situated, almost defiantly, immediately opposite the local church, *cabaret* and *bal public*—the former commonly doubling as the latter—together represented nothing less than "the temple of the enemy," indeed of *the* Enemy himself, where red wine all too often meant red politics as well as Sunday afternoon rowdiness. As far as priests were concerned, dancing, especially those scandalous modern dances like the waltz and the polka where couples actually *held* each other, led, in inevitable concatenation, from flirting to fornication, to extramarital pregnancy or, still worse, to the use of one or another form of contraception (usually what was known as "dry copulation" or withdrawal), which in turn meant parishioners, especially women, not making confession and thus debarring themselves from communion, a further step in the seemingly irreversible process of nationwide dechristianization. The saintly Father Jean-Marie Vianney (1786–1859), curé of the village of Ars just north of Lyon, was celebrated for having successfully banned dancing from his parish, and the curé of Châteauneuf-de-Galaure, a medium-sized village in the department of the Drôme just to the south, was only following solid ecclesiastical practice when, in the early 1900s, he refused to give confession to girls known to have gone dancing: *Je ne confesse pas les danseuses!*

Marthe Robin (1902–81)

For all this, the young Marthe Robin loved, as she later put it, to "turn," and not just at old-fashioned peasant dances like the *rigodon* and the *saut-de-lapin* but to imports from the city like the polka and mazurka, and a kind of waltz known as *la grimacière*.[1] True, she kept her dancing to evenings with relatives and neighbors in the tiny hamlet of Moïlles a couple of miles to the north of Châteauneuf itself, a cluster of buildings on a bleak plateau high above the valley on the Galaure, where her patois-speaking father Joseph Robin (1860–1936), his cousin Ferdinand, and another family, the Achards, had their farms, and, obedient in everything, shunned the public establishments in the French-speaking village below. Neither her father nor her mother Amélie (1865–1940) were especially devout; indeed Joseph liked occasionally to voice antireligious opinions, though a local rhymester insisted that, beneath his *libre penseur* exterior, he was a *clérical* at heart. Marthe herself went to the state primary school in the village, the local Catholic school having been forced to close through inadequate numbers of pupils, a sure sign, like the high rate of civil marriages and funerals, that Châteauneuf, like the whole of the Drôme, was not exactly a hotbed of religious enthusiasm.

Marthe was the youngest of six children (five girls, one boy), and there is some circumstantial evidence that Joseph Robin was embittered when his wife gave birth to yet another girl-child. When Marthe was still not yet two, Clémence (1898–1903), the sister closest to her in age, died of typhoid, almost certainly as a result of drinking polluted water from the farm well; Marthe herself was also infected but appeared to make a complete recovery, though her elder sister Alice (1894–1977), also struck down by the disease, would subsequently always walk with a limp. The family was close, but not incestuously so, unlike the Martins of Alençon and Lisieux, and two of Marthe's surviving sisters would marry in due course, leaving only her grouchy elder brother Henri (1896–1951) to run the farm with his father.

Marthe's childhood and early adolescence were unremarkable—first communion at age ten in 1912, followed by solemn communion two years later in May 1914—though it was noticed that she took communion more frequently than was the practice at the time, and, after she left school in 1916, was often seen telling her rosary beads and reciting the *Ave* while she tended the family's cows and goats out on the high plain above Châteauneuf. Everything about Marthe Robin was *ordinary* and, indeed, everything about her would remain ordinary—whence, in part, her remarkable impact on virtually everyone who subsequently came to know and revere her—even when her life began to take its extraordinary turn in the summer of 1918.

In May of that year Henri Robin was belatedly conscripted into the French army, but there are no grounds for supposing that his departure had any bearing on the illness that struck his younger sister the following August.[2] That the illness was both serious and mysterious is, however, beyond doubt. Over the following months Marthe was subject to ever more agonizing headaches, would frequently vomit and faint, and on 11 November, the day the armistice was signed, collapsed in the farm's kitchen, arousing fears of epilepsy. Further falls occurred on the 25 and 27 of that month, and on 2 December 1918, both legs now completely paralyzed, she was confined to bed in a comatose state that led to extreme unction being administered by the local priest, the aptly named Abbé Payre. By January 1919 Marthe returned to full consciousness, but her appetite and thirst had disappeared almost completely, and the paralysis now extended to her right hand as well as both legs. Extreme unction was again administered in late March 1921, but the following May, after (or so she told her sister Alice) the Virgin Mary had appeared to her in her sleep, she was able to get up, sit in an armchair, embroider, and move around the farmhouse on crutches. Her condition apparently improving, she went on pilgrimages to local Marian shrines in August and September, and on 11 November 1921 was even able to walk down to the village to attend mass.

In the spring of 1922, while staying at the home of her elder sister Gabrielle (1892–1967) who, having borne the illegitimate child of a man killed at Verdun, now lived with her late partner's family, Marthe discovered an antiquated devotional work of which, as she leafed through it, two sentences struck her with particular force: "Why are you looking for happiness, since you are born for suffering?" and "It is necessary to give God everything." With the words "for you it will be suffering" (*pour toi, ce sera la souffrance*) haunting her like some message from beyond,[3] Martha began to experience renewed problems with her legs, which a stay at the nearby spa town of Saint-Péray failed to allay, though she could still—at the age of twenty-one—get around with a walking stick. By 1925 Marthe was eating next to nothing and drinking only the occasional thimbleful of heavily sugared black coffee. Scheduled to join the diocesan pilgrimage to Lourdes, she was asked—and agreed—to cede her place to someone more seriously ill even than herself, and thus for the first time willingly accepted to assume greater suffering for the sake of another: the doctrine of mystical substitution in operation yet again.

Despite deteriorating eyesight, Marthe had been reading some of the "classics" of the mystical life—the *Life* of Saint Teresa of Avila, the *Histoire d'une âme* by her French epigone (canonized on 17 May 1925)—and showed a particular interest in the well-known *Secret de Marie* by Louis-Marie Grignion de Montfort (1673–1716, canonized 1947) whose blend of apocalyptic Marianism reached into every corner of nineteenth- and early twentieth-century French Catholic devotion; it is also possible that she had also heard by now of the "case" of the Bavarian-born stigmatic Therese Neumann (1898–1962) whose condition—paralysis as a result of spinal and head injuries, coupled with allegedly total abstention from food and drink—presented such striking similarities with her own.[4]

This reading is reflected in the first of her "Acts of self-abandonment to the love and will of God" (*Acte d'abandon à l'amour et à la volonté de Dieu*), her version of the traditional "marriage contract" between the bride of Christ and her spouse, written over some months and dated 15 October 1925, the day, not coincidentally, of the feast of Saint Teresa of Avila. Its devotion lies firmly within the double Theresian tradition—Spanish Teresa and French Teresita—differing from the latter only in its emphasis (which, as we saw in chapter 2, Thérèse herself had largely transcended) on self-offering as a "victim for the salvation of souls."

Two years later, a second *Acte d'abandon* was drafted (but still dated 15 October 1925), which recapitulated the main terms of the earlier "contract," while going much further in the direction of total self-abnegation and identification with Jesus: "No more me. . . . No more mine [*plus de mien*]. . . . No more anything [*plus de rien*]. . . . You alone, O my Jesus. . . . Let me say in all truth: My self is Jesus [*mon moi c'est Jésus*], His will, His spirit, infinite Love."[5] By the time of the second "act," Marthe's condition had deteriorated still further, its cycles now strikingly correlated with the calendar of the church, so that a three-week coma in 1926 in the course of which Marthe claimed to have had three visions of the Petite Fleur of Lisieux—"Marthe Robin," it has been suggested, is close to being an anagram of "Thérèse Martin"[6]—began on the first-ever feast day assigned to the newly canonized saint (3 October 1926); when, the following year, Thérèse's "day" was shifted to 1 October, another coma and vision duly ensued. In 1928 Marthe ceased eating even the occasional sweet and gave up her daily thimbleful of coffee (while continuing to pine for its taste), and from that time until her death fifty-three years later is said—and the claim has never been seriously disputed, even by the most skeptical observers[7]—to have consumed nothing except the weekly communion wafer she received which, rather than being swallowed, appeared to dissolve in her mouth. Her intake of liquids was reduced to having her lips and tongue occasionally moistened with a damp cloth, a further consequence being, of course, that she ceased urinating and excreting almost entirely.

In 1928, her legs by now totally and definitively paralyzed, she stopped sleeping (the medical condition known as agrypnia, or total loss of sleep, as opposed to insomnia), and the following year she also lost the use of both hands, her utterances being henceforth transcribed by a succession of "secretaries"; the removal from her finger of the thimble she used for embroidering symbolized the final surrender of the bride's very limited autonomy to her spouse. Even the slightest touch caused her appalling pain, making the changing of her bed linen and nightdress a truly crucifying experience, and she also developed an acute phobia of light. Her world had never extended beyond a few miles from the farmhouse at Moilles. For the next fifty years it would be confined to a single darkened room in which she crouched rather than lay, her paralyzed legs drawn up before her, her back supported by pillows, on a specially constructed divan perhaps five feet in length, with wheels enabling it to be shifted when the room required cleaning. This was the *camera oscura* in which, as close to a human zero as can be imagined,

Marthe Robin would embark on her extraordinary "career" as spiritual counselor, founder of a worldwide lay order of contemplation and charitable works, and, most famously and controversially, bearer of the marks, and weekly reliver, of the Passion of her human-divine spouse.

The bleeding itself—Marthe was always reluctant to speak of stigmatization—appears to have begun in the autumn of 1930. In November 1928 she had been received into the tertiary order of Saint Francis by a visiting Franciscan friar, Brother Marie-Bernard, who, in August 1930, also conducted the rite of the Consecration of Virgins whereby virgins (both male and female) undertake to "follow the Lamb whithersoever he goeth" (Revelations 14:4)—in other words, if necessary, "even unto the Cross." Shortly afterward, Marthe had a vision of Jesus himself, asking her, "Do you wish to be like me?" to which she replied with the *Fiat* of Mary at the Annunciation ("Be it unto me according to thy word," Luke 1:38): "My I is You [*Mon moi, c'est Toi*]. May my life be a perfect and unending reproduction of your life."[8]

At the beginning of October she began to bleed from her hands and feet, from her left side, and finally from her forehead, and embarked on the extraordinary seven-day cycle that she would continue for the rest of her life.[9] Anguish and a feeling of abandonment beginning around 9 P.M. on Thursday evening (corresponding to the Agony in the Garden, when Jesus begs his heavenly Father to "remove this cup from me" and his sweat is "as it were great drops of blood falling down to the ground" [Luke 22:42–45]), bleeding from all of her "wounds" on the morning and early afternoon of "Good Friday," until, around 3 P.M., the traditional hour of Christ's death, she would utter the terrible words, "*Eli, Eli, lama sabachthani?* That is to say, My God, my God, why hast thou forsaken me?" (Matthew 27:46) and, her head falling to one side, fall into a trance or coma that would continue throughout Saturday (the day, traditionally, of the "harrowing of hell" when Christ descends into hell and releases the souls of the "pagans" imprisoned therein) until, on Sunday morning, she would be "resurrected" into full consciousness at a word from the local priest—at first, the Abbé Faure, then the Abbé Georges Finet (see below)—who throughout her "passion" sat at her bedside.

This weekly replication of the Easter triduum always took place in private, with none but the priest (and occasional privileged witness) in attendance, pointing to one fundamental difference, among many, between the hidden Calvary of the stigmatic and the essentially public, indeed theatrical, trance of the "hysteria" (see below). According to Marthe, Jesus told her that "it is you I have chosen to live my passion most fully, after my mother. No one after you will live it as totally."[10] Each week, she said, she, like her spouse, "became sin" in order to take on and take away the sins of the world, reliving Christ's redemptive experience of utter abandonment, even outright rejection, by God in order to "buy back" or "ransom" his flock through the coin of her vicarious suffering. "Don't come near me," she once enjoined the Abbé Finet during her weekly agony, "I would make you dirty and unclean" (Je vous salirais! N'approchez pas de moi).[11]

The difference between the Marthe of Thursday night through Sunday morning and the Marthe of Monday, Tuesday, and Wednesday could not have been greater. Fully conscious, alert, witty, down-to-earth, intelligent, and practical, she received a virtually uninterrupted succession of visitors— up to sixty per day by the 1950s, each in principle allocated ten minutes by her attendants and "secretaries"—to whose questions, doubts, problems, and fears she responded with what appears, from the many accounts that exist, to be truly extraordinary discernment, humor (occasionally sharp-edged), concern, and, above all, patience, irrespective of the social or spiritual status of the individual in question.

To enter Marthe's dimly lit room was, for many, like entering a kind of Catholicized oracle of Delphi where, from out of the darkness, a "young girl's voice" would address them intimately and, it seemed, with an instantaneous understanding not only of their present problem but of the whole of their life history.[12] Gradually they became conscious of the outlines, then of the features of the "diaphanous being" hunched on her divan like the Pythia on her tripod, but speaking not of the future in a visionary trance, but of the problems of the here and now in the homely tones of the peasant woman she remained. In addition, she kept up a massive correspondence via dictation, giving particular attention to the many letters she received from men and women in prison, most notably the condemned murderer Jacques Fesch whose conversion, prior to his execution in 1957 at the age of twenty-seven, has recently made him a candidate for beatification; the last cigarette smoked by another celebrated murderer Roger Bontemps (executed 1972) was reputedly from a packet sent him by Marthe.[13]

Marthe's theology was as simple as her life and largely continues the double Theresian tradition: God's love is unconditional, is not to be won by "good works" or forfeited by sin, and seeks out and sustains even those who are indifferent, even hostile, to the Christian faith. To one nonbeliever searching for mental and spiritual peace, she said, "You would not seek him if He had already found you," a striking parallel to (and, theologically, a crucial reversal of) the celebrated "You would not seek me if you had not already found me" of Pascal's *Penseés,* which she may not even have read:[14] For Marthe, as for Thérèse, the initiative comes always from God. Another striking utterance, made toward the end of her life to the Catholic philosopher Jean Guitton (1901–99), went as follows: "People have often said to me that one cannot see God without dying. But with Jesus one sees God and one does not die. One sees God and one lives."[15] To all who approached her, she gave the reassuring message of the unconditionality of God's love, told them, in effect, to follow the Augustinian precept of "love and do what thou wilt" (*ama et quod vis fac*) and promised to include the "consultant" in her prayers, assuming his or her sufferings into her own. She did not predict the future, nor did she heal. Her body pared down to the absolute minimum, she was essentially a voice, not a *vox clamans in deserto,* but a voice speaking quietly and clearly in a darkened bedroom in a peasant farmhouse in the center of France. It is not difficult to imagine the impact she had on the five thousand or more people who, by the 1950s, were coming to see her each year.

In early 1936, Marthe having asked one of her visitors to send her a picture of Marie Médiatrice, a priest from Lyon known to the visitor was requested to take the picture to Moïlles, simply because he happened to be going that way. The priest was the thirty-eight-year-old Georges Finet (1898–1990) who, once having met Marthe by accident, would henceforth be her inseparable associate—not for nothing, perhaps, was his recently deceased godmother named Marthe—until her death and beyond, listening to and transcribing her utterances, assisting her at her weekly "passion," exercising a large measure of control of who could and could not witness it, and, above all, putting into practice Marthe's plan for a network of so-called Foyers de Charité, the first of which was opened in Châteauneuf itself, on the site of a former dance hall, which had already been converted, at Marthe's instigation, into a Catholic primary school in 1934. Finet conducted the first retreat there in September 1936—some mysterious bangs and other unexplained occurrences were countered by having the premises exorcised by Monseigneur Pic, archbishop of Valence—and a new five-story building constructed on the site, financed by private donations, between 1940 and 1947. In 1941 a second Foyer, devoted like the original center to silent retreats for laypersons and charitable works, was opened by a follower at La-Léchère-les-Bains in the Savoie, since when about eighty Foyers have been founded worldwide, from Martinique and Haiti to Burkina Fasso, Madagascar and Mauritius, from Canada to India, with around fifteen Foyers in France itself.

At the time of their first meeting, Marthe—we have only Finet's account for this—claimed to have already met the priest in November 1930 when a landslide on the celebrated hill-shrine of Fourvière in Finet's then parish in Lyon had killed many local residents, including nineteen firemen sent to rescue them, and would have engulfed Finet himself had not Marthe, as she claimed (and as Finet instantly believed), been praying and suffering on his behalf at exactly that time: a rare case (if one accords the much-retold tale any credence) of what might be called proleptic vicarious suffering, the mystical substitution of self for some as yet unknown beneficiary whom the inscrutable workings of providence will at some point bring into one's life.[16] For Finet, Marthe's anticipatory prayers proved her possession of the rare charismatic gift known as *bilocation,* the ability to be, spiritually if not materially, in two places at once, as though whisked on some angelic magic-carpet from one location to another. It was as though Marthe's body, reduced to the uttermost minimum, had already on this earth become the *corpus subtile* of an angel, able to pass through physical obstacles at will, the gracile, weightless body, *spiritualized matter,* of those resurrected into glory. That, finally, Marthe could pray for him without knowing him was, for Finet, absolute proof of the veracity of the key ultramontanist doctrines of reversiblity and the communion of saints. Mystical substitution must work, or else he, Finet, would be dead.

Finet had been trained at the French seminary in Rome by Father Henri Le Floch (1862–1950), a famed ultratraditionalist and adherent of Action Française who was forced to abandon his post when that organization was condemned by the Vatican in 1926. Marthe undoubtedly shared many of the moral, social, and political preoccupations of the ultra-Catholic right, without being "political" herself, in contrast to several of the mystical stigmatics and anorexics discussed later in this chapter. She condemned Freemasonry and the "atheism" of socialists and communists and was sympathetic, as were almost all French Catholics at the time, to Pétain in the early years of the Occupation, though not to Laval whom she roundly condemned. It is certainly true that she had a following amongst ultratraditionalist priests, including the redoubtable Father Réginald Garrigou-Lagrange whom we have already met through the Maritain circle, but nothing suggests that she and her "message" have been recuperated by the far right, as clearly happened with Mélanie Calvat and a number of the women discussed below.

She may, however, have had some indirect link with a curious occurrence in the autumn of 1943, when, following an alleged Marian apparition in the village of Montmeyran some twenty-five miles south of Châteauneuf, a priest named Michel Collin (1905–74), a refugee from the east of France then based at the Eglise des Recollets in the town of Romans-sur-Isère, approximately midway between the two villages, launched a so-called crusade centered around the figure of a mysterious "chevalier blanc" rumored to be a prince of the old Valois lineage, whose mission, it was said, was to rid France of the German invader. Though there exist photographs of the "chevalier blanc" mounted on horseback and flanked by men wearing crusader-style surplices over their everyday clothes, he has never been identified, and it is just possible that he was the Frère Marie-Bernard who had received Marthe into the tertiary order of Saint Francis in 1928; Collin, calling himself the "Priest of Infinite Love" (*Prêtre de l'Amour infini*) certainly knew Marie-Bernard who was also said to be a scion of the Valois family, and both knew the shadowy Dutch priest, Father Lodsqui, another refugee in Romans, who is responsible for the crude frescoes depicting the chevalier blanc in the chapel of Les Balmes just outside town. Since the files of both the local Vichyist police and the diocese have apparently been "lost," the chevalier and his "crusade" remain as mysterious as ever. Proclaiming himself "Pope Clement XV," Collin later founded his own church and appeared in cassock and cape before a Parisian court some time in the 1960s, charged with evasion of taxes and other financial malpractices; there are reports of the "chevalier blanc" later driving a taxi in Rome. Collin and his "crusade" were condemned as early as September 1943 by Monseigneur Pic of Valence who judged them to be a "dangerous mixture of ostentatious piety and strange political dreams," and it is unlikely that Marthe, who was nothing if not obedient, would have had any truck with something so plainly aberrant.[17] The whole affair—to the extent that it can be known—points to the tenacity of ultra-Catholic royalist chiliasm, even in a department as notoriously dechristianized as the Drôme.

The theory and practice of mystical substitution was, quite literally, the crux of everything Marthe believed in. Running against the emerging current of Catholic humanism, she explicitly placed Christ crucified above Christ in his glory[18] and held that to believe in "the rights of man to happiness" constituted some kind of "blasphemy against suffering [*l'épreuve*]" which, for her, as for the whole ultra-Catholic tradition, was the spiritual stimulus par excellence.[19] She was bitterly opposed to abortion, which, however, she managed to fit into her all-inclusive theology of reversibility by holding, according to Jean Guitton, that "children killed in their mothers' womb (*sein*) prayed to God in the hereafter for their mothers' salvation. For her, the children were in a position similar to her own; that of the innocent, but for that reason alone, redemptive victim. This was the heart of her doctrine: the solidarity of all consciences, the communion of the pure and impure, the final union of the executioners (*bourreaux*) and the victims."[20]

She may even have been an unwitting *bourreau* herself, for in August 1951, her brother Henri—apparently driven to distraction by the never-ending queues of "consultants" at the farmhouse—blew his brains out with his hunting gun. Though orthodox Catholicism held suicide to be among the sins "for which there is no forgiveness," Marthe *knew,* she said, that Henri had been saved,[21] just as she *knew* that her mother (who died in November 1940 lying at the side of her youngest daughter as she underwent her weekly ordeal) had gone directly to heaven, Marthe having performed her purgatorial penance in her stead.[22] From the mid-1930s onward, she (and Finet) were more and more preoccupied with supposed diabolic incursions that they held responsible, in particular, for Marthe's frequent falls off her divan; it was after one such fall, on 6 February 1981 (it was—inevitably—a Friday), that Marthe finally died, having supposedly whispered to Finet in her last moments, *"Il m'a tuée,"* meaning he—the devil—has killed me.[23] "He is always there to massacre everything," she once said, the verb suggesting a *jeu de massacre,* a game of Aunt Sally or skittles, "everything collapses [*ça dégringole*], it descends into chaos."[24]

Out of the massacre of her own body by disease, out of what might have been unmitigated chaos, Marthe Robin had made "something beautiful for God." It is easy to dwell on the extremity of her physical suffering; easy, too, to be repelled by the theology of mystical substitution that enabled her to withstand it. But when, toward the end of her life, Jean Guitton asked what she would do in heaven, Marthe, remembering, no doubt, how she "turned" at the waltz and the polka before the onset of her terrible illness, replied, simply, if untranslatably, *Je gambaderai* (I will frolic, caper, gambol about).[25] It is an extraordinary image, worthy of Thérèse herself, of liberating play, realized, in extremis, by a totally paralyzed woman who, in her spiritual mobility, joins in the endless perichoresis of the three Persons of the Trinity. Ten years after her death, as canon law requires, the process for her beatification was formally begun and will, one assumes, succeed in due course.

Extraordinary Phenomena

All of Marthe's "gifts" (as committed followers might construe them) or "symptoms" (in the eyes of the more skeptical and the frankly disbelieving) belong to what the Catholic Church officially calls "extraordinary phenomena" and toward which it has, by tradition, been markedly reserved, not to say hostile, if only because they seem to bypass established ecclesiastical structures: stigmata, bilocation, agrypnia, inedia (noneating, to be distinguished, as we shall see, from anorexia), glossolalia (speaking in "tongues") and the much rarer xenolalia (speaking in an actual language unknown to the subject), and levitation, among others, the last three being unattested in Marthe's personal case.

If the present discussion of extraordinary phenomena began with Marthe Robin, it is because (setting aside the question of possible bilocation in November 1930) there is in her case nothing "extraordinary" that requires explanation: *All* of her symptoms, including, in all likelihood, her bleeding, can be attributed to a physiological, rather than psychological (even "psychosomatic"), let alone "supernatural," etiology. Her sleeplessness, her inability (*not* her refusal) to eat, her phobia of light and (after 1939) blindness, together with her comprehensive paralysis, can all be explained—and were so as early as 1942 in a report, conducted on behalf of the church, by Drs. Jean Dechaume and André Ricard (Finet's brother-in-law)—as effects of encephalitis, specifically of the *encephalitis lethargica,* popularly known as "sleeping sickness," which claimed no fewer than five million lives worldwide between 1916 and 1927.[26] The disease is transmitted by virus, and the hypothesis is that, having been infected from the same polluted well that killed her sister Clémence in 1903, Marthe partly recovered, but not completely enough to prevent eventual paralysis and blindness, agrypnia, inedia, and intermittent relapses into unconsciousness that she was somehow able to coordinate into her hebdomadal Passion Play, the Church's weekly and annual cycle providing the structure, and her belief in the doctrine of mystical substitution the substance, of a weekly ritual of death followed by resurrection whereby, from the "massacre" of her physical being, she was able—or, as she would see it, God was able—to draw a cosmos of meaning and love.

In particular, Marthe's inability to swallow was caused (as is common with victims of strokes) by damage to the hypothalamus resulting from *encephalitis lethargica*: There is no question of her being anorexic—a psychological rather than physiological/neurological condition—unlike many of the female "mysterics" we shall be discussing shortly. Postponing, for the moment, the question of stigmatization, we might conclude that what is "extraordinary"—truly extraordinary—about Marthe is not her condition per se but the way in which, through personal courage, divine grace, or some unfathomable synergy of the two, she succeeded in transcending the hideous constraints it placed on her freedom, becoming a source of inspiration to thousands rather than an object of impotent pity and resentment to the rest of her immediate family.

"Extraordinary phenomena," especially stigmata and extremes of fasting, are widely attested in France (and in Catholic Europe as a whole) from the early 1800s until the late 1950s, the earliest modern instance to gain widespread notoriety being that of the Westphalian-born Anne Catherine Emmerich (1774–1824), the so-called Living Crucifix whose extraordinarily detailed visions of Christ's Passion—even down to how three special holes were dug for the crosses on Calvary hill—were taken down at her bedside by the poet Clement Brentano and published after her death in no fewer than four volumes.[27] Virtually all of the recorded cases involve women, the only significant exception being that of Padre Pio (1887–1968) of Pietrelcina in southern Italy who received the stigmata in September 1918, ate and slept very little, and allegedly possessed the rare charismata of bilocation and the emission of exquisite perfumes, both before and after his death. Pio, a Capuchin friar, was credited with several miraculous cures and, at the height of his fame, spent eighteen hours a day in the confessional, receiving, hearing, and absolving the thousands of penitents who, despite official Church disapproval, thronged to the monastery of San Giovanni Rotondo.[28]

The object of the discussion that follows is not to "explain" extraordinary phenomena in physiological or psychological terms, and still less to ascribe them to "paranormal" or "supernatural" agencies at work, but to locate them within the Catholic belief-patterns of the time and, beyond these, within the social and political contexts in which they occurred. It is an immense task that may be facilitated by the following table of the principal instances of women presenting one or more of the phenomena in question that are known to have occurred in France between the last years of the Bourgeois Monarchy and the first of the Fifth Republic (c. 1840–1960). The table is based on the biographies brought together in

Jacques Maître's superbly documented *Mystique et féminité* (1997)[29] and attempts to indicate, in necessarily schematic form, the principal "facts" of each case: the dates and origin of each individual; her status (religious, secular, married); a rough indication of her class (upper, middle, lower, peasant); the presence or absence of stigmata, extreme fasting, and other phenomena; the general reaction of the Church; her political tendencies, if any; and, where known or appropriate, the principal intellectual and spiritual influences that acted on her. There follow more detailed, but still brief, discussions of four women of particular interest—Pauline Lair Lamotte, alias "Madeleine Lebouc" (1853–1918), Eva Lavallière (1866–1929), Claire Ferchaud (1896–1972), and, most famously and controversially, Simone Weil (1909–43). These portraits, in turn, point forward to the general consideration of the significance of "holy fasting" and "holy bleeding" given in the conclusion. The names of the women in the table are listed in their order of birth.

The symptoms of the thirty-one women enumerated here (fourteen instances of extreme fasting; nineteen of stigmatization) have no general diagnostic value but are broadly representative of what may have been a much wider diffusion of extraordinary phenomena. A number of general patterns are immediately discernible: (1) socioeconomic status—almost a third of the women concerned are of, crudely, "peasant" origin (nine out of twenty-three whose class is attested), with a further nine belonging loosely to the urban lower classes; only one, Edith Challon-Belval, had links with the aristocracy (though the fathers of two others, Jeanne Bel and Joséphine Raimbault, were employed on aristocratic estates) and four others may be described, again very loosely, of upper- or middle-class origin; (2) geography—the west of France (Britanny, the Vendeé, Mayenne) is comparatively over represented with six cases in all—hardly surprising given the tenacious roots of both Catholicism and royalism in the region—and there is a lesser cluster of instances (four) in the eastern departments where similarly Catholicism was strong; (3) political learnings—the influence of one or another form of royalism (legitimism, Naundorffism, and "Henriquinquisme," the name given to the cause of the Bourbon pretender to the French throne, the Duc de Chambard (1820–83), under the name of Henri V) is attested in no fewer than fifteen instances and may be assumed to be present in others; one lone republican apart (Hélène Villefranche), the link between extraordinary phenomena and royalism in its most extreme, millennialist forms seems to be clearly established; (4) influences—an exacerbated hyperdulia saturates everything; the Mary of the mysteric is Mélanie's Mary, not Bernadette's, La Salette rather than Lourdes. Among intellectual and spiritual influences, the names of Grignion de Montfort and Pierre-Marie Vintras stand out, each bringing his brand of apocalyptic—orthodox if eccentric in Grignion's case; heterodox in the extreme in that of Vintras[30]—to the general mood of millennialist expectation and woe. When the onset of bleeding can be dated, there is a

TABLE 5.1.
French Women and "Extraordinary Phenomena," 1840–1960

| Name | Dates | Town or Department of Origin | Status[a] | Class[b] | Phenomenon | | | Church Reaction[d] | Politics | Influences |
					Extreme Fasting[c]	Stigmata[c]	Other			
Jeanne Boisseau	1797–1871	Loire-Atlantique	S	P		+(1851)	Paralysis of legs miraculously cured, visions, trances	–	Royalist/millennialist	Grignion de Montfort
Thérèse Putigny (Sr. Marie-Catherine)	1803–85	Bas-Rhin	R	P	+	+	Bilocation trances, prophecies, diabolic vexations			
Thérèse Miollis (née Cartier)	1806–77	Var	S/M	L		+	Visions, trances			
Victoire Clair (née Courtier)	c. 1811–83	Ardèche	S/M	P		+(c. 1849)	Marian visions, ecstatic utterances, diabolic vexations			
Rose Tamisier ("Rosette")	1815–99	Vaucluse	S	L	+	+ (c. 1850)	Communion host alleged to "fly" from ciborium into her mouth	– (excom-municated)		Pierre-Michel Vintras
Françoise Barthel	1822–78	Bas-Rhin	S			+	Visions, "visits" to Purgatory			
Caroline Clément	1827–98	Toul	S		+	+	Trances, visions, diabolic vexations			Tertiary order of St. Francis Redemptorist oblate

Mathilde Marchat (St. Marie-Geneviève du Sacré-Coeur)	1830–99	Etampes	R				Visions of Sacré-Coeur	− (excommunicated 1894)	Ultraroyalist /follower of Charles XIe	Cult of Sacré-Coeur Naundorffism
Marie Bergadier ("Berguille")	1830–99	Gironde	S/M	P		+ (1874)	Demonic visions, miraculous cures, visions of Virgin, vision of "Henri V"	+ −	Legitimist/ millennialist	Sacré-Coeur *Le Rosier de Marie* (ultra-royalist weekly)
Joséphine Poirier ("Hélène")	1834–1914	Loiret	S	L	+		Diabolic vexations and possession, visions of Virgin	−	Ultraroyalist	
Delphine Périé ("Pauline")	1838–1915	Lot	S		+	+	Diabolic vexations, trances, visions, telepathy	−	Ultraroyalist	
Edith Challan-Belval (Sr. Marie du Sacré Coeur)	1841–1924	Yonne	R[f]	Minor aristocracy	+		Agrypnia, visions of Sacré-Coeur		Legitimist	Marguerite-Marie Alacoque
Jeanne Bel (Sr. Marie du Coeur de Jésus)	1843–1926	Tarn	R	L		+ (1864)[g]	Diabolic vexations, levitation	−	Legitimist	
Françoise Chambon (Sr. Marie-Marthe)	1844–1907	Chambéry	R	P			Visions, trances, glossolalia (?)	+ (beatification process underway)		

TABLE 5.1.—(cont.)

| Name | Dates | Town or Department of Origin | Status[a] | Class[b] | Phenomenon | | | Church Reaction[d] | Politics | Influences |
					Extreme Fasting[c]	Stigmata[c]	Other			
Mariam Baouardy (Sr. Marie de Jésus-Crucifié)	1846–78	Palestine/ Marseille	R	L		+	Visions, trances, diabolic vexations and possession, "transverberation"[h]	+ (beatified 1983)		
Thérèse Durnerin	1848–1905	Paris	S	M		+	Visions of Virgin prophecies	−	Founder of Société des Amis des Pauvres, legitimist (?)	Grignion de Montfort Sacré-Coeur
Catherine Filljung	1848–1915	Moselle	S	P			Trances, visions, prophecies	−	Legitimist	Joan of Arc
Céleste Fenouil ("Célestine")	1849–1919	Manosque	S	L	+	+	Visions, xenolalia (?)	−		
Marie-Julie Jahenny	1850–1941	Loire-Atlantique	S	P	+	+ (1873)	Trances, visions	−	Legitimist cult of "Henri V"[i]	Joan of Arc
Jeanne Vergne	1853–1927	Paris	S	L	+		Diabolic vexations, miraculous cures	−	Legitimist	
Joséphine Raimbault (née Reverdy)	1854–1908	Cher	S	L	+		Marian visions			

Laurentine Billoquet	1862–1936	Seine-Maritime	S			+		–		
Marie Martel	1872–1913	Tilly-sur-Seulles (Calvados)	S	P			Marian visions	–	Royalist	Pierre-Marie Vintras
Françoise Hellegouarch	1874–98	Morbihan	S		+	+		–		
Hélène Ville-franche (Sr. Marie-Agnès du Coeur de Jésus)	1879–1951	Lyon	R	M	+		Self-inflicted wounds		Republican	
Marie-Antoinette de Geuser ("Consummata")	1889–1918	Le Havre	S	M	+		Visions			
Marie-Thérèse Noblet	1889–1930	Ardennes	S	U		+ (1913)	Trances, visions, diabolic possession, miraculous cures	+		
Reine Colin (Sr. Reine-Marie du Sacré-Coeur)	1898–1935	Haute-Marne	R	L	+		Trances, dialogues with Jesus		Close to Action Française	
Yvonne Beauvais (Sr. Yvonne-Aimée)	1901–51	Mayenne	R			+	Bilocation, diabolic vexations	+– (beatification process interrupted 1960)		

TABLE 5.1.—(cont.)

| Name | Dates | Town or Department of Origin | Status[a] | Class[b] | Phenomenon | | | Church Reaction[d] | Politics | Influences |
					Extreme Fasting[c]	Stigmata[c]	Other			
Marie Danzé (Sr. Marie du Christ-Roi)	1906–68	Finistère	R			+	Diabolic vexations	−	Legitimist	Cult of Christus Rex
Jeanne-Louise Ramonet	b. 1910	Finistère	S	P			Marian visions		Anticommunist/ royalist	Probable links with Michel Collin

Source: Adapted from information compiled in Jacques Maître, *Mystique et féminité* (Cerf, 1997), 345–431.

[a] S = secular; R = religious; M = married.

[b] P = peasant; L = lower; M = middle; U = upper

[c] + = factor present.

[d] − = negative reaction; +− = mixed reaction; + = positive reaction.

[e] Sr. Marie-Geneviève was among the main proponents of the belief that Pope Leo XIII was an imposter and that the "true Pope" had been kidnapped and was languishing in the proverbial Vatican cellars. Three of her supporters, the Comte Vérité de Saint-Michel, a lawyer named Jean-Louis Glénard, and the Abbé Joseph Xaé, actually went to Rome in an attempt to free the "captive," with predictably hilarious consequences that André Gide used as the basis for his novel *Les Caves du Vatican* (1914).

[f] Challan-Belval belonged to an impoverished branch of an aristocratic family, married, and had four children before becoming a nun following her husband's death. An ardent legitimist, she believed in the need for "reconciliation" between the aristocracy and the bourgeois and in the need for both to exercise "a kind of apostolate over the people" (Maître, *Mystique et féminité*, 370).

[g] Jeanne Bel at one time bore the (presumably self-inflicted) words "Fille de réparation" incised, supposedly "with a thorn," on her chest (ibid., 372).

[h] "Transverberation" is the technical name given to the phenomenon of being pierced by the nails of the crucifixion or (in the manner of Saint Teresa of Avila) by the "arrow" of God's love.

[i] Marie-Julie Jahenny has reportedly been "adopted" by the schismatic Lefebvrist tendency of the Catholic Church as one of its principal inspirations (Maître, *Mystique et féminité*, 383).

clear correlation with periods of postrevolutionary reaction (1849–51 and 1870–74): extraordinary phenomena seem to follow, rather than announce, the outbreak of political turmoil. Their general significance, however, is oppositional: they are most commonly attested on the geographical or cultural peripheral; they are more often popular and rural than bourgeois; they are markedly at variance with the democratic, secular thrust of the age; and they are deeply subversive of entrenched notions of what it is to be human and happy. Though their discourse is ultra-Catholic, they run implicitly, and often explicitly, against the authority of the Church that, more often than not, responds with interdict, excommunication, and anathema. With the exception of Mariam Baouardy (1846–78), not a single French woman of the nineteenth or twentieth centuries exhibiting one or another extraordinary phenomenon has been beatified, and of the country's four leading female saints of the period—Catherine Labouré, Bernadette Soubirous, Thérèse Martin, and Elisabeth Catez (Elisabeth de la Trinité, 1880–1906)—not one evinced signs of excessive fasting, unexplained bleeding or ecstasies, transverberation, levitation, diabolic vexations, or whatever. With these general considerations in mind, let us move on to our four individual portraits.

Pauline Lair Lamotte/"Madeleine Lebouc"

Pauline Lair Lamotte (1853–1918) came from a moderately well-off family in Mayenne in the northwest of France and received a Catholic formation that, somewhat unusually, strongly emphasized the Franciscan notion of spiritual and material poverty and placed on its largely middle-class charges the obligation of aiding the poor through prayer, self-denial, and charitable works.[31] But, from an early age, Pauline was determined to take this "option for the poor," as a later age would describe it, far beyond the paternalist concern of contemporary "social Catholicism" and actually to identify with, by living alongside them, those whom the Communard poet Eugène Pottier (1816–87) memorably called "the wretched of the earth."

Having, as a child and adolescent, showed signs of anorexia, religious scruples, and sexual phobias and guilts, and fearing that she "had offended God terribly" (10), she broke with her family and, at the age of twenty, "threw myself headlong on to the path revealed to me by the passion filling my soul, love of the cross and love of the poor" (xx). With the rashness born of that passion and her consuming sense of guilt, she went to live in Bethnal Green in the East End of London, the squalor of which probably exceeded anything she might have experienced in Paris at the time. Living among the poorest of the poor and sharing their condition, she decided, as she later put it, to "become as though dead for the whole of my family"

(27) and, committing a kind of onomastic parricide, began to style herself "Madeleine Tony."

Returning to Paris, it was under this name that, in October 1874, she was arrested, convicted, and jailed on a charge of vagrancy; evidently, the "little ragpicker" (*la petite chiffonnière*), as her elder sister Sophie called her, had been living by begging, often sleeping rough in the warren of lanes on the Butte Montmartre—Martyrs' Mount—which, not coincidentally, she had chosen as the site of her "immolation of myself" (271) for the benefit of mankind. A further arrest on the same charge followed in June 1876 and another in January 1878 when she broke the terms of her parole and returned from Orléans to Paris; in both instances she served her sentence in the tough Saint-Lazare prison in Paris. By now she was calling herself "Madeleine Lebouc," a double identification with the penitent whore of the Gospels and with the scapegoat (*le bouc émissaire*) of Leviticus (16:10) who "shall be presented alive before the Lord, to make an atonement with him," it being her divinely ordained mission to "suffer for myself and all my brothers" by diverting God's righteous anger on to herself.

For the next twenty or so years, Madeleine (as we shall now call her) disappeared almost completely, like the biblical scapegoat whose name she had taken, into the wilderness of the poorest quarters of Paris. Identifying, as ever, with the poor and the suffering, she lived in conditions of destitution, her possessions consisting, she said, of a crucifix, a blanket, a wooden box that served as a pillow and also contained the needles and thread with which she eked out a living, a water jug, and an earthenware pot. For nine years (1878–87) she appears to have lived with, and looked after, a woman named Rosalie Bourland who was suffering from stomach cancer and, after her death, drifted between Montmartre and La Villette, at one time (1895) living on a street we have encountered before, the rue du Chevalier de la Barre, at number 36, opposite where Generals Lecomte and Thomas had been lynched in March 1871 at the start of the Commune (whose enemies would retaliate the following May by executing the leading Communard, Eugène Varlin, on the same spot),[32] the street that, as we have seen, Léon Bloy, author of *La Femme pauvre* (1897), a chronicle of female destitution and religious fervor equal to those of Madeleine, would move to in 1905: there was not a more appropriate place of residence in the whole of Paris for one set on offering her life up as a holocaustal sacrifice.

In January 1893, suffering from excruciating pains in her feet and knees, Madeleine was taken to a hospital in Montmartre where, in May, she was seen by none other than the celebrated neurologist and psychologist Jean-Martin Charcot (1825–93), Freud's mentor, who saw in Madeleine a suitable guinea pig for the electrical therapy he was experimenting with at the clinic of La Salpêtrière on the other side of Paris; terrified at the prospect, Madeleine appears to have discharged herself the following day. She next resurfaced from the anonymity of the streets in November 1894 when she went in person to the Préfecture de Police to deliver a letter denouncing the existence of various "plots," convinced, as she later put it, that a "spider's web" of conspiracy—a crucial image of the plot-obsessed last decade of the century[33]—was enmeshing the nation; that "associations" were engaged in reducing the national birthrate; that there was a citywide commerce in human flesh and, specifically, in female hair, a whole cave-load of which she claimed to have discovered in the wasteland outside the city's fortifications; and that "malevolent microbes" were everywhere abroad (294–95).

Not dissimilar fantasies are to be found throughout fin de siècle rantings about Jews, "internationalists," anarchists, Jesuits, and freemasons, but, unlike Edouard Drumont or Maurice Barrès, Madeleine was adjudged to be a danger to herself and society, and, after being shifted from hospital to hospital, finally ended up, in February 1895, at La Salpêtrière where she became the prize patient of Charcot's successor, the equally formidable Pierre Janet (1859–1947), to whose investigations, published in the first volume of his *Névroses et idées fixes* (1898), we owe almost everything we know about Madeleine (whom he refers to as "Vk") and the extraordinary range of "hysterical" symptoms she displayed.

As well as interviewing his subject and having her photographed during her "ecstasies,"[34] Janet encouraged Madeleine to write, and it is on her disturbingly intimate "confessions," reproduced *in extenso* in Jacques Maître's *Une inconnue célèbre: La Madeleine Lebouc de Janet* (1993), that the following discussion is based. Madeleine's most obvious "symptom" was the bleeding from her feet that had started, she said, on 1 November 1896 after she had attended the Mass for the Dead at the Eglise Saint-Marcel in the southeast of the city (while in prison she had incised the letters IM [Jésus Marie] on her chest, using, it appears, a red-hot poker to do it).[35] Madeleine also claimed to have the ability to "float" or to "fly"; in other words, the extremely unusual charism of levitation, alleged in only one of the instances tabulated above (Jeanne Bel).

Her whole life she describes as a repeated Easter narrative in miniature— "an interminable succession of agonies and resurrections in which my physical being seems to be renewed"—from each of which she emerges "fortified and needing to expend my energies. Surprisingly, I am hungry and I can eat; it's like Jesus Christ returning from the desert after his fast" (71). As this statement indicates, she had continued to suffer from the reduced appetite she had experienced as a girl, and, not surprisingly, her writings are rich in compensating images of eating and drinking and, more generally, of oral gratification. She compares herself to Mary Magdalene kissing the feet of her savior and feeling as though "blood flowed into my mouth, intoxicating me, and Jesus resuscitated came into my arms," and, while she is "flying," "the pleasures [*les douceurs*] that I feel in my mouth are almost continuous, I have the sensation of a perpetual kiss" (307); she receives Christ's blood almost as a fellatrix receiving the semen of her partner, or, of course, as a babe in arms imbibing the milk of its mother ("What is this sweet, intoxicating liquor that fills my mouth?" [308]). But this oral rapture—again, it is almost inevitable that she should use the word *joussance,* the commonest French term, then and now, for orgasm—is purchased at the price of excruciating pain in other parts of her body:

> In my head, it was as though my eyes were being burned with red-hot iron, my ears, nose and throat, everything was seized. . . . My throat contracted, an iron hand grips me, I can't breathe, I give a death's rattle [*je râle*], will it be blocked up for good and all? The torture extends to all parts of my body, what I suffer in the anus, the coccyx, the vagina [*aux parties*] cannot be imagined, large red-hot objects are thrust into me [*on m'enfonce de gros objets rougis au feu*] and electric currents are passed over the wounds. What agony from the whip on my petrified buttocks. My flesh is torn apart in every direction, dogs devour me and chew at my bones. What torture do they not devise, I am suspended from the ceiling by my nipples, it is agonizing. (293)

Agonizing, no doubt, but also intensely pleasurable, for, as she offers up her body to her divine torturer, she experiences "true bliss [*une véritable volupté*] at feeling myself as though crushed [*broyée*] at his feet. Every pain that I feel, I offer to him like a cry of love wrenched from the whole of my being. For me, the great happiness when one loves is to suffer, to endure something painful for the person one loves, I long to obliterate myself [*m'effacer*] before God so as to prove his glory" (270). Once having abased herself lovingly before the divine torturer, she becomes free to "fly" and experiences an extraordinary rapture—the word *"jouissance"* is used over and over again—in the whole of her body, from her mouth down to her "sexual parts" which become as though "spiritual and pure" (300), as though a "thick rope" has been passed between her legs, pushing the "parts"—presumably her labia—up inside her, placing pressure on her bladder, and making her want to urinate, which, of course, is not a pain but a further source of pleasure (306). Restored to a childlike condition of helplessness in which God, characteristically, becomes both her father and mother, she puts her hands together "like a little cross" and cries out "Father, here I am to do your will, Mummy, Mummy [*maman, maman*]!" (315). At this point, she "takes off" into a stratosphere of ecstasy: "You see, the wind carries me away, I am caught and pulled up into the air," she feels weightless, she "comes" (*je jouis*) with her eyes both open and closed, possessed as though by "an urgent need to dance" (cf. Marthe Robin's ecstatic *"je gambaderai"* [loosely translated as frolic, caper, gambol]), as though there is in her "a kind of electricity, of compressed steam that seems on the point of exploding" (308–9). With this, she goes beyond conventional bride-mysticism and actually loses all distinct selfhood in ecstatic fusion with her lover: "My being is purified, transformed, divinized. I participate in the essence of God, I am in God, I am like God, I am . . . no, one mustn't say that, why do I feel that? I am God" (298–99).

It is, she admits, utter madness, divine madness, but, as she says, "is not the Incarnation of the Word anything other than the loving action of a mad God?" (317) What Janet obviously construed as the ultimate in hysterical raving might, in other eyes, have been seen as "the rare and terrible charism of holy folly,"[36] folly for Christ's sake (see 1 Corinthians 4:10), realized to perfection in a hospital in the southeast of Paris: "You are there, I am there, we are people of 1897. But it is the true Christ who is born, the Christ of Bethlehem. You say it's a repetition, but there's no repetition of the true birth of God and it is the true birth. . . . You don't understand, it is a miracle" (310).

Madeleine was released from La Salpêtrière in April 1904 and, apparently no longer afflicted (or blessed) by her remarkable erotico-spiritual ecstasies, spent the rest of her life moving between Brussels and Le Mans (where her sisters now lived), still experiencing some pains in her legs, but devoting herself, as before her lengthy hospitalization, to the needs of the poor. She died in April 1918, aged 64, unknown yet admirable, despite her many afflictions, for her lifelong determination to live her faith to the full.

Eva Lavallière

Unlike Madeleine, Eva Lavallière (1866–1929) did not evince any of the "extraordinary phenomena" considered thus far. She deserves our attention for the impact that she had on her contemporaries in the artistic-intellectual world, notably on Paul Claudel, Jacques and Raïssa Maritain, and the painter and theater designer Jean Hugo (1894–1984), great-grandson of Victor, and another of the Meudon circle's converts to Catholicism.[37]

Born Eugénie Fenoglio at Toulon and brought up in Perpignan close to the Franco-Spanish border, Eva Lavallière's adolescence was marked by an event as traumatic as any imagined in the *romans noirs* of the day: in 1884, when she was eighteen, her father murdered her mother in front of Eva, tried to shoot her, failed, and turned the gun fatally on himself. Shortly afterward she went on stage, taking as her *nom de théâtre* the first name of the original sinner and the surname of Louis XIV's one-time mistress Louise de la Vallière (1644–1710) who, repenting of her early life, entered the Carmel in 1674 and lived an exemplary religious life until her death nearly forty years later. Eva became one of the best-known actresses of fin de siècle, belle époque Paris, due to both her looks and her talent, particularly for *travesti* roles; she was at home both at the traditionalist Théâtre des Variétés (whose owner Fernand Samuel she eventually married) and at André Antoine's avant-garde Théâtre Libre.

Artistic success went along with a turbulent and unhappy personal life, marked by at least one child born out of wedlock, persistent depression, and, it appears, several suicide attempts. In 1917 she signed a contract for a U.S. tour with the great Lucien Guitry (1860–1925), father of Sacha, and she spent the intervening summer at the Château de la Porcherie near Tours. There, according to Raïssa Maritain's account in *Les Grandes Amitiés,* she asked the local curé if she could pick some cherries from his orchard and made some trivial joke about temptation and hell, to which the curé reputedly replied: "Madame, if you had any idea of what hell is like, you wouldn't speak so lightly about it."[38] At this Eva Lavallière burst into tears and that Sunday, after confession, made her first communion in many years, dropped not just her U.S. tour but her entire theatrical career, left Paris for good, and took up residence in the village of Chanceaux-sur-Choisille, also near Tours, accompanied only by her former dresser at the Théâtre des Variétés, known to us only as Léona, who converted to Catholicism along with Eva.

Between 1917 and 1920, Eva attempted in vain to join various religious orders—in a text of 1957, Claudel describes her going from convent to convent like the bride of the Song of Songs (3:2) seeking "him whom my soul loveth: I sought him, but I found him not"[39]—until, in despair, she and Léona decided, in September 1920, to move to the tiny village of Thuillières in the Vosges, close to the spa-town of Vittel. The next village along was Ville-sur-Illon where, by coincidence (or, as she would undoubtedly have believed, by divine preordainment), Charles Henrion, not yet a priest but destined, as we have seen, shortly to play a key role in the Maritain circle, had withdrawn to meditate upon his vocation, and it was to him that the local priest turned for help with his difficult and demanding new parishioner. Somewhat reluctantly, the future Père Charles accompanied Eva to the nearby Marian shrine of Notre-Dame des Bois where, to the amazement of both, the incumbent priest, the Abbé Lamy, "animated by the gift of prophecy, recounted her whole life to her."[40] Shortly afterward she joined the tertiary order of Saint Francis.

The house she and Léona occupied at Thuillières was renamed "Béthanie," and was appropriately adorned with images of Mary Magdalene; Saints Monica, Teresa, and Bernadette; and of the Holy Face, so dear to Thérèse of Lisieux, made popular, as we have seen, by Louis Dupont, the so-called holy man of Tours, close to which city Eva had made her conversion. Thereafter, the two women did the rounds of the holy places of France—Lourdes, La Salette (where Eva wanted to place her pearl necklace around the statue of the virgin; the resident monks refused and sold the necklace instead), Paray-le-Monial, and the huge grotto at la Sainte-Baume near Marseille where Mary Magdalene is said to have lived out her life in penitential weeping, clad, according to legend, only in her long flowing hair, and sustained—inevitably—by the daily communion host brought down to her by angels from heaven.

Erat in civitate peccatrix . . . It was probably inevitable that, as a former woman of the stage with a string of liaisons behind her, Eva Lavallière should identify with the "woman in the city, which was a sinner" of Luke 7:37–38 who washes and anoints Jesus' feet and then wipes them with her hair, to the disgust of some of the disciples who are duly rebuked by their master: "Her sins, which are many, are forgiven; for she loved much." Later identified with Mary of Bethany, sister of Martha and Lazarus, the "woman in the city," her profession, her ointment, her kneeling at Christ's feet, and her passionate unloosening of her hair is an obsessive presence in nineteenth- and twentieth-century French literature, painting, and devotion, and we shall return to her in chapter 7 of this book.

More than any other religious figure of her time, Eva Lavallière—after 1920 Soeur Eve-Marie du Coeur-de-Jésus—identified with the female composite known to Catholic tradition as "Mary Magdalene" (in fact an amalgam of Mary of Magdala, Mary of Bethany, and the "woman in the city"), her particular charism being what that tradition calls the "gift of tears." This was rather more of a curse in Soeur Eve-Marie's case for her continual weeping is said to have caused serious problems with her eyes,[41] though, given the algolagnic tenor of the piety of the time, she may have experienced this as one more sign of God's favor toward her. Abandoning perfume, makeup, and jewelry, and letting her hair—now more than flecked with gray—grow as it would, she may have struck some as the Crazy Jane of the Vosges, but no one could deny that she loved much. Having three times accompanied the now-ordained Charles Henrion to Tunisia in the early 1920s, she died at Béthanie in July 1929, a minor but symptomatic figure of female Catholic devotion of the deeply anti-Catholic French Third Republic.

Claire Ferchaud

It was precisely the "atheism" of "official France," as she called it, that stung Claire Ferchaud (1896–1972) into action and that prompted her, at the lowest point of French fortunes during the First World War, to launch her remarkable personal mission to have the Sacred Heart of Jesus officially added to the red, white, and blue of the national flag. Born in the village of Rinfillières just south of Cholet and a few miles north of the shrine of Grignion de Montfort at Saint-Laurent-sur-Sèvre, Claire came from the heartland of French ultra-Catholicism, the Vendeé, that "permanent antithesis of France," as the region's leading historian has called it,[42] in which the bitter memory of the suppression by the First Republic of the Catholic-royalist uprising of 1793–94 has been sedulously preserved in war memorials (notably at Les Lucs-sur-Boulogne), in the fine stained-glass windows in many village churches (Chanzeaux, Pouzauges, etc.), in the windmills whose sails were used by the insurgents to communicate from village to village (Le Mont des Alouettes), and in a whole mass of devotional activities, pursued with a fervor unequaled anywhere in France: pilgrimages, stations of the cross, and, perhaps most of all, the cult of the Sacred Heart, worn by thousands of insurgents over their own hearts to protect them from enemy bullets. The Vendeé is traditionally the most right-wing region of France— no fewer than thirty members of the Vendéen aristocracy enlisted in Franco's army during the Spanish civil war, seven achieving the obligatory martyrs' death[43]—and it is no accident that the multimedia commemoration of the Vendeé's rebel past, founded in 1977 by the right-wing deputy Philippe de Villiers, is located in the immediate vicinity of where Claire was born, at Le Puy du Fou.[44] The Vendeé has traditionally had close cultural ties with Québec, many French Canadians having distant "roots" in the region,[45] and the region might easily adopt as its own the nationalist motto of their transatlantic cousins: *Je me souviens*. Certainly Claire Ferchaud in her one-woman war against the God-hating Third Republic would never forget what its prototype did in 1793–94 to her ancestors.

As related in her various autobiographical writings (unpublished during her lifetime), Claire's childhood closely resembled that of her heroine and model, Thérèse of Lisieux, whose extended floral imagery, the "poor little country flower," as Claire styles herself, is all too prone to abuse. But the pain beneath the daisies and the lilies is real enough and follows a by-now-familiar pattern: a gentle, loving, devout father whose life was made "a continual martyrdom" by asthma and other pulmonary disorders (1:25)[46] and an anxious, harassed, disciplinarian mother; in short, a kind of peasant version of the Martin household at Alençon and Lisieux where the mother figures the superego and the never-satisfied God of justice and the suffering father the God of forgiveness and love.

It was the former's view of herself that Claire took over from earliest childhood, despite her belief that "Maman doesn't love me" (1:55), and, when she looks into the mirror, it is her mother's image of her, duly diabolized, that she beholds: "a grimacing face, flaming eyes, teeth gnashing between lips from which flames were emerging" (1:67). Sat on her mother's knee, she refuses eat, consenting only when her "sweet little king"—the Child Jesus she "conversed" with throughout childhood and adolescence— urged her to do so; it was the foretaste of eating disorders to come. Internalizing the (imagined) judgment of the maternal superego, Claire begs "God" to punish her for her "sins": "*I want* [Claire's own emphasis] above all that the wrath of the Heavenly Father crush me so justly. . . . I want to be for you [Jesus, whom she probably identifies, as Thérèse did, with her ailing, hemorrhaging father] that embarrassing, humiliating 'thing' people reject, I want to descend with you to the bottom of that ocean of bitterness that submerges you" (1:19). Inevitably, the idea of vicarious suffering and mystical substitution enabled her to rationalize and justify her need to suffer and be punished. She wants to be a "living photograph" of Jesus (1:81) and to offer herself up as a "redemptive coin" (*une monnaie de rachat,* 1:115) to ransom a nation that has been kidnapped by Freemasons and "atheists," though not (or not in so many words) by Jews, for, like the similarly plot-obsessed "Madeleine Lebouc," Claire seems to be untouched by antisemitism.

By 1916, aged twenty, Claire was convinced that France's wartime tribulations were due to a combination of the country's "official atheism" since the separation of church and state in 1905, to the "masonic hords" who had torn the body of the nation limb from limb and, above all, to the absence of the Sacred Heart of Jesus from the national flag. This was a familiar topos in ultra-Catholic discourse, dating back to the vow made in 1689 by the founder of the cult of the Sacred Heart, Marguerite-Marie Alacoque (and whose nonrealization by Louis XIV was the cause, many said, of the fall of the monarchy exactly a hundred years later) and later revived by the battles of Patay and Loigny during the Franco-Prussian war when a company of *zouaves pontificaux*—French members of the Pope's personal guard—had fought beneath such a standard. But, while most Catholic diehards merely complained, Claire Ferchaud decided to act and, like a new Joan of Arc, take the cause of the Sacred Heart to the heart of political power, into the very office of the unbelieving Republic's president, the suitably unbelieving Raymond Poincaré (1860–1934).

On 16 January 1917, Claire wrote to Poincaré, telling him how she had had a vision of the Sacred Heart and how Jesus, pointing to his wounds, had said, "It is France that did this to me." "Raymond, Raymond, why persecutest thou me?" he continues—even a diehard anticlerical would pick up the reference of Saul of Tarsus before he became Paul (Acts 4:4)—at which point Claire turns the screw further and says that the president's mother, safely in heaven, has asked her to save her son's soul and bring him back to the Church, just as he was on the day of his first communion; the price of salvation is, of course, the addition of the Sacred Heart to the national flag (2:14–15).

On 20 February, accompanied by her father and her local priest, the Abbé Audebert, Claire was driven from Rinfillières to Tours in a car belonging to the wife of one of her supporters, a Cholet industrialist named Pellaumail, and from there traveled—first-class, for she had powerful backers, including Bishop Humbrecht of Poitiers—to Paris where the three were put up at a religious house on the Avenue Victor Hugo in the wealthy sixteenth arrondissement. Paris, for Claire, was first and foremost the city of regicide that would never be able to "sleep safely" until it had expiated the crime of January 1793 that had left the nation "disorganized" and "decapitated" (2:172–73). She herself had no intention of sleeping, one of her principal objectives being to spend an all-night vigil in the Basilica of Sacré-Coeur, for which she would need special permission. Realizing that she was sleeping and eating hardly at all, the authorities at the Avenue Victor Hugo residence took steps to compel her to do both, which she did through fear lest her mission be halted and the "*ball* [*la boule*] of hysteria" (2:127, Claire's emphasis) within her bounce out of control.

After receiving a number of rebuffs, Claire was finally authorized to spend the night of 15–16 March 1917 in prayer in the Basilica of Sacré-Coeur, and on the 21 of the month was granted an audience with President Poincaré, thanks to the intervention of a royalist deputy from the Vendeé, the Marquis de Baudry d'Asson. It was not a meeting of like minds, and Poincaré told her straight out that the law was the law and that no modification whatsoever could be made to the national flag. Claire protested, the oleaginous Poincaré praised her courage and commitment and, as an aide ushered her out, gave her a pin to secure the veil she was wearing for the audience. "France didn't want the Sacred Heart," she wrote a quarter of a century later, "Hitler replied with his hell and his swastika [*croix tordue*]" (1:132). Feeling that she had been held up to ridicule (which she had been, by both the Church and the state), Claire retaliated by writing directly to fifteen leading military commanders, including Marshals Lyautey, Pétain, and Foch, reiterating her plea and signing herself "Claire de Jésus Crucifié" (see 2:39–41), only to be rejected as before, with Pétain himself issuing an order that any officer permitting the flying of any religious flag would be charged with "flagrantly violating the freedom of conscience of their men and the religious neutrality of the French state" (2:43).

Rejection by the "official France" she despised merely heightened Claire's outraged sense of mission. Since France, riddled as it was with Masonic influences, had predictably spurned the offer of Christ's Sacred Heart, it was now up to Claire—or "Dolor," as she began to call herself—to make "reparation by substitution, and that substitution [took] me definitively away from my family." Offering themselves up as the inevitable "expiatory victims" (1:103–4), she and ten or so female followers, backed by ultra-Catholic money, acquired a house in the village of Loublande, a few miles east of Rinfillières, and, with the blessing of Monseigneur Humbrecht, constituted themselves as an unofficial religious order, pending what all concerned thought would be automatic Church authorization. If Claire's account (1:126) is to be trusted, huge crowds flocked to the "convent"—not least soldiers on furlough about to return to the front—giving rise to scenes of collective religious fervor of a kind to awaken anxieties in much higher places.

In September 1918 religious manifestations outside the "convent" were banned, and the sympathetic Monseigneur Humbrecht transferred to a diocese on the other side of France. With her fellow "expiatory virgins" (*vierges-expiatrices,* 2:45), Claire now became, as she put it, "an object of veneration and mockery" (1:128)—and of fear, too, for, in March 1920, the Holy Office in Rome issued a formal interdict saying that "the so-called visions, revelations, prophecies, etc., commonly known as the *Loublande events* [*les faits de Loublande*], along with writings relating to them, cannot be approved."[47] The following year the Abbé Audebert was replaced by the far less sympathetic Abbé Girard, through in January 1922 Claire was granted an audience with Pope Benedict XV, thanks to the intervention of the head of the French seminary in Rome, the ultra-Catholic Henri Le Floch, supporter of Action Française and, as we have seen, spiritual father of Marthe Robin's Abbé Georges Finet. Unfortunately for Claire, Benedict XV died shortly afterward, and when she did get to Rome in May 1925, she was granted only a semi-public audience with his successor Pius XI. The ban on Loublande was renewed in 1939 and only relaxed in 1964 when the convent-that-never-was became a public oratory, with Claire still raving on about the "octopus of Freemasonry" (*cette pieuvre de la Maçonnerie*) and how "something of the Fall of Lucifer is being repeated in France" (open letter of 4 June 1959, 2:49–50)—receiving some measure of reluctant recognition from Rome.

Cast, in her own words, as both "comic and diabolic" (1:128), she had been "hoisted up like a rag on a pole" (1:151) and treated "like a piece of lint [*charpie*] destined to draw out the pus of the abscess, and then to be cast into the flames, with the repugnance and disgust that it causes" (2:138). Her solitude was acute as, yet another Mad Meg of ultra-Catholicism, she offered herself up for the deliverance of an utterly indifferent nation: "I feel that, between God and men, I am like a viaduct linking two hills, but across which nobody passes" (2:105). Such support as she had (and continues to have) came from the outermost fringes of the ultra-Catholic right, from diehard defenders of Vichy, and, reportedly, survivors of the pro–Algérie Française military coups of 1958 and 1961 according to whose apocalyptic vision of history France will never be "renewed" until mass is said "in perpetuity" at Claire's one-time "convent" in Loublande.[48]

Simone Weil

Traveling by train from Tours to Paris on the second stage of her "national mission" in February 1917, Claire Ferchaud was taken into the restaurant car and repulsed by the sight of "all those people at table, that animal action that seemed to absorb all those human bodies, that spectacle of carnality from which, however, I could not avert my eyes. I would like to take that heavy mass, those heads flushed red with fine food, and force a bit of God into them [*pour y mettre un peu de Dieu*]."[49] Twenty-five years later, midway through another war and in the midst of a national food crisis of unprecedented severity, Simone Weil (1909–43) was similarly repelled by the sight of people eating. "Eating seemed to Simone a base, disgusting function," wrote her friend Dr. Louis Bercher, "It was a year of 'alimentary restrictions,' to use a euphemism. Consequently, people thought more than ever about food. That disgusted Simone in the extreme. She detested this subject of 'provisions,' on to which, she said, conversation fell, as soon as people met, 'as though by the force of gravity' [*comme par un phénomène de pesanteur*]."[50] Arriving in New York from occupied France in July 1942, she was similarly repelled, this time by what struck her (but not Americans) as a superfluity of food, and, according to the same source, said to her long-suffering parents, " 'I shan't eat any more here than I did in Marseille!' Alas, it is certain that any pretext would have sufficed for her not to eat more than she had in Marseille! Just as, in Marseille, any pretext was enough to eat less than the Marseillais" (JM, 171).

Presumably unknown to each other, Claire Ferchaud, in 1917, and Simone Weil, in 1942, reacted to the sight of people eating in wartime in uncannily similar ways. Each feels endowed with a vocation or mission to suffer on behalf of, or more than, her suffering fellow-citizens, to take on and exceed their privations in order to redeem them ("I cannot," wrote Claire, "think of the salvation of my soul, without adding the salvation of all"),[51] and for each eating—or, rather, *not* eating—becomes the focus of her self-appointed crusade on behalf of the rest of humanity.

There can be no question, here, of giving anything like an adequate exposé of Simone Weil's extraordinary personal and intellectual accomplishments during her brief life: schoolteacher and militant syndicalist, political thinker and activist, philosopher and scholar, and, particularly after her Easter retreat at the Benedictine monastery of Solesmes in 1938, seeker after God through a process of self-emptying even more radical than the *via negativa* pursued by her beloved Saints Teresa of Avila and John of the Cross that led ultimately to her death by self-starvation—or, more probably and precisely, cardiac arrest brought on by her refusal or inability to eat—in a sanatorium in Ashford (Kent, England) in August 1943. As is well known, Simone, the daughter of a nonpracticing Jewish mother and father who claimed never to have entered a synagogue, came to the brink of reception into the Roman Catholic Church, before drawing back for complex reasons briefly considered below. Despite her not being formally a Catholic, it is striking is how closely—on an admittedly disparate level in intellectual and literary terms—her experience replicates that of the three Catholic women we have so far discussed.

The philosopher Gustave Thibon (born 1903), on whose property at Saint-Marcel-d'Ardèche in the south of France she worked as a farm laborer in the summer of 1941, spoke not just of her "vocation for sacrifice" but, still more, of the "vocation for (self-) annihilation" (*sa vocation à l'anéantissement*) that eventually killed her, pointing, in addition, to the contradiction that lay at its heart; detached from every appetite and need, she was not, however, "detached from her detachment" and, though her self (*son moi*) was like "a word she had succeeded perhaps in *erasing*," the word itself remained underlined (*souligné*).[52] "My God, grant that I may become nothing" (Mon Dieu, accordez-moi de devenir rien),[53] she wrote in one of her notebooks, published posthumously as a book, edited by Thibon, entitled *La Pesanteur et la grâce* (1947)—*Gravity and Grace* in the English translation, though "Weight and Grace" would be more accurate. To be saved for Simone is to rise up toward God—almost to levitate—freed from the weight of society, matter, the body, the self, freed, in the first and perhaps last instance, from the primary source of weight that is the food we eat: "There is only one fault," runs one of her extraordinary aphorisms, "not to be able to feed off light alone" (PG 13). "A tragedy of human existence," she writes elsewhere, "is that one cannot look and eat at the same time. . . . What one eats, one destroys" (*Cahiers III,* quoted in JM 157). Sin came into the world when a woman (Eve) ate rather than looked. The world (or at least the finite world of the self) is liberated when another woman (Simone) looks and refuses to eat (see VH 270–71): How scandalized she was, visiting the Abbaye de Sainte-Scholastique at Dourgne in the Tarn on Good Friday 1942, to learn that the nuns, on that day of all days, were not only eating—a bit of dry bread might pass—but eating (as by canon law they were entitled to do) vegetables and *fish* (SP 609). But unlike many of the so-called holy anorexics of the past, alleged, like Catherine of Sienna and Marguerite-Marie Alacoque, to have lived off the communion wafer alone, and unlike even Marthe Robin who, as we have seen, mysteriously "absorbed" the Blessed Sacrament each week, Simone also refused Christ's body as present in the Host. To eat it would be to cannibalize her Savior, to crucify him anew in an act of oral sadism.[54] Instead, she preferred to "attend" (meaning to be attentive to or, her key word, to wait on [*attendre*]) mass, to *look* at the Body of Christ rather than, as Christ enjoins his disciples, to take it and *eat* it. The religious life thus becomes a perpetual Benediction, coupled with a refusal, on principle, of Communion.

In the second of her celebrated letters, written in early 1942, to the Dominican Superior Père Jean-Marie Perrin on the subject of her possible baptism and reception into the church, she rationalized her position as follows:

> It is perhaps not inconceivable that in a being with certain natural propensities, a particular temperament, a given past, a certain vocation and so on, the desire for and deprivation of the sacraments might constitute a contact which was more pure than actual participation.[55]

One can well see, reading this tortuous self-justification, why, for many Catholics, not least the almoner of the Free French Forces in London, the Abbé René de Naurois, who was the last priest to see her, Simone Weil's refusal to eat either of the fruits of the earth or of the Body of Christ was evidence of a hard kernel of spiritual pride beneath the outward appearance of humility.[56] It seemed (and still seems) to many that she was not so much *waiting on* Christ, as she claimed, as putting herself in his place; "every time that I think of the crucifixion," she confessed to Père Perrin, "I commit the sin of envy."[57]

Evidence of eating problems abounds from Simone's earliest childhood. She was born a month prematurely, and though her mother, Selma Weil (1879–1965) continued to breastfeed her through an attack of appendicitis six months after the birth, Simone first became sickly and then, having been weaned at eleven months, fell gravely ill, possibly, the Weils felt (friends of the director of the Institut Pasteur, both parents were obsessed with microbes), as a result of poisoning. At sixteen months, Simone was still refusing to take food from a spoon, forcing her mother to feed her solids through a specially adapted bottle (SP 17): The parallel with Thérèse Martin's early eating problems is striking. During the First World War, Simone and her elder brother, the mathematical prodigy André Weil (born 1906) sent most of the sugar, and all of the chocolate, they received to an "adopted" soldier at the front and are reported to have played a macabre game that consisted of knocking on strangers' doors and screaming "We're dying of hunger! Our parents are letting us die of hunger!" when they were opened (RE 167). Both children wore sandals without socks in even the coldest of weather, and a famous story has Simone, aged six, sitting in the snow and refusing to go on because her parents had given her brother a *heavier* suitcase to carry than her.[58] The mythical heroines with whom Simone most identified were Electra and Antigone, the sister, respectively, of the brother (Orestes) who kills their mother and her lover (Clytaemnestra, Aegisthus) and of the dead brother (Polynices) whom her uncle (Creon) forbids her to bury; though less well documented, the relationship between Simone and André Weil may have been as fraught and problematic as that between Paul and Camille Claudel.

The obsession with food continued through adolescence and into early adulthood. While studying for entrance to the Ecole Normale Supérieure in the late 1920s, she had a brief contretemps with a still more famous Simone, Simone de Beauvoir. The only thing that mattered, said the first Simone when they met one day between classes, is "the Revolution that will feed the whole world" (an appalling famine was devastating China at the time), to which the second Simone replied that "the problem was not to bring about the happiness of men, but to find a meaning for their existence," only to be silenced with the withering (and surely justified) retort that "it's obvious you've never been hungry"; the relationship stopped there and then, and henceforth Simone I would regard Simone II—again not unreasonably at that time—as a "petty bourgeois spiritualist."[59] When, between 1931 and 1932, Simone was teaching at the Lyceé de Jeunes Filles at Le Puy in the Massif Central, she is reported by her roommate at the time to have rejected any fruit that was even the slightest bit blemished; she slept on the floor, with the window open even in the depths of winter, and heated her room only when receiving friends, out of solidarity, she said, with the local unemployed who, as it happened, were not short of fuel (SP 139–40). When her anxious mother had her sent food, clothes, and even some coal, she refused point-blank to use them, and an unsolicited maternal gift of a pair of skis in 1933 earned the following filial rebuke:

> As for the skis, *no* and again *no*. I give you my *word of honor*—do you hear me?—that I will *never* use skis bought without my consent. . . . I *forbid* you to buy me anything whatsoever without my permission. If you do, I shall not eat for a fortnight, or something of that kind. As you read these lines, you must imagine that I am forcing your shoulders up against the wall, and staring at you with fire in my eyes. (SP 274–75, italics in original)

Similar patterns of behavior—minimal eating, sleeping on the floor (when she slept at all), unheated accommodation, all of them now accompanied by frequent lacerating attacks of migraine—continued in her subsequent teaching appointments at Auxerre (1932–33), Roanne (1933), Bourges (1935), and Saint-Quentin (1937), until ill health forced her to give up teaching in early 1938. She had also followed the same demanding regime during the celebrated period in 1934–35—in fact no more than six months from beginning to end, with significant breaks when sick or laid off—that she spent working in various factories in Paris: first on the pressing machine of a company (Alstham) making electrical goods on the rue Lecourbe in the fifteenth arrondissement, then at a foundry at Boulogne-Billancourt in the northeast of the city, and, finally, as a milling-machine operator at Renault, on the basis of which experience she wrote her posthumously published *La Condition ouvrière* (1951), the most lasting of her political and sociological works. Her only indulgence was cigarettes (usually self-rolled, in would-be imitation of the proletariat), and it has been maliciously suggested that, in the unlikely event of Simone's ever being canonized, she would have a packet of Gauloises as her emblem. Even this, though, is more sinister than it appears, for her friend and biographer Simone Pétrement was convinced that the stigmalike red wound that once appeared on her left hand was self-inflicted with a lighted cigarette, as a "punishment" or test of her willpower (SP 62).

Her appearance and dress were similarly disconcerting to friends and enemies alike, though neither would cause much comment today. Both men and women (especially the latter) were shocked by her wiry unkempt hair that stuck out from under her beret (never a hat, at a time when hats for women were obligatory), by her John Lennon–style granny glasses, baggy sweaters, ankle-length black skirts or loose dungarees that concealed any female curves, and the inevitable sockless sandals that, when she was working as a grape picker at Saint-Jean-de-Peyrolas in the south of France in 1941, caused (again stigmatalike) wounds to her feet. She was remarkably antitactile, refusing to kiss or be kissed (even—or especially—when he mother was involved) and, when she could not avoid shaking hands, did so rapidly and perfunctorily, sometimes washing her hands immediately afterward or placing them under her arms. She was renowned for her clumsiness and gaucheness. Her small hands were unsuited to the kind of heavy manual labor she tried to do, and, as a militant syndicalist in Le Puy, she had to force herself to dance with the working men at their local *auberge;* she thought she did well, her partners, though politely complimentary, had a rather different view of the matter.[60]

The obligatory trip to war-torn Spain in the summer of 1936 came to an abrupt end when she stepped in a frying pan full of seething fat and had to be invalided out with a severely burned foot—before, it has to be said, she could do further damage (to herself and her comrades in the dissident Marxist Partido Obrero de Unificación Marxista—the celebrated POUM— rather than to the Fascist enemy) with the rifle she is shown proudly toting in photographs. She was both mocked, feared, and admired by those who knew her and who, in attempt to tie the untie-able down, bestowed on her all manner of nicknames: *la trollesse* (the female troll; cf. *drôlesse*=broad, hussy), *la Vierge Rouge* (the Red Virgin, the name given her by the director of the Ecole Normale Supérieure, Célestin Bouglé), and, most pointedly and perceptively, *la Martienne,* as her philosophy teacher, the great Emile-Auguste Chartier (1868–1951), better known as Alain, dubbed her, not because she was, as it were, "from another planet," but because, like the Martians in H. G. Wells's *The War of the Worlds* (1898), she was—or would dearly have liked to be—"all brain and a look," and no body (SP 49).

Given the sexual, aesthetic, and vestimentary criteria of the time, it was inevitable that Simone would be stereotyped as "masculine," or even, as Georges Bataille, who knew her on the dissident Marxist review *La Critique sociale* in 1933–34 and caricatured her as "Lazare" in his novel *Le Bleu du ciel* (1957), as "asexual, with something sinister about her" (*asexué avec quelque chose de néfaste*);[61] as we shall see in chapter 6, Simone's view of Bataille was even less complimentary. Simone herself spoke tellingly, if rarely, of the "singular misfortune of being a woman" (*une singulière malchance d'être une femme*) and, as her mother proudly declared when her daughter was five, "I am doing my best to foster in Simone, not the graces of a little girl, but the uprightness [*la droiture*] of a boy, even if that comes over as brusqueness" (letter of 21 June 1914, SP 49–50). Simone was known as "Simon" at home and often signed letters to her mother "your respectful son" (*ton fils respectueux*); an early text on working-class conditions (*Sur le tas: Souvenirs d'une exploiteé* [1936]) is signed "S. Galois" as though the author wants both to affirm and then deny her femininity and, more secretly, identify with *and* challenge the mathematical genius of her brother André (the adopted surname is that of Evariste Galois [1811–32], one of the greatest mathematicians of all time) and, more secretly still, put herself forward as a sacrificial victim, Galois having lost his life in a duel at the age of twenty-one.[62] When she became notorious in Le Puy for her syndicalist activities, one local newspaper wrote that "it appears that Antechrist is in Le Puy. He's a woman. She's dressed as a man" (RE 183). The "Vierge Rouge" did not belie either part of her nickname.

She is not known to have had any sexual relationships, either with men or with women, and she herself hints at an incident in early adolescence in the Jardin de Luxembourg—probably a "flasher"—that, she said, made her view with repulsion the idea of being an "object of desire": "As soon as there is *need, desire,* even if it is reciprocal, there is outrage" (SP 330). Like Thérèse Martin, she deliberately masculinized herself, and, not surprisingly, many people identified her with the archetypal symbol of desexed, martialized woman, Joan of Arc. One male teacher who sided with her when her militant activities brought her into conflict with the authorities in Le Puy remarked that he "never understood the story of Joan of Arc before. Now I understand it" (SP 167).[63]

Her refusal of her femininity appears to be linked to her refusal of her Jewishness which, in rabbinical law, is transmitted matrilinearily. As a Jew (according to the definition given in the Vichy regime's Statut des Juifs of October 1940), Simone was barred from occupying any teaching position, and on 18 October 1941 she sent a magnificently sarcastic letter (never replied to, and possibly never read) to Vichy's "Commissioner for Jewish Affairs," the notoriously antisemitic Xavier Vallat, denying any meaning other than religious to the category "Jewish" and, by corollary, denying her own Jewishness since, as she said, "I have never been into a synagogue, I was brought up without any religious practice by free-thinking parents, I have no attraction toward the Jewish religion, no links to the Jewish, and have been nourished [*nourrie,* in her case a highly loaded term] since earliest childhood on the Hellenic, Christian, and French tradition." Nevertheless, she continues, she has conformed to the Vichyist injunction that "Jews" take on (preferably agricultural) work, and thanks Vallat and the regime he represents for giving her this opportunity, since the only people who can be said to "possess" nature and the earth are those "into whose bodies they have entered through the daily suffering of limbs broken with fatigue": "You have also given me the infinitely precious gift of poverty, something you will never possess either" (SP 591–92). As she began to inch closer to Christianity, Simone was at pains to separate the New Testament from the Old, and argued controversially that Christianity had more in common with Platonism, and even with the mysticism of the Upanishads and the Bhagavad Gita, than it did with orthodox Judaism, once even declaring that it was necessary to "purge [again hardly a neutral term in any context, let alone in that of the 1940s] Christianity of the heritage of Israel" (RE 213).

This has led to charges of her being antisemitic—a "self-hating Jew," according to one stereotyped definition—and even pro-Vichy, of having, in the words of one critic (Wladimir Rabi), committed a kind of "spiritual genocide" to set alongside the actual genocide of the Jews, which, remarkably, she seems never to have mentioned in her writings, even though the existence of extermination camps was well attested by the summer of 1942, and she can hardly have been unaware of the ongoing holocaust (RE 211). When Simone offered herself up as, in effect, a holocaustal victim, it was, crucially, on behalf of the suffering *French* people that her self-offering was made, not on behalf of the far more grievously afflicted Jewish people with whom she refused all identification—though critics might say (and some certainly do) that, when she and her parents sailed from Marseille to New York in May 1942, it was not *just,* as she claimed, to enable her circuitously to rejoin the Free French Forces in London.[64]

In her letters of early 1942 to Père Perrin, Simone evokes the various "stations" on her own personal way to the Cross, beginning with how, on holiday in Portugal in the late summer of 1935, she witnessed a religious procession of women in an impoverished fishing-village, "carrying candles and singing what must certainly be very ancient hymns of a heart-rending sadness," at the sight and sound of which, she recounts, "the conviction was suddenly borne in upon me that Christianity is pre-eminently the religion of slaves, that slaves cannot help belonging to it, and I among others." Two years later in Italy—specifically in Assisi, city of *il Poverello,* and not in Rome, city of the institutionalized Church—she describes how

> Alone in the little twelfth-century Romanesque chapel of Santa Maria degli Angeli, an incomparable marvel of purity where Saint Francis often used to pray, something stronger than I was compelled me for the first time in my life to go down on my knees.

But the crucial turning point came, as mentioned earlier, during the ten days that she spent (with her mother) at Solesmes, from Palm Sunday to Easter Tuesday (10–19 April) in 1938. There, despite terrible migraines, she *attended* the entire Easter liturgy, and

> by an extreme effort of concentration I was able to rise above this wretched flesh, to leave it to suffer by itself, heaped up in a corner, and to find a pure and perfect joy in the unimaginable beauty of the chanting and the words. This experience enabled me by analogy to get a better understanding of the possibility of loving divine love in the midst of affliction. It goes without saying that in the course of these services the thought of the Passion of Christ entered into my being once and for all.

While at Solesmes, Simone met a young English Catholic named John Vernon—Simone nicknamed him "angel boy" (in English)—from whom, she told Perrin, "I gained my first idea of the supernatural power of the Sacraments because of the truly angelic radiance with which he seemed to be clothed after going to communion." Vernon introduced her to the poetry of George Herbert (1593–1633), and to the exquisite concluding poem of *The Temple* (1633) entitled, simply, "Love," that Simone learned by heart and, mustering all of her remarkable powers of attention, recited it repeatedly out loud, not realizing that "the recitation had the virtue of a prayer." It was during one such recitation that, as she quietly puts it, "Christ himself came down and took possession of me."[65]

With its emphasis on looking and eating, Herbert's poem could not have been closer to the core of Simone's preoccupations:

> Love bade me welcome: yet my soul drew back,
>   Guiltie of dust and sinne.
> But quick-ey'd Love, observing me grow slack
>   From my first entrance in,
> Drew nearer to me, sweetly questioning,
>   If I lack'd any thing.
>
> A guest, I answer'd, worthy to be here:
>   Love said, you shall be he.
> I the unkinde, ungratefull? Ah my deare,
>   I cannot look on thee.
> Love took my hand, and smiling did reply,
>   Who made the eyes but I?
>
> Truth Lord, but I have marr'd them: let my shame
>   Go where it doth deserve.
> And know you not, sayes Love, who bore the blame?
>   My deare, then I will serve.
> You must sit downe, sayes Love, and taste my meat:
>   So I did sit and eat.[66]

Translated into the terms of *La Pesanteur et la grâce,* grace *descends* into the realm of weight made up by Simone's body, her senses, her intelligence, her social relations, in other words the totality of her self, and urges her— "Descent, precondition of ascent," reads one of her aphorisms[67]—to *ascend* into that ethereal realm inhabited by the Gregorian chant and the song of the Portuguese women: It is a characteristic blend of Christian *agape* and Platonist *eros,*[68] from which, however, Simone will draw literally fatal conclusions. For, alas, "I have no principle of ascension within me,[69] everything weighs me down, even my desire to be weightless," and "this is why one cannot conceive of the descent of God towards man or of the ascension of man towards God except as a rending"[70]—and here Simone uses the word *écartèlement,* the practice—as at the execution of the would-be regicide Damiens in 1757[71]—of "quartering" the body of the condemned criminal after (or sometimes even before) he was killed. The relationship between

God and man replicates that of executioner and victim; man, as it were, is invited by Grace to ascend to the scaffold where, in order to ascend higher, he must be literally taken apart, hanged, drawn, and quartered, to destroy the antidivine principle of weight. It must, says Simone, be possible "to kill all vital energy in oneself while preserving solely the vertical movement. Leaves and fruit are a waste of energy if one only wishes to rise."[72] This is the sense of what Simone Pétrement rightly calls the "terrible prayer" recorded in *Cahiers V*:

> May all this [she means her will, her senses, her intelligence, even her love for God to the extent that is "hers"], may all this be wrenched [*arraché*] from me, devoured by God, transformed into the substance of Christ, and given as food to the unfortunate whose body and soul lack all kind of nourishment. And let me be paralyzed, blind, deaf, an idiot, an imbecile. Father, bring about this transformation now, in the name of Christ. (SP 639)

The difference between this and Herbert's poem could not be more marked. Simone cannot, *will not,* "sit and eat," she cannot bear the thought of tasting the "meat" of Christ's body really present in the Host, while at the same time longing to do so. Instead, she must stand up and be eaten, rise up above the dreaded domain of weight, and offer herself as food for God and suffering humanity; unable to "cannibalize" Christ, she asks Christ to cannibalize her. Hyperactive even as she strains to be passive, intensely self-willed even as she wills the annihilation of her will, she can no more receive the gratuitous gift of Christ's body and blood than she can accept the unsolicited gift of a pair of skis from her mother.

By the early 1940s, Simone was under pressure both from Père Perrin and from herself to confront once and for all the question of her being baptized and becoming a full member, an integral part, not just of "the Church" as mystical Body of Christ but of the existent Roman Catholic Church. (There was never any possibility, it seems, of any other church though, while in New York, she regularly and with much enthusiasm went to a black Baptist church in Harlem; one friend said that, had she remained in America, she would have become black [SP 631].)

It is not possible, or relevant, to review here all the arguments for and against baptism and reception that she rehearses in her letters to Perrin and, later, to Père Couturier, the French priest in New York to whom she was given an introduction by none other than Jacques Maritain, then a refugee from occupied France teaching at Columbia University.[73] Beneath all the ancillary issues that Simone raises (such as the fate of children who die unbaptized), two sets of objection stand out: one consciously thought through, reasonable, and objective; the other, unstated but clearly at the forefront of her mind and inseparable from her deteriorating physical condition. Of the first set of issues—her reservations about the institutional Church, its hierarchies, its social and political record, and the strictures it places on individual intellectual freedom—one can say only that her caution was justified; as she said, the historical Church can only exist as a social structure, but "in so far as it is a social structure, it belongs to the Prince of this World" or, to put it more abstractly, to her negative category of weight.[74] The other issue, of course, involved taking communion (though she never says so in so many words), and her letters to Perrin and Couturier, so dense, so intense, so packed with historical caveats and theological *distinguos,* often read like a complex set of discursive strategies for evading this central dilemma. While attending mass or deep in prayer and meditation, she had never once had, she told Perrin, "even for a moment, the feeling that God wants me to be in the Church," and she accordingly regarded it "as legitimate on my part to be a member of the church by right but not in fact [*en droit et non en fait*], not only for a time, but for my whole life if need be."[75] Given her visceral need for intellectual freedom, not to mention the complexity of her psychological needs, virtual Church membership and virtual communion—standing not sitting, waiting and looking rather than eating—seem not merely the wisest but, in reality, the only option available.

Simone left New York for London in November 1942, accompanied by yet another Simone, Simone Deitz, a Jewish convert to Catholicism, who would be her principal companion during the remaining months of her life. Simone's intention, needless to say, was to play an active, and, ideally, self-sacrificial part in the struggle against Nazism, to be parachuted into France on some resistance mission, and, specifically, to submit to the Free French authorities in London her ideas for a team of nurses—herself presumably among them—to be somehow slipped into France to minister to the Resistance. But, given her temperament, reputation, and obvious physical frailty, she was kept very much at a distance by the Free French, and the winter of 1942–43, which she spent living in a flat in Holland Park, was a period of mounting frustration that frenetic reading and writing, interspersed with visits to the theater, galleries, and East End pubs (which she reputedly adored [SP 666]), could not keep at bay.

She became deeply depressed, ate and slept even less, and in April 1943 she collapsed, stricken with tuberculosis probably linked to her fasting, and was taken in a critical state to Middlesex hospital. Her physical weakness made any treatment a risk, and some of her doctors complained that, by not eating, she was frustrating all their efforts on her behalf and, effectively, collaborating in hastening her death. Still insisting that "I cannot be happy and eat to my fill when I feel that my people are suffering" and asking that the food she rejected be sent to French prisoners of war in Germany (SP 679), she ate virtually nothing—a few cherries, an occasional slice of tinned peach—and, when she refused an operation that would have removed one lung in the hope of rescuing the other, the Middlesex doctors despaired, and Simone was transferred to a private sanatorium in Ashford where, a week later, she died, aged thirty-four, on 24 August 1943, probably of a heart attack brought on by her general condition. The local coroner recorded a verdict of suicide, and the *South Eastern Gazette* headlined its story "Death from starvation: French professor's curious sacrifice" (SP 692). There are unconfirmed rumors that a Catholic patient or nurse in the sanatorium baptized Simone in extremis (as canon law permits a layperson to do), and she was buried in the section of the New Cemetery in Ashford that is reserved for Roman Catholics. The priest who was due to officiate at her burial missed his train, and it was Maurice Schumann, Free French official, future Gaullist minister, and another Jewish convert to Catholicism, who led the prayers at her graveside.

One of Simone's most audacious and influential theological concepts is the idea of creation not as an expansion of God's power but, precisely, as a contraction. In this conception, which owes not a little to various gnostic and cabalistic ideas with which Simone was familiar through her friendship with Simone Pétrement, a leading authority on both subjects,[76] God, who is all in all, somehow contracts into himself and willingly allows something that is not himself to exist in a space of its own. In creating the universe or, perhaps better, in allowing the universe to be created, or to create itself, God, out of love, renounces being a totality. The entire universe results from God's willing self-emptying known in Greek orthodox theology of *kenosis,* a foundational act of self-limitation similar to the cabalistic concept of *Tsimtsoum*—by which God allows something other than himself to exist entirely out of his control;[77] creation is a divine wager in which God can never recover his stake.

From this beginning, Simone might have drawn the conception of the universe as God's play similar to that which, working altogether more intuitively, Thérèse of Lisieux arrived at before the onset of the illness that killed her.[78] The creation has no telos, no point, it is gratuitous, an act of divine folly, the proverbial free lunch on a macrocosmic scale that a God of love freely offers to humans to play with and eat as they will. Unlike Simone, however, Thérèse overcame the eating disorders that plagued her childhood and early adolescence. In contrast, Simone's deduction proceeds differently from that of Thérèse. For her, the universe no sooner comes into being in the space opened out by God's self-limitation than it falls under the sway of what she calls necessity or, more graphically, weight. *Falls* is the operative word, for Simone's universe, like that of the gnostics, is intrinsically fallen, intrinsically weighed down, and oriented away from its divine source, and salvation can consist only in what she calls "decreation," in countering the downward pulsion of weight with the upward pulsion of a self-emptying, self-decreating spirituality modeled on the primordial act of divine self-limitation:

We participate in the creation of the world by decreating ourselves.[79]
God gave me being in order that I should return it to him. . . .

> If I accept this gift, it is evil and fatal; its virtue lies in refusing it [*sa vertu apparaît pour le refus*]. God permits me to exist outside of Him. It is up to me to refuse that permission [*cette autorisation*].[80]

These are terrible words, and, if they are all too consistent with her anorexic condition, they surely run counter to the essence of Christ's teaching: "I am come that they might have life, and that they might have it more abundantly" (John 10:10).

In her extraordinary letter to Père Couturier written in New York between September and November 1942—thirty pages, in standard editions, of dense theological, philosophical, and historical argument—Simone says very significantly that "if the Gospels omitted all mention of the resurrection of Christ, faith would be easier for me. The Cross alone is enough for me."[81] Simone's faith, like that of so many Catholics of her time and others, stopped, so to speak, on Good Friday; she could not get beyond the ultimate divine self-emptying on the Cross to the restored plenitude of Easter Sunday morning when only the tomb is empty. Had Simone been able, metaphorically, to advance from the garden of Gethsemane where, abandoned by both God and his disciples, Christ prays alone to the garden where, after three days, he appears before Mary Magdalene in all his bodily glory, she might have meditated on, with all of her remarkable powers of attentiveness, the story of the meeting at Emmaus, outside Jerusalem, of the resurrected Christ and a handful of still-mourning disciples:

> And while they yet believed not for joy, and wondered, he said unto them, Have ye here any meat? And they gave him a piece of a broiled fish, and of an honeycomb. And he took it, and did eat before them. (Luke 24:41–43)

Not only does the resurrected Christ eat, he feeds and enjoins his disciples to feed each other; the invitation to "come and dine" is immediately followed by the command to "feed my lambs, feed my sheep" (John 21:12–16).

Simone Weil's tragedy was that her illness interrupted and disrupted the endless to-and-fro of reciprocal nourishment that is the central metaphor—and much more than a metaphor—of Christian teaching and practice; she could give but not receive, offer herself up as food but not herself eat. In a sense, she was a fool for Christ's sake, a *stulta propter Christum* (I Corinthians 4:10), who was determined to empty herself out for Christ as Christ had emptied himself out for mankind: "And being found in fashion as a man, he humbled himself [*s'est vidé* in the translation used and quoted by Simone][82] and became obedient unto death, even the death of the cross" (Philippians 2:8) "Mais elle est folle!" De Gaulle reputedly exclaimed when told of Simone's plan for a detachment of nurses to be slipped into France (SP 667), and he was far from the first to utter the word. In her last but one letter to her parents, dated 4 August 1943, Simone describes for their benefit almost the only food that she has been able to take, that staple of English cookery, the fruit fool:

> The name is delicious! But these fools are not like Shakespeare's fools. They lie, making out that they are fruit, whereas in Sh.[akespeare] the fools are the only characters that tell the truth. When I saw *Lear* here, I asked myself how the incomparably tragic character of these had not struck people, myself included, long before. Their tragedy [*leur tragique*] does not consist in the sentimental things that are sometimes said about them, but in this: In this world, only beings that have fallen to the very depths of humiliation, beneath the level of begging, not only lacking in all social consideration, but regarded by everyone as devoid [*dépourvus*] of the most basic human dignity, only such beings have in reality the possibility of telling the truth. Everyone else lies.

She goes on to talk about Velázquez's fools: "Is the sadness in their eyes the bitterness of possessing the truth, to have, at the price of a nameless degradation, the possibility of telling the truth, and of being understood by no-one?" "Darling M. ['Mime,' her mother's pet name]," she concludes, "don't you sense the affinity, the essential analogy between those fools and me?"[83] It is an extraordinary letter, which reaches beyond gooseberry fools, *King Lear* (*leer*=empty?), and Velázquez to embrace the whole Christian tradition of the *stultitia crucis,* the foolishness of the Cross, the foolishness of God, which, says Saint Paul, "is wiser than men," for "God hath chosen the weak things of the world to confound the things which are mighty" (I Corinthians 1:25, 27). But God's fools and the *parvuli,* the little children whom Jesus suffers to come unto him "for of such is the kingdom of God" (Mark 10:14), are of course one and the same, and Jesus gives thanks to his father in heaven "because thou has hid these things from the wise and the prudent, and has revealed them unto babes" (Matthew 11:25).

But if Simone was a fool for Christ's sake, she was, in the last critical analysis, a very serious fool, unable to "play ball" with God, as Thérèse did, or dance, even metaphorically, along with him, as Marthe did: "Je gambaderai!" Simone's last wish, heartrendingly, was, according to Pétrement, for a *purée de pommes de terre* cooked *à la française* "like her mother used to make it," the kind of *purée,* one imagines, that was fed to her at eleven months through that specially adapted baby bottle (SP 690–91). Herbert's great poem had invited her to "sit and eat." This she ultimately could not do, but if her "angel boy" at Solesmes at Easter 1938 had introduced her to a still greater English poet, a few years younger than Herbert, she might also have discovered the following:

"Doth God exact day-labour, light denied?"
I fondly ask. But patience, to prevent
That murmur, soon replies, "God doth not need
Either man's work or his own gifts; who best
Bear his mild yoke, they serve Him best; His state
Is Kingly. Thousands at His bidding speed
And post o'er land and ocean without rest;
They also serve who only stand and wait."

JOHN MILTON (1608–74), SONNET XIX
("WHEN I CONSIDER HOW MY LIGHT IS SPENT")[84]

6

A LAURA FOR OUR TIMES?

Colette Peignot

PARIS — BERLIN — MOSCOW — BARCELONA —
ST. GERMAIN-EN-LAYE, 1903–1938

Colette Laure Lucienne Peignot rarely used her second baptismal name except as an occasional persona in her erotic writings. The woman known to posterity as "Laure" was initially a posthumous creation made jointly by her lover at the time of her death, Georges Bataille (1897–1962) and by his and her friend Michel Leiris (1901–90), with a view to circumventing her family's objections when they published a selection of texts by her in a private edition entitled *Laure: Le Sacré* in 1939, the year following her death from tuberculosis at the age of thirty-five. What one might describe as Colette's negative canonization—her transformation, in the title of Elisabeth Barillé's biography of her (1997), into a "saint of the abyss" (*la sainte de l'Abîme*)[1]—has been the virtual lifework of her nephew Jérôme Peignot (born 1926), who last saw her in the last year of her life in the *chambre de bonne* she was then renting on the boulevard de Lannes just off the Bois de Boulogne in the 16th arrondissement. Readers of André Gide's *La Porte étroite* (1909) will recall the impact of one exotic aunt on another adolescent Jérôme, but the spell that his Aunt Colette cast over the twelve-year-old Jérôme Peignot has been powerful enough to last six decades and more and to have fulfilled one hesitates to say quite how many psychological functions. In his impassioned introduction to his edition of his aunt's writings, first published in 1971 and appropriately entitled "My Diagonal Mother" (*Ma mère diagonale*),[2] Peignot lays his (displaced) Oedipal cards plainly on the table. His lifelong obsession with his aunt has, he says, been a way of "negating my father and replacing him with his opposite," "of not being the son of my father and mother" (9), and of creating for himself a surrogate identity that, paradoxically, is far more "authentic" than anything he could otherwise have or be: "That woman and the love I have for her purifies everything. My passion restores me to my authenticity." Reading "Laure"'s account of her childhood, *Histoire d'une petite fille* (the title was chosen by

Bataille and Leiris when they published it privately in 1940), or discovering how, when she attended her first bullfight in Spain in the mid-1930s, the man sitting next to her "got a hard-on the size of a stallion's" (*bandait comme un cerf*) at the sight of the blood, the young Peignot felt both "ravaged by desire" for his aunt and as though he "had changed sex and rediscovered myself in hers" (25). She is "*my* dead woman [*ma morte à moi*], my everlasting obsession, my true love" through whom he takes "diagonal" revenge on his father, Colette's elder brother Charles Peignot (born 1897): "It is also *against my father* that I love my aunt" (27, Peignot's italics). Not only this, but he also supplants his arch-rival Bataille whose mistress he possesses more fully in her death than Bataille ever did in her life. As an example of parricidal incestuous masturbatory necrophilia, "My Diagonal Mother" can have few equals in psychoanalytic literature. Its effect—and the effect of Peignot's editorial, biographical, and critical work generally—has been to compound the original beatification-in-reverse by Bataille and Leiris and further to conceal the "real" Colette Peignot under the dubious trappings of the *femme fatale* to beat all *femmes fatales,* the modern Lorelei who not only dooms men but dooms herself in the process, the infernal Laura of a succession of vaguely Marxist, vaguely surrealist, sometimes would-be satanic Petrarchs who adored her: the dissident communists Jean Bernier, Boris Pilniak, and Boris Souvarine; the suitably sinister Eduard Trautner, author of *Gott, Gegenwart, and Kokain* (*God, the Present Moment, and Cocain*) and German translator of the alleged memoirs of Charles Sanson, the executioner of Louis XVI; Bataille himself; and the scores of "ordinary men" (*hommes vulgaires,* Bataille's expression, presumably meaning not macho-Hegelians like himself) whom, at one time, she supposedly picked up at random, "making love to them even in train toilets." "But she found no pleasure in this," Bataille reassures us (281).

This chapter attempts, to the extent that it is possible, to disentangle Colette Peignot from "Laure," and to approach her through the fragmentary writings that she left—whether she wanted them published is a major bone of contention among her numerous laureates—rather than through the recollections and fantasies of those who knew, or thought they knew, her. The woman henceforth referred to as Colette gives an appropriately "diagonal" perspective on the concerns of this book in the sense that, given the narrowness of her Catholic upbringing and the unequaled intensity of her attempt to transcend it, she appears as a self-created negation of everything that the other Catholic women discussed here held dear and attempted to stand for, a kind of existential black hole into which they, their lives, their beliefs, and their values, are turned head on their heels, scrambled, shredded, and finally dissolved. Her experience—and sometimes even the details of her biography—both duplicates and subverts that of many of her more devout "sisters."

Coincidentally, she was born at Meudon (on 8 October 1903), many years, of course, before Jacques and Raïssa Maritain moved there, but her family's network of friends overlapped curiously with that of the future Meudon circle: her piano teacher as a child—she was a gifted musician—was the Catalan master Ricardo Viñes (1875–1943), a close friend of Léon Bloy and the Maritains, and her brother married the singer Suzanne Rivière who was close to the composer Georges Auric (1899–1983) who also moved on the fringes of the Maritain circle. More significantly, she suffered and died of tuberculosis like Thérèse Martin (and, saints Bernadette and Elisabeth de la Trinité), she collaborated with Simone Weil on the dissident communist review *La Critique sociale* in the early 1930s and, like her, was a passionate supporter of republican Spain; the two women even had the dubious distinction of appearing together pseudonymously in Bataille's part pornographic, part political novel *Le Bleu du ciel* (written 1935, published 1957), Simone as "Lazare," Colette as "Dorothea," alias "Dirty." Although never declared insane in the manner of her fellow rebel against the narrowness of a Catholic girlhood, Camille Claudel, she had at least one nervous breakdown requiring institutionalization, attempted suicide on, it appears, two occasions, and received regular psychoanalysis from Bataille's friend Antoine Borel. Her relation with her mother and father had much in common with that of Thérèse with hers, though with vastly different long-term consequences. Like Thérèse, too, she was notably thin, though this is more likely to be a consequence of tuberculosis than of an eating disorder. The general argument advanced in this chapter is that, like Bataille (who seriously considered a vocation as a priest or a monk in his late teens and early twenties, before turning violently against Catholicism between 1922 and 1924),[3] Colette remained imprisoned within a Catholic worldview even as she sought to negate and transcend it by sacrilegious inversion, reluctantly recognizing in 1937 that "the religion of crime poisons us just as much as that of virtue" (121). In opposition to almost all writing on the joint subjects of Bataille and "Laure," this chapter takes the view that both remained Catholics, albeit back-to-front Catholics, who realized (but, in Bataille's case, refused to acknowledge it) that they could never get outside or beyond the parameters of the faith they absorbed early on despite doing everything possible, and even "impossible," to use one of Bataille's favorite terms, to destroy them. In what follows, the lives and thinking of Colette and Bataille are shown to be in constant interaction following their meeting in 1931, though with Colette taking the initiative at least as often as she adopted, and adapted, concepts and images first developed by Bataille.

Histoire d'une petite fille

Colette's background was solidly bourgeois—relatively new money rather than old, for it was her grandfather who had established the family fortune in the manufacture of typographical machinery that her father Gustave more than consolidated through the invention of a new typeface for which he was awarded a prize at the Paris Universal Exhibition of 1900. In the year of Colette's birth, 1903, the Peignots moved from the boulevard de Montrouge (now the boulevard Edgar Quinet) by the Cimetière Montparnasse to an unlikely location for a family so wealthy in the 14th arrondissement, on the rue Ferrus midway between the prison of La Santé and the hospital of Sainte-Anne, the latter scarcely less notorious than the former, specializing (as readers of Émile Zola's *L'Assommoir* (1877) will know) in the treatment of the final stages of delirium tremens. The family was obsessively, even oppressively, Catholic, and in her *Histoire d'une petite fille*, written in the mid-1930s, Colette recalls her "sordid, timorous childhood, haunted by mortal sin, Good Friday and Ash Wednesday, a childhood crushed beneath heavy veils of mourning, a child-robbing childhood [*enfance voleuse d'enfants* (54–55)]" in which her mother's idea of a Sunday afternoon treat was to take her children to watch a religious procession on the Ile de la Cité:

> We waited for the procession. I saw the standards and the flags of the sickly little boys and the knock-kneed old men (canes in their hands); I saw the banners and cheap finery of the sweaty priests (their armpits green and malodorous), I saw the filthy scapulars and rosaries of the young girls, the tremulous children of Mary: "Father, I have had sinful thoughts." They were all bawling, their breath reeking to high heaven: We are the ho-o-o-o-pe [*espou a a a re*] of France. Three old crones, their heads nodding under their thick oily hair, revealed beneath their mustaches dentures chock-full of rancid communion wafer. (57)

At once "eternal victim and insane executioner" (56), Jesus stretched out his arms to the already rebellious little girl, Saint Veronica simpered with her "handkerchief oozing of Christ [*linge suintant le Christ*]," painted blood seeped from nails driven into walls, and the Holy Face of Christ—that image so dear to Thérèse Martin, Eva Lavallière, and scores of other Catholic women—"wept tears of oil behind a red lamp that lit all on its own the 'chapel of the Seven Sorrows'" (58).

As a depiction of a certain kind of Catholic childhood, *Histoire d'une petite fille* bears comparison with Arthur Rimbaud's great poem "Les Premières Communions" (1871): one by one, the three Peignot sisters, Madeleine (born 1899), Geneviève (1900), and Colette (1903), go forward to receive "the putrid kiss of Jesus," the blessing of Christ, that "eternal thief of [human] energies."[4] Like the young Rimbaud, too, Colette is obsessed by those other and poorer than herself, workingmen and -women and that rather different creature, the *employé*—shop assistant or metro attendant—to whom her mother spoke in a slightly altered voice and to whom she would never say "Monsieur" or "Madame" and, in the Peignot households, the maids and the washerwomen who, Colette was sure, *could* (unlike her mother) have known joy if only they were given the leisure time and freedom from the terror of dismissal to experience it. The seeds of Colette's future ultraradicalism may have been sown by the suicide of the daughter of one of the servants who threw herself out of a window when her mother was accused of stealing some coal, further proof, if proof were needed, that "mortal sin *really does* kill" (60–61).

Her life is torn between what, following a famous distinction made by the early anthropologist Robert Hertz (1881–1915), Bataille and Leiris would later call, on the one hand, the *sacré de droite*—the noble, positive sacred embodied for Colette in the images of Jesus and Joseph and all the other holy pictures around her, "blue, pink, gilt, surrounded by stars, silk-wrapped and be-ribboned"—and, on the other, the *sacré de gauche*: that which must be shunned and abhorred, bodily products such as mucus, excrement, and sweat, the body itself, and above all its nether regions that God—who sees everything—must never see a little girl touch and examine, even in the attic in which she hides herself away. Between these two modalities, opposed but complementary, of the sacred—the venerated, the forbidden, the pure, the impure—Colette passes her childhood in a sprawling octopus of a city each of whose tentacles "converge on a swollen wet center" (56), every street identical to the next, the houses either with tiny windows (those of the poor) or heavy curtains (those of the rich), a city both oppressively real and hauntingly unreal from which—and here Colette quotes Rimbaud directly—"true life would forever be absent" (d'où la vraie vie serait toujours absente) (60).[5]

Into the stygian gloom of this childhood only Colette's father with his "bright, happy, blue eyes" brought any light. The youngest daughter of three (as Thérèse Martin was of five), she took an "intense joy"—again reminiscent of Thérèse—in "going out alone with my father," an irregular event but one of "extraordinary importance" for her (167). If the huge property on the rue Ferrus was her mother's domain, to her father belonged the family's country retreat at Boissettes on one of the loops of the Seine at Melun, and it was here, encouraged by Monsieur Peignot, that she discovered "nature" with which, anticipating her future "mystical" longings, she longed to merge: "I used to go and disappear, vanish completely, between the wall and the ivy. There I became a spider, a daddy-long-legs, a centipede, a hedgehog, everything you like and perhaps even a ladybird [*bête à bon Dieu*]" (63).

On the other hand, like so many of the mothers discussed in this book, Madame Peignot remained, despite her many servants, "constantly preoccupied with housework, obsessed to the point of anguish by dust, mothballs and floor polish" and shut herself off in "total mistrust of everything that was not family and in ignorance of everything in the world that could be gay, active, moving, living, or simply human" (59). Mother=duty, indoors, superego, death; Father=pleasure, outdoors, ego (let there by no talk of the id!), activity, life.

This is the dichotomy that structured Thérèse's early childhood, and, as we have seen, it was the death of her mother that marked the beginning of her spiritual liberation. Colette's tragedy was that she lost not her death-bearing mother but her life-bringing father, killed on the western front at Givenchy in September 1915, the third Peignot brother so to perish after André (September 1914) and Rémi (May 1915), to be followed not long afterward by the death of a fourth brother, Lucien, in June 1916, at Boissettes, the victim not of a German bullet or shell but of the family curse, tuberculosis, with which Colette herself was diagnosed the following year. The family's tragedy was so great, and its social and political connections so significant, that a commemorative oration was delivered by the former prime minister Louis Barthou, and a street near the Imprimerie Nationale in the 15th arrondissement was renamed the rue des Quartre Frères Peignot. For her part, Colette composed a macabre little rhyme that she included in *Histoire d'une petite fille*:

> Ils sont morts, morts, morts, André et Rémi
> Ils sont morts, morts, morts, Papa, André et Rémi
> Ils sont morts, morts, morts, Papa, André, Lucien et Rémi
>
> (64)

> [They are dead, dead, dead, André and Rémi / They are
> dead, dead, dead, Papa, André and Rémi / They are dead,
> dead, dead, Papa, André, Lucien and Rémi]

When, in the last year of her life, she described for Leiris—author of a celebrated paper entitled "The Sacred in Everyday Life" that he delivered in January 1938 to a study group somewhat portentously known as the Collège de Sociologie that he, Bataille, and the anthropologist Roger Caillois (1913–78) had founded the previous year—what the notion of the sacred meant for her, it was to the departure of her father for the front in July 1915 that she instinctively harked back. It was, she said, an event that "provoked in me a state of total exaltation, made up of a complete premonition of a sacrifice consented to in advance, before the very face of the sacrificial victim [*du sacrifié*]. That, at the age of eleven, mixed with the songs of a delirious crowd, songs in which I join in, my voice suddenly breaking by moments, a sense of total physical upheaval. Inability to resume physical existence. For days on end I bellow out the *Marseillaise* and the *Chant du Départ*. A classmate, met in the Metro, dressed in deep mourning because of having lost her father, makes me feel ashamed" (88). The sacrificial paradigm that would dominate Colette's life had been laid out by the time she was eleven.

After their father's death, Colette and the elder of her two sisters,

Madeleine, would weep in each other's arms, partly in longing for their dead father and partly in horror at their mother who, through the extremity of her mourning, seemed to them "really to want to kill him a second time over" (71). The family's grief was "total, total, eternal" (64), and, banal though it sounds, Colette really did spend the rest of her life trying to replace, compensate for, and take revenge for her lost father (as much against him as against the political and military forces that had killed him), the absence of Father becoming more and more equated with the absence of God. Hatred of mother, longing for dead father: It is a pattern that both replicates and inverts that of Bataille, whose blind, crippled father was effectively abandoned by his wife and son to die in the shelling of Reims at the outbreak of war, it having been his son's unpleasant duty to accompany his father to the WC (water closet; the title in abbreviation of a story Bataille wrote in 1926 and later destroyed) where, "with his great aquiline nose and huge hollow eyes," Jean-Aristide Bataille would "howl like an animal" at the "lacerating pains" of defecation. The "hero" of Bataille's early sacrilegio-pornographic extravaganza *Histoire de l'oeil* (1928) derives his name, Lord Auch, from a combination of Lord (=God) + *aux ch(iottes)* (*chiottes*=toilet, "john"), so determined is the author to collapse the opposition of *sacré de droite* and *sacré de gauche,* to relegate what he calls "the summit" (*le sommet*) to *les chiottes* and raise *les chiottes* to the summit.[6] In a later text, Colette would adopt both Bataille's program and his scatological terms:

> Aux chiottes
> Aux chiottes les sommets . . .
> Aux chiottes
> Aux chiottes
> Les grands sentiments
> Les passions pesantes
> Que tout chavire
> Que nos mères soient maquerelles
> Que nos femmes soient putains
> Nos filles violées
>
> (113)

> [Down the shits / Down the shits with the summits /
> Down the shits / Down the shits / With noble feelings /
> Weighty passions / Let everything capsize, turn upside
> down / Let our mothers be madams / Let our wives be
> tarts / Let our daughters be raped]

Always one to go further, and then further again, Bataille several times describes masturbating over his mother's corpse, and he entitled another of his novels *Ma mère* (1954–55) in which the mother is the object of simultaneous horror and desire. To cap it all, Madame Bataille was baptized Marie-Antoinette, an appallingly apposite first name for the mother of a son who, in adult life, would be obsessed by the execution of Louis XVI (and later his wife) on the renamed Place de la Concorde,[7] and who would, as we shall see, found a secret society called *Acéphale,* the man without a head, with a view, it seems sure, to engaging in some kind of sacrificial ritual.

Following her husband's death, Colette's mother fell more and more under the thrall of the Church and, perhaps in an attempt to provide her children with a surrogate father-figure, frequently invited one particular priest into the family home to give consolation and counsel; as Jérome Peignot says (20), long before there were *prêtres ouvriers* (worker priests) there were *prêtres bourgeois,* the church being greatly concerned at signs of wartime indifference, or even hostility, to religion emerging among the sons and daughters of the *grande bourgeoisie.* The priest in question often features in the literature as "l'Abbé D." (perhaps in deliberate echo of yet another novel by Bataille, *L'Abbé C* [1949]), but his actual name was Marcel Pératé, a follower of the youth movement known as *Le Sillon* founded by the Catholic layman Marc Sangnier (1873–1950) whose commitment to an active "social" Catholicism resulted in conflict with Rome and formal condemnation in 1910. There are schools of psychoanalysis that would attach an overdetermining significance to Pératé's name (*Père athée*=atheist father), and his impact on Colette's life was undoubtedly massive.

In the wake of the suppression of *Le Sillon,* Pératé—that "two-bit Rasputin" (*Raspoutine à la manque* [68]), as Colette later scathingly called him—decided to set up his own youth group, complete with annual camps and so on, and Colette was among a number of Catholic adolescents from good families to be coopted into it. Another was Marcel Moré (1887–1969), a future friend of both Bataille and Leiris who would be present when Colette died, at that time, in his own words, an adherent to a Bloy-derived "absolute" Catholicism, attaching much more importance to the world of the "sacred" (in the sense of mystical, emotional religion) than to that of "morality' " (283), a typical product, in other words, of fin de siècle French Catholicism.

The sacrificial, masochistic bent of Colette's childhood religion would have been further reinforced by membership of the "Groupe Pératé," but it was not so much the group's theology as the behavior of its founder that left its mark on Colette. There seems absolutely no doubt that Pératé sexually abused both Colette and her elder sister Madeleine, causing the latter to attempt suicide by throwing herself into the Seine at Boissettes, and leaving Colette with a lacerating horror both of priests and of sex:

One day, after catechism, "Monsieur l'Abbé" hid behind a door, caught me by the arm, and said: "Nobody must see us," then he placed his lips to mine and ran away. I rubbed my mouth with disgust. He received me in his room without lighting the lamp, I could only see the sinister glow of a coal fire in the hearth. He put me on his knees, lifted my skirts, and placed his hand on my thighs on the pretext of "squeezing those tiny little pimples you have on your skin," then he said, "I do that with your sister," and he half-opened my legs, placed his hand against my sex, I moved sharply and he removed his hand, sweating profusely, he continued to paw at my body and squeeze me tightly in his arms; then he calmed down. (68–69)

Colette runs away in guilt, shame, and horror, much of the future cast of her sexuality already formed in this sordid encounter, and a lifelong loathing of the priesthood surging inside her, a loathing to which her writings, her notably sacrilegious erotic fantasies, and, perhaps, as we shall see, her actions in Spain in May 1936 just prior to the outbreak of the civil war bear eloquent, and sometimes violent, testimony.

In all this, it was not just that Colette, by her late teens, had lost all religious faith (though she had), but that she began, in her hatred and horror, to turn Catholicism blasphemously and scatologically on its head, chanting her own version of the *Ave Maria* ("Hail Mary, shit, God!" [67]), consigning Christ *aux chiottes* and embarking on the path that, in part emulation of *Histoire de l'oeil,* would take her to the identification of sacrament and excrement, chrism and jism, communion and coprophagy that one finds in one of her most extreme texts of the 1930s:

> When she had taken communion and as soon as the spunk [*le foutre*] had been swallowed . . . , Verax and Laure went and calmly shat in the stoups [*bénitiers*] and pissed in the ciboria. . . . The next day she mounted the altar to show her butt to the faithful and, at the moment of elevation, the priest parted her thighs between which the host penetrated, then he licked that divine arse until the choir-boy, kneeling before him, liberated his cock from the lace and gold trimmings of his vestments with a hefty swing of the censer and swallowed the Holy Spunk that gushed on to his face. . . . Finally, the silver Christ could be seen trembling in the shit. (109)

The problem (to anticipate) is that such profanation necessarily confirms by negation the sacredness of that which it profanes or, as Heidegger put it, "beneath all hatred is concealed the most inscrutable dependence on that of which that hatred constantly seeks to make its independent," with the result that "everything which is *anti* remains inextricably caught up within that against which it resolves to do battle."[8] In her determination to "exist *against* and not *with*" (184), she did not realize—or realized only too late—that she could not exist without that which she was implacably against: her family, the bourgeoisie, capitalism, Catholicism, and, ultimately, God. She was, to use one of her favorite images (92, 159, 197), caught up in the "lasso" of an "infernal" figure 8.

Jean Bernier

The *petite fille* became a *jeune fille* and finally a *jeune femme,* and Madame Peignot, anxious that her youngest daughter find a suitable husband, set about organizing, in concert with her son Charles and his wife Suzanne ("Suz"), a series of social events at which Colette could meet an assortment of potential matches. At one such occasion, held in July 1925 at Garches in the western suburbs of Paris so that Colette might make the acquaintance of a scion of the Durand-Ruël art-dealing family, there was also present a handsome thirty-one-year-old writer and journalist Jean Bernier (1894–1975) whom Charles Peignot—a man with a wide network of friends, both male and female, some of them "respectable," many of them not—counted among his acquaintances, along with Jean Cocteau, Drieu la Rochelle, the surrealists Louis Aragon, René Crevel, and Luis Buñuel, Pablo Picasso, and Léon Blum, then *député* for the department of the Seine and also present at the dinner. That a supposedly good Catholic girl like Colette could find herself at table with a future socialist prime minister (and a Jew and a homosexual to boot), a *fils de famille* like the young Durand-Ruël, and a freewheeling adventurer like Bernier says something about the extraordinary interconnectedness of Parisian society at the time. Bernier was not just a man of the left, but of the far left, not, it is true, a member of the French Communist Party, then only five years old, but a writer for *Clarté,* which had been founded as a newspaper by a group of future communists in 1919 and relaunched as a review in 1921. He was a figure on the party's ultraleftist fringes, a veteran of the trenches and author of the inevitable antiwar novel (*La Percée* [1917]), and, in addition, a first-rate rugby player who had recently published a novel about the game (*Tête de mêlée* [1924]). At the time of the dinner at Garches, he was making some money on the side as rugby correspondent of the communist daily *L'Humanité.*[9]

Bernier is of great interest to students of literature and politics in interwar France because it was through him, and, more generally, through *Clarté,* that the highly contentious, and ultimately botched, negotiations between the Surrealist group and the Communist Party were conducted, notwithstanding the fact that he was persona non grata with the party authorities and would shortly join Boris Souvarine, the pivotal figure at *Clarté,* in declaring for the disgraced Trotsky against Stalin. Bernier was a typical figure of the postwar Parisian political-intellectual scene: "antibourgeois" before all else (though himself of impeccable bourgeois origins), antiwar, anticapitalist, antiparliamentary, a Marxist ready to engage with radical non-Marxist movements like surrealism, something of a womanizer, a man who, like his friend Drieu la Rochelle and so many other such rebels, might easily have moved from ultraleft to ultraright as political circumstances changed—in short, precisely the kind of social and intellectual freebooter who would sweep a not-so-dutiful daughter like Colette off her feet. The art dealer's son and the future prime minister of the Popular Front were swiftly pushed to one side, and, after sharing a dance (during which—shades of Sylvia Plath on her first meeting with Ted Hughes—Colette reputedly told Bernier that "I want to drink your blood from your mouth"),[10] they left the gathering and returned, one imagines with some haste, to Paris together.

We need not recount here in any great detail what is known of the affair, which lasted off and on until January 1927, its last month or so being covered by a journal that Bernier kept at the time and which was published in 1978 after his death under a title—*L'Amour de Laure*—that angered many "laureats" because it implied that Bernier, not Bataille, was *the* love of her life; the volume also contained a brief "parallel journal" by Colette that had been discovered among Bernier's papers and had not previously been published. Predictably turbulent, the affair gave Colette the opportunity of breaking more or less permanently with her family when, in April 1926, she left Paris for Corsica, apparently (though this is not fully established) to join Bernier there: "It's not mother [*maman*] that I'm leaving," she wrote provocatively to Suz, "it's *the whole lot of you*," though this did not prevent her from writing affectionately from Bastia and Ajaccio. Colette was not long in returning to France, apparently disappointed at the way the relationship with Bernier was developing, and spent the period from June to November 1926 on an extended trek in the southwest of France, walking great distances in the Pyrenees and Cévennes before returning to Paris where she moved into a grim little hotel on the avenue d'Orléans and the affair with Bernier resumed.

Unfortunately by this time (if not before), Bernier had at least one other girlfriend, a working-class woman named Marie-Louise whom he describes as having drastically lost weight and who, in her desperate desire to marry, had threatened to commit suicide if Bernier refused her and had bought a revolver for the purpose. Bernier's diary shows him vacillating between the two women, desiring and making love to them both, but in neither case with any great love or intensity, and claiming that his feelings for Colette contained "no sensuality," only "pure love, pure eroticism," his main concern being to avoid fathering a child (or, as he put it, "negating the negation" that was Colette herself) by systematically having recourse to coitus interruptus. Colette, who sought a total dialectical synthesis of opposites, told him that "there is only one way that you can be more in me, and that is by coming inside me" (*c'est que tu jouisses en moi*), to which Bernier replied, "Yes, but coming inside you, isn't that the child who destroys love?"[11]

If this was *l'amour fou* as later celebrated by the surrealists, the *folie*, it seems clear, was mainly on one side, with Colette striving after a "total" fusion with the Other just as determinedly as Bernier refused it. There are hints of sadomasochism enjoyed by each party, a sense of passion heightened and exacerbated by the constant invocation of death, a belief, held unambiguously by Colette and by "a part" of Bernier ("which conflicts moreover with another part") that "love is against life, compatible only with a life of revolt, or outside of life,"[12] with Colette knowing how much Bernier is both seduced and terrified by what she calls her "absolute non-conformism": "Was I not eternally unadaptable to everything?"[13] To Bernier, Colette must have been something akin to that utterly ambiguous force that Bataille and Leiris, following Durkheim, would later call *the sacred*: a force both attractive and terrifying, attractive *because* it is terrifying, terrifying *because* it is attractive. Totally to fuse—or, in Bataille's somewhat unusual sense of the term, to "communicate"—with the sacred is held to be impossible short of the extinction of the communicating subject,[14] and, not surprisingly, Bernier drew back. Not so Colette, all too well aware that she was "tuberculoid [*phtisique*] for the whole of a life . . . , I'm tuberculoid, that's all there is to it [*je suis tuberculeuse, et c'est tout*],"[15] and for whom the "impossible" point at which self and not-self merge in ecstatic communion, at which Eros and Thanatos fuse together as one, held an attraction that far outweighed any countervailing concern for the preservation of selfhood. as she would write in a letter of August 1936, prefaced by the not-so-cryptic figure "88," "I speak of 'loving death' because that alone signifies loving life *without restriction*, loving it up to the limit, death included" (132).

Redirecting from God to her lover the sacrificial themes she had internalized from her Catholic formation, Colette duly, and almost inevitably, "offered herself up" as a holocaustal victim to Bernier ("To die=my death will consecrate his life, he will know that I loved him"),[16] and on 9 January 1927, just as they prepared to go to the opera, Charles and Suz were urgently summoned to the hotel on the avenue d'Orléans where they found Colette covered in blood, having narrowly failed to shoot herself in the heart with a revolver—a very real revolver, not a surreal one like André Breton's *Revolver à cheveux blancs* (1932) or the hypothetical one that, notoriously, he would urge those who would accomplish "the most elementary surrealist act" to take down into the street and open fire with at random.[17] Still conscious, Colette begged Charles and Suz to have her taken to a public hospital, not to a private clinic, it being vital to her that, even in extremis, she signal her break from the detested bourgeoisie into which she had been born.[18]

German and Soviet Interludes

The period between Colette's recovery from her self-inflicted wounds and the beginning of her relationship with Boris Souvarine in the spring of 1931 is the most obscure of her life. Like Simone Weil a few years later, she is continually on the move, first within France and Switzerland, where she is reported to be following a course at the University of Geneva, then in Germany (1928–29), and finally in the Soviet Union (1930–31), before being brought back to Paris, gravely ill once again, by her brother in early 1931. Both the German and Soviet "interludes" are replete with controversy, the first because of the nature of Colette's relationship with Eduard Trautner, already referred to, for which there is only a brief text reproduced in the notes of *Laure: Le Sacré* and some additional details in Bataille's *Vie de Laure;* the second, also poorly documented, because of the shifts it brought about in her political positions, shifts that took her in a still more radical direction than before. After spending some time at a sanatorium (Leysin) in Switzerland, Colette moved on to Berlin some time in 1928 where, in her own account, she "threw herself on to a bed as one throws oneself into the sea" and, separating her "real being" from her sexuality and her sexuality from her "real being" attained to some region where "nobody in the world could join me, seek me, find me."

Meeting Trautner, she submitted to his sadistic sexual demands—"there are not many women who like being beaten like that," he tells her—and, fitted with a dog collar and lead (these are details supplied by Bataille), on one occasion ate a sandwich that Trautner "had buttered with his shit" (*un sandwich à l'intérieur beurré de sa merde* [281]), exactly the kind of inversion of sacrament into excrement that could be guaranteed to excite the author of *Histoire de l'oeil.*[19] In her consensual degradation, Trautner encouraged her to believe that there was a subversive political meaning. As a "choice product of a decomposed society" (Trautner's expression), she could hasten the final destruction of that society by pushing her perversion to its "impossible" limit—and make a lot of money for herself (and presumably Trautner) into the bargain (135).

Eventually Colette escaped and, after further wandering (Paris, Switzerland, Paris, Warsaw), made her way to Moscow in July 30. There, thanks to introductions given her by Boris Souvarine, she met the dissident Marxist Victor Serge (1890–1947) and became the mistress of the Soviet novelist Boris Pilniak (1894–1941), later a victim, as the date of his death indicates, of the Stalinist purges. Her six-month stay in the Soviet Union included visits to Leningrad and the Black Sea resort of Sochi and a foray with Pilniak into the region of Kolomna east of Moscow where the ravages of famine and deportation destroyed any illusions that remained about the virtues of "real existing Soviet communism" and propelled her further in the direction of the communist opposition. Back in Moscow, Colette fell seriously ill, and Charles Peignot traveled east to bring her back to Paris by train. Bataille claimed that Colette tried to make love to her brother in the sleeping-car they shared, but "despite their common good will," nothing came of the attempt.[20]

Once recovered, Colette took up lodgings on the rue Blomet in the 15th arrondissement where the painter André Masson (1896–1987), a close friend of Bataille and Leiris, had his studio at the time. It was during this period, according to Bataille (281), that Colette, in a general state of "disgust," took to picking up men more or less at random and making love with them "even in train toilets." Not for the first time were promiscuity and perversion expressions of an underlying asceticism and self-hatred, a sexual bulimia curiously cognate with Simone Weil's self-starvation, and it may have been around this time that, again like Simone, Colette sometimes, as she later confided to Leiris, burned herself with a cigarette "to train herself to withstand pain."[21]

From Souvarine to Bataille

In the circumstances, she was fortunate to form a relationship in the spring of 1931 with Boris Souvarine (1893–1984, born Boris Lifschitz, the name Souvarine being taken from that of the anarchist antihero of Zola's *Germinal* [1885]) who, again according to Bataille (281), treated her "as a patient, a child, was for her more of a father than a lover." As strikingly unattractive as Bernier (and Bataille) were strikingly handsome, Souvarine had been expelled from the barely formed French Communist Party for "indiscipline" (in reality for supporting Trotsky against Stalin) and, as founder of the Cercle Communiste Marx et Lénine in 1926, relaunched as the Cercle Communiste Démocratique (CCD) in 1930, was the fulcrum and cynosure of oppositional (i.e., anti-Stalinist) communism in France, committed, in the words of the CCD's constitution, to the view that "the Russian revolution and Bolshevism have degenerated with the Soviet state which, instead of exercising the dictatorship of the proletariat, is now merely the emancipatory instrument of the Bolshevik party that has become an exploitative and bureaucratic caste."[22] This tallied exactly with Colette's recent experience of the Soviet Union, and shared political convictions and emotional needs made it virtually inevitable that Colette and Souvarine would become lovers. Some time in the spring of 1931 they moved into an apartment on the rue du Dragon just off the Place St. Germain-des-Prés, before decamping westward to the leafy suburbs of Neuilly in the course of the following year. Colette's inherited wealth provided Souvarine with the means to launch a new review, *La Critique sociale,* in March 1931, which would appear, with some irregularity, until March 1934. Colette and Souvarine did the editing together, and Colette also contributed a number of articles, some signed "C. P." and others "Claude Araxe," the reference being to the river Araxes in Armenia which, according to Virgil ("Pontem indignatus Araxes," *Aeneid* 8:728), Alexander had ordered his soldiers to whip when the turbulence of its waters foiled all efforts to bridge it: One can see the appeal of the name, apparently suggested by Souvarine, to the "unbridgeable," "uncrossable" (and at one time, it seems, eminently whipable) Colette.[23]

Bataille

Through *La Critique sociale,* Colette met Simone Weil in 1932,[24] but the decisive encounter of her life happened some months earlier at the famous Brasserie Lipp on the boulevard Saint-Germain when Bataille submitted his first contribution to the publication, a review of Kraft-Ebing's *Psychopathia Sexualis* that sparked off a bitter polemic with Bernier: the spectacle of Colette's former and future lovers arguing about perversion and revolution in the pages of a review she was financing does not lack in piquancy.[25] Since swinging violently against the Catholicism of his late teens and early twenties, Bataille had been living a carefully guarded double life, using his "day job" in the numismatics department at the Bibliothèque Nationale to finance his nighttime activities in such famous brothels of the period as *Le Sphinx* (located, appropriately, on the Place des Pyramides in the 1st *arrondissement*) and the *One-Two-Two* at 122 rue Chabanais, a convenient couple of blocks from his workplace, as well as at a variety of distinctly more down-market establishments in "those propitious streets running from the Carrefour Poissonnière to the Rue Saint-Denis" through which, trousers over arm and erect penis in hand, the "hero" of *Madame Edwarda* (1941) walks at the beginning of the "novel."

In addition to writing various pornographic texts only one of which, *Histoire de l'oeil* (1928) by "Lord Auch," had been published in an edition of 134 copies, Bataille had published extensively in the deluxe cultural review *Documents* (1929–30), to which Leiris had also contributed, and had been ritually hanged, drawn, and quartered by André Breton at the celebrated surrealist "show-trial" (which Bataille refused to attend) at the Bar du Château in Montparnasse in 1929; Leiris, Masson, Robert Desnos, Georges Limbour, and Raymond Queneau were also expelled at the same time, and some of them (but not Leiris) would later gravitate along with Bataille towards *La Critique sociale* and its successors.

By the time Bataille and Colette met, Bataille had developed the main lineaments of his radically anti-idealist "atheology" with its heavy emphasis on violence, transgressive sexuality, and sacrifice. The last was epitomized for him, first, by personally seeing the matador Manuelo Granero being gored to death in a bullfight in Spain in May 1922 (the "tragedy" is treated at length in *Histoire de l'oeil*) and, second, by a photograph, given to him by his friend Antoine Borel (the analyst who would later treat Colette) and reproduced in *Les Larmes d'Eros* (1961), that harrowingly depicts a young Chinese man named Fou-Tchou-Li, having been found guilty of murdering Prince Ao-Han-Ouao, hoisted up on a stake and, still alive, being sliced limb from limb and organ from organ, a look of ecstasy on his face that is for Bataille the very expression of the sacred in all of its glorious horror, beyond pain and pleasure, uniting Eros and Thanatos in a single hallucinating compound:[26] what the ritual dismemberment of the attempted regicide Robert-François Damiens in 1757 was for French writers from Baudelaire, Villiers de l'Isle Adam, and Huysmans to Foucault,[27] the flaying of Fou-Tchou-Li was for the author of *Ma mère* and *Madame Edwarda*.

In the minds of its founders and editors, *La Critique sociale* was always an organ of the revolutionary, anti-Stalinist left, but a dispute between Bataille and Simone Weil revealed cleavages that would have become even more marked had the review long outlasted the fascist riots in Paris on 6 February 1934 and the ensuing alliance of socialists, radicals, and communists that would debouch in the Popular Front victory of May 1936.[28] In an undated and unpublished text, definitely written before the demise of *La Critique sociale* in March 1934, Simone wrote that, for Bataille, revolution is "the triumph of the irrational, for me, of the rational; for him a catastrophe, for me a methodical action in which one must do one's utmost to limit the damage; for him the liberation of the instincts, and notably of those which are currently considered to be pathological, for me a superior morality. What common ground is there between us? [*Quoi de commun?*]"[29] Shortly afterward, Simone made the issues at stake even plainer:

> One cannot be a revolutionary if one does not love life. . . . [R]evolution is a struggle against everything that obstructs life. It has meaning only as a means to an end; if the end pursued is devoid of meaning, the means loses its value. In a general manner, nothing has any value as soon as human life has no value.[30]

The criticism, valid for Bataille, is scarcely less so as far as Colette is concerned, as the political positions she took in the last three years of her life will reveal with some clarity.

That Bataille was moving on to dangerous moral and political ground was revealed by a long article entitled "La structure psychologique du fascisme" that *La Critique sociale* published in its final two numbers (November 1933 and March 1934). Distinguishing between two modes or dimensions of reality, the "homogeneous" (i.e., the normal, unbroken profane order of things) and the "heterogeneous" (i.e., the disruption of that order by the ambiguous force of the sacred), Bataille assigns to each an appropriate form or expression of political power: "bourgeois" (i.e., parliamentary) democracy in the case of the former, revolutionary violence and charismatic leadership in that of the latter, be it the violence of the "Left" or the "Right." Bataille's argument is that fascist power is unquestionably of the heterogeneous variety (even though Hitler had come to power in Germany by electoral means in January 1933), and that that heterogeneity can only be countered by the use of heterogeneous street violence by "the Left." Put simply, it is necessary for "the Left" to "out-fascist" the fascists, to destroy the sacred of the ultraright with the countersacred of the ultra-Left or—to use an expression that Bataille himself never seems to have used, but that was current in the equivocal political world, *ni droite ni gauche,* neither left nor right, in which he would increasingly move—to engage in a form of *sur-fascisme* (superfascism) to combat fascism, just as reality and realism were countered by surrealism.[31] The question raised at the time and still hotly debated today is this: Was the "anti-fascist" Bataille not himself, deep down, a fascist?[32] Is it, by extension, legitimate to ask the same question of Colette, the woman most closely associated with him?

The years 1934–36 are yet another confused period in Colette's life—did she ever know anything other than confusion?—during which she gradually distanced herself from Souvarine (with whom all "sexual exchange," as she put it,[33] had probably ceased by 1934) and reoriented her life around Bataille, finally moving into his apartment on the rue de Rennes in September 1936. It is not possible, even if it were necessary, to pinpoint when she and Bataille became lovers, but, even as late as August 1935, it was still with Souvarine that she made her first visit to Spain; her next visit, however, was with Bataille (April-June 1936).

The shift from Souvarine to Bataille can be followed in detail through the letters, journals, and other documents preserved in *Laure*: *Une rupture* drawn together by Jérôme Peignot and Anne Roche from papers in Souvarine's possession and published in 1999 after his death. It makes depressing reading; for much of the time Colette was institutionalized for psychological as well as medical reasons or receiving psychoanalysis from Borel, having undergone what appears to be a full-scale breakdown some time in 1934 when Simone Weil and Souvarine's sister Jeanne Maurin found her huddled on a divan in Simone's apartment, "foaming at the mouth" (*l'écume aux lèvres*) and sobbing, "I have destroyed Boris, my head is in the basket." "She's talking about the guillotine," said Simone, though whether Colette saw herself as executioner or victim, or both, remains open to doubt.[34] Interestingly and, as we shall see, significantly, Bataille was also using the image of decapitation to characterize the heterogeneous nature of fascist power at exactly this time: "Fascio=executioner's axe / Crucified / Execution [*mise à mort*] of the king / Tragedy."[35]

It is clear from Colette's letters and notes that she felt "smothered" and "crushed" by Souvarine[36] and thought that she might enjoy more "space," both personally and politically, with Bataille whom she both desires and considers a "monster";[37] she is clearly sexually and psychologically disturbed, speaking of her "shame of her nether regions" (*basses régions*)[38] and of her desire to "soil" or "dirty" herself (*envie de me salir*),[39] a significant image if Dirty/Dorothea in Bataille's novel *Le Bleu du ciel* (1935) is indeed modeled on Colette. She does not seem to have played any active part in Contre-Attaque, the short-lived (November 1935–February 1936) "anti-fascist movement" founded by Bataille in conjunction with Breton, Paul Eluard, Benjamin Péret, the novelist and essayist Pierre Klossowski (born 1905), future author of *Sade, mon prochain* (1947) and later a convert to

Catholicism, and Maurice Heine (1884–1940), the leading Sadeian scholar and editor; the absence, once again, of Leiris is to be noted. The triumph of fascism in Italy and Germany and the similar threat in Spain, Austria (the assassination of chancellor Engelbert Dollfuss in July 1934, alluded to in *Le Bleu du ciel* and elsewhere), and France form an ominous backdrop to Colette's life and writings at this time, as, symptomatically, the sound of "ardent, young, beautiful singing" first creeps and then floods into the room of the sanatorium she is staying in at Molveno in Italy in July 1934.[40] It is a two-hundred strong choir of young "blackshirts," aged seven to twelve, and their sudden irruption points forward to the gathering crescendo of the *Hitlerjugend* brass band that brings *Le Bleu du ciel* to its equivocal climax.

Spain 1936

Colette's antifascism, like Bataille's, implied no sympathy either for liberal democracy or orthodox communism (still opposed to so-called social fascists—i.e., socialists—as much as to fascism itself), or, even, a little later, for the Popular Front that swept to power in France in May 1936. It did, however, involve a passionate commitment to republican Spain, and it is surely no accident that Colette and Bataille were in Spain during the period (21 April–19 June 1936) that saw the electoral triumph of the united left in France, followed immediately by the extraordinary wave of sit-in strikes and other autonomous working-class actions that culminated in the Accords Matignon signed on 7 June: Their joint alienation from the realities of French life could hardly be more blatant. The two-month stay in Spain took place during the immediate buildup to the outbreak of civil war in mid-July 1936, and Colette's fragmentary writings leave no doubt as to where her sympathies lay or to what extremes of behavior those sympathies might lead her. This was a time of mounting anticlerical violence among Spanish republicans, pending even greater atrocities after hostilities began, and it is clear that Colette not only witnessed but actively participated in the burning of a Catholic church in the working-class Quatro Caminos district in Madrid on 3 May 1936:

> I was beside myself [*hors de moi-même*] and yet lucid, strangely calm, capable of forming a chain to prevent the firemen from advancing or of poking the fire that was burning a pile of cassocks, of witnessing fairly terrifying scenes but of standing firmly on both legs. . . . What does me good, is that I was truly *with* them [the rioters] and not a spectator and that not for a minute was there mistrust in them or fear or mistrust on my part. (102–3)

Despising the "cowardice [*veulerie*] of leaders and intellectuals" who treat such "healthy" explosions of popular fury as "regrettable excesses of the lumpenproletariat," Colette obviously enjoys the "sacred" experience of togetherness or "communication" as Bataille (not apparently present) would put it as much as any political objective as such. Here she is neither executioner nor victim, but part of the sacrificial mob homing in on its prey, in this instance just a pile of priests' cassocks, or so it would seem, but would she have drawn back if inside the cassocks actual priests were being lynched? Almost certainly not, because what is being incinerated before her eyes is her Catholic childhood, and above all the memory of the detested Abbé Pérate.

While her ecstasy—the word is surely not inappropriate, though no sexual element seems present—may be understandable, how sharply her attitude differs from that of Simone Weil (not yet by any means sympathetic to Catholicism) shortly afterward when she wrote a horrified letter to Georges Bernanos condemning the gratuitous violence meted out by Spanish republicans on their enemies, priests, nuns, and laypersons alike: "never once did I see, neither among the Spanish [republicans], nor even among the French who had come either to fight or to look around [*se promener*]—these last usually colorless, inoffensive intellectuals—never once did I see anyone, even in private, express any repulsion, disgust, or merely disapproval with regard to the blood that had been uselessly shed."[41] For Colette, Spain 1936 was not so much the scene of a political struggle, as it was for Simone, as it was a scene, a spectacle, *tout court,* and the bloodier and more "mystical" the better: "It is Saint Teresa [of Avila] and *les tricoteuses* at every step. Mystical delirium and sacrilege" (102). The orgasmic trances of the visionary saint and the collective *jouissance* at the scenes of ritualized political murder have become one and the same. Colette is equally "turned on" by both the mysticism and the sacrilege, which are no more than differentiated aspects of the object of her ultimate longing, "the sacred." She has aestheticized, sacralized, and perhaps sexualized politics, especially political violence. She is certainly not a fascist ideologically, but her underlying attitude is uncomfortably close to the Spanish fascists' *¡Viva la muerte!*

In the course of her second visit to Spain, Colette attended a number of bullfights, that obsession of French and other writers and artists during the interwar years: Montherlant, Bataille, Masson, Picasso, Hemingway, and, above all, Leiris whose *Miroir de la tauromachie,* first published in 1938 and later dedicated "to the memory of Colette Peignot," is perhaps the most perceptive single discussion of the "sport."[42] The mixture of spectacle, sacrificial violence, and transgressive eroticism could be guaranteed to arouse Colette as much as it did Bataille and Leiris, but whereas it is the matador's possible death that focuses the men's attention and excitement, Colette's identification is rather with the certain death of the bull, whose spitting forth of blood at the moment of the kill and kneeling and "praying," as she says, in the pool of its gore (107), ghoulishly echoes the terrible disease that was ravaging her lungs. Not for nothing did she later describe the scenes around her deathbed as a *"corrida fleurie"* (129), a flower-bedecked corrida, in which she, *toreador* and *toro* at one and the same time, can be certain of death no matter how much strength, skill, and courage she displays.

Acéphale

One other important encounter occurred during the second Spanish trip of 1936, though it is not clear whether Colette was present. In late April, Bataille met André Masson at Tossa de Mar, a sea resort north of Barcelona where Masson was painting at the time, and it was there that the two men decided to launch a new review to be called *Acéphale,* the "logo" for which Masson drew on the spot to Bataille's instructions: a headless (acephalous) man with outstretched arms as though crucified, with a dagger in his left hand and what resembles a flaming Sacred Heart in his right, with stars for nipples, a skull at his crotch, and his intestines showing through his opened belly.[43] The first of the four numbers of the review to appear was published on 24 June 1936, very shortly after Bataille and Colette returned from Spain—an extraordinary achievement in the circumstances. But *Acéphale* was more than "just" a review. It was also the name of a "secret society" whose membership overlapped with, but was not identical to, the contributors to the review and whose activities, now that all, or almost all, of the protagonists are dead, are likely to remain forever shrouded in mystery. Some hints as to its beliefs and objectives are to be found in an article-manifesto that Bataille wrote while at Tossa de Mar and which as published, under the joint names of Masson, Klossowski, and himself, in the first of *Acéphale.* "WE ARE MADLY/WILDLY [*farouchement*] RELIGIOUS," the manifesto declares in capital letters and, declaring a generalized war "on everything that is recognized today," announces the intention to "abandon the world of the civilized and its light." The main, indeed the only, article of faith of the "sacred conspiracy" (*la conjuration sacrée*)—the manifesto's title—is the conviction that the only "grandeur and reality" in life are to be found "in ecstasy and in ecstatic love": "life is not only an agitated void, it is also a dance that has to be danced with fanaticism" (*une danse qui force à danser avec fanatisme*). It is, in short, necessary for man to lose his head like a prisoner his prison, not, to be sure, to find a "God who is the prohibition of crime" somewhere beyond himself but "a being who is ignorant of prohibition":

> Beyond what I am, I encounter a being who makes me laugh because he has no head, who fills me with anguish because he is made up of innocence and crime: he holds an iron weapon in his left hand, and flames resembling a sacred heart in his right. He writes Birth and Death in a single eruption. He is not a man. Neither is he a god. He is not me but he is more me than me: his belly is the maze in which he has lost himself, in which he loses me with him and in which I rediscover myself being him, that is to say as a monster.[44]

"G.B.?" Colette had asked in 1934, and answered, "a monster whom I *must* keep away [*écarter*] from my existence."[45] Now she was not only in Spain with the "monster," but considering moving in with him once they got back to Paris.

The sense of Masson's and Bataille's joint image is not to be doubted.[46] "Acéphale" embodies the triumph of low over the high, of the chthonic principle over the uranian, of matter over spirit, of genitals over head (*testes* over *testa*), of Dionysos over Apollo, id over ego and superego, of animal over human, of the lead over their leaders (*chef* [Latin *caput*], meaning leader in French, still preserves something of its original meaning of "head"), of the Son over the Father and his cognates, *Patrie* and *Patron*. He/It excoriates reason, the principle of individuation (what Bataille would later call the "discontinuity" of separate beings to each other) and the homogeneous or profane order of things. *A contrario,* he/it systematically exults instinct, the ecstatic "communication" (or "continuity") of entities with each other and the heterogeneous or sacred principle of disorder.[47] As a "sacred conspiracy"—bizarrely akin to all other nineteenth- and twentieth-century conspiracies, Jesuit, Jewish, Masonic, "internationalistic"—it sets out to subvert established structures from within. It claims, rightly, to be revolutionary, but the revolution it propounds goes far beyond what it dismisses as mere "political agitation," nor does its revolution have much to do with anything Marx, Lenin, or even Trotsky could endorse. If it is "anti-bourgeois"—and it undoubtedly is—it reminds us, yet again, that to be "anti-bourgeois" is not necessarily the same as being "on the left." Here, if anywhere, is an "anti-fascism" that has spilled over into what it condemns, an antifascist fascism, a "surfascisme" of a most troubling kind.

Who belonged to the "secret society"? About twenty people in all, "headed" (if it is not a contradiction so to put it) by Bataille, with Klossowski and Caillois, his future associate at the Collège de Sociologie, as his principal co-conspirators, though Caillois would quickly distance himself from proceedings. Colette was undoubtedly involved but, equally certainly, Leiris was not. Masson, when in France, also took part, as did the historian Henri Dubief, the economist Georges Ambrosino, and two veterans of *La Critique sociale* and *Contre-Attaque,* Pierre Dugan and Jean Dautry, the likely originators of the "surfasciste" tag (see note 31). The American art critic Patrick Waldberg and his wife Isabelle were occasional participants, as was a still more unlikely figure from across the Atlantic: the Martinican-born Jules Monnnerot *fils* (born 1909, so called to distinguish him from his father, one of the founders of the Communist Party in the island) who in 1932 had been one of the contributors to *Légitime défense,* a strongly Marxist and surrealist-influenced collection of writings often held to be the first expression of literary-political nationalism in the French-speaking West Indies. After the Second World War, Monnerot published an innovative essay entitled *La Poésie moderne et le sacré* (1949) and then veered vertiginously to the far right, finally—and remarkably for a person of color—becoming one of the accredited "philosophers" of Jean-Marie Le Pen's Front National.[48] Another likely member, Pierre Libra, was a former adherent of Action Française destined to become an out-and-out fascist,[49] while Caillois himself, a pupil of the strongly "Teutonophile" anthropologist Georges Dumézil (1898–1986), had published in far-right reviews such as *Volontaires* and *L'Ordre nouveau;* his postwar Gaullism obliterated any trace of his earlier allegiances.[50] "Acéphale," in short, was located on the critical interface of *ni droite ni gauche,* that ideological in-between land in which so much of European, and especially French, fascism had its roots. "Death and sacrifice alone bind together [*soudent*] a community":[51] it is a *Blut und Boden* mysticism, minus the nationalism, that has much more to do with the far right than the left.

So what did the "conspirators" of Acéphale actually do? They certainly commemorated—celebrated rather, for royalists they were not—the execution of Louis XVI every 21 January from 1937 to 1939, foregathering for that purpose around the obelisk on the Place de la Concorde marking the spot where the guillotine had stood.[52] There were also nocturnal meetings—one is tempted to say covens or conclaves—in forests around Paris, and perhaps as far afield at Lyons-la-Forêt in Normandy, the preferred location being the forest of Marly around Saint-Nom-la-Bretèche due west of Paris between Versailles and Saint-Germain-en-Laye. Documents giving terse instructions of how to get to the meeting-place, whose location was never disclosed in advance, have been preserved for what they are worth.[53] Participants should come in groups of not more than three, not speak to each other or to anyone else, and walk through the forest in "Indian file, each several meters distant from the one in front"; it was imperative not to attract attention of any members of the *profanum vulgus* who might be in the forest, and absolute secrecy must be observed vis-à-vis all outsiders. After Patrick Waldberg's death, a text by him entitled "Acéphalogramme" was published in *Le Magazine littéraire* (April 1995) in which the author, speaking as it were from beyond the grave, revealed what few specific details there are concerning the content of Acéphale's sylvan rituals. Having taken their suburban trains to Saint-Nom-la-Bretèche and tramped through damp forest tracks alone or in small groups at night, the "conspirators" convened at their appointed destination, typically—and all testimonies agree on this point—around the mutilated trunk of a massive oak tree that had been struck by lightning long ago, a suitably "acephalous" tree with twisted, charred branches and gnarled roots going down deep into the "telluric" regions below. Torches would be lit revealing Bataille standing holding an enamel dish in which he would ignite several pieces of sulphur; sulphur being, according to the instructions members had received, "an element deriving from the interior of the earth which emerges only through the mouth of volcanoes. This has an obvious significance in connection with the chthonic character of the mythic reality that we are pursuing. It is also significant that the roots of a tree delve deep into the earth."[54] Then, at the ceremony Waldberg is describing, Bataille seized his (Waldberg's) left wrist and rolled his jacket-and shirtsleeve up to the elbow, at which point another "officiant," carrying a dagger identical to the one in the group's logo, made an incision of several centimeters on his forearm, without Waldberg's feeling any pain: "The scar is still visible today."[55] As a ritual of *Blutbruder-schaft,* said Klossowski, interviewed in November 1990 by Bernard-Henri Lévy for his book *Les Aventures de la liberté* (1991), it was all "very beautiful," what with the pelting rain, the "Greek fire" (*feu grégeois*), and the elaborate mise-en-scène.[56] Also interviewed by Lévy, Michel Leiris said it was "puerile"—but he had never been present.[57]

But was this all that happened? Having fled to Latin America even before the outbreak of war, Caillois published a long, penetrating study entitled "Ensayo sobre el espiritú de las sectas" in the Mexican collection *Jornadas* in 1945. In it, he takes Acéphale as a recent example of *Männerbund,* secret society or sect, which he denies having belonged to, though he had—and had obviously been frightened out of his skin by what he had seen. Then Caillois "reveals" that the question of a human sacrifice was raised, and "[W]ould you believe it? It was easier to find a willing victim than a benevolent sacrificer [*sacrificateur*]. Finally, everything remained in suspense. Or at least that's what I imagine, because I was one of the more reticent [here Caillois inadvertently betrays that he was "in the know"], and things perhaps went further than I knew."[58]

That sacrifice should have been discussed is hardly surprising, for ritual immolation—be it Manuel Granero, Fou-Tchou-Li, Louis XVI, or the priest who is degraded and vivisected in *Histoire de l'oeil*—is Bataille's central obsession, and he had only recently contributed a preface to a series of drawings by Masson called *Sacrifices* and depicting the "dying gods" Mithra, Orpheus, "the Crucified," the Minotaur, and Osiris.[59] If the question was raised, so would be that of potential victims and sacrificers, and there is a persistent rumor—unverifiable and unrefutable—that it was Colette who offered herself as the necessary victim. There is a poem by Colette entitled "Le Corbeau" (The Crow) that, according to Bataille and Leiris, "undoubtedly" refers to her association with Acéphale (99). But the date that the poem is given—January 1936—is either wrong, because Acéphale did not exist until April 1936 at the earliest, or the poem refers to some earlier incident. In a later text, written in 1940 after Colette's death, Bataille describes how, in March 1938, he and Colette, by now very seriously ill, had driven from Saint-Germain-en-Laye (where they were now living) to the site of the *arbre foudroyé* (lightning-struck tree), as it is always referred to, having, as they entered the forest, seen two dead crows hanging from the branch of a tree that Colette had immediately "interpreted" as a portent of her impending extinction.

Whatever its date, "Le Corbeau," with its echoes of Edgar Allan Poe and Vincent van Gogh (another exemplary sacrificial victim for Bataille),[60] brings together many of the key images of the Acéphale experience. Deep in the forest, "fairies and ogres . . . / willed that lightning should tear / not far from there / a huge tree / which opened / like a belly / I cried like a deer [*je bramai*]," as though, the victim, she is about to be slain. She then feels a crow brush lightly against her shoulder and wishes that it "would accompany me everywhere and always precede me / like a herald his knight." Entering an abandoned house (which actually existed in the forest of La Bretèche), she goes up into the attic whose walls, covered with strange graffiti, "stripped my life bare": the ritual denuding of the victim prior to sacrifice. At this point the crow flies into the attic with its ravenous beak, and "the black shadow projected over me / seemed to be selecting its prey." Night finds her "strangled at the bottom of the wood," wrapped in a lunar halo and "rocked [*bercée*] in the mist / a white, moving, frosty mist," a mothering shroud for the corpse she has, or shortly will, become. The poem's final words—it is unclear by whom they are spoken or to whom they refer[61]—then produce the all-but-inevitable image of ritual decapitation:

> Lorsque demain à l'aube
> ta tête sera jetée
> au panier des guillotinés
> souviens-toi
> Assassin
> que toi seul
> as bu à mon sein
> "tout le lait de la tendresse humaine."
>
> (96–98)

> [When, tomorrow at dawn, / your head will be cast into
> the basket of those guillotined, / remember, /
> Assassin, / that you alone / drank from my breast /
> "all the milk of human tenderness"]

Whether or not Colette offered herself for *actual* sacrifice will never be known, but as an act of imaginary self-immolation "Le Corbeau" is chilling evidence of the death wish that now consumed her.

In July 1937, Colette and Bataille went to Italy, intending to travel over to Greece from Brindisi, but Bataille decided that it was imperative that they climb Mount Etna in which he discerned yet another "acephalous" structure in direct communication with the chthonic realm of his dreams. During the ascent, in the midst of what Bataille calls an "infernal region" in which "the horrible instability of things" was more than anywhere evident, Colette was suddenly seized by what would now be called a "panic attack," ran away in terror, and, on 14 August, returned to Paris alone, still haunted by what she had "seen" (see 290).[62] In October she took up a post—possibly the first real job she ever had—with the Opera Mundi press on the rue de la Paix, at which she remained for two months, until the call of "the sacred" took her with Bataille and the Sadeian scholar Maurice Heine to another forest, that of Epernon, midway between Rambouillet and Chartres, where Sade had apparently wanted to be buried. It was a day of high winds and snow, they got lost in the wood, and again there was a kind of savagery in the air so that, back in Paris and having dropped Heine, Colette and Bataille joined another couple, the Ivanovs, in what Bataille calls a dinner "no less wild than the wind, Odoïestova, naked, starting to vomit," like some eastern European version of Dirty.[63] All this sounds like some dreadful *folie à deux* in which, egging each other on, the two lovers (and anyone else they can coopt into their madness) try to "spend" themselves in utter self-dissipation[64] in order finally to broach the frontier between sacred and profane and, breaking their "discontinuity" with themselves and the world, merge with the not-self in an absolute "continuity" or "communication" that could only be death.

If this was the case, the dramatic collapse of Colette's health can have been no surprise, and may even, perversely, have been actively sought. On 29 March 1938 Colette was given a pneumothorax in the hope of easing her lungs, whereafter she spent several weeks recuperating at a clinic at Avon near Fontainebleau where her sister Madeleine was now also suffering from the tuberculosis from which she, too, would die in 1944 with, apparently, the Abbé Pératé at her bedside.[65] In mid-July Colette moved into the house in Saint-Germain-en-Laye (59 *bis* rue de Mareil) where Bataille had been living for some months already, and the final stage of her journey began.

The names of Bataille and Colette (or rather of Bataille and "Laure") are now so closely linked with each other that a total unanimity is widely assumed to have existed between them regarding the sacred antiproject they pursued so relentlessly together. Certainly Bataille (aided by Leiris) gave Colette a set of terms, even a coherent discourse, in which she could formulate her experience, while she, for her part, offered him the example of an unstintingly self-dissipatory "sacred" existence that he, quite simply, never had the courage to emulate. Beyond that, there were clear divergences between them, both on a personal and a philosophical level. Bataille himself attests to Colette's "terrible bursts of anger and bouts of hatred against me" (291) when, as she became more and more ill, he responded with what he calls "sickly horror," frequent absences and drinking—something that he did "to excess," but with no more actual enjoyment, in the banal sense of the word, than he transgressed the boundaries of sexual comportment; in a very late letter, Colette expresses disgust at his "drunken returns" (*ton retour d'homme ivre*) and the "atrocious memory" that remained with her (260). She was feeling as "smothered" by Bataille as she had by the far more self-effacing Souvarine. Another late fragment reads "Man—God vis-à-vis woman . . . the one crushes / suppresses / kills / asphyxiates the other," and another: "The God—Bataille / BATAILLE / Replace God . . . by Machiavelli" and use "the force of cynicism" to counter his power (176–77).

An even more revelatory fragment is entitled "Story of Donald" (*Histoire de Donald*)—a mocking echo, perhaps, of *Histoire de l'oeil?*), that is "Donald as in the 2nd of the 3 little pigs of the dairymen at the corner." The half-page story consists of a dialogue between a little girl pig (Colette) and the boy pig Donald (Bataille). Says girl pig to boy pig: "In order to assert your freedom you need to imagine chains, namely me. In that way there is something to break, an order of established things to *transgress*" (girl pig's italics). Boy pig protests, goes on about Sade. Girl pig ripostes: "You take Sade as your witness! [*et tu prétends te réclamer de Sade!*] . . . It's Catholic priests who are your real authority [*Tu te réclames en effet des curés catholiques*]. . . . To me, you're just like a little boy coming out of the confessional and who's going to go back there" (153). Boy pig continues to bluster, but girl pig's barb has struck home: Donald the pig can no more free himself from her than he can from God and the church whom he claims to have transcended but can in reality only transgress, in other words he *needs* God and the Church in order to exist. Each of his sacrilegious acts—or rather each of his sacrilegious *texts,* for Donald, a pusillanimous pig, really, never actually *does* anything, only looks at photographs of other pigs being butchered, or writes dirty books (which he never publishes, at least not as Donald) about pigs rutting and puking—creates taboos and interdicts in order to transgress them, and, having transgressed them, re-creates them anew. Donald, in short, is not the atheistic little pig he claims to be, but an antitheistic theist who is forever caught up in the figure 8 of his self-perpetuating bad faith—bad because he needs good faith in order to exist at all. But, of course, girl pig also needs boy pig, and, like him also needs Big Father Pig up in the sky in order to flout Him, so that boy pig and girl pig are locked together in their sty, forever transgressing its boundaries but returning and re-erecting them in order to transgress them again: 88888 . . . , or until they end up as *saucisse de Toulouse* at the *charcuterie* on the corner.

Marcel Moré, who had known Colette in her teens and was present when she died, wrote how, after hearing Bataille talk about the transgressive character of eroticism in 1944, he was struck by the realization that "remaining hooked [*accroché*] to the notion of sin, [Bataille] was in no way liberated from the Church."[66] The same point was also made by Pierre Klossowski (who, himself now a Catholic, had some back-tracking to do): "Bataille, despite his atheist stance, remains intimately bound up with [*solidaire de*] the whole cultural structure of Christianity."[67] But so too did "Laure."

If Bataille was so often absent during Colette's last months, it was because, nominally with Caillois and Leiris, but in fact largely alone, he was organizing the regular meetings of the Collège de Sociologie, that the three of them, along with Klossowski, Monnerot *fils,* Ambrosino, and Libra had launched in the summer of 1937; in all the Collège held just over twenty lectures-cum-discussions between November 1937 and July 1939. Colette was too sick, or too indifferent, to attend, and indeed there is no record of any female participation; a "negative cathedral," in Denis Hollier's telling description,[68] the Collège was also a *Männerbund* with a vengeance.[69] Since Colette was not a member (though she certainly read Leiris's seminal paper "Le Sacré dans la vie quotidienne," presented in January 1938, and wrote a response to it [85–89]), we need not here discuss in any detail either its membership or the ideological position of its principal animators (Bataille, Caillois, and Klossowski, with Leiris again a rather peripheral figure), except to stress the remarkable diversity of the former and, as with Acéphale, the equivocal character of the latter. Around the central core of Acephale members gravitated a lesser circle of invited lecturers: the Hegelian philosopher Alexandre Kojève; the anthropologist Anatole Lewitzy, a colleague of Leiris at the Museé de l'Homme; the Hellenist René Guastalla; the exiled German political philosopher Hans Mayer; and the director of the *Nouvelle Revue Française,* Jean Paulhan (1884–1968), who lectured on the subject of sacred languages in Madagascar where he had been a teacher before the First World War. In the audience—their presence, of course, not indicating any necessary sympathy with the Collège's character or orientation—were, at one time or another, Drieu la Rochelle (a declared fascist since 1934); the philosopher Jean Wahl; several members of the *Esprit* group, advocates, as "personalists," of a "third way" between capitalism and communism; and, from across the Rhine, now, of course, in exile, three heavyweight Marxists, Theodore Adorno, Max Horkheimer, and Walter Benjamin, who was scheduled to give a paper on his celebrated "Arcades Project" but never did so; contrary to reports, Jean-Paul Sartre had nothing to do with the Collège. The presence in the audience of a number of denizens of the *ni droite ni gauche* (in reality ultraright) fringes of politics—Thierry Maulnier, Arnaud Dandieu, Bertrand de Jouvenel among others—has raised predictable queries about the Collège's own possibly fascist proclivities. Its emphasis on the "resacralization" or "remythologization" of society, plus the underlying language of blood, excess, ecstasy, violence, and sacrifice, seemed to Benjamin in particular all too redolent of what had already happened in his homeland.

What can be said is that, during the Occupation, the core members of the Collège de Sociologie did not distinguish themselves as active resisters. Of the lecturers, only Paulhan and Lewitzky can be called out-and-out resisters: Paulhan as founder and editor of the clandestine *Les Lettres françaises;* Lewitzky as a member of the celebrated resistance network at the Museé de l'Homme—perhaps the first such network in Paris—who was arrested and shot along with six of his colleagues at the fortress of Mont-

Valérien in February 1942, at the very moment, another colleague, Leiris, later learns to his shame, that he, Leiris, was sitting down at the Opéra to enjoy a performance of *Don Giovanni*.[70] Thereafter Leiris, while hardly displaying, by his own admission, a matador's courage in the face of the occupying bull, had an honorable record as an intellectual resister who remained "on the spot," unlike Caillois who fled to Argentina even before hostilities began and duly reinvented himself as a Gaullist and democrat.

The most problematic case, needless to say, is Bataille. Renouncing political activity well before the outbreak of war, Bataille moved more and more into the exploration of what, in his best-known wartime work, he called "interior experience" (*L'Expérience intérieure* [1943]), in which he continued his investigation of moments of sacred or ecstatic "communication" in a notably more individualistic manner than had previously been the case. Thérèse Martin's favorite reading, the visions of Saint Angela di Foligno, was coopted into his still determinedly "atheological" project, but its increasingly internalized character caused Sartre, reviewing his work, to dub him "a new mystic," not exactly a compliment in the new activist world of Liberation and the Purge.[71]

Bataille remained in Paris for most of 1941 and then, partly for reasons of health (he too was now suffering from tuberculosis) and partly the better to pursue his mystical quest, he moved with his new partner Denise Rollin to Vézelay in the Bourgogne, remaining there until after the war; he is buried in the cemetery of the great Basilique Sainte-Madeleine, sacred to the cult of the Penitent Whore, perhaps an appropriate final resting-place for an anti-Catholic who never escaped Catholicism as much as he and others thought and who wrote that a "brothel is my only true church, the only one in which I feel sufficiently ill at ease."[72] There is no question of Bataille's having been pro-Vichy, and still less pro-Nazi, but Leiris, for one, was disgusted when, over lunch in Paris on February 1941, Bataille declared that "what I have always considered essential relates to my interior life; I do not have to concern myself *with what is exterior to me* [*sic*]. In the present time, there is no need to show solidarity [*se solidariser*] with those who are suffering [*qui sont atteints*]."[73]

Colette's Final Days

Colette is in so many ways the reverse image of Thérèse and, just as we did not follow the prolonged agony of the future saint of Lisieux, so the final months of the "saint of the abyss" of Saint-Germain-en-Laye will be dealt with but briefly. In her bedroom at 9 *bis* rue de Mareil, Colette's final "flower-bedecked corrida" lasted several days during which Bataille and her family waged war for control of what remained of her life and, still more, for the image she would present after her death; after all, as she told

Leiris, it is impossible to imagine a bullfight taking place just for oneself (89). When the end came, on the morning of 7 November 1938, the Peignots claimed a deathbed conversion that Marcel Moré, both a Catholic and a friend of Bataille, Leiris, and Colette and, as such, by far the most reliable witness, denies having occurred. Shortly before dying, Colette had, according to Leiris, half-crossed herself in reverse, either as an ambiguous sign of conversion or as an act of auto-damnation which, like all such oppositional gestures, affirms what it negates. Whatever its significance (and neither Bataille nor Moré say anything of it), this valedictory gesture on the part of "one who seemed no longer to exist except in a fabulous distance" caused Leiris to experience a moment of "true sacred horror: a great shudder which ran up my spine and which, shortly afterwards, the intimate companion of the dying woman [Bataille] said he had seen emanating from my head in the form of a bluish flash of lightning."[74]

Writing in the autumn of 1939, and already referring to Colette as "Laure," as though, in death, she had become the marble idol that she once threateningly told her mother she was (72), Bataille says that in that room in which "everything was accomplished" (an echo, surely, of the "it is finished" of Christ on the Cross [John 19:30]), the "obscure resemblance" of her face with that of "an empty and half demented Oedipus" became even more marked; it is, of course, as Bataille himself admits, the face of his blind, deranged, paralyzed father whom he and his mother had abandoned, to die literally *aux chiottes,* amid the ruins of Reims in 1914, the very face of the Sacred that casts such a spell of attraction and dread. But by then Bataille is trying to consign "Laure" (not to mention Colette) to the past, though her presence sometimes overwhelms him "gentle as the flash of an axe in the night" (291). Bataille counters the threat of decapitation by Laure's shade with the "the thought of Denise [Rollin], *alive*" (299, Bataille's italics), her "heavy purity . . . more beautiful than I could ever have dreamed it," a source of intoxication amid the chaos of war. Significantly, these pages on "Laure's death," intended for *Le Coupable* (1944), were excluded from the text that was finally published, and the description of the ascent of Mount Etna in 1937 that is included omits all mention of Colette's terrified presence beside him: All that remains is the confrontation of a solitary I with the "not-I" (*non-je*) of nature at its most alien and terrible.[75] First marmorealized as "Laure," Colette has, by 1943, been written out of the script: There is no "We," only "I" and "not-I."

Before that, however, Bataille had done his utmost to prevent Colette's being "recuperated" by the Church that had so marked and marred her life but from whose grip she, like Bataille, had never liberated herself as much as she thought. Bataille refused to allow a priest into the house, and threatened that, if the Peignots tried to have a requiem mass said for Colette, he would personally shoot the priest at the altar (Moré, 284). An extraordinary scene followed, described by Moré, when the undertakers arrived to place the lid on the coffin. On one side of the bier stood Madame Peignot and Madeleine, dressed in mourning; on the other Bataille, Leiris, and Moré, in light-colored suits, sported "pink and sky blue ties" (*bleu ciel,* as in *Le Bleu du ciel?*) to signal their refusal to mourn. Just before the lid was closed, Leiris took five poker-dice to which he attached an esoteric significance and slipped them "like a talisman or a viaticum" into the coffin.[76] For his part, Bataille's valedictory offering were the pages of a translation of William Blake's *Marriage of Heaven and Hell* (c. 1793) ripped out of a copy of the *Nouvelle Revue Française* and containing one of her favorite quotations, "Drive your cart and your plow over the bones of the dead" (quoted by Colette 106, 115, etc.), along with other aphorisms she surely applauded: "The road of excess leads to the palace of wisdom," "He who desires but acts not, breeds pestilence," "Exuberance is Beauty."[77] Then, remarkably, Madame Peignot asked Bataille, via Moré, to embrace her and, still more remarkably, Bataille agreed, whereupon, in Moré's description, "these two beings who, for several days, had been surveying each other like china dogs, almost with hatred, were seen to move towards each other and, the undertakers' men having withdrawn, to embrace over the coffin" (285); a few days later, Madame Peignot told Moré that she would have welcomed Bataille as a son-in-law. With notable generosity (or perhaps surrendering to Bataille's superior strength of will), Madame Peignot then ceded her daughter's body to her lover for burial, which duly took place at the cemetery of Fourqueux on the outskirts of the forest of Saint-Nom-la-Bretèche. Her grave bears neither a stone nor a date nor a name, just a pile of dirt soon covered in vegetation—a suitably "acephalous" nonmemorial to one who, all her life, had sought to transcend the bounds of identity in nameless "communication" with the anonymity of the sacred.

Was She "Dirty"?

It is widely believed, though without clinching evidence,[78] that Colette was the model for the character of "Dirty" in Bataille's novel *Le Bleu du ciel,* completed in May 1935 but not published until 1957. The novel's central male character is Troppmann, the name, in the first instance, of one of the most notorious multiple murderers of the nineteenth century, Jean-Baptiste Troppmann, executed in 1869 for killing a mother and her five (or, according to some reports, seven) children.[79] Onto this onomastic stem is grafted the idea of the Nietzschean Superman (*trop* + *mann*=Too much man), which is immediately undercut by the missing second letter *p*: *trop* + *p(eu)* + *mann*=too little man). Dirty's "real" name is Dorothea S.: Dorothea (meaning "gift of God") being the Christian virgin and martyr—Dorothea, who was decapitated on the orders of Emperor Diocletian around 303 A.D. Significantly, her feast day is 6 February, the date of the fascist riots in Paris in 1934, the rise of fascism in Germany, Austria, and Spain forming not so much the background to the events narrated in the novel as a closely interlocking obbligato.[80] The other principal character is named Louise Lazare (always referred to as Lazare), in whom it is possible to recognize a stinging portrait of Simone Weil: "ugly and conspicuously filthy," a "skinny, sallow-fleshed Jewess" squinting through steel-rimmed spectacles, her "macabre appearance" all too well summed up in the back-from-the-dead name, anemic ("the thin blood of an unwashed virgin" [29–31]),[81] far to the left of the official Communist Party and with a "hunger for sacrifice" (45) that leads Troppmann-Bataille to make a highly prescient judgment: "I thought, she's a Christian" (63).

The fact that Lazare is so obviously Simone Weil has led to the widespread belief that "Dirty" *must* be Colette Peignot. If this is so, it is an amazingly unflattering portrait by a lover of his mistress of four or so years (or, of course, a highly flattering one, given what Bataille calls the "freakish anomalies" (154) of his thought at the time), for, from the first page of the novel, "Dirty" is shown living a life of continuous boozing, puking, pissing, shitting, belching, bleeding, sweating, and fucking, to the delighted horror of the scarcely less incontinent Troppmann: No novel of comparable length contains so great a volume and variety of human ejecta and effluvia. "Dirty" is marked out from the beginning as a sacrificial victim in the making, wetting and soiling herself in a low dive in London, "beet-red, her eyes twisted upward . . . , squirming on her chair like a pig under the knife" (17).[82] The simile is picked up later on in the image of "the bubbles of blood that form over the hole a butcher opens in a pig's throat" (119) and in the sight, on the Pont du Carrousel, of "the headless necks of flayed lambs" (107) sticking out from under the canvas covering of a butcher's van; the author of a brief article on abattoirs (1929),[83] Bataille was something of a connoisseur of animal carcasses.

After an interval in pre–Civil War Barcelona, Troppmann and Dirty move on to Trèves (Trier) on the German-French frontier and birthplace of Karl Marx where, their bodies "quivering like two rows of teeth chattering together" (it is November now, and snowing), they make love in the mud of the cemetery overlooking the city: "We were as excited by earth as by naked flesh; no sooner was [Dirty's sex] out of sight under her clothes than I hurriedly bared it again" (144–45).[84] Then it is on to Koblenz and Frankfurt where Dirty, having told Troppmann that she wants there to be a war, leaves him and heads off south alone, while Troppmann, quivering now more with horrified excitement, witnesses the "obscene and terrifying" sight and sound of a Hitler Youth brass band made up of boys in "short black velvet pants and short jackets" who, in their "sticklike stiffness," seem "to be possessed by some cataclysmic exultation." In front of them, their leader, "a degenerately skinny kid with the sulky face of a fish," keeps time with a long drum major's stick:

He held this stick obscenely erect, with the knob at his crotch, it then looked like a monstrous monkey's penis that had been decorated with braids of colored cord. Like a dirty little brute, he would then jerk the stick level with his mouth; from crotch to mouth, from mouth to crotch, each rise and fall jerking to a grinding salvo from the drums. (150–51)

It is a typical piece of 1930s Bataille writing: mixing the sexual and political, complicit with what it condemns ("obscene" and "terrifying" are hardly terms of unambiguous criticism in his lexicon), berating fascist irrationalism while indulging in an irrationalism not far from fascism as it does so.

Whether Dirty embodies fascism or antifascism is unclear. She wears "a bright red silk dress" suggestive of the left, but it is "the red of swastikaed flags" (148); it is as though she, like Troppmann, is beyond left and right, just as she is beyond life and death, "too voracious to go on living" (149), doomed to destruction by the very ardor of her passion. What the novel demonstrates is the futility of the couple's mix of violence, eroticism, and politics. "My frenzy was useless" (Je m'agitais inutilement, 99),[85] says Troppmann of his attempt to engage with revolutionary politics in Barcelona, exactly the words he uses to describe Colette's politics in his posthumous tribute to her: "She wanted to become a revolutionary militant, but all she achieved was a vain and febrile agitation" (*une agitation vaine et fébrile*).[86] But, in politics as in everything else (except writing), Colette went further than Bataille but that "further" was never, of course, enough: "We may break all the barriers," she wrote, "we are still *limited*."[87] Ultimately, as André Breton famously said, the real bars are on the *inside* of the cage, and this Colette recognized when she wrote that "it is in oneself that one bears the most dangerous antagonist" (C'est en soi-même qu'on porte l'oppositionnaire le plus dangereux); she also knew that she was prepared to do much more than Bataille, though still not enough, to vanquish that internal enemy. There are times when Colette and Bataille seem like a more intellectual, and decidedly more middle-class, version of Bonnie and Clyde, egging each other on to ever greater extremes, defying the society off which they live (he a librarian, she an heiress), until the inevitable catastrophe that, in their case, is not the mayhem of a final shoot-out, but *une mort très douce* in a bourgeois town outside Paris. But only Bonnie dies, to be reinvented by her lover, friends, and besotted nephew, while Clyde lives on, avoiding the *real* dangers of war and resistance, and ends up, for all the "monstrous anomalies" of his writings, a thoroughly respectable member of society.

7

HOLY TEARS, HOLY BLOOD

Ten women, to whom we shall in due course add an eleventh, one short of a full female apostolic complement. One Carmelite sister, canonized in then record time and recently declared a Doctor of the Church (Thérèse Martin). One a candidate for beatification, who went without food or sleep for close to half a century and who, each week during that time, dramatically reenacted the Passion of her Lord (Marthe Robin). One Jewish convert to Catholicism (Raïssa Maritain), and one who waited on God on the threshold of the Church, refusing the Host as she refused virtually all food (Simone Weil). Two visionaries, one of whom the church repudiated even as it endorsed her vision of the weeping Madonna (Mélanie Calvat), the other whom it first kept at a prudent distance and then effectively silenced, denying her the right to found the religious order she desired (Claire Ferchaud). An artist who was both sacrificed by her lover (and fellow sculptor) and reinvented by her brother as an icon of (un)holy folly and supernatural wisdom (Camille Claudel). Two devotees of Mary Magdalene, in one of whom Eros and Agape met once more in a madness both sacred and profane (Madeleine Lebouc), and of whom the other, repudiating a life spent simulating passion on the stage, gave herself up to shedding holy tears for the sake of suffering, but nonbelieving, humanity (Eva Lavallière). One "saint of the abyss" whose quest for some absolute gratification, beyond all oppositions of life and death, sacred and profane, both repeated and inverted the more orthodox spiritual trajectories of nine of the other ten women (Colette Peignot). Ten lives that, geared without thought of self-preservation toward a perhaps impossible goal, were dominated by pain, tears, blood, illness, and loss, that ended mostly in premature and agonized death and were spent largely in voluntary or involuntary reclusion: in convents, lunatic asylums, hospitals, clinics, prisons or prisonlike family homes, or in self-elected isolation on the margins of society. Having examined these lives separately and diachronically, it now remains to bring them together and draw out synchronically the common themes and images that unite them, to reconfigure them according to certain recurring motifs and metaphors and so discover, perhaps, what lay behind these women's quest for the sacred and why, in so many cases, it both destroyed and inspired them.

"Mysteria"

Confronted with the accounts presented above, the dominant school in nineteenth- and early twentieth-century French psychiatry would have had no hesitation in formulating its diagnosis: all of these women were, at the very least, neurotic, most were hysterical, the physical ailments (notably tuberculosis) from which so many of them suffered were but a somatization of a deep-set psychological disorder, and a good half of them should have been institutionalized after the manner of Camille Claudel. "Many *women Saints* and *Blessed* were nothing other than simple hysterics!" exclaimed Henri Legrand du Saulle, one of La Salpêtrière's squad of hysteria specialists, in 1891, "It is enough to reread the life of Elizabeth of Hungary, in 1207; of Sainte Gertrude, of Saint Bridget, of Saint Catherine of Siena, in 1347; of Joan of Arc, of Saint Teresa, of Madame de Chantal, in 1752; of the famous Marie Alacoque, and of many others: one will be easily convinced of this truth."[1]

Thanks to the work of Jan Goldstein, Ruth Harris, and others on the nineteenth-century French psychiatric profession,[2] it is now possible to view the "hystericization" of a wide range of psychic phenomena previously thought to be supernatural in origin—mystical ecstasies and visions of all kinds, demonic possession, prophetic utterances, extreme fasting, stigmatization—as part of a concerted project, as much political and ideological as scientific and professional, that, in its turn, can only be understood in the context of the "culture wars" that raged in France, particularly between the defeat of 1870 and the religious revival it precipitated and the final separation of Church and state in 1905.

Throughout this period, the sectional interests of the emerging psychiatric profession were congruent with those of the at first struggling and then triumphant secular Republic. Both profession and regime sought to define and consolidate themselves over and against the "clerical enemy" famously designated by Léon Gambetta in 1877, the multifaceted anticlericalism of the Republic having a particular edge for the psychiatric profession to the extent that, even in the 1870s, the Church still dominated the day-to-day care of the mentally ill in both Paris and the provinces. Two thirds of the asylums and hospices in Paris relied on (almost exclusively female) members of religious orders, and one of the first byproducts of the victory of the Republic over its Catholic-royalist rivals in 1877 was the decision, taken by the militantly anticlerical director of La Salpêtrière, Désiré-Magloire Bourneville, the following year, to replace the entire force of *soeurs-infir-mières* in the hospital with licensed, professionally trained (and predominantly male) nurses. As part of the same laicizing project, obligatory church attendance by patients was suppressed in 1883, and hospital buildings were stripped of their religious designations and renamed after leading scientific and medical figures.[3] The "godless asylum" was the psychiatrists' equivalent of the "godless school" (*l'école sans Dieu*) simultaneously promoted by the teaching profession in alliance with the secular Republic.

Nor was it a coincidence that, particularly at La Salpêtrière under Bourneville and the celebrated Jean-Martin Charcot (1825–93), research and therapy were targeted primarily, and certainly most spectacularly, on female patients and that, among those patients, it was those displaying "mystical" symptoms of one kind or another who most attracted the attention of professionals and public alike. The centralization of "mystical" women in psychiatric discourse and practice was, to a considerable degree, a corollary of the centralization, already discussed, of women in nineteenth-century Catholic discourse. If women, as church apologists averred, were more "naturally religious" than men, what better way was there for the Church's opponents to discredit the claims of religion in general, and of the Catholic Church in particular, than to pathologize all those facets of female religiosity, from the extremes of "mystical ecstasy" to simple day-to-day piety, that the Church sought to oppose to the alleged rationalism and materialism of the male sex as a whole? Thus it was, in Cristina Mazzoni's words, that, in the eyes of the psychiatric profession, "anti-religion is to religion . . . as male is to female and . . . as sanity / health is to madness/sickness."[4] "[R]eligion is part of woman's sex," the Goncourt brothers confided to their diary in April 1857,[5] the French word *sexe* hovering between its two meanings of gender and, in this context, of vagina; the formula repeats what was, by then, as much an *idée reçue* among the Church's defenders as among its adversaries. If, by a logical extension, the religious impulse as a whole could be shown to be a displacement of repressed or frustrated female sexuality, the cause of the (male dominated) secular Republic would be served along with, more narrowly, that of the (equally male dominated) psychiatric profession. "Women," the leading republican Jules Ferry (1832–93) had declared in 1870,[6] "must belong to science, or else they will belong to the church." By simultaneously naturalizing, gendering, and pathologizing the supposedly supernatural, the psychiatric profession could make a huge contribution to the broader ideological struggles of the late nineteenth century. Religion would be comprehensively "othered," its supernatural claims systematically debunked, and its innermost character revealed for what it really was: as irrational, sexually supercharged, in a word as *hysterical*.

The late-nineteenth-century assault on "mysteria"—the expression comes from the well-known *Speculum de l'autre femme* (1974) by the feminist psychoanalyst Luce Irigaray[7]—was conducted simultaneously on the historical, collective, and individual levels. The Henri Legrand de Saulle mentioned above was only one of a phalanx of psychiatrists who sought to pathologize the female saints and mystics of the past, and his list of holy hysterics from saints Catherine of Siena and Marguerite-Marie Alacoque to more recent examples such as the Westphalian stigmatic Catherine Emmerich (1774–1824) was routinely repeated by writer after writer. The instance of Saint Teresa of Avila (1515–82), usually mediated through Bernini's openly erotic statue of 1652 in the church of Santa Maria della Vittoria in Rome, was adduced so frequently that Huysmans, among other Catholic apologists, was moved to denounce the virtually automatic assimilation of the doctor-saint's "blessed lucidity and incomparable genius" with the "extravagances of nymphomaniacs and madwomen."[8] Occasions of collective religious "dementia" in the past, either exclusively or predominantly female, were studied as examples of the contagiousness of holy hysteria, from the possessed nuns of Loudun between 1632 and 1640 (the subject, more recently, of a superb study by Aldous Huxley, an opera by the Polish composer Krzysztof Penderecki [b. 1933], a play by John Whiting, and a typically lurid film by Ken Russell),[9] to the Protestant ecstatics of the Cévennes, known as *Camisards* on account of their coarse linen shirts, between the revocation of the Edict of Nantes (1684) and the 1720s and 1730s,[10] with pride of place going to the so-called *convulsionnaires* of the parish of Saint Médard in the south of Paris and elsewhere during approximately the same period.[11] Satanism, demonic possession, and so-called black magic received a similar reductionist treatment in works such as Charcot's *Les Démoniaques dans l'art,* though none possessed the subversive insights of Michelet's much earlier masterpiece *La Sorcière* (1862), according to which both witches' sabbath and the black mass were, in their essence, "the work of Woman, of a desperate woman" and, as such, represented a would-be "redemption of Eve, cursed by Christianity": "Woman in the sabbath fills everything. She is the priesthood, she is the altar, she is the host, which the whole people receives in communion. Deep down, is she not its very God?"[12]

Nor were these instances of collective delirium confined to the past. There were, much closer to hand, a surprising number of outbreaks of (un)holy hysteria, especially between the late 1840s and early 1880s, and not just in remote rural areas but in major cities like Bordeaux (where what was described as collective hysteria gripped a girls' school in 1883) and even in Paris where a group of *premières communiantes* were seized by "convulsions" in Montmartre in 1883.[13] The most striking examples, however, occurred in the same marginal or upland regions as the "extraordinary phenomena" discussed in chapter 5, in the first instance Britanny where the women of the small town of Josselin were reported in 1851 to be barking compulsively like dogs (whence the name *aboyeuses* given them) and where, thirty years later, at the village of Grand-Hirel near Plédran, the seven children of the Moncet family allegedly showed signs of demonic possession, with the three eldest, in the grip of hallucinations of Satan and armies of devils, "climbing up walls and onto roofs, dancing, hurling insults at the curé and stones at passersby"; the medical experts were consulted and produced the predictable diagnosis of "classic hysteria." Similarly, in the villages of Drulhe and Peyrusse in the Aveyron (another remote mountainous department) in 1859–60, a group of girls were seized by convulsions and began to shout, groan, and gesticulate uncontrollably, even (or especially) in church and continued these antics for five months or more before the local curé was able to reassert adult authority. A few years later, in the village of Illfurt near Mulhouse in 1864–65, there was a rare instance of male-led hysteria when two boys, nine-year-old Thiébaut Burner and his seven-year-old brother Joseph, created chaos through their convulsions, blasphemous language in church directed against both priests and sacred objects, and outbreaks of glossolalia in which they supposedly described the demons or monsters who held them in thrall. Attracting enormous public attention, the boys identified with the demon-figures of a conservative rural society (Protestant, Freemasons, and Jews), refused to be exorcised, and were eventually separated, with Joseph remaining at home and Thiébaut being sent to an orphanage at Schiltigheim where, deaf except during his attacks, he, uneducated and speaking a German-based patois, held conversations in French and Latin with visitors. Eventually, both boys consented to undergo the rite of exorcism whereafter they were, apparently, restored to sanity and society.[14]

The most famous nineteenth-century instance of collective hysteria took place, however, in the village of Morzine in the Haute-Savoie, beginning in 1857 (three years before the Savoie was annexed by France in 1860) and continuing off and on for more than fifteen years, the last cases occurring in 1873, during which period the majority of the village's female population seems to have been affected at some time or in some way.[15] Like many such Alpine villages, Morzine survived by exporting virtually its entire adult male population as migrant workers across the nearby Swiss frontier, creating a gynocentric vacuum in which the priest was, in effect, the only male authority figure present. The so-called mal de Morzine began in early 1857 when the ten-year-old "Perronne T." claimed to have received, according to well-known local traditions present, as we have seen, during the events at relatively nearby La Salette eleven years earlier, a letter from the "Santa Vierge" in heaven which she and her sister read out repeatedly and then, supposedly, returned to its sender. Shortly afterward, however, things took a diabolic twist when the two girls began compulsively to scream, swear, gesticulate, and blaspheme when proffered the communion wafer. Convulsions and glossolalia spread to other girls and women in the village as they began to speak with the voice of devils, the damned, and of outsiders in general (Jews, French, woodcutters, shepherds, and hunters), using not the local patois but the French and German that none of them formally spoke. The local priest performed a rite of collective exorcism in 1858, but sporadic outbreaks of "hysteria" continued, and, in April 1864, the bishop of Annecy himself, Monseigneur Magnin, visited the village, only to be greeted by between sixty writhing and cursing women and girls who, when he refused to exorcise one of their number, reviled him with such tirades of abuse as "Wolf of a bishop [*loup d'evêque*], we must tear out his eyes; he hasn't the power to cure the girl; no, he cannot get rid of the devil."[16] By now Morzine was a French village, and eventually a doctor Adolphe Constans was dispatched from Paris to bring the troublesome border *commune* under control, which, by a combination of treatment, threat, and local reforms, he proceeded eventually to do.

Both at the time, and by subsequent historians, the "mal de Morzine" has been interpreted as the response of a dysfunctional and traumatized female community to a series of outside threats over which it had no control: economic poverty whose ostensible solution (male migration) produced problems of social control, the perceived threat of annexation by France, and a sense of cultural exclusion typical, it is said, of remote mountain communities. In this light, the fifteen-year-long trauma was an inchoate and desperate protest of the margins versus the center, of female versus male, of poverty and powerlessness against the perceived loci of authority and wealth; possession, in short, was the only recourse left to the chronically dispossessed. Morzine is, so to speak, La Salette or Lourdes in reverse, a revelation not of the "pure" *sacré de droite* of the Virgin and her son but of the impure and disruptive *sacré de gauche* of their demonic adversaries. Characteristically, the psychiatrists interpreted both as expressions of individual and collective hysteria.

The principal interpretative and therapeutic efforts of such professionals were, however, directed at individual "mysterics," and it was here that the new techniques of photography came into their own. Pierre Janet's photographs of Pauline Lair Lamotte in various poses and postures of mystical "ecstasy" were belated products of a huge iconographic project launched by Désiré-Magloire Bourneville and Paul Reynard at La Salpêtrière between 1876 and 1880. "Mysterics"—always, without exception, women—were urged to "act out," in every sense of the word, their symptoms before the recording lens of the camera, mimicry, histrionism, or, more brutally, "clownisme" being, according to Charcot, one of the defining characteristics of hysteria.[17] Thus subjects such as the famous "Augustine" virtually "danced" before Bourneville, Reynard, and their camera, constituting herself, with their active encouragement, as a spectacle at once grotesque and erotically alluring, until, through the "choreography of her convulsions," she achieved a state of "ecstasy" or possession in which any distinction between the real and the simulated ceased to be operable.[18] The analogies between the gestures and postures of the hysteric and those of the mystic were graphically, if crudely, underlined, not least by the titles of the images collected in the multivolume *Iconographie photographique de la Salpêtrière*: "Ecstasy," "Beatitude," even "Crucifixion."[19] Visiting La Salpêtrière in the mid-1880s, the novelist Alphonse Daudet (1840–97) saw mounted on the walls of Charcot's consulting room numerous photographs of "primitive Italian and Spanish paintings representing saints in prayers, ecstatics, convulsionaries, the great religious nervous disease [*la grande névrose religieuse*], as they say at the asylum."[20] Clearly everything was being done to collapse the distinction between "hysteric" and "mystic" in pursuit of an explicitly ideological and political agenda as well as in the name of scientific research, itself explicitly politicized in the context of the "culture wars" of the late nineteenth century.

Thus the rigorously secularized La Salpêtrière of the 1880s and 1890s came curiously to resemble some kind of a convent to which, Jules Claretie wrote in 1903, countless suffering women came "as to a novena,"[21] much as other women might make a pilgrimage to Fourvière or Lourdes. It also partook of a circus, a (semi-pornographic) photographer's studio, even of a brothel, as female patients posed, paraded, and pouted, often scantily clad, in front of male doctors and visitors. Not only did Charcot come to resemble "the leader of a vast surrogate religion," with his retinue of psychiatrist-priests and student-neophytes (among them, of course, Freud from October 1885 to February 1886), but his weekly public lesson each Friday, with its theatrical display of patients suffering from all manner of psychological disorders, came grotesquely to resemble the ritual exhibition of another sacrificial victim on an earlier Friday on a hill called Golgotha. La Salpêtrière, said Claretie, was a *citta dolorosa* containing at any one time more than four hundred women, a "Versailles of suffering"[22] with its own complex of rituals, regimes, and etiquettes, which both foregrounded women and constituted them as erotico-mystico-hysterical objects. Small wonder, perhaps, that, when Charcot proposed to Madeleine Lebouc in May 1893 that she move from her then hospital to La Salpêtrière to be studied and treated by him, she absconded the following morning rather than fall into his hands.

There was one contemporary "case" above all that fascinated psychiatrists and on which, correspondingly, Church apologists focused in order to refute their enemies' systematic reduction of the supernatural to the pathological. Louise Lateau (1850–83) came from the village of Bois d'Haine in Belgium where an accident at the age of eleven—she was, depending on which version of her story one follows, either trodden on by a cow or gored by a bull—supposedly delayed the onset of menstruation until the age of eighteen, at which point, in January 1868, she began to experience the pain of crucifixion, followed by bleeding from her hands, feet, forehead, and side over the ensuing months. Already at the age of sixteen a member of the Tertiary Order of Saint Francis, Louise is said to have "relived" the Passion, à la Marthe Robin, over eight hundred times between the first onset of bleeding and her death fifteen years later. She is also credited, while in a state of spiritual trance, with the ability to converse in English and Latin, languages that she had never formally learned, and with having taken no food other than the daily communion wafer between 30 May 1871 and her death in 1883 at the Christologically supercharged age of thirty-three years.[23] Even during her lifetime, Louise Lateau's regular reenactment of the Passion inspired a slew of devotional works—*Biographie de Louise Lateau, la stigmatiseé de Bois d'Haine* by H. van Looy (1874), *Louise Lateau, la stigmatiseé de Bois d'Haine* by A. Rohling (1874), and *Louise Lateau, le vendredi saint* by Charles Chauliac (1875), among others—and the huge publicity attaching to her case prompted the arch-anticlerical psychiatrist Désiré-Magloire Bourneville, scheduled to become a republican deputy in 1885, to launch an all-out, no-holds-barred assault on her reputation as a stigmatic and saint in the making. The crux of Bourneville's *Science et miracle: Louise Lateau ou la stigmatiseé belge,* first published in 1875, came in its third chapter, aggressively and confidently entitled "Louise Lateau is a hysteric: a clinical demonstration." Drawing on the cases of "Emilie," "Désirée" (who reputedly embraced in fantasy the naked Christ on the cross and who, at the moment of orgasm, identified with the Holy Virgin suckling her Son), and "Geneviève" (who had actually visited Bois d'Haine to compare her ecstatic trances to those of Louise), Bourneville felt able to assert that Louise's symptoms were absolutely identical to those of successive "hysterics" he had studied; "like all hysterical women," he concluded, "it may very well be that [Louise Lateau] is deceptive—and sometimes even in good faith—and that she lets herself be induced into exaggerating the phenomena she exhibits, seeing the importance that they have in the eyes of her intimate advisors, of whom she is the humble servant and whom she obeys like a slave."[24] In short, Louise is a sick and deeply disturbed young woman requiring institutionalized care, not a deliberate fraud but a deluded (and delusionary) victim who has fallen into the hands of clerical manipulators; all the blood that she is shedding for Christ and humanity stems from the late onset of menstruation caused in its turn by being kicked by a cow. It is difficult to imagine a more comprehensive debunking of the claims being made by the Church on behalf of a possible future candidate for beatification.

The case of Louise Lateau inspired a novel entitled *L'Hystérique* (1885) by the Belgian author Camille Lemonnier (1884–1913), one of a whole series of fictional works that sought to naturalize and pathologize female religiosity under the influence of emerging psychiatric ideas: the Goncourt brothers' *Madame Gervaisais* (1869); Léon Henrique's *Elisabeth Couronneau* (1879), set in the eighteenth-century Paris of the *convulsionnaires* of Saint-Médard; Alphonse Daudet's *L'Evangéliste* (1883), which, interestingly, attacks Protestant, rather than Catholic, religious extremism; and, perhaps most fully and perceptively, Emile Zola's great documentary novel *Lourdes* of 1894. For their part, Church supporters responded either with attacks on their opponents' aims, ideology, and methods such as the Catholic neurologist Antoine Imbert-Goiurbeyre's massive *La Stigmatisation, l'extase divine et les miracles de Lourdes: Réponse aux libres penseurs*, first published in 1873 and still considered authoritative by the Church to this day,[25] and a series of novels, essays, and biographies that sought to reinstate precisely the extreme forms of female religious behavior that the anticlericals sought to discredit, works such as Barbey d'Aurevilly's *Un prêtre marié* (1865), on the subject of stigmatization and the vicarious suffering of a daughter on behalf of her married priest father, Léon Bloy's *Le Désespéré* (1887) and *La Femme Pauvre* (1897), to be discussed shortly. To these may be added Huysmans's hagiological study of Saint Lydwine of Schiedam (1901) and his "conversion novel" *En route* (1895), which, together, can be read as a defense and illustration of virtually every sickly and disturbed female ecstatic, anorexic, or stigmatic in the history of the Church, from Hildegard of Bingen (1098–1179), Angela di Foligno (1248–1309), whose visions, translated by the convert-novelist Ernest Hello (1828–85) in 1868, were read by virtually everyone studied in this book, from Thérèse to Bataille, the Catherines of Sienna and Genoa (1347–1380 and 1447–1510 respectively) to the contemporary or near-contemporary Catherine Emmerich and Louise Lateau. The "culture wars" of the late nineteenth century were, in a very real sense, about the meaning of the ordeal of any number of fasting, bleeding, and otherwise suffering Catholic women. Why were they all so clearly eager to suffer, and what was the meaning of their uncanny ability to go without food, or of the blood that issued, according to some regular rhythm, from their hands, feet, foreheads, and sides?

In the end, after exchanging hundreds of thousands of words of polemic and counterpolemic, neither side budged from its entrenched ideological position. The nature of the church party's case meant that it could do no more than assert and reassert the supernatural character of the "extraordinary phenomena" in question; it could, by definition, "prove" nothing, and indeed the very notion of proof ran counter to the fideistic position it was determined to defend. With their rivals reduced to dogmatic tautology, the nullifidians of La Salpêtrière were ultimately no more scientific when they asserted over and over again the absolute identity of the mystical and the hysterical.

The problem for the psychiatrists was that, in the final analysis, "hysterical" was only a label. Charcot, as Freud said after his death, was not a thinker but a seer, a classifier and categorizer comparable to Adam "when God led before him the creatures of paradise to be named and grouped."[26] Since the Ecole Salpêtrière did not know what *caused* hysteria, or even what constituted it—it was a "sphinx," said Charcot,[27] a "Proteus," said Briquet[28]—or even, finally, whether it existed as an autonomous entity, to equate "mystics" and "hysterics" was, in reality, to say little beyond discrediting the supernaturalist claims of their ideological enemies. As Ruth Harris has written in her fine study of Lourdes, "the word hysteria dismissed as much as it explained," serving as "a catch-all phrase that explained everything and nothing all at once, pinning upon the subject the taint of pathology or susceptibility."[29] The psychiatrists may have naturalized the cause and character of "extraordinary phenomena" without rendering them any less "extraordinary" or, ultimately, demonic; the demon was now merely relocated within the natural-human order rather than without.

Another problem was that though there may have been an *analogy* between what the psychiatrists called the hysterical and the mystical, the one did not always necessarily lead to the other. Of the women discussed in this book, Camille Claudel and Colette Peignot would certainly have been categorized as "hysterical," if not more, by Charcot, Bourneville, and their colleagues, but both, as we have seen, were notable for the intensity of their *anti*religious feelings and opinions. On the other hand, the psychiatrists and their novelistic allies did suggest how the discourse of ultramontanism, with its emphasis on blood, willingly assumed suffering, and the externalization of feeling (especially in the form of tears), could espouse, and lend powerful justification to, disorders of a psychological or physiological nature. Not every "mystical" woman was "hysterical" by any means, but the theology and practice of ultramontanism could and did push mysticism in a pathological dimension, even if it did not cause that pathology itself, as we shall see as we turn our attention to the closely related question of "eating disorders."

"Holy Anorexia"

What "hysteria" was to the 1880s and 1890s, anorexia (in the general sense of prolonged loss of appetite) was, with rather more justification, to the late twentieth century: a way of explaining a range of (almost exclusively female) religious behaviors that were otherwise resistant to rational interpretation. The prodigious ability of female religious of the past to go without food, often allegedly for years, sustained only by daily Holy Communion, was, of course, well known to specialists, but it took the apparent explosion of anorexia among (again) primarily middle-class adolescent females in western Europe and the United States—an index, perhaps, as Maud Ellmann has written, of a culture in which "the kitchen rather than the bedroom has become the theater of temptation and the scene of sin"[30]— to redirect attention toward the medieval and early modern precursors of the "fasting girls" of the present.

The pioneering work in the field, Rudolph M. Bell's *Holy Anorexia*

(1985),[31] dwelt, significantly, on more or less the same "cases" as had the Ecole Salpêtrière a hundred years earlier, perhaps not surprisingly because it was a doctor associated with that school, Charles Lasègue (1816–83), professor of clinical medicine at La Pitié hospital in Paris, who, in 1873, published a seminal article entitled "De l'anorexie hystérique" in the *Archives Générales de Médicine;* anorexia and hysteria were thus linked from the outset.[32] Like Charcot, Bourneville, and their colleagues, Bell foregrounded the lives of the Catherines of Siena and Genoa, Angela di Foligno, and Maria Maddelena de Pazzi (1566–1607), as well as of a number of lesser-known female religious; his conclusion, essentially, was that all these women were clinically diagnosable as anorexics and that current Church practices regarding fasting, (self-) flagellation, and other forms of (self-) deprivation, notably of sleep, gave a supernatural justification to their psychological condition. Two years later, in *Holy Feast and Holy Fast* (1987),[33] Caroline Walker Bynum provided an altogether more subtle and suggestive analysis of the eating and fasting practices of medieval female religious, drawing attention, in particular, to the paradox whereby, in the consecration and taking of communion, traditional or cultural normative gender roles were reversed in such a way that the priest who prepared and consecrated the divine food became the nurturing mother-adult and the woman who received that food in her mouth became both a child accepting nourishment from her mother and who, by swallowing it, then, so to speak, incubated the Body of Christ like a fetus in her stomach-cum-womb. The supposed "eating disorders" of *some* female religious at that time and later were built into this dissymetry between male-female giver and female receiver, though the majority of such women were, in Bynum's analysis, able to transcend this dichotomy and become at once mothers, daughters, sisters, and spouses-lovers of Christ, unions of body and soul, flesh and spirit, who offered themselves up as "living hosts" to a God whom, in their writings and day-to-day devotional practices, they comprehensively maternalized as pure, self-giving, unconditional love.[34]

The present discussion does not seek in any way to equate (as Bell, but not Bynum, is prone to do) the "extraordinary phenomena" of extreme fasting, sleeplessness, visions, and the like with anorexia, nor, above all, does it attempt any "explanation" of that condition itself.[35] It is nonetheless evident that, at some point in their lives, most of the women discussed in this book suffered from what, using quotation marks for the last time, we may usefully describe as "eating disorders": and that these were linked in some way both to the discourse and devotional practices of the Catholic Church and to their family situations, above all to their relationship with their mothers.

The most "spectacular" case of fasting should, however, be eliminated from the outset. Marthe Robin was *not* anorexic but a victim of inedia, the result of brain damage caused by disease—a problem to be treated by medicine, not psychiatry. On the other hand, it does seem appropriate to describe Simone Weil as anorexic and to see her premature death, though technically caused by tuberculosis, as a direct consequence of many years of deliberate self-starvation and other self-imposed deprivations. Thérèse Martin also suffered, as did at least two of her sisters, from intermittent eating disorders, and her lifelong phobia of milk is of particular eloquence given the centrality of the mother-daughter relationship in most discussions of the anorexic condition. Mélanie Calvat—whom even the church accused of "pithiatism," a virtual synonym of hysteria at the time—was also probably a sufferer. Claire Ferchaud relates how, as a child, she refused to take soup fed her by her mother, and her description of herself as a "piece of lint destined to take the pus of the open abscess" of human suffering recalls the extreme forms of self-maceration practiced by Catherine of Siena and Maria Maddelena de Pazzi. Raïssa Maritain was also notably thin, and her recurrent bouts of illness may have been linked to the stringent disciplines she imposed on herself, which, it is reasonable to assume, would have included rigorous fasting. Colette Peignot's apparent willingness to eat an excrement-filled "sandwich" given her by a perverted lover recalls the readiness—the alacrity, even—of Marguerite-Marie Alacoque, among other female saints, to eat the feces, vomit, and pus of the sick in her care,[36] the conduct of the "saint of the abyss," here as elsewhere, sacrilegiously echoing the more egregious forms of Catholic devotion. Camille Claudel's refusal, when institutionalized, to eat anything other than raw eggs and jacket potatoes prepared by herself also points to serious phobias relating to food. Madeleine Lebouc was obsessed with the idea that human flesh was being bought, sold, and consumed in secret all across Paris; anexoria would be consistent with all her other remarkable "symptoms." Louise Lateau, although mentioned only in passing in chapter 2, was without doubt anorexic, as was Catherine Emmerich with whose life almost every person, male and female, discussed in this book, was familiar; Huysmans's Saint Lydwine of Schiedam was one of the most notable holy anorexics of the High Middle Ages. In short, with the exception of Eva Lavallière, *all* of the women under consideration here—along with a number of others only marginally present—showed definite or probable signs of food-related disorders. An epidemic it was not, but it does incite us to look for shared patterns in their histories.

Studies of anorexia commonly focus on three major causative factors, of which the desire to "lose weight" is not necessarily the most important in and of itself: Not one of the women studied here was motivated by concern for her *outward* appearance, in the manner of most "secular" anorexics, but sought through self-deprivation an *inner* identification with the sufferings of Christ. In the first interpretative model, "voluntary" self-starvation—which is not voluntary at all, but deeply compulsive—is seen as a means of asserting control, via control of the intake of food into the body, over one's existence as a whole and, by extension, over reality as a whole. Anorexia is, crudely put, an assertion of identity and autonomy; self-deprivation becomes a deluded form of self-empowerment, though the quest for *total* control over body, self, and world is always, by definition, frustrated.

Of the women considered here, Simon Weil's anorexia most clearly falls into this pattern. By denying herself food (and sleep, warmth, and basic human comforts), she sought to impose mental and spiritual control over what, in due course, she came to define as the domain of weight (*la pesanteur*)—the weight of the self, the weight of society, the weight of the world—which she opposed systematically to the domain of grace. She rationalized this abortive quest for total self-control—abortive, because the more she sought to dominate herself, the less, in reality, was she "in control" of herself—through a series of political, social, and spiritual identifications: first with the material sufferings of the factory workers whose condition she sought voluntarily to assume, then with the sufferings of Christ on the cross, which she came in her last months to equate with the sufferings of the malnourished people of occupied France. The combined effect of these identifications was to legitimate in her own eyes what was, in effect, a protracted act of suicide, which she may at one time have thought she fully controlled but which was clearly controlling her long before she died. The paradox of her situation, as her philosophical mentor, Gustave Thibon, pointed out, was that she was never "detached from her detachment."[37] She wanted to *control* her self-abandonment to God, to create her own self-decreation, to will the relinquishment of her will and her self. Grace, said Georges Bernanos's *curé de campagne,* consists not in hating oneself, but in forgetting oneself,[38] something, it would seem, Simone could never achieve despite—or, rather, precisely because of—the intensity of her own rejection of self; her self-willed effort to transcend the domain of weight had the perverse effect of imprisoning her within it. To eat was to acknowledge dependence, to break the self-enclosed completeness that, while claiming the opposite, she sought to achieve. Above all, as she sought to deny her own body, she could not receive into it the Body of Christ without aborting her whole project. Communion could not be other than a violation of her autonomy—unthinkable, to take the body of her beloved in her mouth—whence her refusal, which she managed (as she always did) tortuously to rationalize to herself, to take communion, supposedly out of love for Christ whose love she was in reality rejecting. Anorexia, gnosticism, and self-excommunication were all of a piece, their interaction leading with appallingly inevitable logic to the hospice at Ashford.

None of the other women studied here sought self-perfection with quite the manic intensity of *la Vierge rouge,* but many shared with her what many writers on the subject regard as the fundamental cause of anorexia: the problematic relationship of daughters and mothers. Of the women discussed in this book, only Marthe Robin, not (to repeat) an anorexic, seems to have enjoyed anything like an untroubled relationship with her mother. Otherwise, it is a depressing tale, in case after case, of early maternal illness and death; of transfer to one or another surrogate mother; of mothers, often themselves unloved or bereaved, unable to love, feed, or even embrace their own daughters; of mothers obsessed with duty, discipline, and religious obligations and guilts who, almost inevitably, contaminate their daughters with their own neurotic compulsions, which, more often than not, are derived from those of *their* mothers. Here, in no particular order, is a compressed version of these mother-daughter tragedies:

- According to Bloy, *Mélanie Calvat*'s mother hated her as soon as she was born with "a strange, hyperbolic, and monstrous hatred"[39] and had effectively repudiated her by the time of the apparition, farming her out as a child laborer in a neighboring village.
- Having lost her own mother at the age of three and also traumatized by the death of her infant son and the suicide of her brother, *Camille Claudel*'s mother sided with her younger daughter (who bore the same first name as herself) against Camille. According to her son Paul, Louise Claudel never embraced any of her children.
- Unable to breastfeed her youngest daughter and obsessed by the earlier deaths of no fewer than four children in infancy, Zélie Martin sent *Thérèse* out to a wet nurse, took her back after a year, and then subjected her to her own guilt-ridden, disciplinarian Catholicism before dying of a protracted painful illness when Thérèse was four.
- *Raïssa* Oumansov (later Maritain) had a relatively trouble-free relationship with her mother, though the earliest memories recorded in *Les Grandes Amitiés* concern pretending that her younger sister is her mother and preferring being rocked in her cradle by her grandfather rather than other members of the family, including her mother. Her conversion to Christianity was, in effect, a rejection of her mother, through whom, by tradition, Jewish identity was transmitted.
- Of Simone and her mother, we need only repeat the letter of 1933, quoted in chapter 5: "As you read these lines, you must imagine that I am forcing your shoulders up against the wall, and staring at you with fire in my eyes."[40]
- Pauline Lair Lamotte broke with her parents when she was twenty and, by changing her name to *Madeleine Lebouc,* symbolically repudiated the whole family heritage. There is some evidence that she was reconciled with her mother prior to the latter's death in 1889, when Madeleine was thirty-six.
- At the age of eighteen, *Eva Lavallière* was present when her father murdered her mother.

- *Claire Ferchaud*'s mother threatened to hand her weeping daughter over to the police[41] and in general treated her with a strictness that, masochistically, Claire came to need and provoke.
- Madame Suzanne Peignot was, in her daughter *Colette*'s account "constantly preoccupied with housework, preoccupied to the point of anguish by dust, mothballs, wax polish,"[42] contaminating the household, servants included, with her death-, duty-, and discipline-obsessed Catholicism. One family servant was driven to suicide, partly through fear of Madame Peignot.
- Finally, although she does not form part of our "sample," it is notable that *Bernadette Soubirous*' mother was unable to breastfeed her, sending her to wet nurse Marie Laguës (whose baby son had just died) in a village nearby. For economic reasons, the Soubirous later handed over their daughter as a servant to her surrogate mother who duly mistreated her, reputedly blaming her for "having taken the milk of her dead baby." Significantly Bernadette, described her vision of 1858 as "bien mignonnette," or, in patois, *no pétito damizéla*, with nothing maternal about her. Bernadette's eating grass when the vision occurred may suggest some eating disorder.[43]

On the other hand, many of the women—Thérèse, Colette, Claire, Raïssa, Camille, even Simone—enjoyed affectionate, even passionate, relations with their fathers, many of whom were themselves sick, anxious, or depressed and toward whom their daughters felt strongly maternal. On the first page of *Les Grandes Amitiés*, for example, Raïssa recalls her father in tears and stresses how she has always had "feelings of protection, of almost maternal compassion" for him.[44] For almost all these women, it was the "masculinized" mother who embodied the values of the superego—in Christian terms, the God of justice, judgment, and vengeance—and the "feminized" father who stood for the god of mercy, compassion, and love. In general, the mothers (or their surrogates) did not nurture the souls of their daughters, and, in rejecting food for their bodies, the daughters were accusing the lovelessness of their mothers—itself, of course, the result of a complex of physical, psychological, and cultural (especially religious) causes—and turning instead to the consolations of a maternalized Father-cum-God.

A third major cause of anorexia is, by widespread consent, the adolescent girl's refusal of sexual maturity, adult autonomy, and, not least, maternity; it is surely significant that, of the women discussed here, only Eva Lavallière (not an anorexic) had a child of her own.[45] Given that it is known that Louise Lateau did not begin menstruating until the age of eighteen, it is possible that some of the other women suffered delayed menarche; Thérèse's attack of scruples in 1885 (when she was twelve) has plausibly been linked to the onset of puberty.

· More to the point, with the exception, once again, of Eva Lavallière, none of the women achieved full personal autonomy, even when, like Simone for a time, they were able to support themselves economically. One remained, for medical reasons, in reclusion and dependence in the parental home (Marthe); two entered a convent (Thérèse, Mélanie); one founded an unrecognized religious community (Claire); while another (Raïssa) lived in what was, in effect, a personal convent with her mother, sister, and husband, with whom she had ceased all sexual relations by mutual consent. Three spent much of their lives in hospital, clinics, or asylums (Colette, Simone, Madeleine); one was permanently institutionalized (Camille); and one (Madeleine again) was imprisoned on at least two occasions. In some cases, this reclusion was involuntary (Camille, Madeleine), in others it was actively sought (Thérèse, Claire, Raïssa), while in others again it may have met an unconscious desire that the subjects did not admit to themselves (Colette, Mélanie, Simone, perhaps Marthe); after a successful and at times spectacular career on the stage, even Eva Lavallière withdrew into her remote Béthanie.

These, in short, were not liberated women or even, in most cases, women who sought liberation in any sense that feminists, either at the time or today, would easily recognize. If they were victims of one form or another of Foucault's *grand renfermement* (great enclosure), it was, for the most part, willingly so. Mélanie Calvat may have been desperate to escape the Carmelite convent in Darlington, but her deepest desire was, like Claire Ferchaud's, to found a religious order of her own. Nor, Simone, Colette, and (possibly) Madeleine apart, were any of these women on the political left. In her misery, Camille seems to have absorbed many of the conspiratorial obsessions of the anti-Dreyfusard camp, while Mélanie and Thérèse were open in support of this or that royalist pretender to power. Raïssa, like her husband, was revolted by the rise of antisemitism and fascism, but was otherwise on the political center-right, and Marthe's support for Pétain appears to have been passionate and ideological rather than merely sentimental or pragmatic. Claire Ferchaud's cause was taken up by the religious and political far right, and she may be assumed to have shared their opinions. Before all else, the majority of the women studied in this book prized inner, spiritual liberation that they equated with love of God, service, and obedience, and the attainment of a condition of spiritual childlikeness foreign to most conceptions of autonomy. Self-starvation may not have been a consciously chosen means to that end, but that was the end to which it commonly led.

There remains, finally, the "Catholic factor" to consider. Although, in both religious and secular life, the nineteenth-century Church discouraged the practice of extreme fasting customary in the past, considering it to be a relic of Jansenism, eating in general, and the eating of the Body of Christ in particular, were still surrounded by enough scruples and taboos both to heighten and legitimate any tendency toward anorexia. Catholicism per se may not have *caused* anorexia, but it provided any nascent case of self-starvation with a massively persuasive justificatory narrative; what the ultraslim supermodel on the catwalk was to teenage girls of the 1980s and 1990s, the great self-denying female saints of the past were to their Catholic counterparts a hundred years earlier.

Even in its modified form, Catholic teaching on food still embodied a tension. On the one hand, as one catechetical work put it, "we can glorify God by eating":[46] eating meant communion with nature and with one's fellow human beings, it was a charitable offering both to oneself and to others and, accompanied by thanks and by prayer, became an act of worship of the ultimate source of the food. On the other hand, there remained the uncomfortable fact, much emphasized by the patristic writers who continued to be read and cited as authorities, that sin had come into the world through the violation of a divine command *not* to eat, and that the original violator was a woman; what one woman had brought about by eating, another woman might remedy by fasting. "The Lord God," wrote Bloy with memorable menace in his first work on La Salette, "is jealous of the human mouth, the children of the new dispensation know why, and it is to the mouth that the serpent addressed himself to bring down the human race."[47] To take pleasure in eating was to renew and exacerbate the primordial sin, whence, for example, Thérèse's practice, even after she had overcome the eating disorders of early adolescence, of finishing each meal with something unpleasant-tasting that would linger in the mouth.

If eating ordinary day-to-day food remained problematic, how much more so was the eating—daily, weekly, or yearly—of the Body of Christ. Officially, and again in reaction against the so-called Jansenist practices of the past, the nineteenth-century Church encouraged frequent, even daily communion, stressing, in one much reprinted work, Monseigneur Gaston de Ségur's *La Très Sainte Communion* (1860), that "one does not take communion because one is good, but in order to become better,"[48] and reprimanding those Catholics who, having confessed their sins, nonetheless felt "unworthy" to approach the communion table.[49] In practice, however, many Catholics took communion with extreme misgivings, even terror, mindful of the threatening words of I Corinthians 11:29: "For he that eateth and drinketh unworthily, eateth and drinketh damnation to himself, not discerning the Lord's body." Many young Catholics must have felt like the future Mère Saint-Jean (Julie Malleval) who, making her first communion at the relatively advanced age of seventeen, tried, as she approached the communion table, to feel "confidence and love" while all the time "she heard within herself what seemed like a sinister voice which replied: *abuse of grace, treachery, sacrilege!*"[50]

When Huysmans first took communion after returning to the Church in the early 1890s, he, too, was driven half crazy by "the all too human aspect of swallowing a God" (*tout le côté trop humain de la dé la déglutition d'un Dieu*): how the communion wafer stuck to the roof of his mouth, how he had to twist his tongue back in order to free it, how all the time he could hear "grumbling in himself the contrary of what he was thinking,"[51] and how, at the end of it all, he felt nothing but spiritual dryness, desolation, and doubt, and all for something that looked and tasted like a miniature cold crêpe. Was it because of this, one may wonder, that Huysmans later refused all treatment and pain-killers for the hideous cancer of the mouth that eventually killed him? Not for nothing did Caïn Marchenoir, Bloy's alter ego in *Le Désespéré* (1887), describe an enemy's mouth as "a rictus, a vagina, a gob, a sucker, a filthy hiatus."[52] The mouth was the locus of sin and remained so, whatever the Church's changed teaching on fasting and frequent communion.

At the Hour of Her Death

By the nineteenth century, dying was no longer the public event that it had been in earlier ages. Though the cult of the dead, celebrated through regular visits to the family tomb, thrived as never before, the actual process of dying was "hushed up" and rendered as socially invisible as possible.[53] This was a general trend and admitted many exceptions, not least in convents and nunneries where dying commonly took place in full view of other sisters who took, so to speak, a theological as well as a humane interest in what was going on on the deathbed. The dying sister was expected to show resignation and contrition, but above all to manifest *joy* at the prospect of imminent reunion with her Bridegroom. Whatever pain or despair she was feeling, it was her duty to console and encourage her *consœurs* in the manner of sister Marie des Anges after she received extreme unction in August 1848:

> "I am truly happy to have received the last rites; but I am sad, am I really that ill?" Then tears flowed from her eyes. That should cause no surprise, her soul was so sensitive, so delicate, so impressionable! But it was only a slight cloud which soon disappeared, leaving no trace behind it. A pure joy continued to shine upon her brow, in her eyes, and over the whole of her face, the freshness of which, emaciation apart, was respected, even after her death, by the horrible disease [tuberculosis] that was consuming her.[54]

The dying sister's words and prayers were eagerly studied, and often noted down for posterity, as was the case with Thérèse's so-called last conversations, preserved—and, in the view of some Theresian scholars, significantly amended and embroidered—by her sister Pauline (Mère Agnès de Jésus) in her famous yellow exercise book.[55]

Intervals of desolation, despair, and even demonic temptation were expected, but only on condition that they be resolved in favor of joyful anticipation. The *total* dereliction of the dying prioress in Bernanos's *Dialogues des Carmêlites* (1949), virtually the last major work to engage with the theology of mystical substitution, could not, however, be condoned: "Why should I, in this hour of my misery, worry about Him! Let Him first worry about me!" (Qu'il s'inquiète donc d'abord de moi!).[56] In the hope of "purchasing" both their own salvation and that of nonbelieving sinners, the dying both expected and wanted to suffer, and they routinely refused the mitigating effects of morphine or chloroform: "You want to prevent me from suffering? Let me merit heaven" (Soeur Eléonore de Gaulmyn [1848]).[57] When death really was imminent, the sister was dressed, if possible, in her most beautiful festal raiment, and at least one (Mère Saint-Jean [1855]) checked her face in a mirror—a banned item in many strict communities—to ensure that her "death's head" (*tête de mort*) was behooving before she took the viaticum:[58] She was, after all, going to meet her heavenly Fiancé. Others, like the above-mentioned Eléonore de Gaulmyn actually saw their divine Bridegroom at or near the moment of death, to the ecstatic consolation of the sisters gathered round their beds:

> What happened at that instant between Heaven and that privileged soul? We would not dare to fathom that secret, but what we do know is that she repeated in ecstatic transports: "I saw Him, my Jesus. . . . Oh! How handsome he was!"[59]

Heroism and joy in the face of death were proof of divine election, and it was around the deathbed that the language of holocaust, victimhood, and vicarious suffering came into its own. The death of a nun was still in other words a spectacular event, and the bed on which she was publicly exhibited before and after her death was tellingly called her *lit de parade,* a stage on which, Christ's actress (one can see the reverberations of Eva Lavallière's profession), she was expected to put on her supreme religious performance.

Thérèse's apart, most of the deaths recorded in this book took place in private, though frequently in conditions involving some ritualization, particularly when the cause of death was tuberculosis. Throughout the nineteenth century, and well into the twentieth, tuberculosis was the commonest cause of death in France as it was in most countries in western Europe (and in the United States), and it is not in this sense surprising that three of the women studied here fell victim to the disease: Thérèse (24), Colette (35), and Simone (34, TB being the immediate cause of her death, aided and hastened by her anorexia), to whom we may add saints Bernadette and Elisabeth (de la Trinité), both killed by the disease at the ages of 35 and 26, respectively.

Readers of Thomas Mann's *The Magic Mountain* (1924) will not need reminding that tuberculosis was as much a way of life as it was of death, indeed not so much a culture as a cult, with its own liturgy, rituals, pilgrimages, and holy places—the clinics and sanatoria in which Colette, in particular, so frequently stayed—and it was in other ways, too, the most "religious" of diseases. More than any other illness, it was believed to "spiritualize" or "dematerialize" its victims,[60] rendering their bodies both "transparent" and "weightless," as befits the common nineteenth-century name for the disease phthisis, from the Greek *phtheien,* to waste away, as in "la négresse phthisique" who, in all likelihood a prostitute, stands ankle-deep in the Parisian mud in Baudelaire's great urban poem "Le Cygne" (1860).

Tuberculosis was also widely associated with artistic creativity, and particularly with the writing of lyric poetry—"when I was young," said Gautier, "I could not have accepted as a lyrical poet anyone weighing more than ninety-nine pounds"[61]—and had reputed links with both sexual passion and its frustration. Above all, in Susan Sontag's words, "the dying tubercular is pictured as made more beautiful and more soulful" than any other terminal sufferer,[62] and, if the dying tubercular was female, she exceeded any other subject in erotic, aesthetic, and spiritual appeal, "the death of a beautiful woman" being, as Edgar Allan Poe wrote in "The Philosophy of Composition" (1846), "unquestionably the most poetical topic in the world."[63]

It is against this complex background—religious, medical, aesthetic, with the erotic hovering, unacknowledged, in the background of the background—that we should approach the deaths of saints Thérèse and Bernadette and of the antisaint Colette Peignot and the posthumous treatment of their remains. Thus the photograph of the dying saint-to-be—such as that taken by Céline Martin (Sœur Geneviève) of her sister on the occasion of the latter's last visit to the Blessed Sacrament on 39 August 1897, a month before her death—plays an important part in the process of informal beatification that is the essential precondition of the formal procedures. Propped up on a veritable Mount Carmel of pillows, Thérèse looks out toward the camera from under the cloisters, crucifix in hand and with petals of roses scattered on the blanket before her. She already belongs to the realm of the dead, and she knows it, and her look displays neither pity for herself nor consolation for the viewer, just the blankness of one who knows her fate is sealed and who, in her own words, can find no *jouissance* at the prospect of the conventional comforts of heaven: Je ne me fais pas une fête de jouir (I can't make a feast of rejoicing [or enjoyment] at the thought of it).[64] As well as consigning her every word to the famous yellow notebook, her sisters even preserved her supposed last tear on a fragment of lace and later had it mounted, surrounded by pearls and ormolu flowers, in a reliquary. The posthumous photograph shows her face smooth and serene, her brow wreathed in flowers, and with lilies bestowed in abundance all around, all trace of physical and spiritual anguish effaced. This may not be the smiling Petite Fleur the world will revere, but she is already, within hours of her death, virtually a saint, abstracted from the flux and depredations of time, the "spiritualization" begun by the disease brought to perfection by the floral and cosmetic skills of her sisters and by the dematerializing agency of the camera lens. The photograph's aura of necrophilia lends itself all too readily to the kind of deconstructive treatment given by the postmodern conceptual artist Jeff Koons (born 1955) in his photograph portraits of the pornographic superstar (and one-time Italian presidential candidate) known as La Ciccolina, similarly bewreathed but only scantily beclothed.

Thérèse's remains were first interred in the regular cemetery at Lisieux, and her grave quickly became a site of pilgrimage and, in May 1908, of the supposedly miraculous restoration of the sight of a blind four-year-old girl. In October 1910 her tomb was opened, as was required by the ongoing beatification procedures, and the fragments that remained (which reputedly emitted the conventional saints' odor of violets) were transferred, after examination, to a new grave nearby. In March 1923, a month before her formal beatification, they were transferred again, amid much ecclesiastical pomp and circumstance, to their present location in the chapel of the Carmel, in a gold casket beneath the marble statue of the saint that itself contains a small number of bones. The golden rose she holds in her right hand was placed there by the papal legate, Cardinal Vico, at the time of her full canonization in September 1925, thus completing the Little Flower's posthumous mineralization.[65] We shall encounter further versions of the petrified, marmorealized woman later in this chapter.

The posthumous fate of Bernadette Soubirous was far more dramatic.[66] Bernadette died of tuberculosis on 16 April 1879, aged thirty-five, sitting in front of a blazing fire in the infirmary of the convent of Saint Gildard in Nevers, which she had entered in 1867. Photographs were taken similar in pose and appearance to those of Thérèse eighteen years later, and, after remaining on display for three days for public veneration, her body was placed in a double coffin of lead and oak and buried in the chapel dedicated to Saint Joseph in the convent grounds. There it remained until September 1909 when beatification procedures required that it be exhumed for inspection by the bishop of Nevers, a tribunal made up of a local priest, the mother superior of the convent and her deputy, and by two doctors, who were all sworn to tell the truth, along with the mayor and deputy mayor of Nevers (required to be present by secular law) and by the two stonemasons and two carpenters selected to do the manual labor. The coffin was lifted and unscrewed to reveal Bernadette's body in a state of almost perfect preservation. The words of the doctors' report require quotation at length:

The head was tilted to the left. The face was dull white. The skin clung to the muscles and the muscles adhered to the bones. The sockets of the eyes were covered by the eyelids. The brows were flat on the skin and stuck to the arches above the eyes. The lashes of the right eyelid were stuck to the skin. The nose was dilated and shrunken. The mouth was open slightly and it could be seen that the teeth were still in place. The hands, which were crossed on her breast, were perfectly preserved, as were the nails. The hands still held a rusting rosary. The veins on the forearms stood out.

Like the hands, the feet were wizened and the toenails were still intact (one of them was torn off when the corpse was washed). When the habits had been removed and the veil lifted from the head, the whole of the shriveled body could be seen, rigid and taut in every limb.

It was found that the hair, which had been cut short, was stuck to the head and still attached to the skull—that the ears were in a state of perfect preservation—that the left side of the body was slightly higher than the right from the hip up.

The stomach had caved in and was taught like the rest of the body. It sounded like cardboard when struck. The left knee was not as large as the right. The ribs protruded as did the muscles in the limbs. So rigid was the body that it could be rolled over and back for washing. The lower parts of the body had turned slightly black. This seems to have been the result of the carbon of which quite large quantities were found in the coffin. In witness of which we have duly drawn up this present statement in which all is truthfully recorded.

NEVERS, SEPTEMBER 22, 1909
Drs. Ch. David, A. Jourdan[67]

The body emitted no odor, and its mummified state was attributed to chemicals in the soil in which it was interred; neither then nor later did the Church lay any claim to miraculous preservation. The body was exhumed again in April 1919 and April 1925, and on neither occasion had any significant change taken place. With beatification imminent, the body was swathed in bandages except for face and hands, returned to the coffin but not reinterred. A precise imprint was made of the face and, with the further aid of photographs, the Parisian firm of Pierre Imans made a light wax mask which, suitably painted, was placed over the wizened features of the corpse. The process was repeated for the hands, and a life-size, glass-sided casket was constructed by the firm of Armand Caillat Cateland in Lyon in which, now beatified, Bernadette's almost preternaturally intact remains were placed for public veneration in July 1925. The saint remains "on view" to this day, as "alive," in the words of the Jesuit author of the official church brochure, as on day one of the apparitions in 1858:

Yes, this is the body of Bernadette in the attitude of meditation and prayer which it adopted in its first coffin. This is the face which was lifted eighteen times to the "Lady of Massabielle," these are the hands which fingered the rosary before and during the apparitions, these are the fingers which scratched the earth and made the miraculous spring appear, these are the ears which heard the message and these the lips which repeated the Lady's Name to Father Peyramale; "I am the Immaculate Conception." This is the heart, too, which bore so much love for Jesus Christ, the Virgin Mary and sinners. One only has to look at the body in the shrine to be present at the wonderful events of Lourdes. Something of the grace of Massabielle strikes the soul.[68]

Thus, although not miraculously, is the visionary made "really present," in principle for all time, a religious version of what Elisabeth Bronfen, in her much-praised book *Over Her Dead Body* (1992) calls the "social sacrifice of the feminine body where the death of a beautiful woman emerges as the requirement for a preservation of existing cultural norms and values or their regenerative modification."[69] Or, in Alain Brossat's words, both Thérèse and Bernadette, victims of the most lethal disease of their time, offered themselves up as *biches émissaires,* "scape-does" (*biche*=female deer, cf. *Bouc émissaire*=scape-goat),[70] whose combined expulsion and preservation both perpetuates and remakes, in this instance, the (male-dominated) order of the Church. Their dying consoles and consolidates against death, their preservation in effigy or mummified form offers hope of miraculous deliverance from the putrefaction, dissolution, and formlessness of mortality.

None of the women studied in this book lived in such continuous proximity to death as did Colette Peignot. Her tuberculosis was diagnosed as early as 1916, when she was thirteen, and she spent the next twenty years in and out of clinics and sanatoria before entering the highly public "flowery corrida"[71] of her final bullfight with death, in which, we may be sure, she sought to be the slain not the slayer. Living so close to death for so long, it is not surprising that, like so many young Europeans, men and women alike, of the late nineteenth and early twentieth centuries, Colette should have been intrigued with the figure usually known as *l'Inconnue de la Seine,* the unknown young woman supposedly found drowned in the Seine some time in the 1880s—nobody knew whether it was accident or suicide—and whose reputed death mask, mass-produced and marketed by a company in Hamburg, was to be found on literally thousands of mantlepieces during Colette's lifetime.[72]

L'Inconnue de la Seine was also a major literary theme, inspiring a superb short story by Jules Supervielle (*L'Inconnue de la Seine* [1931]) a full-length novel by Louis Aragon (*Aurélien* [1944]), as well as a whole raft (so to speak) of works by German writers in the 1930s and 1940s. The death mask, supposedly made at the Paris morgue when the corpse was fished out of the Seine (but also conceivably a forgery by the enterprising Hamburgers), showed a woman in her twenties, hair close to her head and apparently tied up in a bun or tucked in at the back of her neck, eyelids closed but with an enigmatic smile—routinely compared to that of the Mona Lisa or the Sphinx, if not to similarly ever-smiling images of Thérèse—playing unmistakably on her lips. Many young women are said to have modeled their looks and expression on those of *L'Inconnue de la Seine,* and there is indeed some similarity between Colette's usual hairstyle and that of the mask, though nothing so much as a smile, enigmatic or otherwise, is seen on most of the photographs that survive of her.

Colette had every reason to be intrigued by this figure, not least because her elder sister Madeleine had, as we have seen, tried to kill herself by throwing herself into the Seine at the family holiday home at Boissettes; it is conceivably to this that she was referring when, in July 1923, she wrote to her sister-in-law Suzanne Peignot that "I am sending you this letter as I would throw myself into the water" (208). Two other fragments may allude to *l'Inconnue de la Seine* ("the Seine? It didn't seem to me that one could drown in it, but only asphyxiate oneself" [156]; "that corpse floating in the water / floating in time / Life flows / like a great river / Save your soul / Apostle of unhappiness" [172]), and it will be recalled that Colette signed a number of articles "Araxe" after an uncrossable river in Caucasia: if Colette was *l'Inconnue,* she was also implicitly the Seine in which she drowned. But the most suggestive remark is in a letter that Colette wrote to Bataille in July 1934 in which she tells him that "the idea of death followed to the absolute limit, to the point of putrefaction" has always delivered her from the "insurmountable anguish that was you." If she seems to wish Bataille dead, she also wishes for death, perhaps at his hands, saying that "in drowning myself I had summoned to my aid not only a paralytic, but someone who would if need be hit me on the head to force me under and sink me to the bottom" (239): She is now not only dead woman and river but her own hypothetical killer as well.

Part of the appeal of *l'Inconnue de la Seine,* myth and mask, was, in Elisabeth Bronfen's words, that her perfectly preserved features and above all her smile "could assuage the fear of bodily dissolution in death and assure that death was not painful but easy, a promise of peace,"[73] rather as the wax mask over Bernadette's wizened features, or Thérèse's complete marmorealization, offered hope that form will survive the formlessness of death. *L'Inconnue de la Seine* suggested that it was possible simultaneously to be dead and alive, to square the circle of existence and essence, to die and to be fully conscious of one's death, like the heroine of Supervielle's delightful variation on the theme. But Colette longed for the transgression of all limits, all forms, and while *L'Inconnue's* condition of death-in-life and life-in-death might fascinate her, the preservation of her all-too-perfect form could never satisfy her.

A similar tension between form and formlessness is present at her death, funeral, and burial. In the photographs of Colette taken on her deathbed, the *sainte de l'abîme* appears little different from the future saints Thérèse and Bernadette, minus only veil and crucifix; her hair flows freely, a bunch of flowers rests on her chest, her eyes are closed, and her features present the serenity and transparence, even the spirituality, conventionally associated with the victim of tuberculosis. Her funeral both preserves and subverts the Catholic norm: a sacred text (two torn-out pages of William Blake) and a "viaticum" (Leiris's poker dice) are slipped into the coffin in which Colette preserves her human name and form, holding out the hope and possibility of personal survival. But the burial, for which Bataille alone is responsible, systematically negates form, name, and personality. Colette is buried, anonymously, without headstone, beneath a "headless" mound of soil, like the Mount Etna that she and Bataille climbed together or the evocatively named "Mont pourri" she could see from one of the many alpine sanatoria she stayed at (167). No date of birth or death are given: both *inconnue* and *acéphale, la sainte de l'abîme* rots into the not-self in a forest cemetery whose very name—Saint-Nom-la-Bretèche—her unholy anonymity seems called on to flout.[74]

An Androgynous Church

As we saw in our discussion of anorexia, one of the recurring themes of this book has been the "masculinity" of many of its subjects' mothers and the contrasting and complementary "femininity" of the fathers. Almost without exception, it has been the mothers (when they are present) who embody the values of the superego—morality, discipline, justice, judgment, law—while the fathers incarnate love, compassion, mercy, and forgiveness; at the risk of simplification, one might say that the mothers belong to the Old Testament, the fathers to the New, at least in the terms in which Christian apologists of the time opposed the two "dispensations" one to the other. That, for example, we first see Raïssa Oumansov's father in tears is somehow symptomatic:[75] It is the fathers of these supposedly patriarchal families who are more prone to weep, not the stoical, severe, stony-faced mothers.

Concomitantly, a number of the women studied here have cast themselves as "male," or aspired to masculinity, by adopting masculine names or speaking of themselves in masculine terms. Thus, to take the most obvious instance, Thérèse pointedly described herself as *"un* croisé" (a crusader), *"un* martyr," and *"un* admirateur de Jeanne d'Arc" (herself the most masculinized of females) and rechristened one of her sisters "Paulin" and called another "Valérien" or the "valeureux chevalier C. Martin."[76] Similarly, Simone Weil liked to be known as "Simon," signed herself "ton fils respectueux" in letters to her mother (who admitted to bringing her up as a boy) and used the byline "S. Galois" in one of her early articles, in homage to the great martyred mathematician Evariste Galois and, simultaneously, to her brilliant mathematician brother.[77]

The most obvious explanation of these onomastic maneuvers, and certainly not one to be discarded, is that the two young women were engaged in a magical attempt to transcend the social and other limitations imposed on them by their gender. Simone spoke explicitly of the "singular misfortune of being a woman" (*une singulière malchance d'être une femme*),[78] and her neglect of her physical appearance and wearing of masculine clothes (or clothes that obscured her femininity), together, of course, with her anorexia, could be regarded as a sustained and systematic protest against her gendered condition and its social implications. Similarly, Thérèse sometimes spoke regretfully of being forbidden by her gender from becoming a priest.

There are other onomastic oddities, too. Was Camille Claudel given a "unisex" first name in compensation for her parents' earlier loss of a male child in infancy? Why did her brother give the name "Anne" (i.e., the Annas of the New Testament) to the patriarch of *L'Annonce faite à Marie,* and why is the heroine's name Violaine such a tangle of "masculine" and "feminine" phonemes: the male act of *viol*ating set against the maternal substance of wool (*laine*), the name also suggesting, by Claudel's own admission, his own partial namesake, the notoriously bisexual Catholic convert, Paul Verlaine, the first syllable of whose surname is found in that of the patriarch, Vercors? One might even, at a push, add that the name "Marie" (derived from Maria or Marius) is commonly incorporated into male forenames in France.

But these anthroponymic curiosities signal deeper ambiguities. Thérèse, as we have seen, comprehensively feminized the figure of Jesus and, in doing so, continued, probably without knowing it, one of the most ancient devotional topoi of the Catholic Church: the idea of Christ, and of his Father-Mother in Heaven, as both male and female, father and mother rolled into one, who nourishes his/her children with his/her own body and whose bleedings from hands, feet, forehead, and side recall nothing so much as the monthly bleeding of women. Soft-limbed, doe-eyed, with a wispy beard that scarcely masculinizes him at all, the Jesus of tens of thousands of nineteenth-century sacred images points to his rose-red sacred heart as to his (female) genitalia, renewing another age-old mystical topos of the analogy between *vulnus* (wound) and *vulva,* in which the wounded human soul gains redemption through union with the wounds of the Savior, *vulnus vulneri copulatur* (the wound is copulated to the wound).[79] Bataille, it may be noted, both continues and inverts this tradition by speaking almost systematically of both male and female genitalia as *blessures* (wounds) through which otherwise complete beings can "communicate," in his sense of the word,[80] with each other: "To the extent that beings seem perfect, they remain isolated, closed in on themselves. But the wound of incompleteness opens them up. Through what one may call incompleteness [*inachèvement*], animal nakedness, wound, disparate separate beings *communicate,* acquire life by losing themselves in *communication* from one to the other."[81] Splayed on the cross, his masculinity both concealed and metonymically suggested by the loincloth that swathes him,[82] the crucified Christ is pierced like a woman and in death cries out like a woman in orgasm.[83] If Christianity is indeed, as its critics aver, a patriarchal religion, its pivotal figure could hardly be more deficient in traditional male attributes.

From the androgyny of Christ, it is but a step to the androgyny of both his Church and his followers. In Christ, according to Galatians 3:28, "there is neither male nor female," and if women were urged by the Church to deny what was "female" in themselves (other than the ability to bear children) in the service of their Lord, so men were enjoined to "feminize" themselves by rejecting the "male" impulse to power, violence, and control. No two saints were more revered than Saint Francis among men and Saint Teresa among women, and yet, as Huysmans wrote in *En route,* "Saint Francis of Assisi, who was nothing but love, had rather the feminine soul of a woman recluse [*une moniale*] and Saint Teresa, who was the most perceptive of psychologists, had the virile soul of a monk. It would be more accurate to call them Santa Francis and San Teresa [*sainte François et saint Térèse*]."[84]

By extension, the whole Church was identified with the androgynous Body of Christ, a *Mater Ecclesia* "manned" by males who had sacrificed male procreativity (and of whom many had their heads tonsured in token of their symbolic castration), who dressed more like women than like secular men, and who, as we have seen, fulfilled the traditional nurturing role of the mother when they prepared, consecrated, and distributed the communion wafer. Priests were mother-fathers of their flock, just as bishops, archbishops, cardinals, and ultimately the pope were mother-fathers to them; and, as we have seen, almost all the leading "artistic" converts to Catholicism sought, whatever their own sexual orientation, to be both "mothered" and "fathered" by the Church that received them.[85] Not that the androgyny of the Church made it any less powerful; indeed it was precisely in its "femininity" that Baudelaire located the reason for its "omnipotence."[86]

On top of all this, the structure of individual churches and cathedrals was increasingly seen as quintessentially "feminine." As Léon waits for Emma Bovary in Notre-Dame de Rouen, it seems to him that the cathedral is like a "gigantic boudoir" awaiting the arrival of its tutelary goddess;[87] the image of the boudoir was applied independently to churches by Baudelaire and Huysmans.[88] Particularly after 1890, the Gothic cathedral was seen, by Catholics and non-Catholics alike, as much, perhaps more, as the abode of the Virgin as of her Son, the solid, somewhat forbidding Romanesque style appearing to many as the appropriate dwelling-place of the Father. Thus, for Auguste Rodin, every church or cathedral is "shaped like a woman on her knees," the cathedral at Amiens is "a Virgin who makes one think of Demeter," while at Reims the "great maternal voice" of the bells "dominates the city and becomes the vibrant soul of its life."[89] Claudel's response is, as one might expect, far more inventive and profound. The cathedral vaults form a "cavity similar to that of the tomb and the womb of the mother," and it is "pregnant [*grosse*] with something alive"; the "mother-nave" (*nef-mère*) forms the "egg" from which the whole edifice is hatched,[90] while, at Strasbourg, everything coheres together to form "the religious matrix and vessel of our co-presence [*comprésence*] in God."[91]

More often than not, the writer's mode of address is to cathedral and

Virgin interchangeably. Claudel's Chartres is "full of grace" (*pleine de grâce*),[92] while in the beautiful pilgrimage poems that Charles Péguy wrote in the last years of his life, "Présentation de Paris à Notre Dame," "Présentation de la Beauce à notre Dame de Chartres," and "Les cinq Prières dans la cathédrale de Chartres," "Notre Dame" and "Notre-Dame" are effectively identical:

> Etoile de la mer voici la lourde nef
> Où nous ramons tout nus sous vos commandements[93]
>
> [Star of the sea, here is the heavy craft / in which,
> naked, we row under your command]

Mary and her cathedrals are one and the same, so much so that the bombing of Reims cathedral by the German army in September 1914 was almost universally likened to a violation of the Virgin herself or to the martyrdom of her beloved daughter Joan of Arc; how curious that the first published text (in 1918) by Bataille, a resident of Reims from 1899 or 1900 until the outbreak of war, was, ironically for the future author of *Ma mère*, a six-page mediation on, precisely, the destruction of Notre-Dame-de-Reims.[94] The cathedral, like the enfolding body of the mother, offers the overintellectualized (male) Catholic deliverance in the first instance from the travails of thought. Thus "female" metaphors of cooking, weaving, fermenting, and nourishing abound, for example, in Claudel's great essay "Vitraux des cathédrales de France" of 1937: "In the mysterious bosom of the cathedral, there is woven, there simmers, there cooks a wordless poem which nourishes the soul whilst calming the intelligence," the cathedral is a "sacramental tissue of pardons and sins" in which, relieved of any obligation to think, the pilgrim is free simply to abandon himself to "this immense fermentation about you of truth" (*cette immense autour de toi fermentation de la vérité*).[95] In short, the cathedral is that uterine space where the son is reabsorbed into the Mother of Being, in which doubt loses itself ecstatically in faith, in which it is no longer Eros versus Agape, or even Eros versus Thanatos, but Eros, Agape, and Thanatos fusing together to deliver the seeker from himself. How telling that, for Péguy, Chartres should be first and foremost the place where everything is easy: "Voici le lieu de monde où tout devient facile."[96]

All this raises the question, which the present author has discussed more fully elsewhere,[97] of the attraction Catholicism had for French homosexuals, particularly, as far as well-known artists were concerned, in the interwar period. In addition to those already briefly discussed—Jean Cocteau, Max Jacob, Maurice Sachs, Jean Bourgoint, and Jean Desbordes—homosexual converts to Catholicism included the composer Francis Poulenc (1899–1963); the novelist and memorialist Marcel Jouhandeau (1888–1979), whose remarkable *Tirésias,* as lyrical a paean to anal sexuality as there can be, was published anonymously in 1954; Henri Ghéon (1875–1944), a one-time cruising partner of Gide in both Paris and North Africa and a member, as we have seen, of the Maritain circle; the novelist Julien Green (1900–1998); and, rather less well-known, Maurice Rostand (1891–1968), son of the author of *Cyrano de Bergerac* and brother of the celebrated biologist Jean, whose racy *Confession d'un demi-siècle* (1948) concludes with the author of *Le Procès d'Oscar Wilde* (1935) opening himself up to "the sublime hypothesis of God" while criticizing François Mauriac—whose homosexuality was the best-kept secret of the literary world—for making his God so "difficult, His Paradise so painful to gain, what with the *comités d'épuration* He seems to organize at the entrance."[98]

A number of other well-known homosexuals, not necessarily practicing Catholics themselves, were ministers in the strongly pro-Catholic Vichy regime—André Germain, Abel Bonnard, and Abel Hermant, the latter known (untranslatably) in the gay milieu as "la Belle au Bois d'Hermant" (*la Belle au bois dormant*=Sleeping Beauty)[99]—and the prominence of a small number of homosexuals (notably Robert Brasillach, executed for treason in 1945) among out-and-out pro-Nazis gave rise to the myth of the "Gestapette" (*tapette*=queer), of some necessary link between homosexuality and collaboration/fascism that Sartre seems to endorse with his portrait of the gay collaborator Daniel in *Les Chemins de la liberté* (1945–59). In his postwar novel *La Vocation suspendue* (1950), Pierre Klossowski, the former associate of Bataille, now a Catholic, dwelt at length on "the undeniable connection which exists between antisemites and homosexuals,"[100] an assertion as dubious as it is provocative, given the persecution—of which Klossowski was surely aware—of homosexuals as well as of Jews in the name of antisemitic National Socialism, and particularly rich in the light of the martyrdom of Max Jacob—homosexual and Jewish convert to Catholicism—at the concentration camp of Drancy on the outskirts of Paris in March 1944.[101]

The Roman Catholic Church, Mark D. Jordan has written in his outstanding study *The Silence of Sodom: Homosexuality in Modern Catholicism* (2000), is "at once the most homophobic and the most homoerotic of institutions."[102] In France during the period that concerns us, the homophobia was most evident in 1937 when the bishop of Laval, Monseigneur Joseph Marcadé, was caught in the traditional "compromising position" with some officer cadets at nearby Saumur (the French West Point) and was hounded out of his see.[103] Yet this same Church was, in Jordan's words, even then an "empire of closets"[104] in which homosexuals, particularly if they were well-known and of upper-middle-class origin, found a warm and ready welcome in which their sexuality was either taken for granted or passed over discreetly. Jordan speculates that it is the androgyny of Catholicism, particularly as evident in the "beautiful, queer space of liturgy,"[105] that constitutes such a powerful aesthetic-erotic attraction for male homo-sexuals, from "liturgy queens" and adepts of "clerical camp" to the "priestly dandies" who preside over this "officially homophobic religion in which an all-male clergy sacrifices male flesh before images of God as an almost naked man."[106] The "feminization of Christ" conceals the underlying homoeroticism involved in his worship,[107] as anyone familiar with the sacrilegious inversions of Jean Genet's provocatively entitled *Notre-Dame-des-Fleurs* (1944) will hardly need reminding. For further discussion, the reader is referred to the present writer's study of Poulenc (see note 56).

Passion and Pain

"We should let God fuck us," the English sculptor and typographer Eric Gill (1882–1940) wrote, more or less, to the recent convert and future author of a study of Léon Bloy, Rayner Heppenstall, in 1934, adopting, and making explicit, the traditional "female" posture of the Catholic (man or woman) toward his or her male phallic God; it was a posture that Gill notably reversed in his ecumenical relations with most of the female members of his household (including the dog), plus, it is rumored, a random sampling of the cattle and sheep grazing on the South Sussex Downs.[108] Nothing is more common in spiritual writings, from the *Song of Songs* and its multiple commentaries onward, than the overlap and interpenetration of mystical and erotic language and imagery, and, as we have seen, Bernini's great statue of the swooning Saint Teresa of Avila, the angel's arrow aimed unequivocally at her crotch, provided grist for the mill of more than one complex-grinder at La Salpêtrière in the 1880s and 1890s. The agonies and ecstasies of so-called *Brautmystik* (bride-mysticism) are particularly common in the experience and writings of women religious commonly, if loosely, classified as "holy anorexics"—Mechthild of Magdeburg, Hildegard of Bingen, Angela di Foligno, Margaret of Cortona, and Maria Maddalena de Pazzi, of whose visions the following brief extract typifies the whole tradition of epithalmic spirituality:

> I saw Jesus united with His bride in closest embrace. He laid His head over the head of His bride, His eyes upon her eyes, His mouth upon her mouth, His feet upon her feet, all his members upon hers, so that His bride became one with Him and wanted all her Bridegroom wanted, saw all that her Bridegroom saw, and savored all that her Bridegroom savored. And God wants nothing but that the soul unite with Him in such wise, and that He may be utterly united with her.[109]

Angela di Foligno was definitely read by Thérèse and Raïssa, and it was on her *Memoriale* (c. 1292–96) that Bataille based much of his theory concerning the underlying identity of the "erotic" and "religious" ways of being in the world, both opposed by virtue of their openness to pain, horror, suffering, and death to the closedness of the profane order. Improbably enough—or, rather, improbably only to those who resist Bataille's equation of the erotic and the divine—*Madame Edwarda* (1941) was written under the immediate influence of reading the thirteenth-century saint.[110]

Given the strength and admissibility of the *Brautmystik* tradition, we might expect it to be widely in evidence in the writings of the women we have studied. It is indeed present—and with a vengeance—in the "confessions" that Madeleine Lebouc wrote for Pierre Janet, with their repeated use of "voluptés" and "jouissances" in a more or less explicitly sexual sense: "My *jouissances* are real, I assure you, they are not just imaginary," "I experienced a true *volupté* while flying in the air," "I experience *jouissances* which, outside of God, it is impossible for me to know."[111] Rarely has either the pleasure or the pain of religio-erotic experience, or, rather, their fundamental inseparability, been expressed in such openly physical terms, with an emphasis on oral and genital gratification that will shock or surprise only those for whom the whole *Song of Songs* tradition is a closed book. The *Brautmystik* tradition is also represented in a miniaturized, infantilized way in the writings of Thérèse where the ecstatic unions and levitations of Madeleine Lebouc have been replaced by cuddling, petting, and, above all, *playing* with a similarly infantilized Christ; the thematics and language of Eros and Eutrepelia have always been linked, and it is interesting that one of the witnesses of Bernadette's visions said that "it seemed the Blessed Virgin was acting like a mother, when she hides so that her child will look for her."[112]

Other than these two, one is struck by the overwhelming *absence* of pleasure in the spiritual experience of the women we have discussed. Raïssa's Christ was first and foremost a stern taskmaster, and her endless prayers and meditation seem to have brought her little spiritual release, while Simone seems to have little sense of Jesus' humanity, so obsessed is she with the opposition of gravity and grace that the meaning of the Incarnation—the assumption of gravity *by* grace—seems to have escaped her. Mélanie's Christianity was about suffering almost to the exclusion of anything else, as was Eva's and Claire's, while Colette's antireligion, geared at the achievement of some absolute *jouissance* beyond life and death, was, no doubt for that very reason, singularly devoid of enjoyment in the quotidian sense. It seems that puritanism had invaded even the mystical life. These women were passionate in the strictly etymological sense: They suffered with and for Christ, and suffering was not an incidental, but a constitutive, feature of their religious experience. Their Christianity was an unending Good Friday, with no Easter morning to come.

Thus it is to the oxymoronic pain/pleasure universe of the Marquis de Sade, given a theological gloss by the writings of his contemporary Joseph de Maistre on vicarious suffering, that the spiritual lives of these women for the most part belong. Algolagnia rules: There is no pleasure without pain, no meaning without martyrdom, pain is pleasure, pleasure is pain, and only a willingness to suffer endlessly without complaint or rebellion will bring the victim into union with her suffering but sadistic Lord. The victim makes herself not so much a plaything as a thing of suffering in His hands, and subjects herself willingly to His perpetual molestations, suffering when He attends to her, but suffering still more whenever He turns away. This, in short, is the world of *Histoire d'O* (1954), the most unarousing of all pornographic novels, now known to have been written by Dominique Aury (1907–98)—the unisex first name is strangely appropriate—under the name of Pauline Réage, supposedly to rekindle the waning passion of her lover Jean Paulhan, former contributor to the Collège de Sociologie and editor, the years of Occupation apart, of the *Nouvelle Revue Française* from 1925 until 1968; Paulhan was sufficiently impressed to contribute a preface. The curiously timeless sadomasochistic community into which O is inducted by her lover closely resembles an ultrastrict religious order, with its elaborate regulations concerning comportment and dress, the vow of continuous silence to which the victims are constrained in the presence of their torturers, and, not least, the ban on looking their "superiors" in the face; on her arrival in the "convent," O is obliged to remain "half sitting on her heels in the manner of nuns [*religieuses*]."[113] The "name" O is, of course, brilliantly chosen. It is the heroine's fate to be reduced willingly to zero, exactly as Simone sought total "decreation" and self-emptying in order to be free of "gravity" and become a channel of grace; according to Jacques Maître, there was one seventeenth-century anorexic nun who styled herself "Sœur Louise du Néant" (Sister Louise of Nothingness).[114] How ironic, too, that O's principal torturer should be named "Sir Stephen" after the first martyr of the Church.

Like a novice, O is gradually initiated into the Rule of her order, being told like every neophyte that "you are entirely given over to something that exists outside of you."[115] As part of her formation, O is required to take her lover René's cock into her mouth like the Blessed Sacrament, murmuring, "I love you" as she does so, in virtual parody of the "Lord, I am not worthy to receive you" of communion, and then, when he comes, she "receives him as one receives a god," collapsing on the floor after "communicating," for all the world like a Maria Maddelena de Pazzi or Marguerite-Marie Alacoque in ecstasy after taking the Body of Christ into themselves (53–54). The binding and whipping of O, spaced out like the Hours of the Church's day, clearly echo the ritual scourgings of the most extreme religious orders, with O wondering "why so much sweetness was mixed with terror in her, or why she found terror so sweet" (60). She blames herself for the cruelty and perversion of her torturers ("she was profaned and guilty" [71]), and takes their sins upon herself, acknowledging her total dependence on her lover who passes her from man to man like a communion chalice from which they drink their fill. Crucified time after time, she becomes a sacred relic in her lover's eyes, returning at last to him "like an ordinary object that had served a divine purpose and was consecrated thereby" (73). Yet being mocked, bound, stripped, scourged, and crucified day after day is liberation for O: "The chains and the silence, that should have shackled her deep in herself, stifling and strangling her, delivered her on the contrary from herself"; she experiences "a delirious absence from herself, which restored her to love and perhaps brought her close to death" (83). When her lover abandons her, she, like the spiritual bride when her Bridegroom withdraws, becomes "all waiting and all night" (92): The words echo both Simone Weil's *attente de Dieu* and the traditional mystic topos of the Dark Night of the soul: "Blessed night similar to her own night, blessed chains that liberated her from herself" (95). Like a holocaustal victim, O *becomes sin* and suffers joyfully for others, achieving an identity through loss of self, power through powerlessness, redemption through martyrdom and humiliation: "Being every day and as it were ritually besmirched with saliva and sperm, with sweat mingled with her own sweat, she felt that she was literally the receptacle of impurity, the sewer of which Holy Scripture speaks" (91). How not to recall the scatophagia and pus-sucking of a Marguerite-Marie Alacoque, how not to think of Colette Peignot, dog-collared, and that *sandwich à la merde?* But at the end of her novena, O is happy, "illuminated as though from within, and there could be seen a calm in how she acted, and on her face the serenity and the imperceptible inner smile that can be discerned in the eyes of female reclusives [*des recluses*]" (91). Further tortures await her at the hands of Sir Stephen, but already she is redeemed, a "saint of the abyss" whose beatification by blood and tears scarcely inverts at all the traditional "raising to the altar" of her more orthodox sisters in suffering—except that so few of them found, unlike O, any kind of peace in their pain.

Precious Tears

The whole of nineteenth-century French Catholicism bathes in a deluge of liquids. First, in the Precious Blood of Christ, which does not so much flow as it "bursts forth, streams, jets, pushes through the skin of the stigmatics, pulsates through the ventricles of the Sacred Heart."[116] That blood had indeed its principal *fons et origo* in the ecstasies of Saint Marguerite-Marie Alacoque (1647–90), a native of the village of Verosvres in the Charolais, traditional heartland of French beef, whose four great visions of the Sacred Heart in the nearby Convent of the Visitation at Paray-le-Monial in 1673, 1674, 1675, and 1677 Michelet characteristically attributed to the vitality of her blood, itself an emanation of "full-bodied Burgundy [*la vineuse Bourgogne*] where the [female] sex and blood are rich," which had not been "enervated, turned pale early on by a frigid convent regime":

"tardily cloistered, in the full force of youthfulness and life, the poor girl was a martyr to the superabundance of her blood [*sa pléthore sanguine*]. Each month, it was necessary to bleed her."[117]

But blood was far from the only liquid to course through the body of the Church. There are the springs and streams of countless Marian sites, the spas of Cauterets and Bagnères-de-Bigorre in the Pyrenees where hundreds of Catholics went for spiritual as well as physical healing before the advent of Lourdes, the waters of the once dried-up stream of Sézia supposedly released by the Virgin at La Salette in 1846, and above all the healing waters uncovered by Bernadette Soubirous at the behest of her *pétito damizéla* at the grotto of Massabielle in 1858. Interestingly, the patois word for spring or fountain—*hount*—that Bernadette would have used also means eye[118] and provides us with a link to our present subject, tears—that other liquid externalization of what lies hidden within. Jesus wept at the sight of Mary of Bethany weeping over her brother Lazarus's death, and the latter-day Marys and Marthas discussed in this work wept at the thought of his weeping, uncontrollably. The nineteenth-century French Catholic woman was in the first instance *celle qui pleure*, she who weeps copiously and compulsively in emulation of the weeping Mother and her Son, but whose tears have a double meaning, both negative and positive, that we can best begin to explore through the work of Charles Baudelaire, whose Catholic formation and androgynous, sadomasochistic sensibility bring him surprisingly close to the spiritual *mundus muliebris*, or female world, of the age.

Baudelaire was not an admirer of women's writing in general—he considered George Sand a "latrine"[119]—but he made an exception for the poetry of Marceline Desbordes-Valmore (1786–1859), whose imaginary landscape he evoked as follows in his great series of critical essays *Réflexions sur quelques-uns de mes contemporains* of 1861:

> The observer, contemplating these expanses in their widow's weeds [*voileés de deuil*], feels *hysterical tears* [in English in the original] rise to his eyes. The flowers, vanquished, bow down, and the birdsong becomes low. After a premonitory flash of lightning, a crash of thunder resounds: it is the explosion of lyricism [*l'explosion lyrique*]; at last an inevitable deluge of tears restores all these things, prostrated, suffering, and discouraged, the freshness and solidity of new youth![120]

These are the same creative and fertilizing tears that literally *explode* at the beginning of the great poem *Le Cygne*, Baudelaire's inexhaustible mantra of modern urban exile, written two years earlier in 1859, where the memory of the Trojan queen Andromache weeping in captivity over the death of Hector her husband, mingled with the image of the poet's own doubly widowed mother, unleashes a flood of associated images and memories amid the barren cityscape of contemporary Paris:

Andromaque, je pense à vous! Ce petit fleuve,
Pauvre et triste miroir où jadis resplendit
L'immense majesté de vos douleurs de veuve,
Ce Simoïs menteur qui par vos pleurs grandit,

A fécondé soudain ma mémoire fertile,
Comme je traversais le nouveau Carrousel.
Le vieux Paris n'est plus (la forme d'une ville
Change plus vite, hélas! Que le coeur d'un mortel);

[Andromache, I think of you—this meager stream,
This melancholy mirror where had once shone forth
The giant majesty of all your widowhood,
This fraudulent Simois, fed by bitter tears,

Has quickened suddenly my fertile memory
As I was walking through the modern Carrousel.
The old Paris is gone (the form a city takes
More quickly shifts, alas, than does the mortal heart);][121]

They are the tears that flow from the widows' eyes in "Les Petites Vieilles"
("Ces yeux sont des puits faits d'un million de larmes" / "These eyes are
wells, made of a million tears"),[122] or from the blank, unseeing eyes of the
female statue in "Un masque" who weeps because she has lived and must
live on more:

Pauvre grande beauté! Le magnifique fleuve
De tes pleurs aboutit dans mon coeur soucieux;
Ton mensonge m'enivre, et mon âme s'abreuve
Aux flots que la Douleur fait jaillir de tes yeux!

[O beauty, how I pity you! The great
Stream of your tears ends in my anxious heart;
Your lie transports me, and my soul drinks up
The seas brought forth by Sorrow from your eyes!][123]

Tears, then, are pregnant with potential, and the fact that they are "hysterical tears" only makes them more powerful. They are both male and female, stemming from the very matrix of being and able to inseminate the
waiting soil of the imagination: well before the La Salpêtrière school and
well before the surrealists, Baudelaire had realized, in every sense of the
word, the creative potential of "hysteria."[124] But if the woman's tears do
not flow "naturally," the poet-lover is all too ready to wring them from her
so as relaunch his desire and fecundate the parched wasteland of his imagination:

Je te frapperai sans colère
Et sans haine, comme un boucher,
Comme Moïse le rocher!
Et je ferai de ta paupière,

Pour abreuver mon Saharah,
Jaillir les eaux de la souffrance.
Mon désir gonflé d'espérance
Sur tes pleurs salés nagera

Comme un vaisseau qui prend le large,
Et dans mon coeur qu'ils soûleront
Tes chers sanglots retentiront
Comme un tambour qui bat la charge!

[I'll strike you without rage or hate
The way a butcher strikes his block,
The way that Moses smote the rock!
So that your eyes may irrigate

My dry Sahara, I'll allow
The tears to flow of your distress.
Desire, that hope embellishes,
Will swim along the overflow

As ships set out for voyaging,
And like a drum that beats the charge
In my infatuated heart
The echoes of your sobs will ring!][125]

Tears, then, like everything else in Baudelaire' universe, have a double meaning as an index of man's fallen but redeemable condition:

When an exquisite poem brings tears to the eyes, those tears are not the proof of an excess of enjoyment, they are much more the evidence of a frustrated melancholy, a nervous impulse, of a nature in the imperfect and which would like to take possession immediately, on this very earth, of a revealed paradise.[126]

More generally, tears were precious for the nineteenth-century French Catholic imagination because they are the price (*pretium*) man has paid for his fall from perfection, and the further price that he must pay to be "redeemed"—bought back—from the eternal damnation that otherwise awaits him. The only release from suffering is to suffer more;[127] only the shedding of more tears will staunch their flow, provided they are offered up in sacrifice to the God of Judgment and Mercy. And it is above all women—just as it is their tears that inspire the (male) artist—who must weep for men, substituting themselves as victims so that God's mysterious soteriological project may be realized.

Thus when Eugénie Fénoglio changed her name to Eva Lavallière, she launched herself, perhaps not yet fully consciously, on a lifetime's vocation of vicarious redemption through tears. As Eva, she acknowledged herself and her sex as authors of sin and, as Lavallière (after the ex-royal mistress and Carmelite nun Louise de la Vallière), announced her intention to exacerbate her sin so that her repentance might be more salvifically effective. Her sins cause her to weep, but it is those very tears that, offered up to God for the sake of sinful and nonweeping mankind, become the means and price of others' salvation. At the end of her days, according to a well-worn Catholic topos of reversion, *Eva* becomes *Ave,* and the erstwhile sinner, still weeping, takes up residence in Bethany, where her tears help purchase the release of the countless Lazaruses of fallen humanity.

Three quarters of a century after the publication of *Les Fleurs du Mal,* a latter-day Baudelairean, E. M. Cioran (1911–95), still writing in his native Romanian, published a book in Paris entitled *Lacrimi si sfinti* (1937).[128] It is a sequence of provocative aphorisms in the style that Cioran would later perfect in works in French such as *Précis de décomposition* (1949) and *De l'inconvénient d'être né* (1973), titles that well indicate the blend of irony and despair that is Cioran's forte. In this early work, an astonishing achievement for a writer in his mid-twenties, Cioran's subject is the inseparability of saintliness and suffering, a subject for which he had studied the lives and works of many of the female saints, mystics, and stigmatics that feature in this book: Angela di Foligno, Catherine Emmerich, the inevitable Catherines of Genoa and Siena, the equally inevitable Marguerite-Marie Alacoque, Mechthild of Magdeburg, Teresa of Avila, and, not least, Thérèse of Lisieux. Quoting Marguerite-Marie's dictum "none of my sufferings has been equal to that of not having suffered enough," Cioran begins by declaring that "without the *voluptuousness of suffering,* saintliness would not interest us any more than a medieval political intrigue in some little provincial town. Suffering is man's only biography, its *voluptuousness* the saint's" (9). Saintliness is "the negation of life through heavenly hysteria" (10), the "cosmic apogee of illness": "Illnesses have brought the heavens close to the earth. Without them, heaven and earth would not have known each other" (22). The saint's obsession—it should be stressed that almost all Cioran's examples are women—is "fighting illness with *illness*" (36), in other words, combating the contingent sufferings of the world with absolute, voluntarily assumed suffering. Although the suffering of the saints is predicated on what they suppose to be the still greater suffering of Christ on the cross, Cioran argues, skirting sacrilege as he does so, that "whenever I think about the infinity of suffering to which the saints' perverse transcendence has led, the agony of Jesus strikes me as merely sad. The cross broke apart and fell into the saints' souls, and its nails bore into their hearts all their life, not for just a few hours on the hill. The ultimate cruelty was that of Jesus: leaving an inheritance of bloodstains on the cross" (39).

Thus it is that the Son of God is a "Dealer in Pain" (49), a "heavenly Don Juan" (41) who causes countless holy Annas, Elviras, and Zerlinas to fall madly in love with him before abandoning them to their misery and tears that, of course, they, like their profane sister-in-suffering O, are all too happy to assume: "for the saints the end of suffering is the loss of grace" (42). Saintliness, in short, is a "celestial vice"; it "cannot exist without the voluptuousness of pain and a perverse refinement of suffering" (59). All this might suggest that Cioran is attacking the orthodox conception of saintliness in the name of some alternative spiritual ideal. But, though plainly no Christian, Cioran equally plainly admires and commends the tears of his saints. Without them, existence would be bland, and devoid of the algedonic voluptuousness after which he aspires; as much as Baudelaire, he believes in the power—at once moral, aesthetic, and erotic—of "la fertilisante douleur" (fecundating pain)[129] whose "aristocratic beauty"[130] is infinitely superior to the democratic banalities of mere earthly happiness.

Everything that Cioran so trenchantly expresses is of obvious relevance to the themes of this book. But so too are the young Romanian's politics at the time, which he and his admirers have subsequently carefully covered up, in common with those of other 1930s intellectuals to whom Cioran is temperamentally and philosophically so close: Bataille, Caillois, Blanchot, Klossowski, and others. For Cioran—like his fellow Romanian Mircea Eliade (1907–86), the much-praised scholar of comparative religion, autobiographer, and mystic—was close in the 1930s to the extremist Legion of the Archangel Michael, better known as the Iron Cross, "a populist movement with strong mystical characteristics," bent on bringing about "moral and spiritual change [in Romania], ethnic 'regeneration' [i.e., antisemitism] by returning to Orthodox Christian values, and 'salvation' through asceticism and sacrifice."[131] Not to put too fine a point on it, Cioran was a typical 1930s neither-right-nor-leftist—that is, in effect, a fascist—and his *Romania's Transfiguration*, also published in 1937, is a Nietzschean blueprint for the regeneration of his country which argues that "all means are legitimate when a people opens a road for itself in the world. Terror, crime, bestiality and perfidy are base and immoral only in decadence, when they defend a vacuum of content; if, on the other hand, they help in the ascension of a people, they are virtues. All triumphs are moral."[132]

All this falls all too neatly and predictably into one of the principal patterns revealed by this book. Adepts of the doctrine of vicarious suffering— both the (usually) female sufferers and their (usually) male panegyrists—are almost always on the political far right: Mélanie Calvat, Thérèse Martin, and Claire Ferchaud among the "sufferers" discussed here, de Maistre,

Bonald, Blanc de Saint-Bonnet, Barbey, Baudelaire,[133] Bloy, Huysmans, and Bernanos amongst the hagiographers. Ultraroyalism, in particular, and mystical substitutionism are all of a piece. Images of each other, Jesus and Louis XVI die on the cross and the guillotine, and their followers, particularly their *female* followers, assume and atone for their sufferings with their tears, all this for a kingdom of God that suspiciously resembles the lost kingdom of pre-1789 France. The effect of the doctrine of vicarious suffering is to legitimate, perpetuate, and often exacerbate the miseries of the last, the least, and the lost; it almost invariably validates hierarchy, (male) order, and inequality. Adherents of the doctrine would, of course, argue that, in so doing, it ensured the salvation of men and women whose souls would otherwise have been lost. This may be so, but others will look more to Jesus' healing mission on earth and less to his supposedly expiatory sufferings on the cross and, above all, not take the latter, as did most of the French Catholics discussed in this book, as the indispensable paradigm for the Christian life.

Mary Magdalene

"Others by Dayes, by Monthes, by Yeares / Measure their Ages, Thou by Teares" (Richard Crashaw [1612–49], "The Weeper").[134] In view of the volume of tears shed in nineteenth-century literature, it is hardly surprising that, of all the female saints, it was Mary Magdalene who was the most popular among French Catholics, both men and women, of the time. A composite (in the western Church but not in the eastern)[135] of at least three biblical women—Mary Magdalene herself, Mary of Bethany, and the anonymous "woman in the city, which was a sinner" of Luke 7:37 (the "magna peccatrix," or great sinner, of medieval iconography)—Mary Magdalene had scarcely ever gone out of devotional favor, such was the rich complex of images and themes that clustered about her protean figure: the washing of Christ's feet with her tears and then the drying of them with the flowing locks of her hair; the anointing of his head from her "alabaster box" (Matthew 26:7, Mark 14:3); the casting out of seven devils from her (Mark 16:9, Luke 8:2); the witnessing of the crucifixion, at which, contrary to the biblical narrative that has her and the other women "beholding afar off" (Matthew 27:55), she is traditionally represented kneeling at the foot of the cross, often with her knees placed either side of the base; her discovery, weeping still, of the empty tomb; the meeting with the resurrected Christ whom she takes for a gardener; his asking her why she is weeping (the "Quid ploras?" of John 20:15); her recognition of him and addressing him as Rabboni "which is to say, Master," followed by the terrible order not to touch him (*Noli me tangere*: "her *tangere* had a tang to it," said the great Anglican divine Lancelot Andrewes);[136] and, finally, the taking of the news to the craven male apostles that made her—a woman and hence, by definition, suspect as a witness—the "apostle of the apostles" (*apostola apostolorum*) and thus, in the eyes of many recent feminist theologians, as much the founder of the Church as Saint Peter.

The cult of Mary Magdalene peaked in France at the time of the Counter-Reformation, as it did everywhere in Europe, thrived in the late seventeenth and eighteenth centuries, but went into temporary abeyance during the revolutionary and Napoleonic periods, mainly because of the dechristianization campaign and the consequent vandalization of the principal shrines of the cult. There were two of these, bitter rivals ever since the Middle Ages for primacy in France: Vézelay in the Bourgogne and Saint-Maximin-la-Sainte-Baume between Aix-en-Provence and Marseille (*baume* means cavern in Provençal but is suggestively identical to the French word for balm) where Mary Magdalene was believed to have lived and died, clad only in her flowing locks like a holy Lady Godiva and living off the Blessed Sacrament alone, brought to her daily by angels, after she, her brother Lazarus, and two other biblical Mary's, Mary Salome and Mary Jacobus, had fled the Holy Land by sea, landing at the celebrated gypsy pilgrimage center of Saintes-Maries-de-la-Mer in the Camargue at the mouth of the Rhône. With the restoration of the monarchy in 1815, the cult briefly revived, its traditional focus on repentance for past sins being given a political edge by the events of the previous twenty-five years. At Whitsun 1822, 140,000 people were said to be present at the mountain grotto when a newly constructed chapel containing a statue of the Penitent Whore was consecrated, but still the pilgrimage languished and, visiting the site in 1848, Henri Lacordaire, the restorer of the Dominican order in France and a leading devotee of the Magdalene, was distressed to find the grotto once more abandoned and dilapidated.[137]

The revival of the cult of Mary Magdalene during the post-1870 ultramontanist upsurge was in considerable part inspired by the hagiography that Lacordaire wrote on his deathbed (*Sainte Marie-Madeleine* [1860]). By the turn of the century, Saint-Maximin and the grotto in the mountains above were attracting thousands of pilgrims, tourists, and Provençal nationalists, including the founder of the Provençal literary movement, Le Félibrige, Frédéric Mistral (1830–1914), for whom the site was a shrine, above all, of a distinctive regional identity. The pilgrims, then and later, included a number of figures already mentioned in this book and others closely linked to them: Huysmans's curious housekeeper and live-in mystic Julie Thibault (1839–1907) who, "Madame Bavoil" in his novels, "did" all the major Marian and related shrines in western Europe, traveling everywhere on foot with just a bundle of clothes and her umbrella and living exclusively off a diet of bread, milk, and honey;[138] Eva Lavallière, a frequent visitor to the grotto "where Sainte Madeleine expiated and loved, so much, so much!!! Such delicacy on Jesus's part! He has so many, so many!!!";[139]

Jacques Maritain and others of the Meudon circle; Cocteau's ex-lover Jean Bourgoint, who spent much time there discovering his religious vocation; and Jean Hugo (1894–1984), great-grandson of Victor and a distinguished painter and stage decorator who, converting to Catholicism in the early 1930s, provides yet another link between the world of the fashionable nightclub Le Boeuf sur le Toit and the Catholic Church.[140]

The pilgrimage to Vézelay also revived, thanks to the almost complete reconstruction of the great ruined basilica undertaken in the 1840s by Viollet-le-Duc (1814–79) at the behest of the Bourgeois Monarchy's Inspector of Public Monuments, the novelist Prosper Mérimeé (1803–70); it was Viollet's first public commission and marked the beginning of a meteoric career as the restorer and, in many cases, the virtual re-creator, of the Gothic cathedrals of France.[141] As well as reestablishing itself as a major pilgrimage center, particularly for Catholic students in the region for whom, at Easter, the basilica became what, inspired by Péguy's famous pre-1914 pilgrimages by foot, Chartres cathedral became for their counterparts in Paris, Vézelay attracted a remarkable number of literary pilgrims and/or residents, not all of them Catholics: Paul Claudel,[142] the novelist Romain Rolland (1866–1944), the poet Max-Pol Fouchet (1913–81), and the Algerian-born novelist Jules Roy (1907–2000), author of the rhapsodic *Vézelay ou l'amour fou* (1989). The graveyard adjoining the basilica contains the remains of the dissident Catholic novelist and essayist Maurice Clavel (1920–79), the closest recent equivalent of a Bernanos or Bloy, the title of whose essay *Dieu est Dieu, nom de Dieu!* (1976) gives some idea of the apoplectic tone of his writings, of the woman who inspired the figure of Ysé in Claudel's great drama of illicit love *Partage de midi* (1905–6), and, not least, of Georges Bataille who moved to the town with his new partner, Denise Rollin, in 1943 and spent the remaining years of the Occupation and the immediate *après-guerre* living in a house on the Rue Saint-Etienne where he met the woman, Diane Kotchoubey de Beauhamais (b. 1920) whom he would marry in 1951.

All these, Catholics and non-Catholics alike the *magna peccatrix* gathered symbolically about her, but her influence spread far beyond those who, for whatever reason, made the pilgrimage to Saint-Maximin or Vézelay. The Magdalene features, in one guise or another, in a host of nineteenth- and twentieth-century literary works: in Zola's early novel *Madeleine Férat* (1869); in Maurice Maeterlinck's play *Marie-Madeleine* of 1913; in the poetry of Pierre Emmanuel (the pseudonym of Noël Mathieu [born 1916]), a convert from Protestantism to Catholicism; in a typically incisive and subversive story, "Marie-Madeleine or le salut" in Marguerite Yourcenar's *Feux* (1936); and in a range of late-twentieth-century feminist novels in which the Magdalene is cast both as an icon of female strength and resourcefulness and—following the very different works of D. H. Lawrence (*The Man Who Died* [1929]) and Nikos Kazantzakis (*The Last Temptation of Christ* [1951])—as the site of a possible reconciliation between spirituality and sexuality, Agape and Eros. There is also an abundance of paintings, most, but not all, of them saccharine at best,[143] and two works that, each in its way, make explicit the eroticism that is never absent from even the chastest treatment of the Magdalene theme. Rodin's sculpture "Le Christ et la Madeleine" dates from 1892–94—in other words, from the stormiest years of his liaison with Camille Claudel (whose own sculptures "L'Age mûr" [1899] and "L'Imporante" [1905] are secular variations on the Magdalene theme)—and, in the words of his famous secretary Rainer Maria Rilke, shows the crucified Jesus, "his outstretched arms resembling a signpost at the crossroads of all pain," while, coiled about his waist, the naked, swooning Magdalene "surrounds him with a disconsolate and entreating movement, and with a gesture of hopelessness she looses her hair in order to bury Christ's tormented heart in it."[144] Could the sculpture represent, if only unconsciously, Rodin's sense of being "crucified" and suffocated by Camille's jealous and possessive love, along the lines suggested in Rilke's poem "Pietà" of 1906?

> Doch, siehe, deine Hände sind zerrissen:
> Geliebter, nicht von mir, von meinen Bissen.
> Dein Herz steht offen und man kann hinein:
> Das hätte dürfen nur mein Eingang sein.
>
> [But, look, how torn your hands have come to be:
> Not from my bites, beloved, not by me.
> Your heart stands open now for all to share:
> I only should have had the entry there.][145]

Even more explicit, indeed grotesquely so, is the series of etchings on the Magdalene theme done by Baudelaire's Belgian friend Félicien Rops (1833–98) in the halcyon days of Decadence in the 1880s. In the five etchings of *Les Sataniques* (1882–83), it is not Christ that the Magdalene-figure embraces, but Satan as either crucified or sacrificer. In "L'Idole," a naked woman, legs splayed in an obscene exaggeration of the traditional Magdalene pose, mounts a statue of the devil on the peristyle of the Grand Temple devoted to his worship, while two phallus-shaped lampades ejaculate flames on either side; "in a superb rush of passion," runs Rops's commentary, "the possessed woman throws herself headlong on to the impassive idol and abandons herself, crazed and subjugated. The deed is done, the *Woman* belongs to *Satan!*" "Le Sacrifice" shows the same woman impaled by Satan's coiling, snakelike penis on an altar ("His monstrous force animated by every kind of violence and lust spreads the *Woman*'s flanks and seems to drink the blood that gushes from them and stains the steps of the altar red"), while, in "Le Calvaire," Satan "attached to the cross in a diabolic travesty of a scene from the Passion" towers above a naked woman standing arms outstretched at his feet, "hypnotized, her head beneath the exultant sex of the Master"; the woman's mouth opens just beneath the devil's testicles, above which his narrow, circumcised penis rises dramatically to just beneath his solar plexus.[146] Two years later, in 1885, Rops went still further down the path of blasphemous inversion with two "before and after" etchings in which it is neither Christ nor the devil that is nailed to the cross, but a severed cock and balls, the former erect in the first etching, detumescent in the next, while at the foot of the cross, a naked Mary Magdalene is shown recumbent, first masturbating and then lying head and hair flung back, though more perhaps in frustration than in post-orgasmic bliss.[147] Inadvertently, Rops seems to have discovered the secret meaning of the Magdalene cult: its introversion, narcissism, and ultimate sterility.

These and other works show that it was not only, or even primarily, to women that the Magdalene theme appealed. Indeed the Magdalene-Christ dyad permitted all kinds of gender-bending transpositions and androgynous trochilics, as in two extraordinary stanzas in an early Baudelaire poem inspired by his probable first sexual partner, and likely origin of the syphilis that eventually killed him, a Jewish prostitute in Paris known in the milieu as "Sara la Louchette" (Squint-eyed Sarah):

> Elle n'a que vingt ans; sa gorge—déjà basse
> Pend de chaque côté comme une calebasse,
> Et pourtant me traînant chaque nuit sur son corps,
> Ainsi qu'un nouveau-né, je la tète et la mords—
>
> Et bien qu'elle n'ait pas souvent même une obole
> Pour se frotter la chair et pour s'oindre l'épaule—
> Je la lèche en silence avec plus de ferveur,
> Que Madeleine en feu les deux pieds du Sauveur[148]
>
> [She is only twenty years old; her already sagging
> breasts / hang like gourds on each side, / and yet,
> crawling each night over her body, / like a newborn
> baby, I suck and bite at her breasts— / and even
> though she often does not have a penny to her name / to
> rub her body and anoint her shoulders— / I lick her
> in silence with far greater fervor / than Mary
> Magdalene on fire at the two feet of the Savior]

Here it is Baudelaire who becomes the male-female prostitute, and the prostitute who becomes the female-male Christ. The author of three explicit poems, two of them banned, on the subject of lesbianism, who first gave the title *Les Lesbiennes* to the future *Les Fleurs du Mal,* Baudelaire might be described as a male lesbian, a woman in male form who desired other women, not as same unto other, but as like unto like.

It will not be surprising, therefore, to find many gay writers, Catholic and non-Catholic, openly attracted to the Magdalene theme. Here, for example, is Max Jacob's remarkable "Mise au tombeau" ("The Entombment"), published in 1919, four years after his reception into the Church:

> Your [*ton*] dead body! To have loved it so much when it was alive! But still stone-like flesh is still yours, my beloved! My God! There is still blood on his pretty forehead: it all seems to sweat but is nonetheless hard. It is your corpse! My pretty God [*mon Dieu joli*] reduced to a corpse. . . . Your belly is hard too: that is the most surprising thing about corpses. I had never seen how delicate your feet are. . . . Alas! I have never felt how much I love you since your death: I am in love with your corpse and I see how much I loved you without realizing I did. . . . Here are your pierced feet. Oh! The swine! How they made you suffer: they pierced you, you, God, you a more than charming young man, more than seductive, more than genial. That unique marvel, God descended to earth, they destroyed it in their wrath.[149]

Of course, such ecstatic sensuousness is hardly unparalleled in devotional writing, even in that of heterosexual men, but it is difficult not to link it to Jacob's own sexuality. His rapturous, agonized voice is that of a Mechtild of Magdeburg, an Angela di Foligno, or a Marguerite-Marie Alacoque as he transposes himself into one of the Holy Women on Calvary, a male-female mourner distraught before the still seductive body of a male-female Christ. More haunted by the Passion than any other French Catholic poet, Jacob commonly casts himself as Veronica wiping her Lord's face on his way to the cross or, more commonly still, as Mary Magdalene who, after anointing Christ's feet and wiping them with her hair, is the agonized witness of his death on the cross and then, three days later, afraid, amazed, and overjoyed, of his glorious resurrection. More remarkably still, when Cocteau told Jacob of Radiguet's death in December 1923, Jacob tried to console him with the image of Mary at the foot of the cross: Radiguet as crucified Christ, Cocteau as his lover-cum-mother.[150] Four years later, Jacob wrote to Cocteau of his *amour-admiration*—though much more than mere admiration was involved—for one Louis Vaillant, a young man of Saint-Benoît, describing it as "genre Madeleine-Christ," like that of Mary Magdalene for Christ, the same love that Cocteau had felt for Radiguet.[151] At a much lower literary level, Jean Desbordes (another future martyr) fantasizes in his mystical-masturbatory farrago *J'adore* about "the hand of Mary Magdalene who touches men's genitals [*le sexe des hommes*] for their pleasure and the garment of Christ for His light" as he longs for a watery *Liebestod* in which, like an "ecstatic swimmer," "Greek lover," or "dream girl," he would merge with the floodtides of Life.[152]

In their different ways, Jacob, Cocteau, Green, Sachs, and Desbordes (and also Bourgoint, another devotee of Mary Magdalene) were all seeking—and failing—to marry the Eros and Agape that the institutional Church was committed to keeping rigidly apart. Mary Magdalene may be an unlikely "gay icon," but her presence, as an embodiment of spirituality and sexuality reconciled and conjoined, in gay French Catholic discourse in the interwar years, gives an added pungency to the coincidental prominence of the *quartier de la Madeleine* in the gay life of the city at the time, just a few blocks from Le Boeuf sur le Toit and, according to Jean Hugo (not a homosexual, but familiar with the milieu), a "black temple" where every sect and denomination could find satisfaction.[153] And it also helps explain why, of all the churches in Paris, it is to La Madeleine that Genet's Divine always takes her beloved Mignon to Mass, Mignon, that "earthly expression, [that] symbol of a being (perhaps God), of a heavenly idea,"[154] on whose naked chest she fantasizes about consecrating the host, and whose cock, the be-all and end-all of her world, she anoints, impenitent whore that she is, as ardently as Mary Magdalene ever did the feet and head of her Master and Savior.

All this would have raised more than one Carmelite eyebrow, but who would have expected Lacordaire, no less, to have written as follows to his fellow Catholic Charles Montalambert in 1832: "I kiss your [*tes*] pieds, I wash them with my tears; I bring together at one time all my caresses of three years, all my concerns for you, all my joys, all my humiliations that I prefer to everything"?[155] Thérèse and her sisters would have felt on safer and more familiar ground, had they been able to read it, with a remarkable, but unfortunately anonymous, seventeenth-century sermon that the Abbé Joseph Bonnet discovered in the Imperial Library in Saint Petersburg in 1909. It was translated into German in 1911 by Rilke—decidedly the greatest non-Catholic devotee of the Magdalene—under the title of *Die Liebe der Magdalena* (*L'Amour de Madeleine*), and, although its composition greatly predates our period, it is discussed here because, perhaps more than any other text, it brings out the core of Magdalenian spirituality.

In common with all meditations springing from the *Song of Songs* tradition of bride-mysticism, *L'Amour de Madeleine* effectively makes no distinction between Agape and Eros. It begins with a bold and unambiguous declaration that love alone, not faith or "works," was the essence of the Magdalene's being: "Madeleine, the holy lover [*sainte amante*] of Jesus, loved him in his three conditions. She loved him living, she loved him dead, she loved him resurrected."[156] In loving him, she gives herself unstintingly, with a prodigality and unconcern for self-preservation that make of her an early example of Bataille's notion of *dépense* ("spending," self-dissipation, or-dilapidation), hardly surprisingly since he formulated that idea in part through his reading of Angela di Foligno, herself, predictably, one of the pillars of Magdalenian erotic spirituality:[157]

At every moment, she dies, and at every moment, kissing the feet of Jesus, takes on a new life, only to immolate it immediately afterwards. She gives and dissipates [*prodigue*] everything: her perfumes, her hair, her tears, her signs, and her very heart. It seems she wants to exhaust herself in favor of her Beloved. Nonetheless, she fears exhaustion, because she wishes to give without measure. (32)

Her prodigality is both selfish and selfless, for she loves Jesus with a "furious hunger" and "insatiable love" (34); as Jesus himself says (Luke 7:45), "this woman since the time I came in hath not ceased to kiss my feet." She is at once possessed and possessive, and, tearfully kissing her Beloved's feet, they present a "truly admirable spectacle":

Madeleine captive of Jesus, and Jesus captive of Madeleine. Placing her head at Jesus' feet, she declares herself sufficiently his captive; but holding the feet of Jesus, she makes him her captive. How does she hold the feet of Jesus? She holds them with her mouth, by kissing them thousands upon thousands of times; she holds them with her eyes, by drenching them with her tears; she holds them with her hands, by embracing and anointing them. But that is not enough, and there must be chains. Loosen your hair, O Madeleine, and bind with them the feet of Jesus. O the delicate chains that Madeleine prepares for her conqueror, whom she wants to make her captive! (26)

But Jesus, in the manner of Cioran's "heavenly Don Juan," *plays* with Mary Magdalene, indeed "plays hard to get," first approaching then withdrawing, appearing to give himself only forthwith to retract the gift, luring his lover into further ecstatic and desperate longing:

What are you thinking of, O Jesus Christ, drawing hearts so strongly to you, binding them so closely to yourself, and then withdrawing in so unforeseen a fashion? O how you are cruel? O how strangely you play with the hearts that love you! (38)

Jesus is to Madeleine as her lover is to O: She loves him, he hurts her, she suffers, but what she dreads most is his indifference, the end of her pain. O, Madeleine, and the bride of the *Song of Songs* cry out in one voice *Revertere, revertere,* come back, come back (*Song of Songs* 2:17 [44]) to their capricious and fugitive lover:

It is Jesus Christ's method, it is his ordinary conduct. He draws hearts powerfully to him, he makes them avid and insatiable, he defeats them, he masters them, he binds them, he gives himself to them in a thousand ways that commit them in such a way that their every breath is him; and as soon as they are committed with no possibility of retraction, he draws back, he slips off, he tests them with flights and terrible privations. They complain, and Jesus laughs at their plaints; he lets them exhaust and consume themselves in inexpressible greedy longing [*avidités inexprimables*]. He himself lays his hands upon them in order to enflame them, and he looks at them from afar, playing [*se jouant*], so to speak, with their passions and furies. (38–40)

Finally, Madeleine's agony of ecstatic desire is brought to an appallingly nonclimactic climax when, having recognized Jesus in the garden and hailed him as her Master, she is ordered not to touch him; "God," says the sermonist, "communicates himself only by hiding; not in order to satisfy but to frustrate love" (*non pour assouvir, mais pour irriter l'amour*) (60). Thus it is that, though Madeleine's life is, in Bataille's terms, one of unstinting *dépense,* an endless holocaust of herself for the sake of her Beloved, "there is," in the sermonist's words, "almost never a moment of pleasure" (58)— and the word he uses is none other than *jouissance,* which even in the seventeenth century had a strong sexual nuance. It seems a fitting comment on the almost always frustrated lovemaking of the ravenous Brides of Christ described in this book. They glimpse the Bridegroom and, besotted, go to embrace him, giving themselves, hair loosened, tears flowing, yet forever he withdraws, lures them on and abandons them, leaving them, having been played with, playing with themselves, as the vulgar phrase has it, like Rops's Mary Magdalene at the foot of the cross, with all too little hope of finding fulfillment.

Victim and Visionary: Anne-Marie Roulé

It is at this point that we can introduce our eleventh and final portrait, that of Anne-Marie Roulé (or Roulet, 1846–1907), first mistress and then mystagogue to Léon Bloy, in whom virtually every theme, image, and symptom so far discussed is represented with almost preternatural clarity; only anorexia is not clearly documented, and though it would be rash to assume its presence from other aspects of her case, it would by no means be inconsistent with them.

Anne-Marie was born at Rennes on 25 February 1846, a few months before Bloy (11/12 July) whose own date of birth, as he characteristically put it, occurred "sixty-eight days"—"exactly the number of the brothers of the faithful Obed-edom chosen with him by King David to be the guardians of the ark of the Covenant"[158]—before the event that in many ways dominated his existence: the apparition of the virgin at La Salette on 19 September that year. Anne-Marie was the illegitimate daughter of a woman in her forties who abandoned her at birth to public assistance, and she was brought up in an orphanage in Rennes named Les Catherinettes until 1860 when she was belatedly recognized and removed by her mother; she never knew the identity of her father. In 1867, aged twenty-one, she sought, but failed to be granted, entrance into a convent at Tours, and was back working as a needlewoman in Rennes when her mother died in 1874. Thereafter, for reasons unknown, her fortunes, never good, underwent a dramatic decline, and she is next heard of living in and around the Latin Quarter in Paris and, it is clear, making what living she could as an occasional prostitute.

Whether she first met Bloy in a professional capacity is unclear but remains the most likely reason for their encounter; when it occurred, in February or March 1877, they were living within ten or fifteen minutes' walking distance from each other, she on the rue Saint-Jacques, he on the rue Rousselet in the seventh arrondissement. In *Le Desespéré* Bloy gives Anne-Marie the name of Véronique Cheminot (curiously, Bloy was employed by the Compagnie des Chemins de Fer du Nord when he met her and was thus in a sense a *cheminot* [railway worker] himself) and the professional nickname "La ventouse," meaning both a glass for the "cupping" of blood and the sucker of a leech: Véronique is a bloodsucker, but potentially a healing one, who will free Bloy's alter ego Caïn Marchenoir of the "bad blood" that makes him, like his name sake, a "black walker," "a fugitive and a vagabond in the earth" with God's ambiguous mark on him that both singles him out as the murderer of his brother and protects him "lest any finding him should kill him" (Genesis 4:14–15).

Two or three months into the liaison, in mid-May 1877, Léon-Caïn became, in his own eyes, a parricide (D 23) as well as a fratricide when his father died in impoverished circumstances in Périgueux. Bloy was absent from his deathbed and arrived too late for the funeral. Determined to atone for these sins of omission, Bloy seems to have decided there and then to convert Anne-Marie to his faith and, renouncing all sexual relations, pursue a religious vocation.

In pursuit of the first part of this expiatory project, in June 1877, Bloy took Anne-Marie to the principal center of Marian devotion in Paris, the Notre-Dame des Victoires that Thérèse and her father would visit ten yeas later en route for Rome, where Anne-Marie was enrolled as member number 997,631 in the Archiconfrérie du Très Saint et Immaculé Coeur de Marie, dedicated to "the conversion of sinners," of which the church was the national, and indeed international, headquarters. "That day," Bloy later wrote, "our way of life changed completely and for ever. It was the first divine prodigy observed by me" (letter of August 1880, B 311). Perhaps so, but it did not halt sexual relations between "Caïn" and "La Ventouse."

Bloy still had thoughts of a religious vocation, and he spent ten days in the austere monastic conditions at La Grande Trappe at Soligny near Mortagne-au-Perche, at the end of September 1877. It was a miserable time, and Bloy suffered terrible toothache until a "providential brother" extracted the bad tooth, the possible significance of which will become clear in due course. Back in Paris, and having jettisoned the idea of a vocation, Bloy resumed his relationship with Anne-Marie and was pressured to marry her by his new spiritual adviser, the famous Abbé Tardif de Moidrey (1828–79), who would have a huge impact on Louis Martin when he gave a conference at Lisieux on the subject of freemasonry, that "hideous nihilistic spectre: negation of all authority, social equality, levelling of the sexes."[159] In November 1877, Bloy's mother died (at least this time he made it to her funeral) and, giving up his job, Bloy abandoned the *chemin de fer* for his own highly individual *chemin de la croix* on which he would be accompanied for the next four years by a very bizarre Saint Veronica indeed, who would regularly wipe his face on his way to the cross, while following an even more extreme Via Dolorosa herself.

At this point it becomes increasingly difficult to distinguish the "real" Anne-Marie from the "fictional" Véronique, particularly as the former left no writings—nor even, it appears, a picture—of her own. Caïn—or Marie-Joseph-Caïn, to give him his full name, as though he is to be the future mother-father of Christ as well as the author of the first murder—transforms his *Magna Peccatrix* into a virgin, while she, in her turn, identifies explicitly with Mary Magdalene (D 213, 388) in tears at the feet of her two virtually indistinguishable "Saviors," Caïn and Jesus, "both of you in agony for me and both of you so poor" (D 389): "The two feelings, natural and supernatural, had become so perfectly amalgamated and blended in her in the unique thought of one Savior that there was no longer any way of separating them, for this simple soul, who did not believe she was paying for the recovery of her innocence too dearly by pouring [*déversant*] of the glory of the heavens on the painful human *resemblance* of her Redeemer!" (D 290–91).

After a further stay at La Trappe in August-September 1878, Bloy accompanied Anne-Marie to Sacré-Coeur and it was there, in his words, that she underwent her "true conversion," her "road [*chemin*] to Damascus, for the love of God descended on her like a lightning bolt. From that day began that extraordinary story of brother-sister relations, of prayers without ceasing, of communication with the supernatural and sufferings the detailed story of which would stretch all credibility" (letter of August 1880, B 311). There seems no reason to doubt Bloy's insistence that, from September 1878, their relationship ceased to be sexual. Anne-Marie began praying ten to fifteen hours a day, crying continually so that (like Eva Lavallière) her eyesight was affected, and she was no longer able to take in needlework to sustain her and her currently unemployed "Savior."

In late August 1879, leaving Anne-Marie in Paris, Bloy and Tardif de Moidrey made the pilgrimage—Bloy's first—to La Salette together. In the course of their stay, Tardif became seriously ill with what transpired to be the contagious skin disease popularly known as St. Anthony's fire and, sending Bloy back to Paris, died on the "Holy Mountain" itself on 28 September 1879; it was—how could it not have been?—the feast of Notre-Dame-des-Sept-Douleurs. Bloy was devastated by Tardif's distinctly untardy death and became more and more entrenched in his conviction that "everything on earth is ordered for Pain" (D 177), that Pain, not Love, is the force that moves the sun and other stars, placing on human beings the obligation to suffer and atone for each other and, in a vast network of solidarity encompassing the saints, complete the work of suffering and expiation that, if Colossians 1:24 was to be believed, Christ had left *unfinished* on Calvary hill. It was a belief that Anne-Marie, in her turn, would adopt with a vengeance and that the fictional Véronique would push to unimaginable extremes—unimaginable, that is, by anyone other than Bloy.

During Lent 1880, Bloy and Anne-Marie made four separate visits to the shrine dedicated to Saint Joseph (cf. Caïn's second given name) at Antony on the southern outskirts of Paris. It was during this period that Anne-Marie began to have visions of an apocalyptic character, suggestive, on the one hand, of her impending mental collapse and, on the other, of contact with the ideas of Pierre-Eugène-Michel Vintras (1807–85) and his schismatic Oeuvre de la Miséricorde.[160] Like Vintras and his followers, Anne-Marie proclaimed the imminent arrival, after the reigns of God the Father and God the Son, of God the Holy Spirit. She prophesied that Jesus was about to be released from the cross by Elias, and that a "secret," akin to the one given to Mélanie at La Salette but still more momentous in purport, was about to be revealed, with her, naturally, as its prophet. The fact that both Anne-Marie and Bloy were now aged thirty-three, the age traditionally attributed to Christ at his death, and that thirty-three years had elapsed since the Virgin's apparition at La Salette, convinced both of them that the Endtime was at hand. Bloy recognized that, by any secular standards, Anne-Marie was "absolutely mad" (B 426) and was staggered when, waking one night, he saw Anne-Marie standing in tears before her image of the Holy Face so dear to Thérèse to which she (Anne-Marie) was speaking "as to Jesus really present and visible for her." She was not, however, thanking, praising, or entreating her Savior but upbraiding for his treatment of her other "Savior"—Léon-Caïn—"like a master speaks to an unfaithful servant or like a cruel executioner [*bourreau*] speaks to his victim" (letter of April 1880, B 429). In the fictional version of this episode Caïn looks at his exmistress as, unaware of his presence and with "her magnificent eyes dilated by all the stupefactions of dementia," she pledges to go to hell if Jesus will come to his aid, and thinks: "I am her executioner" (*bourreau*). The whole cosmos, from the lowest animals, victims and torturers of each other before becoming sacrificial victims of men,[161] to the saints and Jesus himself is an interlocking chain of executioners and victims in which each being is now in the one role, now in the other, and sometimes in both roles simultaneously; "it might," said Baudelaire, like Bloy a sado-Catholic to the core, "be agreeable [*doux*] to be alternatively victim and executioner."[162]

In September 1880, Bloy and Anne-Marie, convinced that the apocalypse, or something like it, really was at hand, decided to *walk* to La Salette (the *chemin* image again) and, though they eventually took this and that form of transport, "pitched their beggars' tent," in Bloy's words, on the

Holy Mountain on the 17th of the month, fully expecting that, two days later, on the anniversary of the apparition, nothing less than "the secret that is Lucifer's despair" (B 436) would be revealed, through them, to humanity. When nothing happened, both were predictably devastated, and Anne-Marie's final descent into madness can be plausibly dated from her bitterness that the God to whom she was prepared to sacrifice everything had, when it most mattered to her, remained silent.

Her escalating decline is not clearly documented, but by June 1882 even Bloy had to bow to reality. Anne-Marie was examined by a Dr. Gervais who ordered her immediate internment at the hospital Sainte-Anne, thereby depriving Charcot and the Ecole Salpêtrière of a prize addition to their collection of religiohysterical specimens. At Sainte-Anne, Anne-Marie was diagnosed as suffering from "persecutory delirium and religious monomania," and in September 1882 she was transferred to the Maison du Bon Sauveur at Caen. She was still a patient, her condition unchanged, when, in 1889, Thérèse's father was placed in the same institution for a period of three years. Anne-Marie died, aged sixty-one, on 7 May 1907, of a tumor of the stomach and, on the 11, presumably unaware of her death, Bloy wrote in his diary: "We can pay for others, not for ourselves. The communion of the saints. I suffer. It is no use my needing to expiate, my suffering is not given to me for my sake. I am only the trustee [*le dépositaire*] of that treasure."[163] Anne-Marie had suffered for Bloy, and, in a way, had enabled him to become the writer he was, sustaining him in the darkest years of his life and, not least, providing him with the model for the most memorable character in his work. Unlike her ex-lover, she paid the price to the full.

The relationship between Bloy and Anne-Marie, at least as narrated in the former's letters, is transposed with few additions or subtractions into that of Caïn and Véronique in *Le Désespéré*. The novel's most extraordinary episode is, however, of Bloy's own invention and may have had something to do with the impromptu dental work that he had done at La Trappe in September 1877. The scene in question has already featured in *Blood in the City*,[164] and is returned to here not so much on account of its horrific, but of its exemplary, nature. The fictional Véronique habitually visits this or that Parisian church at random, enters the confessional, and, "thirsting after contempt, desperate to be trampled underfoot," announces to the bewildered priest, "Mon père, je suis une sale prostituée" (Father, I am a dirty prostitute) (D 252–53). Even when the priest agrees to hear her confession, the penances imposed on her are never hard enough, so Véronique decides to take the business of expiation into her own hands. First—the reference to the repentant Magdalene is obvious and explicit—she hacks off her magnificent blond hair and then, feeling that she has still not humbled herself enough, goes to a backstreet fence-cum-pimp-cum-abortionist—it being 1887, his name is, inevitably, Judas Nathan—whom she asks, at a price, too pull out all her teeth without any anesthetic whatsoever. There follows one

of the most appalling scenes in the whole of French literature as Véronique
settles into a leather armchair, tilts back her head to expose a "double row
of luminous teeth" to the attentions of her chosen "torturer" (*tortionnaire*).
Sade and de Maistre meet as "streams of foaming blood" froth from her
mouth onto the canvas apron Nathan has tied round her neck. After the top
row of teeth has been completely removed, the "executioner" wants to stop,
but the "astounding martyr" (*l'étonnante martyre*) signals to him to press
on. When the ordeal (*supplice*) is over, Véronique looks at her "mutilated
martyr's head" (*tête mutilée de martyre*) and, "with that frenzy for humiliation which is one of the features of mystical love, picked up the hand of the
filthy bandit (*l'immonde bandit*) through which every kind of foulness had
passed, and kissed it—as the instrument of her martyrdom!—with her
bloody and misshapen lips" (D 219–21).

After this "astounding hostocaustal prank" (*étonnante fredaine d'holocauste,* D 257) the once "flamboyant sea-swell" of Véronique's hair grows
back as best it can, but henceforth she keeps it tied up in a "despotic and
monstrous chignon," held in check by all manner of pins, combs, and grips
so as not to offend God with the former exuberance of its growth. Her
mouth, however, the site of the first sin and, in the words of Colossians 3:8,
of "anger, wrath, malice, blasphemy, filthy communication," not to mention of old-fashioned gluttony and lust, is damaged beyond repair if not, in
Bloy's soteriological vision, beyond redemption. The "bestially exquisite
lips" that used to "crush the nerves, gobble up the bone-marrow [*fripait les
moelles*] [and] unhinge the brains" of every man that they touched have
now become the flabby embouchure of a toothless hag, and "the demon of
Lechery [*Stupre*], long since expropriated from [his] former patrimony, has
at last irrevocably removed himself from these ruins amongst which there
was no longer even a humble stump of a tooth on which he could sit himself
down" (D 260–61). With her shorn locks and ravaged mouth, Véronique
resembles the victims of a future real holocaust, hair and gold teeth removed for sale at a profit, except that Véronique has undergone this savage
coiffure and dentistry willingly and while still alive and that, perversely, her
"dentist" is a Jew named, with vile Christological symmetry, Judas Nathan,
son of David and betrayer of Christ.

Hair, Holiness, and Sacrifice

The fate of Véronique's magnificent locks may suggest to the reader how
often hair—primarily, but not exclusively, female hair—has featured in this
book. Here, supplemented where appropriate with additional examples, are
the principal instances:

Camille Claudel. Writing eight years after her death, in 1951, Paul
Claudel recalled his sister's "powerful fleece of hair of the chestnut brown

the English call *auburn,* which went down to her hips." In addition, she was renowned, particularly after the break with Rodin, for her extravagant taste for hairstyles and hats incorporating "ribbons or plumes combining the gaudiest and least harmonious of colors," in keeping, perhaps, with her increasingly wayward behavior; it is thus that she represented herself in a plaster model entitled "Autoportrait avec coiffure de feuilles et de fruits" of which only a photograph now survives. Her hair and hairstyles are caricatured in the snakes writhing on the decapitated head of the Medusa—conceivably a self-portrait—in her *Persée et la Gorgone* of 1902 and in the remarkable spider's web of hair, resembling nothing so much as the matted dreadlocks of a Rastafarian, that sprouts from the head of the aged crone Clotho, one of the Three Fates, in her great marble of that name (now lost) sculpted in 1895, inspired by, but surpassing, the filthy, tangled hair of Donatello's emaciated *Maddalena* of c. 1455. Yet when her brother last saw her, at the asylum at Montdevergues, all that appeared beneath the "vague bonnet" she was wearing was "this skull, like a disaffected monument, whose magnificent architecture [was] revealed to me."[165]

Simone Weil. Both men and women were shocked by Simone Weil's frizzy unkempt hair sticking out from under her beret almost as much as they were by her shapeless clothes and generally unwashed appearance. In *Le Bleu du ciel,* "Lazare's short, stiff, uncombed hair" sticking out "like crow's wings on each side of her face" set the seal on her "macabre appearance":[166] this really is someone back from the dead or shortly bound to join them.

Colette Peignot. Dirty's hair is quite different: "Her shoulders were bare to the point of indecency. In that light I found the glitter of her blond hair unbearable." Like some drunken parody of the Magdalene, "she was sobbing so hard her hair was drenched in tears."[167] In some fragmentary notes, Colette Peignot refers to Bataille and herself as "Vérax and La Chevelure in search of the world and life,"[168] and there is also a poem in praise of a circus performer named Esmerelda who, naked, rides a horse bareback with "her long broad / red hair / falling and merging with / the mane / the tail [*la queue*=penis]" of the horse.[169] While they were living together, Bataille published an article entitled "Chevelures" (December 1937) in which "useless hair" (*l'inutile chevelure*), unloosed and free-flowing like water or fire, is seen as an expression of self-dilapidation and *dépense,* "like the irremediable losing of self that is a river."[170] Colette usually wore her hair short or tightly pinned up. The last photograph of her on her deathbed, however, shows her hair flowing down to her shoulders, as though she had found in death the release and fulfillment that eluded her in life. On the other hand, like many women of her time, she appears to have revered the image of the *Inconnue de la Seine* whose neatly coiffured hair symbolized the triumph of form over the dissolving powers of the water in which she met her death.

Thérèse Martin. When Thérèse, aged fourteen, went to Bayeux in October 1887 to seek the bishop's permission to enter the Carmel underage, she abandoned the little-girl curls that symbolized her dependence on her father, put her hair up, and was transformed from a prepubescent girl into a confident young woman. When she took her final vows, her hair was shorn but, in keeping with Carmelite custom, the tresses were kept as a memorial of her sacrifice.

Mary Magdalene. Mary Magdalene's hair was as charged with sacred mana as her tears, and writers and artists dwelt almost fetishistically on its abundance and beauty. In his would-be naturalistic updating of the Magdalene theme, *Madeleine Férat* (1869)—the surname suggests ferocious or feral—Zola, following Flaubert's earlier practice in *Madame Bovary,* ties up or loosens his heroine's magnificent head of hair in accordance with the state of her passions—"a single thick and fiery tide" of red hair falling, scarcely checked, onto her shoulders when she is erotically restless, the same hair "carefully plaited" when she first marries and then loosened again as she falls into adultery.[171] Writing much later and from a very different perspective, the Catholic poet Pierre Emmanuel sees the unfettering of her hair as the very essence of "the great power of self-abandonment / Of being Mary Magdalene"; in the same work "Acathiste de Madeleine" (1973), Emmanuel even calls the Magdalene the "Sainte de l'abîme," the name Leiris and others had given to "Laure."[172] The Magdalene's hair links up with other talismanic fin de siècle and belle époque locks. Lacordaire's image of the *Magna Peccatrix* wiping Christ's feet "with the linen of her hair"[173] unexpectedly suggests "La fille aux cheveux de lin" of Claude Debussy's first book of *Préludes* (1910), which, in its turn, suggests the still more famous tresses of *Pelléas et Mélisande* (1902, based on play by Maurice Maeterlinck of 1893) which, says Pelléas to their owner, "flee from me into the branches of the willow . . . they quiver, flutter, tremble in my hands like golden birds; they love me, they love me, a thousand times more than you!"[174]

Madeleine Lebouc. As befits her name, Madeleine Lebouc was obsessed by human hair (not so much by her own, which, in the photographs taken at La Salpêtrière, is straight, short, and sparse) as by the "piles of women's hair" that, in her fantasies, she discovered in a cave in the fortified zone on the outskirts of Paris: "It was for me a revelation of the unspeakable crimes that are committed each day in Paris."[175] Jacques Maître makes the comparison with the mountains of human hair discovered in concentration camps half a century later.[176]

Eva Lavallière. After her conversion and, specifically, after reading a passage from Angela di Foligno in which Christ tells the saint that he has "expiated" for all her perfumes and cosmetics, Eva Lavallière, that other devotee of the Magdalene, threw all her toiletries into the fire and let her hair grow as it would, back into its *"true* color, and white predominates: so what?"[177]

The examples given so far suggest a relatively straightforward opposition: long, free-flowing hair is equated with life, passion, self-abandonment, love, while cropped or tightly restrained hair connotes repression, self-denial, self-enclosure, death. Let us add density, complexity, and precision by bringing in some of the second-string characters, most of them men, who have appeared now and then in this book.

First, three close-cropped writers, two of them world-famous, one less well known:

Baudelaire. Some time in October 1857, just weeks after, first, the condemnation of *Les Fleurs du Mal* and, second, the publication of his first poems in prose that included the famous "Un hémisphère dans une chevelure" (then simply entitled "La Chevelure"), Baudelaire was seen by the Goncourt brothers at the Café Riche "tieless, bare-necked, head shaven, truly dressed like a condemned man awaiting the guillotine" (*en vraie toilette de guillotiné*). With "the head of a madman," he defended himself against the charge of obscenity, "striving for the tone of a Saint-Just and attaining it,"[178] victim and executioner characteristically rolled into one.

Jean Genet. The work of the one-time jailbird Jean Genet (1910–86) contains, not surprisingly, a gallery of cropped pates. *Miracle de la Rose* (1946) begins with a batch of prisoners being transferred at a station from train to Black Maria (*panier à salade*) en route for the Centrale of Fontrevault, a former monastery near Saumur now used as a prison; Genet is struck by "the sadness of young shaven-headed lads watching the girls going by."[179] Each week, the prisoners have their hair cropped by a fellow inmate, and they resemble nothing so much as a group of "monks and nuns" performing some "forgotten liturgy."[180] Tonsured, the prisoners are the Carthusians and Trappists of the modern secular state: "The Centrale lived like a cathedral at Midnight Mass. We continued the tradition of monks getting up in the middle of the night, in silence. We belonged to the Middle Ages."[181] The hair of the condemned murderer Harcamone has been allowed to grow—possibly to permit the ritual *toilette du guillotiné* in due course—"the curls were entangled on his brow with the canny cruelty of the twists of a crown of thorns":[182] every *guillotiné* renews the Passion of Christ.[183] The close-cropped hair that Genet retained for a lifetime may plausibly be "read" as a memorial to his years in Fontrevault and Fresnes and as an act of homage toward such *guillotinés* as Harcamone and Maurice Pilorge (1914–39), the hero of Genet's long poem *Le Condamné à mort* of 1942.[184] (Women prisoners, it seems, did not have their hair cropped but wore it tucked up into bonnets that hid it and made them virtually identical to each other—again in the manner of the nuns in the former convents that now served as prisons.)[185]

Michel Leiris. In *L'Age d'homme* (1939), Bataille's close friend, the former surrealist Michel Leiris (1901–90) describes how, in the early 1920s, he had his hair closely cropped and asked a painter friend, probably André

Masson who later illustrated his great essay on bullfighting *Miroir de la tau-romachie* (1938), to "trace with a razor a line [*une raie*] running from the nape of my neck to the middle of my forehead" as an image—Leiris was deeply "into" esotericism at the time—of "the geometrical figure that I would like to have been, a sort of divine Adam or constellation." A (highly intellectual) skinhead *avant la lettre,* Leiris describes this striking coiffure as "a symbolic attempt at *mineralization,*"[186] a quasi-magical means of countering what was soft, fleshy, and merely material both within and without him and so of "spiritualizing" both body and world which, in tune with the gnostic philosophy he was reading, he viewed as irremediably fallen and corrupt. Nor was his "mineralizing" project, in fantasy at least, confined to himself: as he puts it in *Le Point cardinal* (1927), "the advance to perfection proceeds by way of mineralization." In his surrealist "novel" *Aurora* (first published in 1946, but written in the 1920s), Leiris's anagrammatic alter ego Damoclès Siriel not only shaves his head so as to have "mineral rather than vegetable hair,"[187] but has his (female) sexual partners—women being that much more "vegetable" than men by dint not only of their normally longer hair but of the cyclicity of their periods—"delicately shaved and de-pilated to rid them of anything animal." Making love, himself auto-petri-fied, to these "alabaster women with skulls more naked than pebbles," it seems to "Siriel" that he has transcended matter entirely and gained access, while still alive, to the mineralized realm of the dead, cheating death magically by simulating the stonelike condition of a corpse. But the moment of orgasm is "a great debacle"—the word in French also means the melting of ice—and "Siriel" and his partners are instantly restored to the condition of "flexuous humanity" and the "dirty waters" it consists of.[188]

On the other hand, Leiris—he was hardly alone in this[189]—was obsessed as a child, adolescent, and young man with the story of Samson and Delilah. It was not just that, conventionally enough, he saw in the latter's cutting of the hair of the former a figure of decapitation and castration[190] but that, in the performance of Saint-Saëns's *Samson et Dalila* (1877) that he saw as a boy, the part of the "killer" (*tueuse*), as he calls her, was played by none other by his own "Tante Lise," by no means a bald prima donna, whose impressive physique, passionate delivery, and, not least, her flowing black hair will, in *Fibrilles* (1966), the third volume of his autobiographical tetralogy *La Règle du jeu,* make of her the very incarnation of artistic authenticity. In real life, Leiris was also, by is own admission, strongly attracted to women, particularly women of color, whose cropped or shaved heads conferred on them an "inhuman beauty," a "shattering distinction,"[191] women such as Emawayish, the adept of the Ethiopian possession cult *zâr* whom Leiris, an anthropologist by profession, met and fell in something like love with at the conclusion of the trans-African Dakar-Djibouri mission of 1931–33 recorded in *L'Afrique fantôme* (1934), or Khadidja, the *fille à soldats* met while on military service in North Africa in 1939–40 and evoked with a wonderful blend of tenderness, lyricism, and irony in the second volume of the tetralogy, *Fourbis* (1955).

It is, therefore, of no little significance that if there was one part of Colette Peignot's person that summed up her truly sacred potency for Leiris, it was, precisely, her *forehead*. In *Fourbis,* immediately after recalling how he and Khadidja, his "angel of death," once urinated together after drinking, he evokes an earlier occasion with a drunken woman in Montmartre when he steadied her and helped her vomit by placing his hand in reassurance on her forehead. The woman is, of course, Colette in her "dirty" days, and it is a gesture that he repeats when, a few years later, death has already consigned her—she who boasted to her mother that she had a heart of marble, not of stone, "because it's colder"—to a definitive condition of "marble-like impenetrability."[192] Finally, to complete the nexus of images, it is logical that Leiris's earlier emblem of artistic authenticity, the matador, should be evoked essentially in terms of a mineral-like sculptural hardness. "Like a stone causing the water to ripple,"[193] he stands up to the bull—that is, nature, destiny, death—with all the "rigidity of a man on his own" (*roideur d'homme seul*)[194] in the middle of the arena, and often, in the course of the faena, his headgear comes adrift, or is thrown off, to reveal, not a bald pate, but a close-cropped head haloed in sweat, ready to "receive / the crown with its nerve-veins of anguish."[195] A sacrificer who runs the risk of being sacrificed himself, the matador offers himself up for a crown of glory and triumph, knowing that his fate may be a crown of thorns instead.

The connection between cropped hair, sacrifice, and death seems clearly established. The shaven-headed man or woman stands at the portals, either as sacrificer or victim, or both, of the domain of the dead. How appropriate, to say the least, that the paradigmatic sacrifice of Christ was staged at "the palace Golgotha, which is, being interpreted, The place of a skull" (Mark 15:22, cf. Calvary derived from *calvus,* Latin for bald).

Joan of Arc. Now, if ever, is the moment to bring in the most famous urchin-cut in history. For Joan of Arc's accusers at her trial in January through May 1431, the fact that, in the words of the charge sheet, she wore her hair "cropped short and round in the fashion of young men" fits the rest of her male appearance and dress-shirt, breeches, doublet, mantle, leggings, "a close-cut cap, tight-fitting boots or buskins, long spurs, sword, dagger, breastplate, lance and other arms in the style of a man-at-arms"—and proved beyond doubt that here, truly, was a heretic, a witch, and a deliberate flouter of natural and divine law: "Doth not even nature itself teach you, that, if a man have long hair, it is a shame unto him? But if a woman have long hair, it is a glory to her: for her hair is given her for a covering" (I Corinthians 11:14–15).[196]

Many of the most famous nineteenth- and early twentieth-century images of Joan do indeed depict her with short (but not cropped) hair,[197] but many do not, including the most famous of all, Jean-Dominique Ingres's imposing painting of 1854 depicting Joan at the coronation of Charles VII at Reims in 1429, haloed, clad in armor, and holding her battle-standard, with her hair, admittedly in a kind of pigtail, descending well below the nape of her neck.[198] Indeed, many artists follow Rubens's great painting of 1620 of the Maid at prayer and give her the flowing auburn locks of a Mary Magdalene in armor; significantly, when Thérèse played the role of Joan in the play she had written in 1894 (and almost burned to death in the process), photographs show her wearing a black wig over her *toque,* the white canvas cap that Carmelite sisters wore under their veils.[199] Nor do the vast number of late nineteenth- and early twentieth-century literary works devoted to Joan—works by Péguy, Bernanos, Claudel, and Anouilh, to name only the best and best-known French treatments of the theme[200]—dwell unduly, if at all, on the cutting of her hair, perhaps so as not to detract from the femininity of the Maid, which is of crucial significance for at least the first three writers concerned. Even Bloy's wartime *Jeanne d'Arc et l'Allemagne* (1915), replete though it is with explicit analogies between Joan, "the highest miracle since the Incarnation," and Christ[201] and with parallels too numerous and obvious to detail between Calvary and the "appalling combustion of the Place du Vieux-Marché [in Rouen],"[202] makes no mention of the Maid's hair, long, short, or cropped. It seems, in short, that between 1431 and the first Joan-inspired films of the twentieth century, no one paid much attention to the length or quality of her hair. Its talismanic significance is largely an invention of the cinema, for reasons that are worth briefly considering.

It appears that over thirty films, perhaps many more, have been made about Joan,[203] from Georges Méliès's pioneering fifteen-minute sequence of twelve tableaux from her life made in 1900 to Luc Besson's *Jeanne d'Arc* of 1999, at 167 minutes over ten times as long, but a mere *court métrage* compared to Jacques Rivette's interminable five hours plus *Jeanne la Pucelle* of 1994. Some of the greatest as well as some of the most pretentious directors have treated the theme—Cecil B. DeMille (*Joan the Woman* [1916]), Carl Theodor Dreyer (*La Passion de Jeanne d'Arc* [1927–28]), Victor Fleming (*Joan of Arc* [1948]), Otto Preminger (*Saint Joan* [1957]), and Robert Bresson (*Le Procès de Jeanne d'Arc* [1962])—and, except in the first, the cutting of Joan's hair is one of the film's pivotal scenes. Sometimes the results are merely cute (Fleming's Ingrid Bergman) or grotesque (Besson's strapping, bug-eyed Milla Jovovich) or simultaneously sexy and sinister, as in Preminger's Jean Seberg, chosen, aged seventeen, as Joan was by God, after a much publicized international "search" involving eighteen thousand wannabe Maids, and fated, after her still greater urchin-cut triumphs in Godard's *A bout de souffle* (1959), to descend into depression, alcoholism, and eventual suicide, aged forty-one, in 1979: No head, it seems, can be shorn with impunity.

From all the hours upon hours of film about Joan, the present discussion will limit itself to the searing eighty-five minutes of one of the first, and without question the greatest, cinematic treatments of her story, *La Passion de Jeanne d'Arc,* made in 1927 and first shown the following year, by the Danish director Carl Theodor Dreyer (1889–1968). Using French actors and based on a text by Joseph Delteil (1894–1978), briefly a member of the Surrealist group from which he was expelled when his novel-cum-hagiography *Jeanne d'Arc* won the Prix Fémina in 1925, the film is a masterpiece of silent cinema, which, in the version currently available on video, reconstituted from original footage previously thought to be lost, truly is silent, with the Albinoni *Adagio* and music by Vivaldi, Scarlatti, Bach, and Palestrina that the film historian Lo Duca had substituted for Dreyer's original plain-chant in his 1952 re-creation of the original now completely removed. The experience of watching this "cinematic poem," as Marina Warner rightly calls it,[204] is all the more intense as a result.

The principal themes and images of *La Passion de Jeanne d'Arc* are contained within its title. The deeds of derring-do are over, and this is Joan's Passion, closely modeled on the Passion of her Savior, with virtually every frame replete with Christological parallel and allusion. Thus Joan's trial repeats that of Jesus before the Sanhedrin in which, with all the meekness and defiance of her Savior, Joan refuses to defend herself but turns her accusers accusations back on them in the manner of Jesus's "Ye say that I am" to the priests and the scribes (Luke 22:70). In a scene inspired by the traditional theme of the mocking of Christ, and particularly by the well-known depictions of Christ as Holy Simpleton by Hans von Memling and Hieronymus Bosch, a wicker crown that Joan has been fashioning is placed lopsidedly on her head by her jailers, and a feathered arrow, like the reed of the Passion (Matthew 27:29), is placed in her right hand in lieu of a scepter. A superscription reminiscent of Pilate's "This is the King of the Jews" is nailed to the stake on which she is burned, proclaiming her heresy and apostasy, and the soldiers' attack on the protesting crowd after her death recalls the Massacre of the Innocent: The final image of the film is the nail driven into the stake. But it is the image of the bald head, endlessly repeated, varied, and transposed, that, in the present context is the most arresting cinematic motif. During her trial, Joan's hair is short, cut close to her head, but not yet shaved or cropped. Her head is continually juxtaposed and contrasted to the tonsured and bald pates of her judges, to the round metal helmets of the guards, barely distinguishable from the standard French army helmet of the Great War, and to the skull-caps both of the clerics and of the acrobats who entertain the crowd outside the court, twisting their limbs into grotesque parodies of a body being tortured or crucified. The replication of the motif is made even more effective by Dreyer's frequent practice of directing the camera just above or just below the eyes of his actors; the top of the head, covered or uncovered, is somehow sliced apart from the rest of the head and body that bear it. Joan is eventually shorn as close to the head as is possible, rendering the actress, Renée Falconetti, even more naked and exposed, tears not so much streaming as running one by one down her cheeks, as the camera's interrogation of her face becomes at once more cruel and more loving. What remained of her hair is swept into a dustpan along with her "crown," and she is led out from the courtroom onto the set version of the Place du Vieux-Marché in Rouen. Her bald head is again echoed in the rounded domes of the church and other buildings on the square, in the head of a baby sucking at the dome-shaped breast of its mother in the crowd, and even in the convex curve of the cobblestones over which she and her guards move to the pyre. The film becomes a kind of cubist painting in which a geometrical form, the dome or the curve, is virtually detached from the objects that sustain it, making the film both brutally realistic and sublimely spiritual and abstract, with the unforgettable face of Falconetti etched, like that of a Flemish painter's Christ crowned with thorns with all the suffering, sadness, and sins of the world.

"Joan of Arc's chief attraction [for film-makers]," the film historian Robin Blaetz has written, "may lie in the chance to pornographically depict the death of this potent female with chains, ropes, and lascivious camera work."[205] There is indeed an uncomfortable similarity, even in the greatest film versions of the theme, between Joan's humiliation, torture, and death and such scenes as the following in the inevitable *Histoire d'O* in which Sir Stephen belies his martyr's name and takes on the role of chief martyrizer, having already branded her with his initials (SS ?):

> He fixed the nails. At the end of the handles of the scourges and riding whips there were rings which could be attached to the hooks of the nails, making it easy to remove and return each of the whips; with the handcuffs and the coiled ropes, O would thus have, opposite her bed, the complete panoply of her instruments of torture. It was a handsome panoply, as harmonious as the wheel and the pincers in pictures representing the martyr Saint Catherine, as the hammer and the nails, the crown of thorns, the lance and the scourges in pictures of the Passion.[206]

Almost all these motifs are present in *La Passion de Jeanne d'Arc,* even the Saint Catherine's Wheel that, as in the Golgotha and hell-scenes of Brueghel and Bosch, pushes into the sky at the place of execution. In Dreyer's film, unlike others, we do not see Joan being tortured, but the sight of blood being drawn from her inner arm when she faints stands for all the blood she has shed (and, be it added, caused to be shed) in the service of her Lord. For Joan is in love with her Bridegroom and, like O, positively welcomes suffering as expression and proof of her love. Ultimately, the tears of Agape are never far removed from the tears of Eros (cf. Bataille, *Les Lames d'Eros* [1961]), and no treatment of the Joan theme is ever entirely free of its sado-masochistic component.

One of Falconetti's fellow actors in *La Passion de Jeanne d'Arc,* playing the role of Jean Massier, one of the few officials at Joan's trial to show her any sympathy, was Antonin Artaud (1896–1948), not with the long lank black hair of the familiar photographs, but tonsured, with a face already as replete as Falconetti's with desolation and loss. A far less well-known, but, if anything, even more troubling image of Artaud than the usual ravaged, flop-haired look was taken on his arrival, in February 1943, at the asylum in Rodez where he would spend the next three years of his life. The photograph, taken by the asylum's director Gaston Ferdière, who doubled as an alienist and would-be surrealist poet, shows Artaud with closely cropped hair, the result of a shearing during his previous internment in the asylum of Ville-Evrard (where Camille Claudel was also interned in 1913–14) in the eastern suburbs of Paris; it is presumably with this institutional coiffure that Artaud underwent electroshock treatment on no fewer than fifty-one occasions between June 1943 and December 1944.[207] Artaud in turn suggests Vincent Van Gogh, "society's suicide" and subject of his lacerating text of 1947,[208] and the terrifying sequence of self-portraits of, in particular, 1887–89, each showing a doomed man in virtual *toilette de guillotiné,* culminating in the almost completely shaven skull that stares out from the 1888 self-portrait now in the Art Museum in Cambridge, Massachusetts: perhaps the closest approximation to a living death's head in art, an *écorché* flayed and still palpitating before us.[209] And what of Artaud's great champion, Michel Foucault (1926–84), whose unforgettable Kojack-style profile seems eerily fitted to the pattern of sadomasochistic activities, "alternatively victim and executioner" in authentic Baudelairean fashion, that surely contributed to his AIDS-related death in 1984? Not for nothing is James Miller's excellent and revealing biography of the philosopher entitled *The Passion of Michel Foucault.*[210]

To this impressive list of individuals may be added whole communities of cropheads. Reporting on the penitentiary colony in Cayenne (French Guiana) for *Le Petit Parisien* in 1923, the great investigative journalist Albert Londres (1884–1932) encountered squads of convicts with hair "cut in jagged lines [*en escalier*] and totally naked," as well as similarly shorn individuals, one "a billiard ball endowed with eyes," another in a prison performance of Dumas *père*'s melodrama *La Tour de Nesle* (1832), in drag but wigless, "her" head shaven and arms covered in tattoos, playing the part of the infamous Marguerite de Bourgogne (c. 1290–1315) who, having taken her fill, reputedly had her lovers bound and thrown from the tower into the Seine and who, in retribution, was shorn as an adulteress, repudiated and strangled on the orders of her multiply cuckolded husband, King Louis X.[211] Soldiers in the French army were not normally shorn, except those drafted, for persistent indiscipline, into the notorious Bat' d'Af' (Bataillon d'Afrique) in which beards and mustaches, as well as hair, were removed:[212] even in Cayenne convicts could have beards. Most humiliating and threatening of all was the shearing of concentration camp prisoners who, in the words of David Rousset, a veteran of the camps, became "strangers to themselves" once shorn of their hair as they entered *l'univers concentrationnaire*.[213] Another, Edmond Michelet (1899–1970), interned in Dachau from 1943 to 1945, wrote of his and his fellow prisoners' sense of an "immense denudation," a "total bereavement" (*dépouillement*), at the loss of one of the principal signs of their personal and civic identity; echoing Genet's analogy of prison and monastery, Michelet, a Catholic (and possible candidate for sainthood) and future Gaullist minister who entered Dachau, as he says, on the feast of Notre-Dame des Sept Douleurs, describes the camp as the "Saint John of Latran, the mother church of all concentration camps" in which the prisoners, involuntary monks, tonsured and clad in coarse Lenten dress, do penance under the less than charitable surveillance of their sadistic superiors.[214]

To move, after such historical horrors, to the annual midsummer ritual of the Tour de France might seem an unpardonable levity, had not many French writers, from the Tour's very inception (1903), perceived some subliminal analogy between the ordeal of its unrelenting daily stages and Christianity's foundational sacrifice. A year after investigating the convict settlements of Cayenne, Albert Londres turned his attention to another form of hard labor, that of "the convicts of the road," *les forçats de la route*, those crusaders (*croisés*) on two wheels who, every year, set out on what they themselves call the *Tour de souffrance* on, still more evocatively, the *Calvaire du Tour de France*. The contestants are not of course necessarily cropheaded, but their close-fitting caps, "soiled, stained and reddened with blood," remind Londres of "the bandages of the war-wounded"—no trivial comparison in 1924.[215] Wearing the sacramental *maillot jaune* (yellow jersey), the Tour leader is a miraculously triumphant sacrificial victim whose Via Dolorosa through the ancient provinces of France is watched or followed by the bulk of the nation as, stage by stage, and station by station, he heads toward the Jerusalem of Paris, binding, as he does so, the *sacrifiants* into a cohesive communal unity as occurs in any sacrificial rite. Still more potent is the cyclist who never wins, the eternally second- or third-placed like the great Raymond Poulidor (born 1936), who, in the words of the novelist Antoine Blondin (1922–91), *L'Equipe's* chief commentator on the Tour from 1954 to 1983, became for his countless admirers "a kind of Christ of the outrages of fate, a Christ of the everyday who came down to earth to redeem their petty miseries, with no message, but not without 'passion,'" his endlessly postponed Eldorado the very image of "our abortive dreams and disappointed ambitions."[216]

Many years before "Poupou" began his annual ascent of Calvary, Alfred Jarry (1973–1907), in a text entitled "La Passion considérée comme course de côte" (The Passion Considered as a Mountain Climb), recast the entire Crucifixion narrative in terms of a cycle race up the "fourteen bends" of Mount Golgotha. Barabbas declares forfeit, Pontius Pilate signals the start and keeps time with a water-clock (in which from time to time he washes his hands), Saint Matthew reports the event for the Judeo-Roman version of *L'Equipe,* the two thieves make an early break when Jesus sustains a puncture—thorns on the road—and has to carry his bicycle, crosslike, up the hill, falling at the third, seventh and eleventh bends, until his trainer, Simon of Cyrene, relieves him of the burden; Veronica, an ambitious young reporter, does not wipe his brow with her handkerchief but captures his image with her Kodak. By the time they reach the "twelfth bend," Jesus and the two thieves are running dead heat, but all three then undergo "the deplorable accident of which everyone has heard," whereafter Jesus definitely breaks free from the *peloton* of mere mortals and triumphs by ascending into heaven "like an aviator."[217] Mere facetious blasphemy? Certainly, but no one who has seen film of the British cyclist Tommy Simpson, high on a lethal cocktail of amphetamines and alcohol, pushing himself literally to death on the redoubtable Mont Ventoux in 1967 will balk at the Christological comparison, Simpson, that "expiatory victim in the midst of lies [about drug use on the Tour]" who "died for all the other [drug-using cyclists]" (Jean-Emmanuel Ducoin, *L'Equipe,* 21 July 2002).[218] In his classic essay "Le Tour de France comme épopée," written ten years before Tommy Simpson's drug-induced "martyrdom," Roland Barthes prophetically likened Mont Ventoux to a "veritable Moloch," "a god of Evil to whom sacrifice must be offered."[219] To complete the network of images, the cyclists themselves call the mountain *le Chauve* (the "Bald One," cf. Calvary) on account of its total absence of vegetation and cruelly reverberating light, a "chalky mass tonsured like a monk" (Ducoin, *L'Humanite',* 22 July 2002),[220] at whose summit the Simpson memorial stands littered with the impromptu instruments of his "passion" left there by admirers: a water bottle, an inner tube, a floppy white cap . . .

Les Tondues

Everything that precedes is obviously leading up to the *tondues* (and very occasional *tondu*) and *tondeurs* (and occasional *tondeuses*) of 1944–45. Since the publication of Alain Brossat's pathbreaking *Les Tondues: Un carnaval moche* in 1992, the phenomenon of the "shearing" (*la tonte*) of the hair of women accused of sleeping with German men or of otherwise "collaborating" with occupiers has inspired an abundance of writing, much of it excellent, in which, however, empirical evidence still lags behind theoretical speculation. From the best writers on the subject—Brossat himself, Fabrice Virgili,[221] Corran Laurens,[222] the late Claire Duchen,[223] Hanna Diamond[224]—the broad lineaments of the phenomenon are now clear, though some dispute remains as to the centrality of gender to the issues at stake. Shearing incidents are reported as early as March 1944 (three months before D-Day), peaked in June and July of that year, and briefly recrudesced in 1945, after the return to France of concentration camp deportees. Shearing occurred in seventy-seven of the then ninety departments of France, in both rural and urban contexts, and figures of between 100,000 and 300,000 victims have been mooted. The shearing of men is reported in seven departments, but the overwhelming majority of victims were women, with the unmarried, divorced, widowed, poor, and poorly educated most likely to be targeted. The shearers, correspondingly and conversely, were overwhelmingly men, though cases of *tondeuses* are certainly reported. Many shearings were sanctioned and performed by accredited resistance organizations, but, equally, many were spontaneous and unstructured, with, by widespread repute, individuals with less than spotless resistance records likely to be in the van of the new-style witch hunts. Any hint, however insubstantial, of "horizontal collaboration" with the enemy was grounds for retribution, and women were also singled out as informers, blackmarketeers, and companions of *miliciens*. Daughters, sisters, and other relatives were also liable to be, quite literally, tarred with the same brush, the daubing of swastikas on foreheads, shoulders, and backs being a routine component of the ritual. On the other hand, female "horizontal" collaborators were much less likely to be killed than the male "vertical" variety, leading Brossat to call shearing a "décapitation douce,"[225] a "gentle" decapitation in which the shearing of the hair simulates—but does no more than simulate—actual beheading. Shearing is, again in Brossat's words, a carnivalesque occasion, an "ugly carnival," to be sure, but one that, however extreme, remains *just* this side of actual shedding of blood, which is in no way to minimize its short- or long-term consequences for the victims (or "patientes" as they were sometimes archly called).[226] *La tonte* is thus, in a sense, a perversion of the play principle, a ludic event that *alludes* to decapitation and creates an *illusion* of bloody tragedy but in which the victim finally *eludes* mortal retribution, at the cost, it is true, of many months, years, or even a lifetime of reclusion, rejection, and humiliation; the sight of *la femme au turban*, a woman wearing a bandanna or headscarf, was long a stimulus to derision and abuse, even if the woman so attired had conventional-length hair and was innocent of any form of collaboration, horizontal or otherwise.[227] An ugly carnival, shearing is ultimately "only" vicious sport, the Tour de France being, "accidents" notwithstanding, a version of the bullfight in which, as Albert Londres said,[228] there is no *mise à mort* at the end of the corrida.

Shearing was a traditional punishment for female adultery, administered to Marguerite de Bourgogne among others, and female heretics were also punished in this way, the shedding of their hair being regarded as the necessary precondition of a possible "rebirth" into orthodoxy;[229] it is striking that *tondues* became, inter alia, fully grown newborn babies, hairless and vulnerable, pending a *possible* reincorporation into the "believing" community from which they had been incompletely and temporarily expelled. More recently, French women had been shorn for sleeping with Germans in those parts of France occupied during the First World War, and, correspondingly, German women had been similarly treated for sleeping with French soldiers—some of them, still more scandalously, *tirailleurs sénégalais*—during the postwar occupation of the Rhineland; republican women were shorn by nationalists in the Spanish civil war, and the tarring and feathering of Ulster Catholic women suspected of "horizontal collaboration" with British soldiers was at one time a regular feature of the Northern Ireland crisis.[230]

All this, plus the unquestionable fact that the *tondeurs* were, in their overwhelming majority men (with women commonly looking on, sometimes in complicity with the shearers, sometimes in covert sympathy for the victim, occasionally in open hostility to the whole persecutory ritual,[231] and, not infrequently, with a conflicting combination of these emotions), clearly points to the centrality of the issue of gender: Women were punished *as women*, predominantly by men acting *as men*. Given the traditional figuration of France as a woman, the *tondue* may be seen as an anti-Marianne—in at least one Liberation poster, Marianne was represented with the stigmata of Christ[232]—a slut on whom men take revenge for their own failure, in 1940, to protect their own womenfolk against the invader; it is as though, four years later, the *tondeurs* "take the place of the powerful (and attractive?) male invader in a symbolic re-enactment and reworking" of the earlier invasion,[233] fictively reoccupying and repossessing "their" women in a sordid mini-blitzkrieg of their own. It has been argued that, in view of the frequent absence of men as prisoners of war and conscripted laborers in Germany, French women were, to repeat and half-parody a famous statement by Sartre, "never so free as they were under the Occupation."[234] Now, in 1944, men reoccupy the sexual space of which they had been (partly) dispossessed by the Germans, the Resistance is defined as "male," collaboration as "female," and the gender boundaries, disturbed and partly abolished by the defeat of 1940 that, so to speak, "feminized" French men, were reestablished to the evident advantage of men. The *tondues* were both dehumanized and desexed, rendered almost identical and interchangeable, indistinguishable from each other save by such clothes as were left on their body, and marked with the swastika that, like the mark of Cain, both stigmatized them and, paradoxically, protected them from death. They came, curiously, to resemble concentration camp survivors, shaven but alive, living corpses whose mortification—rather than actual *mise à mort*—permitted, like every sacrificial ritual, the reconstitution of the community to the obvious advantage, to repeat, of the traditionally dominant element, men.

Only Brossat points out, and then merely in passing,[235] how closely the notion and action of shearing repeats one of the key texts and images of Christianity, namely Acts 8:32: "He was led as a sheep to the slaughter; and like a lamb dumb before his shearer, so opened he not his mouth." The Vulgate makes the parallel even more stark: *Tamquam agnus coram tondente se obmutuit et non aperuit os suum.* In their humiliation and rejection, the bald women repeated in miniature and in part the paradigmatic sacrifice on the bald skull of Golgotha, the swastikas daubed on their bodies miming both the crown of thorns and marks of the nails and Pontius Pilate's so-called superscription "in letters of Greek, and Latin, and Hebrew" above the cross (Luke 23:38), *I-N-R-I,* "THIS IS THE KING OF THE JEWS," this is, or was, the whore of the Boches. Like "the stone which the builder rejected" (Matthew: 22:42, etc.), the *tondue* was first symbolically cast out and then brought back as an unacknowledged "head of the corner" of the reconstituted male republican order, just as, in due course, Christ was reincorporated by the very power—Rome—that, infinitely more than the by now almost mythical "Jews," had been responsible for his death in the first place. And, just as Rome made discursive concessions to the teachings of Christ while using them to shore up its secular power, so in 1944 the male republican order conceded suffrage to women, confident, surely, that they could deflect it to their own political and ideological advantage; the benefits of rituals of sacrifice seldom accrue to the human category from which the victims are taken but, almost invariably, to the *sacrificateurs.*

Similarly—and here we touch on dangerous ground—no writer really confronts the erotic appeal of the partly clad, humiliated, and submissive *tondue.* Leiris says nothing of *la tonte,* not surprisingly given how closely its shaven, sculpturelike, and usually inexpressive victims conform to his erotic ideal. Remarkably, though, the penultimate section of *L'Age d'homme,* first published in 1939, is entitled "La femme turban" and features a dream, part erotic, part mystical, about a woman in a turban; in republishing the section in the 1946 edition of the book, did Leiris not even consider its new contemporary vibrations? Still more remarkable is the parallel with that other postwar sadomasochistic "classic," Pauline Réage's *Histoire d'O. La tonte* was a politicized version of the humiliations and tortures undergone, albeit willingly, by O; like the *tondues,* O does not die, but, unlike her bald sisters, she does, so to speak, "keep her hair on," so great is its fetishistic appeal to her lovers-cum-torturers. Or, to be pruriently and pornographically precise, she keeps the hair of her head, for at the end of the novel O undergoes a variety of *tonte* of her own in preparation for the so-called Commandant's masked ball. In the first place, O's face and head are concealed, but for eyes, mouth, and chin, by the extravagantly plumed screech-owl mask she selects, and she then visits her regular beautician to have her legs depilated, choosing, needless to say, treatment by wax, which, as it is ripped away, is "no less lacerating than the crack of a whip." At first, O intends only to have her legs "done," but, as the beautician goes about her task with O "spread-eagled [*écartelée*] as though making love," she comes to feel that there is "something shocking in the contrast between the fur [*fourrure*] of her belly and the plumes of her mask." She realizes that, in order to be complete, the "aspect of an Egyptian statue" (shades of Leiris again!) that her mask and the impressive curves of her body confer on her, "requires that her flesh be totally smooth." She then thinks of a fellow willing victim named Anne-Marie and how her "master" wants her to be completely depilated "because it was only in that way that she was totally naked." O is afraid that Sir Stephen—who is in the habit of seizing her by her "fleece" (*toison*) and pulling her to him—would not appreciate the all-over, toes-to-chin treatment, but she goes ahead anyhow. Contrary to her fears, Sir Stephen is absolutely delighted and "caresses her timidly like a beast one is about to tame." At the masked ball, O is duly revealed, mask apart, in all her smooth, shaven glory, in a manner that fulfils the Leirisian ideal down to the last image: "Was she then made of stone or of wax, or even a creature from some other world?"[236]

If the severed head was the dominant image of *Blood in the City,* it is, therefore, its shaven equivalent that takes central place here. Not that the severed head has been absent from the pages that precede. Thérèse compared her "definitive" conversion to Judith emerging from the tent of Holophernes, revealing an unexpected link with Michel Leiris whose *L'Age d'homme* is structured around the opposition of Judith and Lucretia, respectively the woman who kills, or is killed, after making love.[237] She also prayed for the conversion of the convicted murderer Pranzini and adopted as one of her spiritual models Saint Théophane Vénard, decapitated in Indochina in 1861. As Rodin's model and as a sculptor herself, Camille Claudel was first transformed into marble by her lover and then, so to speak, marmorealized herself, resulting, inter alia, in two memorable images of her decapitated head: the Medusa in the already mentioned *Persée et la Gorgone* (1902) and Rodin's earlier *La Pensée* (1886; cf. the female character Pensée de Coûfontaine in her brother's historical trilogy) in which the bonneted head emerging directly from the marble is that of Camille. Marthe Robin prayed for the souls of many convicted murderers, most notably that of the Catholic convert Jacques Fesch, guillotined in 1957, and Claire Ferchaud was obsessed with the execution of Louis XVI; Georges Bataille named the "hero" and "heroine" of *Le Bleu du ciel* after the decapitated murderer Troppmann and the martyr Dorothea, and called his review *Acéphale.*

It is nonetheless with an image, by far the best known, of one particular *tondue* that the present study may appropriately close.[238] Taken by the great American photographer Robert Capa (1913–54), it shows a shaven woman, with a white housecoat over her day clothes, walking along a crowded cobblestoned street "somewhere in France." A representative sample of French provincial humanity is accompanying her, at a distance, for, like all sacrificial victims, she is dangerous to approach, along her Via Dolorosa that resembles any other street in the country. Her bald head is curiously replicated and set off by the bald heads of at least two men in the crowd, and is both contrasted and linked to the headgear of the three men closest to her: a middle-aged man wearing a béret walking in front of her carrying a bundle, perhaps her meager possessions, a gendarme in a képi looking back at her with what looks like a leer on his face and, walking next to her, staring into her face and apparently addressing her, another gendarme or fireman with a metal helmet on his head. For her part, the *tondue* is looking into the eyes of a baby, evidently the fruit of her traitorous liaisons, cradled in her arms in a shawl, with a full head of hair and apparently asleep. The photograph was taken on either 18 or 23 August 1944,[239] at any rate in the octave of the Feast of the Assumption of the Blessed Virgin Mary, and the street is the rue du Cheval Blanc in Chartres: Chartres, site of the greatest cathedral in France, dedicated to Our Lady and one-time home of the Black Virgin, Notre-Dame-de-Sous-Terre, Chartres, goal of the annual Easter pilgrimage from Paris and spiritual capital of its founder, Charles Péguy. And here are the new Mother and Child, for whom there is truly no place at the inn, totally alone on a French provincial street, with the three unwise men, béret, képi, and helmet, the Herods of the new order, driving them into who knows what flight into Egypt. The baby, if still alive, would be about sixty now: what, one wonders, has become of him—or her?

Coda

For all their differences, the eleven women studied in this book had one thing in common: they suffered, and suffered acutely, almost all of their lives. Only one married (Raïssa Maritain), and she abjured marital relations after a few years of marriage, and only one had a child (Eva Lavallière), and that outside marriage, at a time when illegitimacy carried real stigma. Otherwise, whether they were Brides of Christ (Mélanie, Thérèse, Marthe, Claire, Anne-Marie, Madeleine, Simone) or Brides of Antichrist (Camille, Colette), all the women betrothed themselves to suffering and had suffering as offspring, and they did so willingly, even enthusiastically, passionately, in both the commonplace and etymological senses of those words, for, in the case of the believers, all they wanted to do was to identify with God by reliving and repeating the Passion of His Son. Or, in the words of Marie Noël (1883–1967), poet and mystical Bride of Christ:

All our sufferings were integrated in the Passion of Christ, at the immense hour of Gethsemane, and are, in and through his, salvific [*salvatrices*], either for a single beloved soul—spouse, child, brother, friend [all in the masculine gender in the French]—or, more broadly, for a people, for a Church, for a Fatherland [*une Patrie*]. All you who suffer, innocently, as suffered the Innocent-God [*l'Innocent-Dieu*], we are all martyrs, we are all communion hosts [*des hosties*], we are all Savers and Redeemers. But it is necessary to consent to it. It is necessary to give to suffering the loving "yes" of marriage [*le "oui" d'Amour du mariage*]. Empty, the suffering that is not accepted, the suffering that is rejected, the suffering that is hated. If Christ, in the sacred garden, had said No! if He had hated his cross, He would perhaps have been crucified, He would not have redeemed mankind.[240]

Taking as their text the notoriously obscure verse 24 of the first chapter of Paul's letter to the Colossians ("It makes me happy to suffer for you, as I am suffering now, and in my own body to do what I can to make up all that has still to be undergone by Christ for the sake of his body, the Church," Jerusalem Bible translation),[241] the Brides of Christ studied here believed, in accordance with a powerful current in Catholic, and especially Ultramontanist, theology, that Christ's Passion was somehow incomplete and that since he, ascended into heaven, could not, by definition, be suffering any more, it was necessary for them to suffer in his stead on behalf of both sinners and innocent nonbelievers whose souls would otherwise be sold off to the devil. It was their task to buy back, *redeem,* those souls in the coin of freely assumed suffering, by taking on the sins and sufferings of the world in an exact and complete imitation of Christ and to share in the cup of suffering that he himself, though sorely tempted, did not finally abjure.

Such, then, was the doctrine of vicarious suffering, or mystical substitution, that guided the lives of so many of the women discussed in this book, a doctrine summed up as follows by its chief contemporary expounder and proselyte, Léon Bloy: "We have learned from . . . Saint Paul that there is still something lacking in the sufferings of Jesus Christ, and that this something must be made up for [*accompli*] in the living members of his Body,"[242] in other words in the sufferings of those Christians here and now on earth. In willingly choosing suffering as their spiritual Bridegroom, the Brides not only gave direction, meaning, and hope to their lives but answered one of the great conundra of Christianity: Why, if Christ has been born and has lived among us, has given us his teaching, has redeemed us through his sacrificial death, has been resurrected, and has ascended to heaven, why, if, following all this *and* the descent of the Holy Spirit at Pentecost, does humanity still suffer, Christians and non-Christians alike, why, more than that, is it that, in the words of Romans 8:22, "the whole creation groaneth and travaileth in pain together," and not just "until now," as Paul optimistically puts it, but, to all appearances, interminably? The doctrine of vicarious suffering justified the omnipresence of suffering and pain, or at least made them less scandalous and hopeless, the whole and only difference between "B.C." and "A.D." being, according to Bloy, that "before" human being suffered without hope and "after" they suffered with hope, the incarnation, death, and resurrection of Christ having changed everything and nothing. Of the women studied here, only Thérèse, and then only incompletely, pointed the way beyond the doctrine of vicarious suffering with her belief in the unconditionality of God's love, mediated through Christ, for each of his creatures. Otherwise, God's love and salvation had to be bought, and bought at the price, in the women studied here, of lifelong misery and pain.

But if the Brides suffered with and for the sake of their Bridegroom, who was it, in immediate human terms, who reaped the benefits of their suffering? The answer is stark and straightforward: the men in their lives or, more generally, the male-dominated order of things, particularly in the Church, if only in the sense that they gave (and continued to give) inspiration, literary and/or spiritual, to men who did not go nearly as far along the Via Dolorosa as they did. Thus Claudel gained from Camille's beauty and madness (just as, in *L'Annonce faite à Marie,* Anne Vercors and Pierre de Craon gain from the sacrifice of Violaine); Bloy found inspiration, and a literary model, in the religious mania of Anne-Marie Roulé; and Bataille profited from the willingness of Colette Peignot to go much deeper into the agonies and ecstasies of "interior experience" than he. Jacques Maritain's exploitation of Raïssa's suffering was far less blatant, but he certainly derived inspiration and illumination from her formidable gifts of concentration and prayer; Pierre Janet turned Madeleine Lebouc's ecstatic sufferings to considerable scientific, professional, and personal advantage. With Mélanie, Thérèse, Eva, Marthe, and Claire, there is no individual man who derived obvious advantage from their sufferings, but each in her way gave inspiration and succor to a male-dominated Church or to particular male-dominated sections within it. It is striking how many of the alleged stigmatics and ecstatics tabulated in chapter 5 espoused, or were coopted by, ultraroyalist politics, and one well-known study of women in nineteenth-century lunatic asylums has argued that "the major catalyst of female fantasies at the time was the Duchesse de Berry," the deluded leader of a royalist uprising in the Vendeé in 1832 and mother-figure to the whole ultraroyalist movement; the famous and rebellious Hersilie Rouy signed herself "a sister of King Henri V" when, in 1863, she sent a secret letter to the wife of the Prefect of the Seine in protest against the conditions in which she was being held.[243] Mélanie, Thérèse, and Claire each sympathized with the ultraroyalist or ultrarightist movements of their day, and Marthe Robin was undoubtedly a far more ardent supporter of Pétain and Pétainism than her current hagiologists allow. Only Simone Weil was openly on the left, and even her writings, with their stress on "rootedness" and "community," not to mention their marked anti-Judaical, if not antisemitic, animus, lend themselves to recuperation by the far right. Politically and ideologically, the Brides' willingness to suffer with and for, and to subordinate themselves to, their mystical Bridegroom reinforced the patriarchal principle in operation both in the Church and, more loosely and less obviously, in French society at large. Indeed, many of the Catholic men discussed in this book felt that women were the spiritually superior sex precisely because of their willingness to suffer and so—though this was never openly said—to sustain, directly or indirectly, the male order of things.

This is the implicit meaning of *L'Annonce faite à Marie* and the explicit message of Bloy's novel *La Femme pauvre,* his last and, in many ways, most successful fictional work, published in 1897. After the internment of Anne-Marie Roulé, Bloy had had a relationship with a woman named Henriette Vilmont who had died of—almost inevitably—tuberculosis in 1883. Not long afterward Bloy met, as was his wont, another woman on the streets, not a prostitute this time, but a beggar, clad in tatters and weeping. Her name was Berthe Dumont, in her mid- to late twenties, a gilder (*une doreuse*) by trade, and addicted to the morphine that she took to ease the suffering caused by the metal poisoning she had contracted through her profession. For once gainfully employed, Bloy took the woman under his wing, a relationship began, and lasted for just over a year when, in May 1885, Berthe died after suffering horrifically from what Bloy calls "the most abominable death known to medicine, death by *tetanus* . . . which people in the middle ages attributed to diabolic possession, such is its terror." In the early 1890s, by now married to Johanne Molbech, daughter of the Danish poet and dramatist Christian Molbech, Bloy used Berthe, as he had earlier used Anne-Marie, as the model for the heroine of the novel he had originally entitled *La Dés-espéreé,* the female equivalent of his earlier *Le Désespéré.* The novel became *La Femme pauvre,* and the heroine mutated from Clotilde Lecopieux into Clotilde Maréchal, a fusion of Véronique Cheminot and Caïn Marchenoir, whose sufferings exceed those of both.[244]

Alternatively rabid and sublime, and, at his best (and worst), sublimely rabid and rabidly sublime, Bloy it is who deserves the last word in this book. The scene is in an anonymous Parisian parish church and, reduced to vagrancy after a life of appalling privations and suffering, Clotilde is found by "a true priest" in tears before the exposed Blessed Sacrament. "You must be truly unhappy," he says, to which she replies that, no, she is perfectly happy: "One does not enter Paradise tomorrow or the day after tomorrow, or in ten years' time, one enters it *today,* when one is poor and crucified." "*HODIE mecum eris in paradiso,*" murmurs the priest, these being the words of Christ to the penitent malefactor being crucified beside him, "*To day* shalt thou be with me in paradise" (Luke 23:43), and goes away "overwhelmed with love." Then Bloy delivers his message, with whose every italicized and capitalized word our Brides of Christ would have been in, literally, passionate agreement:

> By dint of suffering, this living and strong Christian [cette chrétienne vivante et forte; i.e., Clotilde] has divined that, *especially for women* [italics added], there is only one way of entering into contact with God, and that this way, completely unique, is Poverty. . . . she has even understood, and this is not far short of the sublime, that Woman only truly exists on condition of being without bread, without home, without friends, without husband and without children, and that it is only like that that she can force her Savior to descend. . . . "*There is only one tragedy,* she has said . . . , *it is the tragedy of NOT BEING SAINTS.*"[245]

CHRONOLOGY

YEAR	PRINCIPAL EVENTS MENTIONED IN TEXT	SELECT CONTEMPORANEOUS EVENTS
1830	Marian apparitions at rue du Bac (Catherine Labouré)	July Revolution Beginning of Bourgeois Monarchy
1831	Birth of Mélanie Calvat	
1835	Birth of Maximin Giraud	
1840		Return of Napoleon's remains to France
1844	Birth of Bernadette Soubirous	
1846	Marian apparition at La Salette (19 SEPTEMBER)	
	Birth of Léon Bloy and Anne-Marie Roulé	
1848		February Revolution Proclamation of Second Republic
1851		Coup d'état by Louis Napoleon (2 DECEMBER)
1852		Proclamation of Second Empire
1853	Birth of Pauline Lair Lamotte	

1854	Proclamation of doctrine of Immaculate Conception	
1858	Marian apparitions at Lourdes	
1864	Birth of Camille Claudel	Promulgation of Syllabus Errorum
1866	Birth of Eva Lavallière	
1868	Birth of Paul Claudel	
1870	First Vatican Council Promulgation of doctrine of Papal Infallibility	"L'Année terrible" Franco-Prussian War Proclamation of Third Republic
1871	Marian apparition at Pontmain	Paris Commune
1873	Birth of Thérèse Martin	
1874	Death of Maximin Giraud	
1878	Death of Pope Pius IX	
1879	Death of Bernadette Soubirous	
1881–82		Creation of secular state primary schools
1882	Birth of Jacques Maritain	
1883	Birth of Raïssa Maritain	
1886	"Conversion" of Paul Claudel "Complete conversion" of Thérèse Martin	Secularization of teaching profession in state schools
1877	Bloy, *Le Désespéré*	
1888	Thérèse Martin enters Carmel at Lisieux	
1894–95		Dreyfus affair
1896	Birth of Claire Ferchaud	
1897	Death of Thérèse Martin Birth of Georges Bataille Bloy, *La Femme pauvre*	
1902	Birth of Marthe Robin	
1903	Birth of Colette Peignot	

1904	Death of Mélanie Calvat	
1905		Separation of church and state
1909	Birth of Simone Weil	
1912	Claudel, *L'Annonce faite à Marie*	
1914		Outbreak of First World War
1917	Death of Léon Bloy Claire Ferchaud's audience with President Poincaré	
1920	Canonization of Joan of Arc	
1923	Beatification of Thérèse	
1923	Canonization of Thérèse	
1926		Papal condemnation of Action Française
1929	Death of Eva Lavallière	
1934		Fascist riots in Paris (6 FEBRUARY)
1935	Bataille, *Le Bleu du ciel*	
1936		Popular Front Outbreak of Spanish civil war
1938	Death of Colette Peignot	
1939		Outbreak of Second World War
1940		Defeat of France Inauguration of Vichy Regime
1943	Death of Camille Claudel Death of Simone Weil	
1947	Weil, *La Pesanteur et la grâce*	
1955	Death of Paul Claudel	
1960	Death of Raïssa Maritain	

1962	Death of Georges Bataille	Opening of Second Vatica Council
1972	Death of Claire Ferchaud	
1973	Death of Jacques Maritain	
1981	Death of Marthe Robin	

NOTES

Unless otherwise stated, all works in French are published in Paris and those in English in London; where there is more than one place of publication, only the first is given.

Introduction

1. For the term "ugly carnival," see the brilliant study by Alain Brossat, *Les Tondues: Un carnaval moche* (Editions Manya, 1992), copiously drawn on in chapter 7 of this book.

2. See Richard Griffiths, *The Reactionary Revolution: The Catholic Revival in French Literature* (Constable, 1966), still far and away the best study of the subject.

3. See Anne Delbée's vivid biography *Une femme* (Presses de la renaissance, 1982), a development of an earlier play of the same title, which won the 1983 Grand Prix des Lectrices d'*Elle*.

4. See Richard D. E. Burton, *Blood in the City: Violence and Revelation in Paris, 1789–1945* (Ithaca: Cornell University Press, 2001), esp. 44–53.

5. On Blanc de Saint-Bonnet, see Richard D. E. Burton, " 'La douleur est donc un bien . . . ': Baudelaire et Blanc de Saint-Bonnet. Contribution à l'étude du politique et du religieux chez Baudelaire," *Les Lettres romanes* 47, no. 4 (1993): 243–55.

6. Quoted in Annette Becker, *La Guerre et la Foi: De la mort à la mémoire, 1914–1930* (Armand Colin, 1994), 34.

7. Georges Bernanos, *Les Enfants humiliés* (1949; reprint, Folio, 1991), 10 and 15.

8. Jean-Paul Sartre, *La Mort dans l'âme* (Gallimard, 1949), 243. Unless otherwise noted, all translations are my own.

9. Pierre Taittinger, *Les Leçons d'une défaite: Ce que le pays doit savoir* (1941), quoted in Gérard Miller, *Les Pousse-au-jouir du Maréchal Pétain* (1975; reprint, Seuil, 1988), 54.

10. Ibid., 47.

11. Georges Bernanos, *Dialogues des Carmélites* (Seuil, 1996), 57. For a discussion of the theology of text and opera, see Richard D. E. Burton, *Francis Poulenc* (Bath: Absolute Press, 2002), 92–105.

12. For an illuminating comparison with the churches in Britain, see the superbly documented study by Callum G. Brown, *The Death of Christian Britain: Understanding Secularization 1800–2000* (Routledge, 2001).

13. George Bernanos, *Sous le soleil de Satan* (Presses Pocket, 1996), 21.

14. For a summary, see Claude Langlois, "La 'déchristianisation,' " in *Histoire de la France religieuse,* ed. Philippe Joutard, vol. 3: *Du roi Très Chrétien à la laïcité républicaine (18e–19e siècle)* (Seuil, 1991), 240.

15. Brown, *Death of Christian Britain,* 73.

16. Ibid., 41.

17. Quoted in Gérard Cholvy, *Etre chrétien en France au XIXe siècle, 1790–1914* (Seuil, 1997), 36. Most of the details that follow are taken from pages 36–48 of this valuable book, supported by Claude Langlois, "Le renouveau religieux au lendemain de la Révolution," in *Histoire de la France religieuse,* ed. Joutard, 3:422–23.

18. On the "Charlottes," see Yvonne Turin, *Femmes et religieuses au XIXe siècle: Le féminisme "en religion"* (Nouvelle Cité, 1989), 148–50.

19. Quoted ibid., 352.

20. Brown, *Death of Christian Britain,* 58.

21. Ibid., 59.

22. See Cholvy, *Etre chrétien en France,* 40.

23. Brown, *Death of Christian Britain,* 58.

24. See Philippe Boutry, *Prêtres et pariosses au pays du Curé d'Ars* (Editions du Cerf, 1986), 490–91.

25. Ibid., 491.

26. Philippe Boutry, "Le mouvement vers Rome et le renouveau missionnaire," in *Histoire de la France religieuse,* ed. Joutard, 3:435.

27. On Pontmain, see the excellent summary in Joachim Bouflet and Philippe Boutry, *Un signe dans le ciel: Les apparitions de la Vierge* (Grasset, 1997), 158–63. Jeanne-Marie Lebossé retracted her testimony in 1920.

28. Ruth Harris, *Lourdes: Body and Spirit in the Secular Age* (Allen Lane, 1999), 214.

29. Ibid., 235.

30. See, for example, *Pauvre Belgique!* in Charles Baudelaire, *Oeuvres completes,* ed. Claude Pichois (Gallimard, 1976), 2:949. Baudelaire is speaking here of Jesuit churches in Belgium, but the image of the boudoir is applied to Parisian churches (especially new ones such as Saint-Philippe du Roule and the Eglise de la Trinité) by Huysmans among others.

31. Ernest Renan, *Souvenirs d'enfance et de jeunesse* (Folio, 1992), 4–5.

32. Baudelaire, *Fusées,* in *Oeuvres completes,* ed. Pichois, 1:650.

33. André Gide, *Les Nouvelles Nourritures* (1935), in *Les Nourritures terrestres* (Livre de poche, 1966), 200.

CHAPTER 1. *She Who Weeps*

1. For convenient summaries of the rue du Bac apparitions, see Yves Chiron, *Enquête sur les apparitions de la Vierge* (Editions J'ai lu, 1995), 189–95, and Joachim Bouflet and Philippe Boutry, *Un signe dans le ciel: Les apparitions de la Vierge* (Grasset, 1997), 108–15. See also Richard D. E. Burton, *Blood in the City: Violence and Revelation in Paris, 1789–1945* (Ithaca: Cornell University Press, 2001), chap. 6, 118–29.

2. The best short account of the apparition at La Salette is to be found in Bouflet and Boutry, *Un signe dans le ciel,* 126–50. I have also used Yvonne Estienne, *Lourdes et La Salette* (Nouvelles Editions Latines, 1958) and Charles de Salmiech, *Voyants de La Salette* (Nouvelles Editions Latines, 1980), as well as the texts by Huysmans, Bloy, and Massignon discussed later in this chapter. Notes and references are kept to the bare minimum.

3. See Michael P. Carroll, *The Cult of the Virgin Mary: Psychological Origins* (Princeton: Princeton University Press, 1986), 152–55. According to Carroll, the Virgin at La Salette is "modeled upon Maximin's perception of his highly punitive stepmother" (155), an interpretation that could be extended to Mélanie's image of her supposedly cruel mother.

4. The link with the Magnificat is made by Joris-Karl Huysmans in *Là-haut or Notre-Dame de La Salette,* ed. Michèle Barrière (Nancy: Presses universitaires de Nancy, 1988), 108, and also by Bloy in his *Introduction à la vie de Mélanie* (1911), in *Oeuvres de Léon Bloy,* ed. Jacques Petit (Mercure de France, 1970), 10:25–26.

5. For a full and insightful discussion of the progressive textualization of the La Salette "event," see Bouflet and Boutry, *Un signe dans le ciel,* 129–41. The original of the "relation

Pra" has now disappeared and is known thanks to a copy published by the Abbé Rousselot in his *La Vérité sur l'événement de La Salette* of 1848.

6. Quoted in Salmiech, *Voyants de La Salette,* 17. Salmiech does not indicate from which of Maximin's several accounts this statement is taken.

7. The present summary is based essentially on Mélanie's 1879 account, reproduced in *Témoignages historiques sur Mélanie Calvat, bergère de la Salette* (F.X. de Guibert, 1993), 9–24. For the patois original, see Bouflet and Boutry, *Un signe dans le ciel,* 139–40.

8. This account of the early years of the pilgrimage is based on Estienne, *Lourdes et La Salette,* 39–51.

9. The Virgin's down-to-earth comments led to all kinds of hermeneutic ingenuity among the symbolically minded. See, for a late example, Paul Claudel's complex allegorization of potatoes in "Le Symbolisme de La Salette" (1952) in Claudel, *Oeuvres complètes* (Gallimard, 1953), 5:297–98.

10. According, at least, to the account given in Salmiech, *Voyants de La Salette,* 96. According to Yves Chiron (*Enquête sur les apparitions de la Vierge,* 433), Pius IX was the first, and perhaps only, reader of the complete text prior to its publication in 1879. It should also be added that Maximin also wrote down his "secret" at the same time and that it too was dispatched to Rome; its contents have never been revealed, and the document itself, like Mélanie's own testimony, is now officially "lost."

11. Léon Bloy, *Celle qui pleure* (1907), in *Oeuvres de Léon Bloy,* 10:146.

12. One particularly violent attack on La Salette was published by a renegade priest named Déléon under the title of La Salette-Fallavaux (Fallax-Vallis) or la Vallée du Mensonge in 1852–53. Déléon claimed that the Belle Dame was none other than a well-known local eccentric (and former Sister of Providence), Mlle. de La Merlière, who had waylaid the children and regaled them with her own religious fantasies. In 1857 Mlle. de La Merlière took Déléon to court and her lawyer, the celebrated republican Jules Favre, proved without difficulty that she was somewhere else at the time of the "event"; the judge, however, declined to award her the damages she sought. (See Estienne, *Lourdes et La Salette,* 64–65).

13. Quoted in Salmiech, *Voyants de La Salette,* 37–38.

14. Huysmans, *Là-haut,* 118.

15. This account of Maximin's life is based on Salmiech, *Voyants de La Salette,* 57–80. On the complex and obscure question of Maximin's interview with the Curé d'Ars, see Estienne, *Lourdes et La Salette,* 65–70.

16. Most of the details in this account are taken from Salmiech, *Voyants de La Salette,* 96–120. Some of Salmiech's facts and interpretations should be treated with caution.

17. Bloy, *Oeuvres,* 10:311. This observation occurs in a note to *Celle qui pleure* (1907).

18. See Salmiech, *Voyants de La Salette,* 113.

19. All quotations from the secrets are taken from *Témoignages historiques sur Mélanie Calvat,* 14–17.

20. I have based the terms "La Salette I" and "La Salette II" on the distinction Catholic scholars sometimes make between "Fátima I" (the apparitions of 1917) and "Fátima II" (the "secrets" supposedly imparted to the three children who claimed to have witnessed them). See Bouflet and Boutry, *Un signe dans le ciel,* 212–24.

21. See Bouflet and Boutry, *Un signe dans le ciel,* 130.

22. See Jacques Maritain's letter of protest to the review *Vie spirituelle* in October 1946, reproduced in *Témoignages historiques sur Mélanie Calvat,* 72–74.

23. Bloy, *Celle qui pleure, Oeuvres,* 10:276.

24. For a masterly exposition of the doctrine of vicarious or expiatory suffering and its impact on fin de siècle French Catholicism, see Richard Griffiths, *The Reactionary Revolution: The Catholic Revival in French Literature 1870–1914* (Constable, 1966), 149–217.

25. Bloy, *Symbolisme de l'apparition* (written 1879–80, published posthumously 1925), *Oeuvres,* 10:20–24.

26. Bloy, *Introduction à la Vie de Mélanie* (1911), *Oeuvres,* 10:274.

27. Bloy, *Celle qui pleure,* 190.

28. Ibid., 137.

29. Letter of 21 December 1906 to Pierre Ternier, quoted by Jacques Petit in his introduction to vol. 10 of *Oeuvres de Léon Bloy*, 7.

30. On Tardif de Moidrey, one of the most powerful influences on the French Catholic revival, see Griffiths, *Reactionary Revolution*, 49–52.

31. For an account of Huysman's "back-to-front conversion," see Burton, *Blood in the City*, chap. 9.

32. Huysmans, *Là-haut*, 142.

33. Ibid., 140–42.

34. Bloy, *Celle qui pleure*, 171–72.

35. Bloy, *Introduction à la Vie de Mélanie*, 271–73.

36. Ibid., 265.

37. Bloy, *Celle qui pleure*, 147.

38. Bloy, *Symbolisme de l'apparition*, 24.

39. On Naundorff, see Claude Guillet, *La Rumeur de Dieu: Apparitions, prophéties, et miracles sous la Restauration* (Imago, 1994), 109–12.

40. See Bloy, *Le Fils de Louis XVI* (1900), in *Oeuvres de Léon Bloy*, 5:105–8. According to Bloy, Naundorff was a "monster of misfortune" whom "it pleased God to crush in a mortar in expiation for the crimes of his Race" and who, hounded from country to country "like a Cain vomited forth by the whole of humanity," is a figure both of the Man of Sorrows and of the Wandering Jew.

41. Bloy, *Celle qui pleure*, 189–90.

42. The comparison between Mélanie and Marie-Antoinette is made in Massignon's article "Notre-Dame de La Salette" published in the review *Dieu Vivant* in 1946 and reprinted in *Témoignages historiques sur Mélanie Calvat*, 60–71. On Massignon and Marie-Antoinette, see his monograph *Un voeu et un destin: Marie-Antoinette, reine de France* (Chantenay, 1955). Bloy had also cast Marie-Antoinette as an emblematic sacrificial victim in his early essay *La Chevalière de La Mort* (written 1877, first published 1891). For the whole ultra-Catholic cult of Marie-Antoinette, see Richard D. E. Burton, "From Scapegoat to Martyr: The Image of Marie-Antoinette in Nineteenth-Century Catholic-Monarchist Thought," *Australian Journal of French Studies* 34, no. 2 (1997): 196–201.

43. Massignon, "Notre-Dame de Salette," 68.

44. Ibid., 63–66.

45. Ibid., 60.

46. Ibid., 70.

47. Ibid., 61–62.

48. Bloy, *Celle qui pleure*, 164.

49. Ibid., 150.

50. Claudel, "Le Symbolisme de La Salette," 302.

51. Massignon, "Notre-Dame de Salette," 68.

CHAPTER 2. *Little Flower*

1. For a full discussion of Paul Claudel's "conversion," see Richard D. E. Burton, *Blood in the City: Violence and Revelation in Paris, 1789–1945* (Ithaca: Cornell University Press, 2001), chap. 8, where full references are given.

2. See David Usborne, "Saint Who Stopped the Traffic on Fifth Avenue," *The Independent,* 19 October 1999, 1–2.

3. See the testimony of her sister Simone Berteaut, reproduced in Guy Gaucher, *Histoire d'une vie: Thérèse Martin* (Editions du Cerf, 1982), 241.

4. Sainte Thérèse de L'Enfant Jésus, *Manuscrits autobiographiques* (Office central de Lisieux, 1980), 86. Though still available as such, the much-edited *Histoire d'une âme* has now been superseded by the full manuscripts usually referred to as A (1895), B (September 1896), and C (June-July 1897). All quoted passages are translated by me, and all emphases are in the original unless otherwise stated.

5. Hans Urs von Balthasar, *Thérèse de Lisieux: Histoire d'une mission,* trans. Robert Givord (Médiaspaul, 1996), 40.

6. Vita Sackville-West, *The Eagle and the Dove: A Study in Contrasts* (Michael Joseph, 1943), 146.

7. On Isidore Guérin and the political-religious conflicts in Lisieux in the 1880s and 1890s, see Jean-François Six, *Vie de Thérèse de Lisieux* (Seuil, 1975), 84–98.

8. See Pierre Descouvemont and Helmut Nils Loose, *Thérèse et Lisieux* (Cerf, 1991), 8. On the iconographic significance of the flags flown at Loigny, see Burton, *Blood in the City,* 180.

9. Jacques Maître, *"L'Orpheline de la Bérésina," Thérèse de Lisieux (1873–1897): Essai de psychanalyse socio-historique* (Cerf, 1996), 31. This excellent study has greatly influenced the argument advanced in this chapter.

10. On this subject, see Pierre Pierrard, "L'âge d'or des pèlerinages nationaux français (1871–74)," in *Les Chemins de Dieu: Histoire des pèlerinages chrétiens des origines à nos jours,* ed. Jean Chélini and Henry Branthomme (Hachette, 1995), 319–32.

11. See Six, *Vie de Thérèse,* 20.

12. See von Balthasar, *Thérèse de Lisieux,* 197. Thérèse's *pratique* is illustrated in Descouvemont and Loose, *Thérèse et Lisieux,* 55.

13. See Descouvemont and Loose, *Thérèse et Lisieux,* 248. For a detailed discussion of the personality and health of Thérèse's elder sisters, see Six, *Vie de Thérèse,* 35–49.

14. On the differences between Thérèse's and Pauline's forms of devotion, see Six, *Vie de Thérèse,* 320.

15. See Maître, *"L'Orpheline de la Bérésina,"* 154–56.

16. Six, *Vie de Thérèse,* 35.

17. Maître, *"L'Orpheline de la Bérésina,"* 356.

18. Ibid., 138.

19. Account based on Six, *Vie de Thérèse,* 13–15 and 50–53.

20. See Maître, *"L'Orpheline de la Bérésina,"* 210.

On Rose Taillé as "the *unconscious figure* of the *mercy* of God" in Thérèse's thinking, see Denis Vasse, *La Souffrance sans jouissance ou le martyre de l'amour: Thérèse de l'Enfant-Jésus et de la Sainte-Face* (Seuil, 1998), 51. The present chapter was written before I consulted this valuable study by a leading Christian psychoanalyst.

21. *Manuscrits autobiographiques,* 29.

22. Ibid., 240–41.

23. All details from Six, *Vie de Thérèse,* 56–63. For an important discussion of the psychological impact of the death of the mother, directly relevant to the case of Thérèse, see André Green, "La Mère morte," in *Narcissisme de vie, narcissisme de mort* (Les Editions de Minuit, 1988), 222–53.

24. *Manuscrits autobiographiques,* 45.

25. Ibid., 19.

26. On Marie de Gonzague (Marie Davy de Virville), see Descouvemont and Loose, *Thérèse et Lisieux,* 114.

27. *Manuscrits autobiographiques,* 69

28. Ibid., 203.

29. *Manuscrits autobiographiques,* 200.

30. See Six, *Vie de Thérèse,* 41.

31. *Manuscrits autobiographiques,* 46.

32. Six, *Vie de Thérèse,* 74.

33. *Manuscrits autobiographiques,* 54–55.

34. Ibid., 60–61.

35. See Six, *Vie de Thérèse,* 188–89, and Maître, *"L'Orpheline de la Bérésina,"* 141 and 176.

36. See Six, *Vie de Thérèse,* 188–89, and Maître, *"L'Orpheline de la Bérésina,"* 141 and 176.

37. *Manuscrits autobiographiques,* 47.

38. Ibid., 200.

39. See Descouvremont and Loose, *Thérèse et Lisieux,* 202.

40. *Manuscrits autobiographiques,* 224.

41. See Descouvremont and Loose, *Thérèse et Lisieux,* 215.

42. For the testimony of Marie and others, with comments, see Maître, *"L'Orpheline de la Bérésina,"* 195–99 and 203.

43. On Notre-dame des Victoires and its Archiconfrérie, see Claude Guillet, *La Rumeur de Dieu: Apparitions, propheties, et miracles sous la Restauration* (Imago, 1994), 146–49.

44. See *Manuscrits autobiographiques,* 80–82.

45. See Descouvemont and Loose, *Thérèse et Lisieux,* 55.

46. *Manuscrits autobiographiques,* 93.

47. Ibid., 72.

48. Ibid., 124.

49. Ibid., 102.

50. See Six, *Vie de Thérèse,* 114–15.

51. *Manuscrits autobiographiques,* 106.

52. All quotations in ibid., 115–16.

53. *Derniers entretiens* (Desclée de Brouwer, 1971), 312 (8 August 1897). The quotation is a translation from the Vulgate of Judith 15:11.

54. *Manuscrits autobiographiques,* 117.

55. See the well-known photographic portrait, taken shortly after her return from Bayeux, in Descouvemont and Loose, *Thérèse et Lisieux,* 95.

56. *Manuscrits autobiographiques,* 117.

57. On Louis Martin's illness, see Six, *Vie de Thérèse,* 158–61. The detail concerning Anne-Marie Roulé is in Descouvemont and Loose, *Thérèse et Lisieux,* 147.

58. Monica Furlong, *Thérèse of Lisieux* (Virago Press, 1987), 89. The text of Thérèse's *billet de profession* is given on page 90.

59. Furlong, *Thérèse of Lisieux,* 90. According to Carmelite practice, the ceremonial cropping of the hair should have occurred in January 1889 but was postponed because of fears that, because of anticlerical agitation, the Carmel might have to disband and go into exile. For a photograph of Thérèse's hair, reconstituted in 1913 by Soeur Marie de la Trinité, see Descouvemont and Loose, *Thérèse et Lisieux,* 143.

60. See especially chaps. 4 and 6.

61. On *La Croix,* see the authoritative study by Pierre Sorlin, *La Croix et les Juifs* (Grasset, 1967).

62. The report in *La Croix* is reproduced in part in Descouvemont and Loose, *Thérèse et Lisieux,* 79. Not surprisingly, Thérèse was the preferred intercessor of *condamnés à mort* in France, above all of Jacques Fesch (executed 1 October 1957 at the age of 27) who became a Christian while awaiting execution and whose beatification is reportedly "under consideration" (see the testimony written on the last night of his life, reproduced in Gaucher, *Histoire d'une vie,* 239).

63. All quotations relating to Pranzini in *Manuscrits autobiographiques,* 117–19.

64. Pranzini pleaded his innocence to the end, though Thérèse does not seem to have known this.

65. This passage is greatly influenced by Six, *Vie de Thérèse,* 132–37.

66. On Pichon, see Descouvemont and Loose, *Thérèse et Lisieux,* 125.

67. *Manuscrits autobiographiques,* 199–200.

68. See Descouvemont and Loose, *Thérèse et Lisieux,* 268–69.

69. Quoted in ibid., 186.

70. See her letter of 14 October 1890 to Céline, in *Correspondance générale* (Desclée de Brouwer, 1973), 2:620–21.

71. See Descouvemont and Loose, *Thérèse et Lisieux,* 137, and Maître *"L'Orpheline de la Bérésina,"* 73. On Dupont and Marie de Saint-Pierre, see Guillet, *La Rumeur de Dieu,* 149–57.

72. On Thérèse's opposition to *voies extraordinaires,* see Six, *Vie de Thérèse,* 208 and 330. On pilgrimages, see ibid., 171.

73. On the controversies of 1889, see Burton, *Blood in the City,* chap. 10.

74. See the letters in *Correspondance générale,* 484–88.

75. *Manuscrits autobiographiques,* 200.

76. For an authoritative discussion of the origins and development of this spiritual theme, see Caroline Walker Bynum, *Jesus as Mother: Studies in the Spirituality of the High Middle Ages* (Berkeley: University of California Press, 1982), esp. 110–69.

77. See the characteristic passage quoted in Maître, "*L'Orpheline de la Bérésina,*" 55.

78. I have adapted this formulation from ibid., 14.

79. *Manuscrits autobiographiques,* 301.

80. For a valuable discussion of the theme of spiritual childhood, see Leah Sinanaglor Marcus, *Childhood and Cultural Despair: A Theme and Variations in Seventeenth-Century Literature* (Pittsburgh: University of Pittsburgh Press, 1978).

81. See Descouvemont and Loose, *Thérèse et Lisieux,* 46.

82. Ibid., 224.

83. See *Manuscrits autobiographiques,* 300.

84. See *Correspondance générale,* 2:1377, and *Derniers entretiens,* 887.

85. *Manuscrits autobiographiques,* 218.

86. *Correspondance générale,* 2:1377, and *Derniers entretiens,* 887.

87. Charles Péguy, *Le Porche du mystère de la deuxième vertu,* in *Oeuvres poétiques complètes,* ed. Marcel Péguy (Gallimard, 1975), 625.

88. Péguy, "Le Mystère des Saints Innocents," ibid., 693.

89. See note 73 above.

90. See, for example, the oil painting that Thérèse produced in 1894 to commemorate Pauline's (Mère Agnès) first year as prioress, reproduced in Descouvemont and Loose, *Thérèse et Lisieux,* 157.

91. *Manuscrits autobiographiques,* 212. The escutcheon is reproduced in color in Descouvemont and Loose, *Thérèse et Lisieux,* 157.

92. See Descouvemont and Loose, *Thérèse et Lisieux,* 160–61.

93. See ibid., 141 and 206.

94. See, among numerous references, *Manuscrits autobiographiques,* 259–61.

95. Hugo Rahner, *Man at Play, or Did You Ever Practise Eutrepelia?* trans. Brian Battershaw and Edward Quinn (Burns and Oates, 1965), esp. 1–11.

96. Henry Vaughan, "Childe-hood," quoted in Marcus, *Childhood and Cultural Despair,* 156.

97. On her playing at Semallé, see Six, *Vie de Thérèse,* 54, and on her subsequent inability to play, *Manuscrits autobiographiques,* 48, 85, and 97.

98. Quoted in *Thérèse de Lisieux, Pensées,* ed. Conrad de Meester (Descleé de Brouwer, 1980), 3:37. See also von Balthasar, *Thérèse de Lisieux,* 199.

99. *Derniers entretiens,* 226.

100. Quoted in von Balthasar, *Thérèse de Lisieux,* 200, to which the present paragraph is greatly indebted.

101. See, among many other references, Thérèse's letter of 17 November 1894 to Mme Guérin, *Correspondance générale,* 2:798.

102. See Therese's letter of 18 November 1889 to Mme Guérin, ibid., 1:511.

103. Georges Bernanos, *Les Enfants humiliés* (Folio, 1991), 26.

104. The present paragraph leans heavily on Maître, "*L'Orpheline de la Bérésina,*" 239–40, Six, *Vie de Thérèse,* 206–11, and Von Balthasar, *Thérèse de Lisieux,* 175–77.

105. See Six, *Vie de Thérèse,* 70.

106. *Manuscrits autobiographiques,* 145, 275, 201, 145.

107. Ibid., 61.

108. Quoted in Six, *Vie de Thérèse,* 210.

109. *Manuscrits autobiographiques,* 232.

110. Ibid., 242.

111. Letter to Céline, 2 August 1893, *Correspondance générale,* 2:715. Thérèse would have found the thematics of hiding richly developed in the work of Saint John of the Cross (see Descouvemont and Loose, *Thérèse de Lisieux,* 170).

112. See the stimulating essay by Julia Kristeva, "*Ego affectus est*: Saint Bernard: l'affect, le désir, l'amour," in *Histoires d'amour* (Folio, 1985), 190–215.

113. See *Manuscrits autobiographiques*, 193.

114. Ibid., 300–01.

115. Thérèse sometimes signed her letters "Thérésita" before she entered the Carmel.

116. *Manuscrits autobiographiques*, 219.

117. Ibid., 240–41.

118. See von Balthasar, *Thérèse de Lisieux*, 210.

119. *Manuscrits autobiographiques*, 261.

120. The concept of *Gelassenheit* ("releasement," "letting be") was central to the spiritual teaching of Meister Eckhart and was taken over, with a somewhat different sense, by Heidegger. See John Gray, *Enlightenment's Wake: Politics and Culture at the Close of the Modern Age* (Routledge, 1995), 182–83.

121. See, inter alia, John Saward, *Perfect Fools: Folly for Christ's Sake in Catholic and Orthodox and Orthodox Spirituality* (Oxford: Oxford University Press, 1980), and Jacques Heers, *Fêtes des fous et carnavals* (Fayard, 1983). In his Annotations on the New Testament, Erasmus noted that the Greek word *nepiois* which the Vulgate translates as *parvuli* "has the sense of both fool and infant," whence the equation "parvulis . . . hoc est stultis." (See M. A. Screech, *Ecstasy and the Praise of Folly* [Duckworth, 1980], 31.)

122. Quoted in Maître, "*L'Orpheline de la Bérésina*," 66.

123. See Descouvemont and Loose, *Thérèse de Lisieux*, 184 and 234.

124. See Maître, "L'Orpheline de la Bérésina," 107.

125. See Six, *Vie de Thérèse*, 233.

126. *Manuscrits autobiographiques*, 207.

127. *Derniers entretiens* (4 August 1897), 302.

128. Simon Tugwell, *Ways of Imperfection: An Exploration of Christian Spirituality* (Darton, Longman and Todd, 1984), 228.

129. *Manuscrits autobiographiques*, 227. On the importance of the distinction Thérèse is making here, see Vasse, *La Souffrance sans jouissance*, 89.

130. See Descouvemont and Loose, *Thérèse et Lisieux*, 219. On the frequency of fire imagery in her last writings, see von Balthasar, *Thérèse et Lisieux*, 261.

131. The text in question is reproduced in *Manuscrits autobiographiques*, 307–9.

132. Ibid., 245 and 248.

133. Ibid., 247.

134. *Derniers entretiens*, 786. Thérèse's words are quoted in part in von Balthasar, *Thérèse de Lisieux*, 271, to which the whole of this discussion is greatly indebted.

135. See Descouvemont and Loose, *Thérèse et Lisieux*, 247.

136. *Derniers entretiens*, 787.

137. See Six, *Vie de Thérèse*, 275, and his comments on the "presence-absence" of God, 170.

138. *Derniers entretiens*, 241 (7 July 1897). The Jerusalem Bible translates this verse as "Let him kill me if he will; I have no other hope than to justify my conduct in his eyes."

139. *Manuscrits autobiographiques*, 245. On this whole question, see Six, *Vie de Thérèse*, 269–73.

140. Quoted in von Balthasar, *Thérèse de Lisieux*, 271.

141. *Manuscrits autobiographiques*, 246.

142. *Derniers entretiens*, 239 (6 July 1897).

143. See Six, *Vie de Thérèse*, 267, and von Balthasar, *Thérèse et Lisieux*, 270.

144. *Correspondance générale*, 1:494.

145. *Manuscrits autobiographiques*, 208.

146. Ibid., 200.

147. According to Six (*Vie de Thérèse*, 329–30), it was the Prioress, Mère Marie de Conzague, who rejected the doctor's advice that Thérèse be given morphine.

148. The film starred Catherine Mouchet in the title role and was awarded the Prix du Jury de Cannes in 1986.

149. See Descouvemont and Loose, *Thérèse et Lisieux,* 298.

150. See Maître, *"L'Orpheline de la Bérésina,"* 30. On Thérèse's recourse to "baby-talk" and patois during her final illness, see ibid., 325–30.

151. See Descouvemont and Loose, *Thérèse et Lisieux,* 299.

152. On Taxil and the "Diana Vaughan" hoax, see Eugen Weber, *Satan franc-maçon* (Julliard, 1964).

153. Account based on Six, *Vie de Thérèse,* 252–56.

154. *Manuscrits autobiographiques,* 245. See Descouvemont and Loose, *Thérèse et Lisieux,* 283.

155. These and all subsequent details are taken from Descouvemont and Loose, *Thérèse et Lisieux,* 312–25, and Gaucher, *Histoire d'une vie,* 222–34.

156. Quoted in Annette Becker, *La Guerre et la foi: De la mort à la mémoire 1914–1930* (Armand Colin, 1994), 76.

157. On the revival of anticlericalism after the war, provoked mainly by the resumption of diplomatic relations with the Vatican in 1920, see René Rémond, *L'Anticléricalisme en France de 1815 à nos jours* (Brussels: Editions Complexe, 1985), 236–47.

158. On Suhard's record under the Occupation, see Jacques Duquesne, *Les Catholiques français sous l'Occupation* (Points, 1996), 44–45 and 385–86.

159. On the two Piuses and Thérèse, see John Cornwell, *Hitler's Pope. The Secret History of Pius XII* (Viking, 1999), 174.

160. Pierre Mabille, *Thérèse de Lisieux* (Editions Allia, 1996), 9.

161. Ibid., 15.

162. Ibid., 31–2.

163. Ibid., 105.

164. Ibid., 70, 15.

165. Ibid., 85.

166. Ibid., 41.

167. Ibid., 134.

168. Ibid., 138, 36.

169. Ibid., 46.

170. Georges Bernanos, *La Joie* (Points, 1983), 84. For an exhaustive discussion of Bernanos's borrowings from Thérèse's writings, see Guy Gaucher, "Bernanos et Sainte Thérèse de l'Enfant-Jésus," *Revue des lettres modernes* 56–57 (1960): 229–68.

171. Georges Bernanos, *L'Imposture* (Points, 1985), 292.

172. Ibid., 268, 270, etc.

173. Bernanos, *La Joie,* 193.

174. Ibid., 91.

175. Ibid., 97–98.

176. *Derniers entretiens,* 221. See Gaucher, "Bernanos et Sainte Thérèse," 229–30.

177. For a succinct discussion of Bernanos's politics, including an assessment of his antisemitism, see Michel Winock, "Le cas Bernanos," in *Nationalisme, antisémitisme, et fascisme en France* (Points, 1990), 397–415.

178. In August 1935 Claudel had written a poem "Sainte Thérèse de Lisieux" that was included in his sequence *Visages radieux* (see Claudel, *Oeuvres complètes* [Gallimard, 1952], 2:316–17). For a valuable discussion of French Catholics and the Spanish civil war, see René Rémond, *Les Crises du catholicisme en France dans les anneés trente* (Points, 1996), 171–99.

179. Georges Bernanos, *Les Grands Cimetières sous la lune* (Livre de Poche, 1977) 139. A first version of this work was published as articles in the Dominican weekly *Sept* between June 1936 and February 1937, Bernanos having embarked on a new polemical work prior to the outbreak of hostilities; the definitive version was written between May 1937 and April 1938 and was published by Plon in May 1938. *Nouvelle histoire de Mouchette* was published in May 1937.

180. Interview with André Rousseaux in *Candide,* 17 June 1937, quoted in Georges Bernanos, *Oeuvres romanesques,* ed. Albert Béguin (Gallimard, 1961), 1853.

181. Bernanos, *Les Grands Cimetières,* 140.

182. Ibid., 296–98.

183. Ibid., 303.

184. Ibid., 316, 297.

185. Ibid., 330, 332, 310.

186. Ibid., 332.

187. Ibid., 329, 104.

188. Bernanos, *Les Enfants humiliés,* 164.

189. Bernanos, *Les Grands Cimetières,* 297.

190. Ibid., 260.

191. Ibid., 325.

192. *Manuscrits autobiographiques,* 289–90.

193. Paul Claudel, *Trois figures saintes pour le temps actuel,* in *Oeuvres complètes,* 24:419. "Making up what is lacking in the passions of Christ" is a translation from the Vulgate of Colossians 1:24 (*adimpleo quae desunt passionum Christi*), the text usually cited in support of the doctrine of vicarious suffering.

194. Julian of Norwich, *Revelations of Divine Love,* trans. Clifton Walters (Penguin, 1980), 84.

195. Ibid., 198.

196. I have preferred the traditional translation to that offered by Walters (*Revelations of Divine Love,* chap. 27).

CHAPTER 3. *Brother and Sister*

The present chapter was written before the publication of Danielle Arnoux's challenging study *Camille Claudel: L'Ironique Sacrifice* (EPEL, 2001). Taking her point of departure from Jacques Lacan's 1961 seminar on Paul Claudel's trilogy of historical plays ("Le Transfert dans sa disparité subjective, sa prétendue situation, ses excursions techniques"), Arnoux subjects the life and work of both Camille and Paul to a searching interactive reading and traces the major themes of both sculptor and poet-dramatist back to the oppressive family climate that reigned at Villeneuve-sur-Fère. Camille's eventual insanity is linked to similar cases in the Claudel and Cerveaux families, and Arnoux brings out with force the deep melancholy afflicting Louise-Athanaïse Claudel (née Cerveaux, 1840–1919), mother of Camille, Paul, and Louise, traumatized, it is plausibly claimed, by the death of her own mother in 1843 when she was three, barely a month after the birth of her younger brother Paul-Louis, after whom the poet-diplomat was named. This early loss was followed in due course by the death of her own infant son, Charles-Henri Claudel, in 1863, and by the suicide, by drowning, of her brother Paul-Louis Cerveaux at the age of twenty-two in 1866, barely a month after she had given birth to her second daughter Louise. Arnoux gives greater prominence than I do here to the virtual certainty that Camille underwent an abortion in 1892, in the eyes of her brother a sin against God as well as a criminal act for which her madness and internment were expiatory retribution (31). Arnoux also, as the subtitle of her work indicates, dwells insistently on the theme of sacrifice discussed here, establishing both the parallel and the "sharp chiasmus" between brother and sister: whereas the Catholic Paul becomes the successful creator of a work founded on the idea of sacrifice, Camille is fated to make a holocaustal sacrifice of both her work and her sanity (281). To take into account all of Arnoux's ideas would require a substantial rewriting and expansion of this chapter and, in the absence of any fundamental clash between our interpretations, I have decided not to do so. I have, however, included some of her ideas at appropriate points in chapter 7.

1. Paul Claudel, *Mémoires improvisés* (Gallimard, 1969), 12.

2. Paul Claudel, *Contacts et circonstances*: *Ouevres complètes* (Gallimard, 1959), 16:197–203. The reference to "the vocation of the Universe" is from Paul Claudel, *Journal,* ed. François Varillon and Jacques Petit (Gallimard, 1968), 1:636 (July 1924). For a discussion of Claudel's conversion, see Richard D. E. Burton, *Blood in the City: Violence and Revelation in Paris, 1789–1945* (Ithaca: Cornell University Press, 2001), 149–58.

3. Claudel, *Mémoires improvisés,* 13.

4. Claudel, *Journal,* 2:214–15 (December 1937).

5. Claudel, *Mémoires improvisés,* 18–19, and Henri Guillemin, *Le "Converti" Paul Claudel* (Gallimard, 1968), 44.

6. See Guillemin, *Le "Converti,"* 44–45.

7. See Varillon, *Claudel* (Descleé de Brouwer, 1967), 15–17.

8. Claudel, *Journal,* 2:247. (See also 1198 n. 4.)

9. Ibid., 863 (20 June 1929).

10. Paul Claudel, *La Ville* (Folio, 1982), 105.

11. Almost all the details in the paragraphs that follow are taken from Reine-Marie Paris, *Camille Claudel* (Gallimard, 1984). In addition to the biographical study by Mme Paris (who is Paul Claudel's granddaughter), the essay by François Lhermitte and Jean-François Allilaire on "Camille Claudel malade mentale" (155–92) is of particular value and interest. References are kept to a necessary minimum.

12. See Guillemin, *Le "Converti,"* 54.

13. Claudel, *Mémoires improvisés,* 28.

14. Ibid., 20.

15. Reproduced in Paris, *Camille Claudel,* 56.

16. Quoted in ibid., 82.

17. All quotations from "Camille Claudel," in Paul Claudel, *Oeuvres complètes* (Gallimard, 1960), 17:247–56.

18. "Camille Claudel statuaire" (1905), reproduced in Paris, *Camille Claudel,* 11–16.

19. See Paris, *Camille Claudel,* 92, 122, etc.

20. Claudel, *Journal,* 2:103–4. For new evidence on Camille's original internment in 1913, see Eric Favereau, "Camille Claudel, asile année zéro," *Libération* (15 September 2000): 44–45.

21. The paragraphs that follow lean heavily on the model study by Bernard Howells, "Le bouclier en miroir de Persée: Sur la trace de Camille Claudel dans l'oeuvre de son frère," in Paris, *Camille Claudel,* 313–51.

22. For a discussion of this controversial subject, see Peter Ackroyd, *T. S. Eliot* (Hamish Hamilton, 1984), esp. 149–50, 167–68, and 233–34.

23. Claudel, "Camille Claudel," 247–51.

24. See Guillemin, *Le "Converti,"* 121.

25. See Howells, "Le bouclier," 336–37.

26. "La Messe là-bas," in Paul Claudel, *Ouevres complètes* (Gallimard, 1952), 2:49, 53.

27. See Howells, "Le bouclier," 337–42.

28. Paul Claudel, *Théâtre,* ed. Jacques Madaule (Gallimard, 1956), 1:564.

29. Ibid., 590.

30. Ibid., 550.

31. See Michel Autrand's preface to *L'Annonce faite à Marie* (Folio, 1993), 14.

32. Claudel, *Théâtre,* 1:649.

33. Ibid., 580.

34. Ibid., 2:30.

35. Claudel, *Journal,* 2:315 (May-June 1940). Cf. also "Ô mon Jésus de lait! O mon petit enfant de lait pur!" (Quoted in Guillemin, *Le "Converti,"* 75.)

36. For a full discussion of the theme of vicarious suffering in Claudel, to which the present paragraph is greatly indebted, see Richard Griffiths, *The Reactionary Revolution: The Catholic Revival in French Literature, 1870–1914* (Constable, 1966), 198–210.

37. Claudel, *Théâtre,* 1:621.

38. Ibid., 2:89, 2:75.

39. Ibid., 2:31, 2:105–6.

40. Ibid., 2:74–75.

41. All quotations from ibid., 2:104–12.

42. Ibid., 1:615.

CHAPTER 4. *Beggars of Heaven*

1. On the controversy surrounding the naming of the rue du Chevalier de la Barre, see Richard D. E. Burton, *Blood in the City: Violence and Revelation in Paris, 1789–1945* (Ithaca: Cornell University Press, 2001), 183.

2. See Léon Bloy, *Journal* (Mercure de France, 1958), 2:269 (entry for 5 August 1905). Bloy would develop these ideas in the *Le Sang du pauvre* (1909).

3. Bloy's letters are reproduced in Raïssa Maritain, *Les Grandes Amitiés* (Desclée de Brouwer, 1949), 126–28.

4. All details from Jean-Luc Barré, *Jacques et Raïssa Maritain: Les mendiants du ciel* (Stock, 1996), 20–33.

5. Ibid., 82–83. On Psichari's homosexuality, see Frédérique Neau-Dufoun, *Ernest Psichari: L'ordre et l'errance* (Cerf, 2001), 109–15.

6. All details from Raïssa's own account of her childhood and adolescence in *Les Grandes Amitiés,* 13–46. For a discussion of the conditions of eastern European Jewish migrants to France in the late nineteenth and early twentieth centuries, see Burton, *Blood in the City,* 209–10.

7. R. Maritain, *Les Grandes Amitiés,* 105.

8. Ibid., 90.

9. Ibid., 83–89.

10. Quoted in ibid., 117.

11. Ibid., 231.

12. This account was first published as the introduction to Bloy's *Lettres à ses filleuls: Jacques Maritain et Pierre van der Meer de Walcheren* (1928) and is reproduced in *Les Grandes Amitiés,* 129–31.

13. This paragraph repeats the argument, and some of the phrasing, of Richard D. E. Burton, "Baudelaire, Belgians, Jews," *Essays in French Literature* 35, no. 6 (1998–99): 69–112.

14. This issue is discussed with great insight in Hyam Maccoby, *The Sacred Executioner: Human Sacrifice and the Legacy of Guilt* (Thomas and Hudson, 1982).

15. Léon Bloy, *Le Salut par les Juifs,* in *Oeuvres de Léon Bloy,* 9:51.

16. R. Maritain, *Les Grandes Amitiés,* 491–92.

17. Ibid., 135.

18. Ibid., 133.

19. Ibid., 149–50.

20. Ibid., 151–54.

21. Raïssa bitterly resented Jeanne Bloy's action at the time—presumably because she was not yet formally a Christian—but seems retrospectively to have attributed her recovery to it (see *Les Grandes Amitiés,* 182). In the summer of 1904, she had had an emergency operation for pharyngeal blockage that appears to have been purely physiological in character, but after which, she says (ibid., 113), her health was never what it had been.

22. On Véra Oumansov, see Jacques's memoir, "Our Sister Vera," in Jacques Maritain, *Notebooks,* trans. Joseph W. Evans (Albany, N.Y.: Magi Books, 1984), 186–218.

23. R. Maritain, *Les Grandes Amitiés,* 187–88.

24. Ibid., 192.

25. Ibid., 297.

26. Quoted in Barré, *Jacques et Raïssa Maritain,* 119.

27. J. Maritain, *Notebooks,* 41.

28. See Barré, *Jacques et Raïssa Maritain,* 193–97. For Maritain's article of 1946 on La Salette, see *Témoignages historiques sur Mélanie Calvat bergère de la Salette* (F. X. de Guibert, 1993), 72–74.

29. For the circumstances of this visit, which are connected with Péguy's conversion, see Barré, *Jacques et Raïssa Maritain,* 113–17.

30. See J. Maritain's letter to Massis, quoted in ibid., 146–47.

31. R. Maritain, *Les Grandes Amitiés,* 316.

32. Ibid., 317–22.

33. On this whole question, see Barré, *Jacques and Raïssa Maritain,* 145–48.

34. See R. Maritain, *Les Grandes Amitiés,* 260–70.

35. A discussion of Maritain's philosophy lies outside the purport and competence of this work.

36. R. Maritain, *Les Grandes Amitiés,* 515.

37. Ibid., 412–13.

38. Raïssa Maritain, *Poèmes et essais* (Descleé de Brouwer, 1968), 89. The translation is that given in Judith D. Suther, *Raïssa Maritain: Pilgrim, Poet, Exile* (New York: Fordham University Press, 1990), 69, to which the comments that follow are indebted.

39. On the Eiffel Tower and the horror it excited in conservative Catholics like Huysmans and Bloy, see Burton, *Blood in the City,* 191–97.

40. Maurice Sachs, *La Décade de l'illusion* (Gallimard, 1950), 185.

41. Maurice Sachs, *Le Sabbat* (Gallimard, 1960), 156–57.

42. The biblical passages are quoted by Sachs in *Le Sabbat* (155) from which the other details are also taken.

43. Quoted in Francis Steegmuller, *Cocteau: A Biography* (Macmillan, 1970), 335.

44. Sachs, *Le Sabbat,* 155–56.

45. Raïssa Maritain, *Journal de Raïssa* (Descleé de Brouwer, 1963), 137.

46. On Rouault and the Maritains, see *Les Grandes Amitiés,* 248–58.

47. On the overlapping of these different worlds, see Richard D. E. Burton, *Francis Poulenc* (Bath: Absolute Press, 2002), 46–54. The present discussion repeats the argument and some of the phrasing of these pages.

48. The present account is based on Barré, *Jacques and Raïssa Maritain,* 244–305, and Steegmuller, *Jean Cocteau,* 321–64; only essential references are given. Laloy's presence at the Meudon *soirées* is attested by Maurice Sachs (*La Décade de l'illusion,* 190).

49. Jean Cocteau, *Lettre à Jacques Maritain,* in *Oeuvres complètes* (Maiguerat, 1950), 9:278. See also Steegmuller, *Jean Cocteau,* 336.

50. For the relevant letters, see Barré, *Jacques et Raïssa Maritain,* 252–53.

51. Sachs, *Le Sabbat,* 173.

52. *Journal de Raïssa,* 177.

53. See Raïssa's account in *Les Grandes Amitiés,* 324–28, which, according to Steegmuller (*Jean Cocteau,* 335), "makes painful reading for agnostics"—and doubtless for many Catholics as well.

54. See Sachs, *Le Sabbat,* 142.

55. See Steegmuller, *Jean Cocteau,* 360.

56. The expression is Cocteau's, quoted in ibid., 342. It seems that Bourgoint and Sachs were both secret visitors to the clinic (ibid., 340).

57. All details on Henrion from R. Maritain, *Les Grandes Amitiés,* 419–23 and 428, and Barré, *Jacques and Raïssa Maritain,* 268.

58. Cocteau, *Lettre à Jacques Maritain,* 284–85, translation as in Steegmuller, Jean Cocteau, 344–45. The word "groggy" is in English in the original.

59. *Journal de Raïssa,* 167.

60. Jacques Maritain, *Réponse à Jean Cocteau* (1926), quoted in *Les Grandes Amitiés,* 435.

61. *Journal de Raïssa,* 167.

62. All information and quotations from *Journal de Raïssa,* 167–68. The story about Reverdy and the earphones comes from a footnote by Jacques.

63. See Steegmuller, *Jean Cocteau,* 6 (footnote).

64. Quoted in Barré, *Jacques et Raïssa Maritain,* 299.

65. Cocteau, *Lettre à Jacques Maritain,* 283.

66. So Steegmuller conjectures in *Jean Cocteau,* 357.

67. Jean Bourgoint and his sister Jeanne are the models for the incestuous siblings Paul and Elisabeth in Cocteau's novel *Les Enfant terribles* (1929). On Christmas Eve 1929, Jeanne Bourgoint committed suicide, in emulation, it was said, of Elisabeth's self-inflicted death in the novel. Cocteau had introduced Jeanne, as well as her brother, to opium, and some people held

him morally responsible for her death by encouraging her to imitate the fictional heroine she had inspired. For Bourgoint's later life, see Jean Mouton's introduction to his often moving, and always interesting, letters published under the title of *Le Retour de l'enfant terrible* (Desclée de Brouwer, 1975).

68. See Barré, *Jacques et Raïssa Maritain,* 298.

69. Jean Desbordes, *J'adore* (Grasset, 1928), 132–33. The abridged translation quoted here is taken from Steegmuller, *Jean Cocteau,* 390.

70. Quoted in Barré, *Jacques et Raïssa Maritain,* 375.

71. Quoted in Steegmuller, *Jean Cocteau,* 390.

72. Quotations from Barré, *Jacques et Raïssa Maritain,* 375–77.

73. Jean Cocteau, *Le Livre blanc* (Passage du Marais, 1992), 85. Jean-Jacques Cambacérès, a well-known homosexual and jurist, was instrumental in the effective decriminalization of homosexual acts in the Napoleonic penal code of 1810.

74. On Desbordes' death, see Steegmuller, *Jean Cocteau,* 447–49.

75. The present section is based on Sachs's own account in *Le Sabbat,* supported by Steegmuller, *Jean Cocteau,* and Jean-Michel Belle, *Les Folles Anneés de Maurice Sachs* (Grasset, 1979).

76. The best account of this episode is in Barré, *Jacques et Raïssa Maritain,* 329–34. Not surprisingly, Sachs himself denied the whole business.

77. Interestingly, his partner-in-crime was Violette Leduc (1907–72), the acclaimed lesbian author of the autobiographical *La Bâtarde* (1964).

78. Raïssa Maritain, *Les Grandes Amitiés,* 291–92.

79. See Bernard E. Doering, *Jacques Maritain and the French Catholic Intellectuals* (Notre Dame: University of Notre Dame Press, 1983), 36–44.

80. Ibid., 95.

81. For a full discussion of Maritain and the Spanish civil war, see ibid., 85–125.

82. See ibid., 114–16.

83. Quoted in Barré, *Jacques et Raïssa Maritain,* 454.

84. On Garrigou-Lagrange, see ibid., 464–65. Garrigou-Lagrange was to become an ardent Pétainist, declaring support for De Gaulle to be a mortal sin, and denouncing Maritain's work as a perversion of the "true spirit" of Thomism; relations between them were only partly restored by the time the Dominican died in 1964.

85. For a full discussion of Jacques's campaign against the rise of antisemitism, see Doering, *Jaacques Maritain,* 126–67.

86. See Barré, *Jacques et Raïssa Maritain,* 552.

87. *Journal de Raïssa,* xix.

88. "Et le Verbe s'est fait chair" (1958–59[?]), *Journal de Raïssa,* 361. All subsequent references to this work are contained in the text, together with the year in question.

89. R. Maritain, *Poèmes et essais,* 161–70.

90. The only passing allusion to a maternal dimension in God comes in a description of the statue at Chartres representing God forming Adam: "Ah! To remain always like that beneath his gentle hand, head resting on his *maternal* knees, and to let oneself go [*se laisser faire*], forever" (1917, 39, italics in original).

91. R. Maritain, *Poèmes et essais,* 339. This is Raïssa's own translation of the French original.

92. "Avertissement," *Journal de Raïssa,* 8–9.

93. R. Maritain, *Les Grandes Amitiés,* 112–13.

94. Suther, *Raïssa Maritain,* 47 and 126.

95. R. Maritain, *Les Grandes Amitiés,* 471.

96. Ibid., 228.

97. Ibid., 13–14, 18–19.

98. Ibid., 35–36.

99. Steegmuller, *Jean Cocteau,* 9.

CHAPTER 5. *Fasting, Bleeding, Seeing*

1. See Jean Guitton, *Portrait de Marthe Robin* (Grasset, 1985), 93. The bibliography on Marthe Robin is considerable, and not all of it of high quality, and I have drawn heavily on Guitton's study, as on Jean-Jacques Antier's *Marthe Robin: Le Voyage immobile* (Librairie académique Perrin, 1991), the fullest of the many biographies. I have also used Bernard Vandewiele's stimulating Lacanian study, *Le Salut précaire de Marthe Robin* (Romans-sur-Isère: L'Autre incertain, 1994) despite its tendency to psychologize Marthe's "condition" to the extent of saying virtually nothing of her physical illness. Only essential references are given.

2. A connection is posited by Bernard Vandewiele (*Le Salut précaire,* 65–66), following similar speculations in Gonzague Mottet's *Marthe Robin, la stigmatiseé de la Drôme: Etude d'une mystique du XXe siècle* (Toulouse: Editions Erès, 1989). I have not managed to locate a copy of this latter work.

3. See Antier, *Marthe Robin,* 52.

4. Therese Neumann "received" the stigmata in the spring of 1926, whereafter she "relived" the Passion each Friday until her death in 1962. Friedrich von Lama's study of her "case" was translated into French in 1938 as *Thérèse Neumann: Une stigmatiseé de nos jours* (Mulhouse: Salvator). On Neumann, and on the question of stigmatization, see Ian Wilson, *The Bleeding Mind: An Investigation into the Mysterious Phenomenon of Stigmata* (Paladin, 1991), 47–54.

5. Quoted from Henri-Marie Manteau-Bonamy, *Marthe Robin sous la conduite de Marie 1925–1932* (Editions Saint-Paul, 1995), 30, where the full text of the second "act" is reproduced (29–33).

6. See Vandewiele, *Le Salut précaire,* 79.

7. For a full and fair-minded discussion, see Antier, *Marthe Robin,* 258–61.

8. Quoted in Antier, *Marthe Robin,* 93.

9. The following summary is based on Antier, *Marthe Robin,* 96–100, supported by the Abbé Georges Finet's detailed "timetable," reproduced in Monique de Huertas, *Marthe Robin: La Stigmatiseé* (Editions du Centurion, 1990), 110–12. There were variations in the basic chronology given here, and it appears that there was no bleeding at all between 1936 and 1939 (Antier, *Marthe Robin,* 100); otherwise, all accounts concur as to the weekly pattern of Marthe's life.

10. Quoted in Antier, *Marthe Robin,* 96.

11. Quoted in Huertas, *Marthe Robin,* 115.

12. The present section is based on the chapter entitled "Témoignages" in Antier, *Marthe Robin,* 197–233.

13. See Huertas, *Marthe Robin,* 160.

14. See Antier, *Marthe Robin,* 229.

15. Guitton, *Portrait de Marthe Robin,* 104.

16. See Antier, *Marthe Robin,* 124–27.

17. The present account is based on the brief notice in Jeanne Deval, *Les Anneés noires: Romans/Bourg-de-Péage 1939–45* (Romans-sur-Isère: Editions Deval, 1984), 103–4 (where the photograph is reproduced), and on a notice in the chapel of Les Balmes. The Marian apparition at Montmeyran (to a girl named Thérèse Raillon) is discussed in Bouflet and Boutry, *Un signe dans le ciel,* 290–91, where further unverifiable details on the "Chevalier Blanc" are provided. See also Jacques Maître, *Mystique et féminité: Essai de psychanalyse sociohistorique* (Cerf, 1997), 311–13.

18. See Antier, *Marthe Robin,* 218.

19. Ibid., 69.

20. Guitton, *Portrait de Marthe Robin,* 217.

21. See Antier, *Marthe Robin,* 184–85.

22. Ibid., 149.

23. Ibid., 240.

24. Quoted in Huertas, *Marthe Robin,* 218.

25. Guitton, *Portrait de Marthe Robin,* 105.

26. The report is reproduced extensively in Antier, *Marthe Robin,* 159–74. Antier (271–79) makes a pertinent connection with Oliver Sacks' well-known study of *encephalitis lethargica,* and of the belated recovery, after many years of "sleeping," of some of its victims, in *Awakenings* (Duckworth, 1973).

27. See Wilson, *The Bleeding Mind,* 30–32, 76.

28. Ibid., 6–8, 119–22.

29. I have omitted those instances for which only scanty information is provided by the author or which do not fit readily into the categories I have chosen. The women discussed in the text do not figure in the table.

30. On Vintras and his followers, see the discussion in Burton, *Blood in the City,* 163–65, where full references are provided.

31. All of the information and quotations in this section are from Jacques Maître, *Une inconnue célèbre: La Madeleine Lebouc de Janet* (Anthropos-Economica, 1993). In order not to overburden the notes, I have placed page references in parentheses in the text that follows.

32. See Burton, *Blood in the City,* 181.

33. See ibid., 189, for a characteristic image of the period.

34. On the use of photography at La Salpêtrière, see the well-known study by Georges Didi-Huberman, *Invention de l'hystérie: Charcot et l'iconographie photographique de la Salpêtrière* (Macula, 1982). A selection of the photographs of Madeleine is reproduced in Maître, *Une inconnue célèbre* (plates 4, 6, 7–8, 10).

35. See plate 4 in Maître, *Une inconnue célèbre.* Cf. the similar markings self-inflicted by Jeanne Bel and Hélène Villefranche.

36. John Saward, *Perfect Fools: Folly for Christ's Sake in Catholic and Orthodox Spirituality* (Oxford: Clarendon Press, 1980), ix.

37. The principal source for information about Eva Lavallière's spiritual history is Omer Englebert's introduction to her *Ecrits spirituels* (Editions franciscaines, 1939). She is mentioned in many studies of the Parisian theater, and I am grateful for the many references given me by my former colleague Beynon John.

38. Raïssa Maritain, *Les Grandes Amitiés* (Descleé de Brouwer, 1949), 425.

39. Paul Claudel, "Eva Lavallière," in *Trois figures saintes pour le temps actuel, Oeuvres complètes* (Gallimard, 1963), 24:471.

40. See Jean Hugo, *Le Regard de la mémoire* (Babel, 1983), 368.

41. See R. Maritain, *Les Grandes Amitiés,* 428.

42. See Jean-Clément Martin, *La Vendeé de la mémoire (1800–1980)* (Seuil, 1989) for a searching and well-documented discussion of this subject.

43. Ibid., 194.

44. See the excellent study by Jean-Claude Martin and Charles Suaud, *Le Puy du Fou, en Vendeé: L'Histoire mise en scène* (L'Harmattan, 1996).

45. See Martin, *La Vendeé de la mémoire,* 181–83.

46. All parenthetical page references in the following text are to the two volumes of Claire Ferchaud, *Notes autobiographiques* (Téqui, 1974).

47. Quoted in Maître, *Mystique et féminité,* 416.

48. See ibid., 417–18.

49. Ferchaud, *Notes autobiographiques,* 2:74.

50. Quoted in Simone Pétrement, *La Vie de Simone Weil* (Fayard, 1997), 564–65 (first published 1973, henceforth referred to in parentheses in the text as SP). The bibliography on Simone Weil is vast and, apart from Pétrement's biography, I have used extensively three works that deal directly with her eating disorders: Ginette Raimbault and Caroline Eliacheff, *Les Indomptables: Figures de l'anorexie* (Editions Odile Jacob, 1996), 155–229 (henceforth referred to as RE); Jacques Maître, *Anorexies religieuses, anorexie mentale: Essai de psychanalyse sociohistorique* (Editions du Cerf, 2000), 143–85 (henceforth referred to as JM); and, in English, Judith Van Herik, "Simone Weil's Religious Imagery: How Looking Becomes Eating," in *Immaculate and Powerful: The Female in Sacred Image and Social Reality,* ed. Clarissa W. Atkinson, Constance H. Buchanan, and Margaret R. Miles (Crucible, 1987), 260–82 (henceforth referred to as VH).

51. Ferchaud, *Notes autobiographiques,* 2:74.

52. Thibon's assessment of Simone, one of the sharpest ever written, is reproduced in Simone Weil, *Oeuvres,* ed. Florence de Lussy (Gallimard, 1999), 1256–59. The text dates from 1952, and the present quotation is on page 1257.

53. Simone Weil, *La Pesanteur et la grâce* (Union générale d'éditions, 1966), 43 (first published 1947 and henceforth referred to as PG).

54. "Cannibalism. Communion, 'this is my blood, this is my body.' The urge to destroy what one loves in order to fulfill that love (child who breaks its toys). Sadism." (*Premiers écrits philosophiques,* quoted in JM, 160).

55. Simone Weil, *Waiting on God* (*Attente de Dieu* [1950]), trans. Emma Craufurd (Collins, 1983), 23.

56. The Abbé de Naurois later denied making such a charge, at least openly to Simone herself, but a number of other priests—not including Père Perrin and Père Couturier, the priest she consulted in New York—had similar feelings (see SP 675–76).

57. Weil, *Waiting on God,* 49.

58. See Bernard Halda, *L'Evolution spirituelle de Simone Weil* (Beauchesne, 1964), 8.

59. Simone de Beavoir, *Mémoires d'une jeune fille rangeé* (Folio, 1996), 331 (first published 1958).

60. For a fascinating working-class man's view of Simone in Le Puy, see the testimony of Jean Duperray in Weil, *Oeuvres,* 1250–52 (first published 1964); even the local Fred Astaire, a man nicknamed Le Boul Chapuis, could not get her to dance in time to the music.

61. See Bataille's testimony in Weil, *Oeuvres,* 1252 (first published 1949).

62. See Weil, *Oeuvres,* 67, and SP 381.

63. She is also reported to have joined a rugby team in 1930, hardly a common leisure pursuit of French women at the time—not that Simone would ever have done anything for pleasure (see Weil, *Ouevres,* 47).

64. En route for New York, the Weils were detained for just over two weeks in a camp outside Casablanca, where numerous Jews (mainly Polish) were also in detention (SP 620). Simone must have been fully aware of what was happening to "her" people.

65. All quotations from Weil, *Waiting on God,* 33–35.

66. See *The English Poems of George Herbert,* ed. C. A. Patrides (Dent, 1981), 192.

67. Weil, *La Pesanteur et la grâce,* 97.

68. For this distinction, see the classic work by the Swedish Lutheran scholar, Andreas Nygren, *Agape and Eros,* trans. P. S. Watson (Society for the Promotion of Christian Knowledge, 1953).

69. Weil, *La Pesanteur et la grâce,* 104.

70. Ibid., 94.

71. On Damiens, see the celebrated opening to Michel Foucault, *Surveiller et punir: Naissance de la prison* (Gallimard, 1975), 9–13.

72. Weil, *La Pesanteur et la grâce,* 93.

73. It is not clear from the standard biographies of either Simone or the Maritains whether they actually met in New York; if they did, there is no evidence of it in the writings of any of the three. Simone was strongly anti-Aristotelian and reportedly hostile to the Aristotelianized Christianity of Aquinas (see Halda, *L'Evolution spirituelle,* 106).

74. Weil, *Waiting on God,* 22.

75. Ibid., 41.

76. The present discussion leans heavily on Pétrement's admirable exposition of the concept in SP 646–55.

77. On the concept of *Tsimtsoum,* see the classic essay by Hans Jonas, *Le Concept de Dieu après Auschwitz,* trans. Philippe Ivernel (Editions Payot et Rivages, 1998), 37–38.

78. See chapter 4.

79. Weil, *La Pesanteur et la grâce,* 42.

80. Ibid., 48.

81. Weil, *Lettre à un religieux,* in *Oeuvres,* 1004.

82. Simone quotes this passage in *Lettre à un religieux* immediately after the comment on

the Resurrection cited above: "It is this," she says, "that compels me to believe" (*Oeuvres,* 1004). Simone probably also knew the passage in Origen's *Homilies on the Song of Songs* in which it is said that "nos inanes, et ille [Christ] exinanivit semetipsum formam servi accipiens" (quoted in M. A. Screech, *Ecstasy and the Praise of Folly* [Duckworth, 1980], 24).

83. Weil, *Oeuvres,* 1236. See RE 199.

84. Milton, *Poetical Works,* ed. Douglas Bush (Oxford: Oxford University Press, 1979), 190.

CHAPTER 6. *A Laura for Our Times?*

1. Elisabeth Barillé, *Laure: La Sainte de l'Abîme* (Flammarion, 1997). Most of the biographical information contained in this chapter is taken from this well-documented study. I have also drawn with profit on Sharon Louise Black's as yet unpublished thesis "Laure: Life under a Black Sun" (Ph.D. thesis, University of Sussex, 1998). The term "sainte de l'abîme" seems to be Leiris's invention (see Michel Leiris, *Frêle bruit* [Gallimard, 1976], 345).

2. The story of the gradual publication of Laure's writings—always challenged by the Peignot family, notably her brother Charles—is complex and troubled. The edition used here is the "definitive" version of *Ecrits de Laure,* ed. Jérôme Pedignot (Pauvert, 1977, reprinted 1985). All page numbers in parentheses in the text refer to this edition.

3. See Michel Surya, *Georges Bataille, la mort à l'oeuvre* (Editions Garamont-Frédéric Birr, 1987), 36, 49, 61–62.

4. Arthur Rimbaud, *Oeuvres,* ed. Suzanne Bernard (Garnier, 1960), 125–26.

5. "Le vraie vie est absente [ou *ailleurs*]," "Délires" (I), in *Une saison en enfer,* ibid., 224.

6. All the quotations from Bataille in this paragraph are taken from his brief essay *Le Petit* (1943), in *Oeuvres complètes* (Gallimard, 1971), 3:59–61.

7. For a discussion of Bataille's essay on the Place de la Concorde ("L'Obélisque" [1938]), see Burton, *Blood in the City,* 70–71.

8. Quoted in Philippe Sollers, *L'Année du tigre: Journal de l'année 1998* (Seuil, 1999), 260–61.

9. On Bernier, see the extremely informative introduction by Dominique Rabourdin to Jean Bernier, *L'Amour de Laure* (Flammarion, 1978).

10. See the testimony of the Swiss photographer Ella Maillart who had it from Bernier himself, quoted in Barillé, *Laure,* 100.

11. Bernier, *L'Amour de Laure,* 68–69. There is some suggestion that Colette may have had, or have feigned, an ectopic pregnancy (ibid., 74).

12. Ibid., 64.

13. Ibid., 89.

14. On the idea of "communication," see Georges Bataille, *L'Expérience intérieure* (1943; Gallimard, 1983), 74: "There is no longer subject=object, but a 'gaping breach' [*brèche béante*] between one and the other and, in this breach, subject, object are dissolved, there is passage, communication, but not from one to the other: *the one* and *the other* have lost distinct existence."

15. Bernier, *L'Amour de Laure,* 95.

16. Ibid., 95.

17. André Breton, *Second Manifeste du Surréalisme* (1930), in Breton, *Manifestes du Surréalisme* (Pauvert, 1962), 155.

18. Jérôme Peignot in Bernier, *L'Amour de Laure,* 194–95.

19. According to Sharon Black (*Laure,* 113), "Bataille's fascination with Laure—on a textual level—would seem to focus on her involvement with coprophagy." One wonders whether the qualification "textual" is necessary.

20. This "detail" is omitted from the text of Bataille's *Vie de Laure* given in the *Ecrits de Laure* but is reinstated in Jérôme Peignot's year-by-year account of his aunt's life provided in Anne Roche and Jérôme Peignot (eds.), *Laure: Une rupture 1934* (Editions des Centres, 1999), 157.

21. Michel Leiris, *Journal 1922–1989*, ed. Jean Jamin (Gallimad, 1992), 318.

22. Quoted in Catherine Maubon, "L'Expérience 'politique' de Colette Peignot," in *Des années trente: groupes et ruptures*, ed. Anne Roche and Christian Tarting (Editions du C.N.R.S., 1985), 192.

23. See Roche and Peignot (eds.), *Laure: Une rupture*, 159–60.

24. See Corinne Devaux-Mandelli, "Simone Weil et Colette Peignot," *Cahiers Simone Weil* 7, no. 3 (1983): 243–50.

25. On this exchange, see Jean-Michel Besnier, "Georges Bataille et *La Critique sociale*: Marxisme et perversion," in Roche and Tarting, *Des années trente*, 175–86.

26. On the photograph of Fou-Tchou-Li, see Surya, *Georges Bataille*, 103.

27. For a discussion of this, see Burton, *Blood in the City*, 98, where a full list of sources is given.

28. On these events, see ibid., 65–67, where again full references are given.

29. Quoted in Simone Pétrement, *Simone Weil* (Fayard, 1973), 306.

30. Ibid., 309.

31. Surya (who denies any fascist complicities in Bataille's politics) attributes the term "surfascisme" to either Jean Dautry or Pierre Dugan (*Georges Bataille*, 229 and 249.

32. The bibliography on the question of Bataille's "fascism" is now rather substantial. For a succinct, penetrating discussion, see Denis Hollier, "On Equivocation (Between Literature and Politics)," *October* 55 (1990): 3–22, to be supplemented by Susan Rubin Suleiman, "Bataille in the Street: The Search for Virility in the 1930s" in *Bataille: Writing the Sacred*, ed. Carolyn Bailey Gill (Routledge, 1995), 26–45. The whole question of the "neither left nor right" origins of fascism, especially in France, has its origins in Zeev Sternhell's controversial study, *Ni droite ni gauche: L'idéologie fasciste en France* (Seuil, 1983). For a vivid and incisive discussion of this whole intellectual milieu, see Daniel Lindenberg, *Les Années souterraines 1937–1947* (Editions La Découverte, 1990), 58–85. For a full bibliography on Bataille's politics, see Suleiman, "Bataille in the Street," 43–45.

33. See Roche and Peignot (eds.), *Laure: Une rupture*, 94–95.

34. Details in a letter, dated 1989, from Jeanne Maurin to Charles Ronsac, quoted in ibid., 16.

35. Notes to unpublished article "Le Fascisme en France," written in 1934 and reproduced in Bataille, *Oeuvres complètes* (Gallimard, 1970), 1:436.

36. See, for example, Peignot and Roche (eds.), *Laure: Une rupture*, 444, 75, 101.

37. Ibid., 100–101.

38. Ibid., 96.

39. Ibid., 44.

40. Ibid., 38.

41. The scenes referred to were seen by Simone in August 1936; the letter itself dates from 1938. See Simone Weil, *Oeuvres* (Gallimard, 1999), 408.

42. For a full discussion of bullfighting and French intellectual life, see Burton, *Blood in the City*, 319–21.

43. See Bataille, *Oeuvres complètes*, 1:444. The image exists in various forms and another version, also by Masson, is reproduced in *Ecrits de Laure* (191), with leafy branches replacing the hands and the feet firmly rooted in the ground (cf. the tree image in Colette's letter [1934?, 254]).

44. All quotations from ibid., 443–45.

45. Peignot and Roche (eds.), *Laure: Une rupture*, 100.

46. For a fully documented discussion of the image, see Carlo Pasi, "Acéphale ou la mise à mort du chef/du père," in Roche and Tarting (eds.), *Des anneés trente*, 207–22.

47. Bataille would develop this idea fully in his wartime texts *Le Coupable* (1943) and *Sur Nietzsche: Volonté de chance* (1945).

48. Surya (*Georges Bataille*, 253) considers Monnerot to be only a possible member. Monnerot is briefly mentioned in Hollier, "On Equivocation," 3, but an in-depth study of his remarkable intellectual-political trajectory remains to be done. It has been reported that Monnerot eventually left the Front National.

49. See Lindenberg, *Les Anneés souterraines,* 80–81.

50. Ibid., 76–79. Caillois's prewar career is also discussed in Denis Hollier, "Mimesis and Castration 1937," *October* 31 (1984): 3–15.

51. Quoted in Lindenberg, *Les Années souterraines,* 80. It is necessary, to repeat, to distinguish Acéphale, the secret society, from *Acéphale,* the review, to which totally nonfascist antifascists such as Leiris and Jean Wahl were contributors.

52. See Bataille's article "L'Obélisque" (in *Mesures,* 15 April 1938), reprinted in Bataille, *Oeuvres complètes,* 1:501–13. The article and related issues are discussed in Burton, *Blood in the City,* 70–71.

52. See Bataille, *Oeuvres complètes,* 2:277–78, and *Ecrits de Laure,* 99–100.

54. Bataille, *Oeuvres complètes,* 1:278.

55. Quoted in Barillé, *Laure,* 328–29.

56. Bernard-Henri Lévy, *Les Aventures de la liberté* (Grasset, 1991), 172.

57. Ibid., 175. Leiris is here referring to the proposed celebration of the execution of Louis XVI, but the judgment extends to the whole of Acéphale's activities.

58. Roger Caillois, "L'Esprit des sectes," in *Instincts et société* (Conthier, 1964), 67.

59. See "Sacrifices" (1936), in Bataille, *Oeuvres complètes,* 1:89–96.

60. See his article "La Mutilation sacrificielle et l'oreille coupeé de Van Gogh" (1930), reprinted in *Oeuvres complètes,* 1:258–70, and discussed in Burton, *Blood in the City,* 325–26.

61. It is striking that the basket and guillotine images repeat those applied to *Souvarine* in the incident discussed above (see note 34).

62. For the full account, originally written for *Le Coupable* (1944) but eventually omitted, see Bataille, *Oeuvres complètes,* 5:499–500.

63. For the full account, see ibid., 524–25.

66. On Bataille's concept of "spending" or "expense" (*dépense*), see his innovative article "La Notion de dépense" (*La Critique sociale* 7 [January 1933]), reprinted in *Oeuvres complètes,* 1:302–19.

65. Barillé, *Laure,* 344–45.

66. Marcel Moré, "Georges Bataille et la mort de Laure," *Cahier des Saisons* 38 (1964), reprinted in *Ecrits de Laure,* 283–87. The present quotation is on page 287.

67. Pierre Klossowski, "La Messe de Georges Bataille" (review of *L'Abbé C*), in *Un si funeste désir* (Gallimard, 1963), 128. The quotation continues: "The *priest,* the *mass,* the *sacraments,* all the accessories of worship, just as much as the *name of God* are indispensable to Bataille's *expression.*"

68. Denis Hollier, ed., *The College of Sociology (1937–39),* trans. Betsy Wing (Minneapolis: University of Minneapolis Press, 1988), xi.

69. For an interesting sociology of the Collège de Sociologie, see Michèle Richman, "The Sacred Group: A Durkheimian perspective on the Collège de Sociologie (1937–39)," in *Bataille,* ed. Bailey Gill, 58–76.

70. Leiris, *Journal,* 351.

71. Jean-Paul Sartre, "Un nouveau mystique" (1943), in *Situations* (Gallimard, 1947), 1:133–72.

72. Georges Bataille, *Le Coupable* (1944; reprint, Gallimard, 1961), 9.

73. Leiris, *Journal,* 336–37.

74. Michel Leiris, *Fourbis* (Gallimard, 1955), 225. The incident is also recalled in *Frêle bruit,* 344–45.

75. Bataille, *Le Coupable,* 166.

76. Leiris, *Fourbis,* 225.

77. William Blake, *Selected Poems and Letters,* ed. J. Bronowski (Penguin, 1966), 96–98. See Bataille's essay on Blake in Georges Bataille, *La Littérature et le mal* (Gallimard, 1967), 89–116.

78. Jacques Chavy, an associate of Bataille on *Contre-Attaque,* spoke for many when he affirmed the identity of "Dirty" and Colette (see Barillé, *Laure,* 296). The identification is, however, queried by Anne Roche in her preface to *Laure: une rupture* (22, n. 33).

79. On the execution of Troppmann, the subject of a celebrated article by Turgenev, see Burton, *Blood in the City,* 111–13.

80. For a brief discussion of the politics of the novel, see Philippe Sollers, "Une prophétie de Bataille," in *La Guerre du goût* (Gallimard, 1994), 455–59.

81. All numbers in parentheses refer to the English translation of *Le Bleu du ciel: Blue of Noon,* trans. Harry Mathews (Marion Boyars, 1986).

82. On the pig as traditional sacrificial victim, see the remarkable study by Claudine Fabre-Vassas, *La Bête singulière: Les juifs, les chrétiens et le cochon* (Gallimard, 1994), and the comments in Burton, *Blood in the City,* 42, 59 and 333.

83. "Abattoir," *Documents* 6 (November 1929), reproduced in Bataille, *Oeuvres complètes,* 1:205. Colette was also fascinated and appalled by abattoirs (see *Ecrits de Laure,* 256).

84. The English translation has "Dorothea's cleft" for *le sexe de Dirty;* I have given an accurate translation.

85. Georges Bataille, *Le Bleu du ciel* (Gallimard, 1997), 138.

86. Bataille, "Vie de Laure," in *Ecrits de Laure,* 281.

87. Letter to Suzanne Peignot (1926?), ibid., 223.

CHAPTER 7. *Holy Tears, Holy Blood*

1. Henri Legrand du Saulle, *Les Hystériques: Etat physique et état mental: Actes insolites, délictueux et criminels* (1891), quoted in Cristina Mazzoni, *Saint Hysteria: Neurosis, Mysticism, and Gender in European Culture* (Ithaca: Cornell University Press, 1996), 3. The present section leans heavily on Mazzoni's insightful and well-documented study.

2. See Jan Goldstein, *Console and Classify: The French Psychiatric Profession in the Nineteenth Century* (Cambridge: Cambridge University Press, 1987), and Ruth Harris, *Murders and Madness: Medicine, Law, and Society in the Fin de Siècle* (Oxford: Oxford University Press, 1989).

3. See Mazzoni, *Saint Hysteria,* 26.

4. Ibid., 71.

5. Edmond and Jules de Goncourt, *Journal,* ed. Robert Ricatte (Robert Laffont, 1989), 1:248. This entry is cited in Mazzoni, *Saint Hysteria,* 67.

6. Quoted in Goldstein, *Console and Classify,* 374.

7. Luce Irigaray, *Speculum de l'autre femme* (Editions de Minuit, 1974), 238–52. A combination of "mystère" and "hystérie," the neologism is also intended to suggest the idea of "je m'hystère" (i.e., "I hystericize myself"). For a discussion, see Mazzoni, *Saint Hysteria,* 150–55.

8. See Mazzoni, *Saint Hysteria,* 38.

9. On nineteenth-century discussions of Loudun, see the typically well-documented study by Frank Paul Bowman, "From History to Hysteria: Nineteenth-century Discourse on Loudun," in *French Romanticism: Intertextual and Interdisciplinary Readings* (Baltimore: John Hopkins University Press, 1990), 106–21. See also the now classic study by Michel de Certeau, *La Possession de Loudun* (1970; reprint, Gallimard/Julliard, 1980).

10. Nineteenth-century writers on the Camisards included Balzac, Dumas *père,* Suë, Béranger, and Michelet. For a full discussion, see Philippe Joutard, *Les Camisards* (1976; reprint, Gallimard/Julliard, 1994).

11. See Catherine-Laurence Maire, *Les Convulsionnaires de Saint-Médard: Miracles, convulsions et prophéties à Paris au XVIIIe siècle* (Gallimard/Julliard, 1985).

12. Jules Michelet, *La Sorcière,* ed. Paul Viallaneix (Garnier-Flammarion, 1996), 126.

13. See Catherine-Laurence Maire, *Les Possédées de Morzine 1857–1873* (Lyon: Presses universitaires de Lyon, 1981), 120.

14. All these, and similar, incidents are discussed in chapter 5 ("The Possessed") of Judith Devlin's admirable *The Superstitious Mind: French Peasants and the Supernatural in the Nineteenth-Century* (New Haven: Yale University Press, 1987).

15. This paragraph is based on Catherine-Laurence Maire's full-length study *Les Possédeés*

de Morzine (see note 13), supported by the typically searching study by Ruth Harris, "Possession on the Borders: The "Mal de Morzine" in Nineteenth-Century France," *Journal of Modern History,* 69 (1997): 451–78. Only essential references are given.

16. Quoted in Harris, "Possession on the Borders," 472.

17. See Goldstein, *Console and Classify,* 327, and Georges Didi-Huberman, *Invention de l'hystérie: Charcot et l'iconographie photographique de la Salpêtrière* (Macula, 1982), 113. The present paragraph is strongly influenced by Didi-Huberman's study.

18. See Didi-Huberman, *Invention de l'hystérie,* 165–68.

19. See Mazzoni, *Saint Hysteria,* 23.

20. Alphonse Daudet, "A la Salpêtrière," *Chronique médicale* (January 1898), quoted in Goldstein, *Console and Classify,* 372.

21. Jules Claretie, "Charcot, le consolateur" (1903), quoted in ibid., 382–83.

22. Quoted in Didi-Huberman, *Invention de l'hystérie,* 18.

23. Account based on Ian Gibson, *The Bleeding Mind: An Investigation into the Mysterious Phenomenon of Stigmata* (Paladin, 1991), 143.

24. Quoted by Eléonore Roy-Reverzy in her introuction to Camille Lemonnier, *L'Hystérique* (Séguier, 1996), 17.

25. See Mazzoni, *Saint Hysteria,* 25.

26. Freud, "Charcot" (1893), quoted in Goldstein, *Console and Classify,* 383.

27. Quoted in Didi-Huberman, *Invention de l'hystérie,* 73.

28. Quoted in ibid., 28.

29. Ruth Harris, *Lourdes: Body and Spirit in the Secular Age* (Allen Lane, 1999), 356.

30. Maud Ellmann, *The Hunger Artists: Starving, Writing, and Imprisonment* (Virago, 1993), 22.

31. Rudolph M. Bell, *Holy Anorexia* (Chicago: University of Chicago Press, 1985).

32. For an excellent history of ideas concerning anorexia, see Walter Vandereysken and Ron Van Deth, *From Fasting Saints to Anorexic Girls: The History of Self-Starvation* (Athlone Press, 1994). Lasègue is discussed on pages 155–57.

33. Caroline Walker Bynum, *Holy Feast and Holy Fast: The Religious Significance of Food to Medieval Women* (Berkeley: University of California Press, 1987).

34. See, in addition to Bynum's *Holy Feast and Holy Fast,* Caroline Walker Bynum, *Jesus as Mother: Studies in the Spirituality of the High Middle Ages* (Berkeley: University of California Press, 1982).

35. The bibliography on anorexia is vast, and I have read only a tiny fraction of it. For what it is worth, I have derived particular profit from, in English, Kim Chernin, *The Hungry Self: Women, Eating, and Identity* (Virago, 1985) and, in French, Ginette Raimbault and Caroline Eliacheff, *Les Indomptables: Figures de l'Anorexie* (Editions Odile Jacob, 1989), already much used in the discussion of Simone Weil. It should be stressed that what follows is concerned only with the possible causes of *female* anorexia.

36. See Jacques Maître, *Anorexies religieuses, anorexie mentale: Essai de psychanalyse sociohistorique* (Editions du Cerf, 2000), 103. This admirable work has greatly influenced the present discussion.

37. See his discussion of Simone reproduced in Simone Weil, *Oeuvres* (Gallimard, 1999), 1257.

38. Georges Bernanos, *Journal d'un curé de campagne* (1936; reprint, Livre de poche, 1971), 316.

39. Léon Bloy, *Introduction à la vie de Mélanie* (1912), in *Oeuvres de Léon Bloy* (Mercure de France, 1970), 10:265.

40. Quoted in Simone Pétrement, *La Vie de Simone Weil* (Fayard, 1973), 275.

41. Claire Ferchaud, *Notes autobiographiques* (Téqui, 1974), 1:39.

42. Colette Peignot, *Histoire d'une petite fille,* in *Ecrits de Laure* (Pauvert, 1979), 59.

43. All details from Harris, *Lourdes,* 46–47 and 70–77.

44. Raïssa Maritain, *Les Grandes Amitiés* (Descleé de Brouwer, 1949), 13.

45. The child, Jeanne Louveau, was born illegitimately in 1895, when her mother was 29. See Eva Lavallière, *Ecrits spirituels* (Editions franciscaines, 1939), 14.

46. A. Curé, *Les Repas* (no date), quoted in Odile Arnold, *Le Corps et l'âme: La vie des religieuses au XIXe siècle* (Seuil, 1984), 129.

47. Léon Bloy, *Le Symbolisme de l'Apparition* (1879–80), in *Oeuvres complètes*, 10:74.

48. Quoted in Gérard Cholvy, *Etre chrétien en France au XIXe siècle, 1790–1914* (Seuil, 1997), 115.

49. See the sermon of 1862 by the well-known Père d'Alzon quoted in Gérard Cholvy and Yves-Marie Hilaire, *Histoire religieuse de la France contemporaine* (Toulouse: Privat, 1985), vol. 1 (1800–1880), 173.

50. Abbé Dabert, *La Bonne Mère Saint-Jean, ou Vie de Mme Julie Malleval* (1885), quoted in Arnold, *Le Corps et l'âme,* 131.

51. Joris-Karl Huysmans, *En route* (Folio, 1996), 372–73 and 407.

52. Léon Bloy, *Le Désespéré* (Union Générale d'Editions, 1983), 408.

53. This is the familiar thesis advanced in a range of works by Philippe Ariès, most fully in *L'Homme devant la mort* (Seuil, 1977). The Parisian cult of the dead is discussed fully in Richard D. E. Burton, *Blood in the City: Violence and Revelation in Paris, 1789–1945* (Ithaca: Cornell University Press, 2001), 130–35.

54. Quoted in Odile Arnold, *Le Corps et l'âme,* 269. The present discussion leans heavily on this admirable work.

55. On this complex controversy, see Claude Langlois, *Les Dernières Paroles de Thérèse de Lisieux* (Editions Salvator, 2000), published after the chapter on Thérèse in this book was written.

56. Georges Bernanos, *Dialogues des Carmélites* (Seuil, 1996), 49. I have discussed the theology of this work through Poulenc's opera of the same name in Richard D. E. Burton, *Francis Poulenc* (Bath: Absolute Press, 2002), 95–108.

57. Quoted in Arnold, *Le Corps et l'âme,* 273.

58. Ibid., 276.

59. Ibid., 279.

60. All the ideas, examples, and quotations in the following are taken from Susan Sontag's classic essay *Illness as Metaphor* (1978; reprint, Penguin, 1983), 17–21.

61. Quoted in ibid., 34.

62. Ibid., 21.

63. Quoted in Elisabeth Bronfen, *Over Her Dead Body: Death, Femininity, and the Aesthetic* (Manchester: Manchester University Press, 1992), 59. The following discussion owes much to this widely praised study.

64. *Derniers entretiens,* 13 July 1897, quoted in Langlois, *Les Dernières Paroles,* 150. The question of Thérèse's feelings on her deathbed is discussed with great sensitivity and insight in this work.

65. All details from Pierre Descouvement and Helmuth Nils Loose, *Thérèse de Lisieux* (Editions du Cerf, 1991), 306–10 where the relevant photographs may be found.

66. All details and quotations in this paragraph are taken from the official church brochure *The Body of Saint Bernadette* by André Ravier S. J. (Baume-les-Dames, I.M.E., 1986).

67. Ibid., 4–5.

68. Ibid., 14.

69. Bronfen, *Over Her Dead Body,* 181.

70. Alain Brossat, *Les Tondues: Un carnaval moche* (Editions Manya, 1992), 73.

71. *Ecrits de Laure* (Pauvert, 1985), 129.

72. I owe the original reference to *l'Inconnue de la Seine* to Sharon Louise Black, "Laure: Life under a Black Sun" (Ph.D. thesis, Sussex University, 1998), 200–201. The figure is discussed in A. Alvarez, *The Savage God: A Study of Suicide* (Weidenfeld and Nicolson, 1971), 115–16, and Elizabeth Bronfen, *Over Her Dead Body,* 206–8; the mask of *l'Inconnue* is reproduced on 207.

73. Bronfen, *Over Her Dead Body,* 206.

74. The actual cemetery, as noted earlier, is that of Fourqueux in the forest of Saint-Nom-la-Bretèche. For a description and photograph, see Black, *Laure,* 215–16.

75. R. Maritain, *Les Grandes Amitiés,* 13.

76. For full references, see chapter 4, pp. 29–30.

77. See chapter 5, pp. 138–39.

78. Quoted in Pétrement, *La Vie de Simone Weil*, 49.

79. The expression comes from the *Stimulus Amoris* of the medieval mystic James of Milan and is quoted in Wolfgang Riehle, *The Middle English Mystics*, trans. Bernard Standing (Routledge and Kegan Paul, 1981), 46, where the whole vulnus/vulva theme is discussed with great insight.

80. See chapter 6, p. 000.

81. Georges Bataille, *Le Coupable* (Gallimard, 1944), 31.

82. On this topos, see the outstanding study by Leo Steinberg, *The Sexuality of Christ in Renaissance Art and in Modern Oblivion* (New York: Pantheon/October Books, 1983).

83. For a remarkable, extended parallel between crucifixion and copulation, see the passage from Léon Bloy quoted in Burton, *Blood in the City*, 316. Here the cross itself figures the woman, with the man in the posture of the crucified Jesus.

84. Huysmans, *En route*, 387.

85. On the conversions of Claudel and Huysmans, see Burton, *Blood in the City*, 149–58 and 159–73, respectively.

86. See introduction, p. 000 (note 32).

87. Gustave Flaubert, *Madame Bovary* (Folio, 1988), 311.

88. See, for example, Charles Baudelaire, *Pauvre Belgique!*, in *Oeuvres complètes*, ed. Claude Pichois (Gallimard, 1976), 2:949–50.

89. Auguste Rodin, *Cathedrals of France*, trans. Elizabeth Chase Geissbuhler (1914; reprint, Boston: Beacon Press, 1965), 54, 143, 162.

90. Paul Claudel, "Développement de l'Eglise," in *Art Poétique* (1903; reprint, Gallimard, 1984), 140–44.

91. Paul Claudel, "La Cathédrale de Strasbourg," in *L'Oeil écoute* (Gallimard, 1995), 165 (written in 1937).

92. Claudel, "Développement de l'Eglise," 148.

93. Charles Péguy, "Présentation de Paris à Notre-Dame," *Oeuvres poétiques complètes*, ed. Marcel Péguy (Gallimard, 1994), 893.

94. The text in question is reproduced in translation in Denis Hollier, *Against Architecture: The Writings of Georges Bataille*, trans. Betsy Wing (Cambridge, Mass.: MIT Press, 1989), 15–19, and forms the basis of Hollier's challenging interpretation of Bataille's thought.

95. Claudel, "Vitraux des cathédrales de France, XIIe et XIIIe siècles," in *L'Oeil écoute*, 121, 126.

96. Péguy, "Prière de résidence," in *Oeuvres poétiques complètes*, 908.

97. See Burton, *Francis Poulenc*, esp. 56–58.

98. Maurice Rostand, *Confession d'un demi-siècle* (La Jeune Parque, 1948), 341, 323. On Rostand, see Christian Gury, *L'Extravagant Maurice Rostand: Un ami de Proust et de Cocteau* (Editions Kimé, 1994). On Mauriac's homosexuality, see the typically waspish pages in Roger Peyrefitte, *Propos secrets* (Albin Michel, 1980), 2:204–20.

99. See Christian Gury, *L'Honneur flétri d'un évêque homosexuel en 1937* (Editions Kimé, 2000), 30.

100. Pierre Klossowski, *La Vocation suspendue* (1950; reprint, Gallimard, 1990), 30–31.

101. On the death of Max Jacob, see Burton, *Blood in the City*, 183.

102. Mark D. Jordan, *The Silence of Sodom: Homosexuality in Modern Catholicism* (Chicago: University of Chicago Press, 2000), 8.

103. For a detailed study of this widely reported "affair," see Christian Gury, *L'Honneur flétri d'un évêque homosexuel en 1937* (Editions Kimé, 2000).

104. Jordan, *The Silence of Sodom*, 89.

105. Ibid., 159.

106. Ibid., 8.

107. Ibid., 204.

108. Quotation (adapted) from Fiona MacCarthy, *Eric Gill* (Faber, 1989), 162.

109. Quoted in Nicolas James Perella, *The Kiss Sacred and Profane: An Interpretative His-

tory of Kiss Symbolism and Related Religio-Erotic Themes (Berkeley: University of California Press, 1969), 297.

110. See Michel Surya, *Georges Bataille, la mort à l'oeuvre* (Editions Garamont-Frédéric Birr, 1987), 309.

111. Quoted in Jacques Maître, *Une inconnue célèbre: La Madeleine Lebouc de Janet* (Anthropos, 1993), 312.

112. Fanny Nicolau, quoted in Harris, *Lourdes,* 70.

113. Pauline Réage, *Histoire d'O* (Livre de Poche, 1997), 39. The present discussion is greatly indebted to Jessica Benjamin, *The Bonds of Love: Psychoanalysis, Feminism, and the Problem of Domination* (Virago, 1990), esp. 56–60.

114. See Maître, *Une inconnue célèbre,* 12. The nun in question was Louise de Bellère du Tronchay (1639–94).

115. Réage, *Histoire d'O,* 51. All numbers in parentheses refer to this edition.

116. Frank Paul Bowman, "'Precious Blood' in Religion, Literature, Eroticism, and Politics," in Bowman, *French Romanticism,* 81. The thematics of blood are discussed at length in Burton, *Blood in the City,* 309–33, to which the interested reader is referred.

117. Jules Michelet, *Histoire de France* (Lausanne: Editions Rencontre, 1966), 9:338–39.

118. See Harris, *Lourdes,* 290, where an informed and insightful discussion of the thematics of water is given. On the cultural history of tears, see Anne Vincent-Buffault, *Histoire des larmes, XVIIIe-XIXe siècles* (Editions Rivages, 1986), and Tom Lutz, *Crying: The Natural and Cultural History of Tears* (New York: Norton, 1999), both of which have influenced the present discussion.

119. Baudelaire, *Mon coeur mis à nu,* in *Oeuvres complètes,* 1:686.

120. "Marceline Desbordes-Valmore," in *Oeuvres complètes,* 2:149. For a further elaboration of the themes of this paragraph, see Richard D. E. Burton, *Baudelaire in 1859: A Study in the Sources of Poetic Creativity* (Cambridge: Cambridge University Press, 1988), esp. 34–35.

121. Text and translation from Charles Baudelaire, *The Flowers of Evil,* trans. James McGowan (Oxford: Oxford University Press, 1993), 173–75. For further discussion, see Burton, *Baudelaire in 1859,* 149–69.

122. Baudelaire, *Flowers of Evil,* 182–83.

123. Ibid., 42–43.

124. In "Cinquantenaire de l'hystérie" (1928), André Breton and Louis Aragon famously described hysteria as "the greatest poetic discovery of the late nineteenth century" (quoted in Didi-Huberman, *L'Invention de l'hystérie,* 147). For a full and insightful discussion of hysteria and the nineteenth-century French literary imagination, see Janet Beizer, *Ventriloquized Bodies: Narratives of Hysteria in Nineteenth-Century France* (Ithaca: Cornell University Press, 1994).

125. Baudelaire, *Flowers of Evil,* 154–57. The title of the poem, "L'Héautontimorouménos," means "self-executioner" in Greek.

126. Baudelaire, "Notes nouvelles sur Edgar Poe" (1857), in *Oeuvres complètes,* 2:334.

127. See Harris, *Lourdes,* 319, for a broader development of this notion.

128. E. M. Cioran, *Tears and Saints,* trans. Ilinca Zarifopol-Johnson (Chicago: University of Chicago Press, 1995), 12. All subsequent numbers in parentheses refer to this translation.

129. Baudelaire, "Un mangeur d'opium" (1860), in *Oeuvres complètes,* 1:444.

130. Baudelaire, "Hégésippe Moreau" (1861), in *Oeuvres complètes,* 2:160.

131. Leon Volovici, *Nationalist Ideology and Anti-Semitism. The Case of Romanian Intellectuals in the 1930s* (Oxford: Pergamon Press, 1991), quoted by Ilinca Zarifopol-Johnston in her introduction to Cioran, *Tears and Saints,* xv–xvi. For a detailed and revealing discussion of Cioran's and Eliade's fascist sympathies, see Alexandra Laignel-Lavastine, *Cioran, Eliade, Ionesco: L'Oubli du Fascisme. Trois intellectuals roumains dans la tourmente du siècle* (Presses Universitaires de France, 2002), published after this manuscript was completed.

132. Quoted in introduction to Cioran, *Tears and Saints,* xix.

133. On Baudelaire's politics in his later years, see Richard D. E. Burton, *Baudelaire and the Second Republic: Writing and Revolution* (Oxford: Oxford University Press, 1991), 356–66.

134. *The Poems of Richard Crashaw,* ed. L. C. Martin (Oxford: Oxford University Press, 1957), 83.

135. The bibliography on the cult of Mary Magdalene is vast, with Susan Haskins, *Mary Magdalene: Myth and Metaphor* (Harper Collins, 1993) being by far the best overall work; it has been copiously drawn on here. For a consideration of the origins of the devotional figure of Mary Magdalene, see chap. 1 of this work, "De Unica Magdalena," 3–32.

136. Lancelot Andrewes, *Ninety-Six Sermons* (Oxford: John Henry Parker, 1841), 3:29 (sermon preached on 1 April 1621).

137. All details from Jean-Paul Clébert, *Marie Madeleine en Provence: Lieux et figures* (Philippe Lebaud, 1998), 96–98.

138. See Burton, *Blood in the City,* 165, where full references are provided.

139. *Ecrits spirituels d'Eva Lavallière,* 92.

140. See Jean Hugo, *Le Regard de la mémoire* (1983; reprint, Actes Sud/Labor, 1989), 365–67.

141. On Vézelay, see Guy Lobrichon, "Vézelay," in *Les Lieux de mémoire,* ed. Pierre Nora, vol. 3: *Les France* (Gallimard, 1992), 316–57.

142. See his text entitled "Vézelay" in Paul Claudel, *Oeuvres complètes* (1948; reprint, Gallimard, 1969), 17:240–46.

143. The French exceptions to the rule would include two paintings on the theme by Corot (1833 and 1853) and a curious Magdalene of 1869–70 by the unclassifiable Pierre Puvis de Chavannes (1824–98).

144. Rainer Maria Rilke, "Rodin" (c. 1905), quoted in Haskins, *Mary Magdalen,* 360–61.

145. Rainer Marie Rilke, *Neue Gedichte,* English translation in Rilke, *Selected Works,* trans. J. B. Leishman (Hogarth, 1960), 1:155.

146. For illustrations and texts, see Thierry Zeno, *Félicien Rops* (Brussels: Editions Jacques Antoine), 124–29.

147. For a reproduction of the first of the etchings, see Klaus Theweleit, *Male Fantasies,* trans. Stephen Conway et al. (Polity Press, 1987), 1:350.

148. Baudelaire, "Je n'ai pas pour maîtresse une lionne illustre," in *Oeuvres complètes,* 1:203.

149. Max Jacob, *La Défence de Tartuffe* (1919; reprint, Gallimard, 1964), 197–98. This discussion is closely based on Burton, *Francis Poulenc,* 59–60.

150. Letter of 27 December 1923, in Max Jacob/Jean Cocteau, *Correspondance 1917–1944* (Editions Paris-Méditeraneé, 2000), 180.

151. Letter of 12 April 1927, in ibid., 529.

152. Jean Desbordes, *J'adore* (Grasset, 1928), 54.

153. Hugo, *Le Regard de la mémoire,* 151.

154. Jean Genet, *Notre-Dame-des-Fleurs* (Folio, 1998), 89. To make the gender-bending criss-cross of images even more telling, when Divine is arrested while drunkenly singing the *Veni Creator* on the boulevards, she faints and is revived by the *gendarmes'* fanning her with their handkerchiefs, like so many "Holy Women who were wiping my face, my divine Face" (*"Ils étaient les Saintes Femmes qui m'essuyaient la face. Ma Divine Face,"* 82).

155. Quoted by Jacqueline Klein in her introduction to Henri Lacordaire, *Sainte Marie-Madeleine* (Grenoble: Jérôme Millon, 1998), 8.

156. Rainer Maria Rilke, *L'Amour de Madeleine/Die Liebe der Magdalena* (Bar-le-Duc: Arfuyen, 2000), 14. Numbers in parentheses are to this edition, which includes the French original as well as Rilke's translation.

157. See Haskins, *Mary Magdalen,* 177 and 179.

158. Letter to Mme Roselly de Lorgues of 18 December 1879, quoted in Joseph Bollery, *Léon Bloy: Essai de biographie* (Albin Michel, 1947), vol. 1: *Origines, jeunesse et formation, 1846–1882,* 414. Although seriously dated, this biography reproduces in toto a large number of original documents and is the principal source for what follows; all numbers in parentheses preceded by the letter *B,* refer to vol. 1 of this work. All numbers preceded by the letter *D* refer to the edition of *Le Désespéré* cited in note 52. Only essential references are given.

159. See Jean-François Six, *Vie de Thérèse de Lisieux* (Seuil, 1975), 83. Six dates the conference as February 1881, but Tardif had died at La Salette in 1879.

160. On Vintras and his followers, see Burton, *Blood in the City,* 163–65, where full references are provided.

161. On Bloy's view of animals as sacrificial victims, see the remarkable pages in *La Femme pauvre* (1879; reprint, Folio, 1980), 129–33.

162. Baudelaire, *Mon coeur mis à nu,* in *Oeuvres complètes,* 1:676.

163. Léon Bloy, *Journal,* ed. Pierre Glaudes (Robert Laffont, 1999), 1:643.

164. See Burton, *Blood in the City,* 316–17. The present discussion repeats in part the pages in question.

165. Paul Claudel, "Camille Claudel," in *Oeuvres completes,* 17:247–48. On the motif of hair in Camille's work, see Danielle Arnoux, *Camille Claudel: L'Ironique Sacrifice* (EPEL, 2001), 75–79.

166. Georges Bataille, *Le Bleu du ciel* (Gallimard, 1997), 40–41. (*Blue of Noon,* trans. Harry Matthews [Marion Boyars, 1986], 29–30.)

167. Ibid., 18–20 (*Blue of Noon,* 12–14).

168. *Ecrits de Laure,* ed. Jérome Peignot (Pauvert, 1985), 169.

169. Ibid., 142.

170. Georges Bataille, "Chevelures," in *Oeuvres complètes* (Gallimard, 1970), 1:495–96.

171. Emile Zola, *Madeleine Férat,* in *Oeuvres complètes,* ed. Henri Mitterand (Cercle du Livre Précieux, 1966), 1:757, 766, 795.

172. Pierre Emmanuel, "Acathiste de Madeleine," in *Sophia* (Seuil, 1973), 156 and 167.

173. Lacordaire, *Sainte Marie-Madeleine,* 52.

174. Maurice Maeterlinck, *Pelléas et Méelisande* (1893; reprint, Lacomblez/Lamm, 1902), 52 (act 3, scene 2).

175. Maître, *Une inconnue célèbre,* 295.

176. Ibid., 117.

177. Lavallière, *Ecrits spirituels,* 129.

178. Goncourt, *Journal,* 1:301.

179. Jean Genet, *Miracle de la Rose* (1946; reprint, Folio, 1998), 12.

180. Ibid., 223.

181. Ibid., 18.

182. Ibid., 25.

183. For a full discussion of this theme, see Burton, *Blood in the City,* 113–15.

184. On Genet and Pilorge, see François Sentein, *L'Assassin et son bourreau: Jean Genet et l'affaire Pilorge* (Editions de la Différence, 1999).

185. My only authority for making this statement is Edmond de Goncourt's documentary-style prison novel *La Fille Elisa* (1877; reprint, Calmann-Lévy, no date), 70, where the heroine is relieved *not* to have her hair cut when entering prison.

186. Michel Leiris, *L'Age d'homme* (1939; reprint, Gallimard, 1964), 201.

187. Michel Leiris, *Le Point cardinal,* in *Mots sans mémoire* (1927; reprint, Gallimard, 1969), 48–49.

188. Michel Leiris, *Aurora* (Gallimard, 1946), 86–88.

189. On the diffusion of the Samson/Delilah motif in fin de siècle European culture, see Bram Dijkstra, *Idols of Perversity: Fantasies of Feminine Evil in Fin-de-Siècle Culture* (Oxford: Oxford University Press, 1986), 375–76.

190. Leiris, *L'Age d'homme,* 104.

191. Michel Leiris, *L'Afrique fantôme* (1934; reprint, Gallimard, 1951), 206 (cf. 155 and 157).

192. See Leiris, *Fourbis,* 214, and "Histoire d'une petite fille," *Ecrits de Laure,* 72. The importance of the forehead motif is well brought out by Sharon Black (*Laure,* 125–27).

193. Michel Leiris, "Tiers de a mort," in *Albanico para los toros, Haut mal* (1943; reprint, Gallimard/Poésie, 1969), 148. On Leiris and bullfighting, see Burton, *Blood in the City,* 320–21.

194. Michel Leiris, *Tauromachies,* in *Miroir de la tauromachie* (1937; reprint, Guy Lévis-Mano, 1964), 11.

195. Leiris, "Tiers de la mort," in *Haut mal,* 148.

196. The charges at the trial are quoted from Marina Warner, *Joan of Arc: The Image of Female Heroism* (Penguin, 1983), 149. The Pauline text is appositely quoted on page 152.

197. In order not to overburden the text, I have not given examples, but the interested reader may refer to the many images conveniently brought together in Régine Pernoud, *J'ai nom Jeanne la Pucelle* (Gallimard/Découvertes, 1994), especially, in the present context, Jean-Jacques Scherrer's painting *Entrée de Jeanne à Orleans* (1887, 42–43), Maurice Denis's *Sainte Jeanne d'Arc pendant le sacre* (c. 1920, 57), and Louis-Ernest Barrias's sculpture *Jeanne d'Arc prisonnière* (1903, 74).

198. For illustration, see Robert Rosenblum, *Jean-Auguste-Dominique Ingres* (Thames and Hudson, 1967), 161 (color plate 45).

199. See Pierre Descouvemont and Helmuth Nils Loose, *Thérèse et Lisieux* (Editions du Cerf, 1991), 219–23.

200. Respectively, *Jeanne d'Arc* (1897) and *Le Mystère de la charité de Jeanne d'Arc* (1910) by Charles Péguy, the first, loosely socialist and humanistic in orientation, the second explicitly Catholic; *Jeanne, relapse et sainte* (1929) by Georges Bernanos; *Jeanne d'Arc au bûcher* (1938–39), Claudel's text set to music by Arthur Honegger; and *L'Alouette* (1953) by Jean Anouilh. For a good general discussion of the earlier works, see the chapter entitled "Jeanne d'Arc et les écrivains française de 1870 à 1920" in Marie-Claire Bancquart, *Les Ecrivains et l'Histoire* (A. G. Nizet, 1966), 293–378.

201. Léon Bloy, *Jeanne d'Arc et l'Allemagne*, in *Oeuvres completes*, 9:162.

202. Ibid., 155.

203. For a useful summary and discussion, see Warner, *Joan of Arc*, 325–27.

204. Warner, *Joan of Arc*, 47. The present discussion has derived much from Warner's brief analysis of the film. I have also used with profit David Bordwell's *Filmguide to "La Passion de Jeanne d'Arc"* (Bloomington: Indiana University Press, 1973).

205. Quoted in *The Observer*, 14 November 1999.

206. Réage, *Histoire d'O*, 268. It is worth noting that the "real" Pauline Réage, Dominique Aury, edited an *Anthologie de la poésie religieuse française* (1943).

207. See Stephen Barber, *Antonin Artaud: Blows and Bombs* (Faber and Faber, 1993), 105–7. The photograph is reproduced between pages 86 and 87.

208. See Antonin Artaud, "Van Gogh le suicidé de la société," in *Oeuvres complètes* (Editions K, 1947), 13:13–64. On Van Gogh, see Burton, *Blood in the City*, 325–26.

209. The self-portraits, or a selection of them, are reproduced in most books on Van Gogh. A powerful selection opens the well-illustrated study by Pascal Bonafoux, *Van Gogh, le soleil en face* (Gallimard/Découvertes, 1987). The 1888 self-portrait is reproduced on page 128.

210. For a discussion of Foucault's private life, see James Miller, *The Passion of Michel Foucault* (New York: Simon and Schuster, 1993), esp. 13–36 and 259–61.

211. See Albert Londres, *Au bagne* (1923; reprint, Le Serpent à Plumes, 1998), 155, 170, 162, respectively.

212. See Georges Darien, *Biribi* (1890; reprint, Jérome Martineau, 1966), 90.

213. David Rousset, *Les Jours de notre mort* (1947; reprint, Union générale d'éditions, 1974), 1:73.

214. Edmond Michelet, *Rue de la Liberté: Dachau 1943–1945* (1955; reprint, Seuil, 1998), 69–71.

215. Albert Londres, *Les Forçats de la route* (1924; reprint, Arléa, 1996), 54, 31, 13, respectively.

216. Antoine Blondin, *Oeuvres,* ed. Jacques Bens (Robert Laffont, 1991), 1401 (originally published in *L'Equipe*, 15 July 1968). On 14 July that year, Poulidor, with his best chance ever of winning the tour, was knocked down by a passing motor vehicle and failed to finish in the first three. Describing the incident as the "Poulidorian calvary," Michel Chemin (*Libération*, 18 July 2003) says that, at that moment, the whole French nation "literally communed with the wounded national icon."

217. Alfred Jarry, "La passion considérée comme course de côte," reproduced in *Le Tour (1903–2003). Une histoire de France*, ed. Jean-Emmanuel Ducoin (*L'Humanité*, June 2003), 77. I have been unable to trace the date and place of the original publication.

218. Quoted from ibid., 91.

219. Roland Barthes, *Mythologies* (1957; reprint, Seuil, 1970), 113.

220. Quoted from *Le Tour (1903–2003)*, 82.

221. Fabrice Virgili, "Les 'Tondues' à la Libération: le corps des femmes, enjeu d'une réappropriation," in *Histoire femmes et sociétés, résistances et libérations,* ed. Françoise Thébaud (Clio, 1995), 1:111–27.

222. Corran Laurens, " 'La femme au turban.' Les Femmes tondues," in *The Liberation of France: Image and Event,* ed. H. R. Kedward and Nancy Wood (Oxford: Berg, 1995), 155–79.

223. Claire Duchen, "Crime and Punishment in Liberated France: The Case of *les femmes tondues,*" in *When the War Was Over: Women, War, and Peace in Europe, 1940–1956,* ed. Claire Duchen and Irene Bandhauer-Schöffmann (Leicester: Leicester University Press, 2000), 233–50.

224. Hanna Diamond, *Women and the Second World War in France, 1939–1948: Choices and Constraints* (Longman, 1999), 134–42. In all of what follows, references are kept to a minimum.

225. Brossat, *Les Tondues: Un carnaval moche* (Manya, 1992), 212.

226. See Laurens, " 'La Femme au turban,' " 157.

227. Ibid., 174.

228. Londres, *Les Forçats de la route,* 38.

229. Diamond, *Women and the Second World War in France,* 136.

230. See Duchen, "Crime and Punishment in Liberated France," 246.

231. See the incident discussed by Diamond, *Women and the Second World War in France,* 138.

232. The poster was by Paul Colin and, in the words of a fellow *affichiste,* depicts a "tricolour image, in the blue of a cloudless sky, where France, with her hands crucified only yesterday, lifts her gaze beyond her own ruins towards the future" (quoted and discussed in Michael Kelly, "The Reconstruction of Masculinity at the Liberation," in *The Liberation of France,* ed. Kedward and Wood, 118).

233. Duchen, "Crime and Punishment in Liberated France," 237.

234. See Kelly, "The Reconstruction of Masculinity" (note 27 above). My reference is to the celebrated opening line of Sartre's 1944 article "La République du silence."

235. Brossat, *Les Tondues,* 243.

236. All quotations from Réage, *Histoire d'O,* 304–10. Tenses have been changed from the past to the present.

237. In an entry in his diary dated 5 October 1979, Leiris notes the importance of *le thème de l'acéphale* in the literature and painting of the 1920s and 1930s, instancing, in addition to *Acéphale* itself and various minor works, Robert Desnos's poem "Les sans cou," Max Ernst's painting "La femme 100 [=sans] tête" and, interestingly, his own work on possession cults of *zâr* and *vaudou* in which the adept "loses his or her head during the trance" (*Journal de Michel Leiris (1922–1989)* [Gallimard, 1992], 721–22).

238. The question of photographs of *tondues* is almost as controversial as the phenomenon itself. For good general discussions, see the articles by Duchen and Laurens.

239. Various dates for the photograph are given: 19 June 1944 (Laurens, an obvious error), 18 August 1944 (Brossat), 23 August 1944 (Duchen).

240. Marie Noël, *Notes intimes* (1959; reprint, Stock, 1998), 297.

241. The French Jerusalem Bible translation closely resembles the English, and both are close to the Vulgate version with which most of the women studied here would have been familiar. The translation of the Authorized Version is practically incomprehensible ("and fill up that which is behind of the afflictions of Christ") and gives some idea of the obscurity of Paul's thinking at this point.

242. Léon Bloy, *La Femme pauvre* (1897; reprint, Folio, 1980), 374.

243. See Yannick Ripa, *Women and Madness: The Incarceration of Women in Nineteenth-Century France,* trans. Catherine du Peloux Menagé (Cambridge: Polity Press, 1990), 20–21.

244. Details and quotations from Joseph Bollery, *Genèse et Composition de La Femme pauvre: Archives des lettres modernes,* 99 (1969): 8–12.

245. Bloy, *La Femme pauvre,* 392–93.

INDEX